GOING GREEK

GOING GREEK

JEWISH COLLEGE FRATERNITIES
IN THE UNITED STATES,
1895–1945

Marianne R. Sanua

WAYNE STATE UNIVERSITY PRESS DETROIT

AMERICAN JEWISH CIVILIZATION SERIES

EDITORS
MOSES RISCHIN
San Francisco State University

JONATHAN D. SARNA
Brandeis University

Library of Congress Cataloging-in-Publication Data

Sanua, Marianne Rachel.
Going Greek : Jewish college fraternities in the United States, 1895–1945 / Marianne
R. Sanua.
p. cm. — (American Jewish civilization series)
Includes bibliographical references and index.
ISBN 978-0-8143-4419-4 (paperback); ISBN 978-0-8143-4418-7 (ebook)
1. Greek letter societies. 2. Jewish college students—United States—Conduct of life.
3. Jewish youth—United States—Societies, etc.—History. I. Title. II. Series.
LJ51 .S38 2003
378.1′98′55—dc21   2002007160

NATIONAL ENDOWMENT FOR THE
Humanities

THE
ANDREW W.
MELLON
FOUNDATION

The publication of this volume in a freely accessible digital format has been made
possible by a major grant from the National Endowment for the Humanities and the
Mellon Foundation through their Humanities Open Book Program.

http://wsupress.wayne.edu/

To my mother,
Stella Sardell Sanua

AND

To my father,
Victor D. Sanua

The world stands out on either side
No wider than the heart is wide;
Above the world is stretched the sky,—
No higher than the soul is high.
The heart can push the sea and land
Farther away on either hand . . .

    "Renascence" by Edna St. Vincent Millay (1917)

Plus ça change, plus ça reste la même chose
The more things change, the more they stay the same.

. . . And when the former high priest Jason rose against Menelaus, who was appointed after him, the populace was divided between the two, the Tobiads being on the side of Menalaus, while the majority of the people supported Jason; and being hard pressed by him, Menelaus and the Tobiads withdrew, and going to Antiochus informed him that they wished to abandon their country's laws and the way of life prescribed by these, and to follow the king's laws and adopt the Greek way of life. Accordingly, they petitioned him to permit them to build a gymnasium in Jerusalem. And when he had granted this, they also concealed the circumcision of their genitals in order to be Greeks even when unclothed, and giving up whatever other national customs they had, they imitated the practices of foreign nations.

    Josephus, "The Hellenizers Appeal to Antiochus Epiphanes,"
    in *Jewish Antiquities XII.* 240–243 citing I Maccabees, i.11

"A cow can sooner jump over a roof than a Jew get into a Russian university! They guard their schools from us like a bowl of cream from a cat."

    —Tevye in Sholom Aleichem's *Tevye the Dairyman*

Oy yoy yoy, Zeta Beta Toi
What have you done to my little Yiddish boy?
I sent him off to college to learn to read and write
Now he dates a *shiksa* every Friday night
I sent him off to college to learn to read and spell
Now he thinks *boruch atoh* is a college yell!
I sent him off to college to learn the Jewish way,
Now he thinks a *hora* is a girl who's gone astray . . .

    —Popular American Jewish folksong, c. 1920s–1930s

Contents

Illustrations

Sigma Delta Tau at Indiana University in 1940

Alpha Epsilon Pi's national convention, 1940

Executive head of Phi Sigma Delta formally pledges a local group of
    Jewish students, University of Connecticut, 1942

At the University of Michigan, c. 1940s, outside the women's dormitory

Sigma Delta Tau at the University of Nebraska in the 1940s

Sigma Delta Tau at the University of Iowa in front of their chapter
    house in 1942

The Sigma Delta Tau pledge class at Penn State in 1942

Founding chapter of Sigma Delta Tau at Penn State University in 1943

Mrs. Margaret Rossiter, for decades the administrator of Zeta Beta
    Tau's national office

Alumni of Zeta Beta Tau celebrate the end of World War II in the fall
    of 1945

A Star of David in a field of crosses at a military cemetery in
    Margraten/Maashricht, Holland, 1945

Annual formal dinner dance of the Marquette University chapter of
    Alpha Epsilon Pi, 1947

Phi Epsilon Pi members at the formal dance of the University of
    Pittsburgh chapter, 1948

"Parisian Night" at the Wayne State University chapter of Alpha
    Epsilon Pi, c. 1952

Formal dance night at the Vanderbilt University chapter of Zeta Beta
    Tau in 1940

Formal initiation dinner dance at the Hotel Syracuse, April 6, 1940

Junior Prom weekend at Rutgers University, Phi Epsilon Pi chapter
    house, March 1962

Advertisement urging Phi Epsilon Pi members to send in reservations
    and "date requests" for the 1950 convention

Jewish National College
Fraternities and Sororities, c. 1930

Fraternities

Name	Founded	Status
1. Pi Lambda Phi	1895, Yale	Still in existence
2. Zeta Beta Tau	1898, JTS/CCNY	Still in existence
3. Phi Epsilon Pi	1904, CCNY	Merged w/ZBT 1970
4. Sigma Alpha Mu	1909, CCNY	Still in existence
5. Phi Sigma Delta	1910, Columbia	Merged w/ZBT 1969
6. Tau Epsilon Phi	1910, Columbia	Still in existence
7. Tau Delta Phi	1910, CCNY	Ceased operations by 1973
8. Beta Sigma Rho	1910, Cornell	Merged w/PiLamPhi 1972
9. Kappa Nu	1911, U. Rochester	Merged w/ PhiEpPi 1961
10. Phi Beta Delta	1912, Columbia	Merged w/PiLamPhi 1939
11. Omicron Alpha Tau	1912, Cornell	Merged w/TauDeltPhi 1934
12. Phi Alpha	1914, G. Washington U.	Merged w/PhiSigDelt 1959
13. Alpha Epsilon Pi	1914, NYU Square	Still in existence
14. Alpha Mu Sigma	1914, Cooper Union	Ceased 1963, absorbed by others
15. Sigma Omega Psi	1914, CCNY	Merged w/AEPi 1940
16. Sigma Lambda Pi	1915, NYU	Ceased 1932, absorbed by others
17. Sigma Tau Phi	1918, U. Penn	Merged w/AEPi 1947

Sororities

Name	Founded	Status
1. Iota Alpha Pi	1903, Hunter [formerly Normal College]	Disbanded 1971
2. Alpha Epsilon Phi	1909, Barnard	Still in existence
3. Phi Sigma Sigma	1913, Hunter [formerly Normal College]	Still in existence
4. Sigma Delta Tau	1917, Cornell	Still in existence
5. Delta Phi Epsilon	1917, NYU Law	Still in existence
6. Pi Alpha Tau	1919, Hunter [formerly Normal College]	Became inactive nationally by 1950

The Greek Alphabet

ALPHA	A	α	NU	N	ν
BETA	B	β	XI	Ξ	ξ
GAMMA	Γ	γ	OMICRON	O	o
DELTA	Δ	δ	PI	Π	π
EPSILON	E	ε	RHO	P	ρ
ZETA	Z	ζ	SIGMA	Σ	σ
ETA	H	η	TAU	T	τ
THETA	Θ	θ	UPSILON	Y	υ
IOTA	I	ι	PHI	Φ	φ
KAPPA	K	κ	CHI	X	χ
LAMBDA	Λ	λ	PSI	Ψ	ψ
MU	M	μ	OMEGA	Ω	ω

Preface

Higher education has long played a defining role in shaping the lives of young American Jews and their families. Just how high a value they have placed upon it and how far its influence has extended beyond the classroom first became apparent to me during my own undergraduate years. The phenomenon was far too much taken for granted to be ignored, and as a theme it called for a historian's closest attention. But how could one best document an experience that was by its nature so fleeting?

Years later in New York, as a graduate student in history researching the subject of U.S. Jews and higher education, I encountered in the reference section of the Jewish Theological Seminary Library a short 1923 history of the Zeta Beta Tau Fraternity. Founded in 1898 by students attending both the Seminary and New York area colleges, ZBT turned out to be the first of an entire system of some two dozen national Jewish Greek-letter fraternities and sororities that had once flourished, separate from Gentile fraternities, throughout the U.S. and Canada. Although the system as a whole had collapsed by the late 1960s, as individual groups a number of the historically Jewish fraternities and sororities continued to exist into the present day.

That such a thing as "Jewish Greeks" could exist in modern times struck me at first as ironic. Greek-letter fraternities had not existed at all at the college I attended, although it had a club system that was similar in many respects. I had never encountered their Jewish variants either through family ties or through historical literature. That very term our ancient history class at the Seminary was immersed in the fierce battle between Jews and Hellenizers culminating in the Maccabean victory of 163 B.C.E., an event commemorated annually in the triumphant festival of Hanukkah. Hadn't that particular religious and cultural confrontation been resolved a long time ago? Yet here a modern, syncretistic form of Jewish Greekdom had apparently been resurrected on twentieth-century North American college campuses. Surprisingly, while these institutions did seem to have bred some excellent athletes, they did not appear to have encouraged mass swine-eating, idol worship, or wholesale apostasy among their adherents. A remarkable number of my academic associates—future rabbis, cantors, teachers, and loyal Jewish communal supporters—turned out to be the children or grandchildren of couples that had met through fraternity auspices, if not members themselves. Verbal inquiries elicited a torrent of information on how important these fraternities had been in people's lives. Stories from those whose families originated from the Midwest, the West Coast, or areas beyond Metropolitan New York were especially vivid.

The written records of this historic Jewish Greek system, it turned out, were the perfect screen upon which to track the precise movements of American Jews as they took up higher end professional education and to shed light on unanswered questions. Other works of scholarship, for example, had described how Jewish students suffered from limited means, antisemitism, restrictive quotas and other obstacles on the ladder to success. How was it, then, that so many were able to get their education and prosper within one or two generations anyway? What was life like *after* they got past the barriers at the admissions office? What specific techniques had they used to transform themselves so quickly?

As a research tool the archives, magazines, yearbooks and photographs of the historically Jewish fraternities and sororities avoided major methodological problems in exploring these and many other questions of historical and sociological interest. The blessing of separation of church and state that American Jews enjoy, coupled with their own natural reticence, has always meant as well that any research project on them can turn into a major ordeal. Census and other official records did not include religious affiliation, and many college Jews thought it wiser to be discrete about their identity. They or their fathers could change their names. They could try and leave any reference to their Jewishness off the application form, off the registration card during freshman week, and out of the class yearbook when they graduated. When the young men went off to do their duty in World War II they could decide, as many did, that it was preferable to leave the telltale "H" for "Hebrew" off their dog tags in the event that they were captured by the enemy. The omission might save their lives but it could also have serious consequences if and when they needed burial services and their deaths recorded. Choices such as these left legions of researchers guessing for years afterward.

With these fraternities, however, there was no need to guess if a member was or was not Jewish. Conversations and writings about matters of identity were much freer when the subjects believed the words were only among themselves and Gentiles were not listening. Basic demographic data abounded. Campus investigation reports from across the country included detailed information and population estimates not just for the college but for the Jewish community surrounding it, and rejections carried as much if not more information than the acceptances. Changes of name for purposes of business or marriage, weddings, births, professional school acceptances, occupations, job promotions, and communal achievements all appeared in alumni columns and articles. (Unlike college clubs, fraternity and sorority affiliation was meant to endure one's entire life.) Precisely *which* fraternity or sorority someone belonged to in the early years of the system was a probable key to his or her socioeconomic status as well. American Jews were never a monolithic group. Class, economic, and sub-ethnic divisions among them could be examined through the variety of Greek-letter groups that sprang up to service them, and the rhetoric used by the members of one group to reject members of another.

Finally, college fraternities appeared as a useful way to examine an underreported but extremely important sector of the American Jewish population. These young people of the 1910s through the 1930s did not fall into the category of rabbis, labor leaders, Zionist leaders, Bundists, Yiddishists, radicals, New York intellectuals, or any of the other fascinating groups that have tended to draw scholars' attention. Interwar fraternity students and alumni adumbrated what would in fact become the majority profile of mid-to late-twentieth century American Jews. It is not known how many of them left the community altogether. Those that remained for the most part aimed straight for the middle or upper-middle classes, went to college, married, raised families in the suburbs, succeeded in their professions and businesses, became officers in Jewish organizations, or otherwise quietly took up their places within the bourgeois community structure. These were the generations that faced and fought World War II. It was into their mature hands that the reins of world communal and philanthropic leadership passed even before the war ended and they knew that the great centers of European Jewish life were gone.

In setting parameters for this study I decided to focus on what are known in the Greek-letter world as national—that is, multi-chapter—college social fraternities, to the exclusion of Greek-letter local, honor, recognition, city, professional, and high school fraternities, or youth organizations such as Aleph Zaddik Aleph (AZA) and B'nai B'rith Girls (BBG), which themselves graduated thousands of members. To examine in detail every single historically Jewish fraternity or sorority was, regretfully, not possible, and future researchers are likely to come across groups that are not mentioned here. In addition, while material on both college fraternities and sororities is included, the balance of this study focuses on the men's groups, which were older and more numerous than the women's groups. There were indeed major differences between the men's and women's organizations, and gender was a significant variable influencing the fact, location, and nature of college attendance. However, Jewish college fraternities and sororities were at all times closely related. Here I chose most of the time to deal with themes common to both groups. The records of Jewish college sorority women alone represent an unmined treasure trove of information, and they deserve to receive their own full historical treatment.

A full comparative analysis of Jewish and non-Jewish fraternities has also been beyond the scope of this study. To map out the Jewish Greek world alone was a task of sufficient complexity. That the Jewish fraternities on the whole consumed alcoholic drinks and indulged in brutal hazing practices to a lesser extent than the Gentile fraternities was accepted as a truism in the American college Greek world before the 1970s, though concrete data on the subject is not easy to obtain. Another truism—that the Jewish fraternities demonstrated a higher level of scholarship—is far more easily documented. From the 1910s through the early 1960s individual university and supra-fraternal councils, in particular the NIC (National Interfraternity Conference) kept careful annual records of fraternity members' academic grades. The results were commonly used as a basis for disciplinary action. While individual chapters might perform abysmally, national Jewish fraternities inevitably ranked at or near the top of their lists.

Fraternity terminology and slang is complex, beginning with the names of the groups themselves, composed of Greek initials meant to denote the organization's secret motto. Each had its own customary shorthand designations. For example, Zeta Beta Tau members became "ZBTs" or "Zetes" or "Zebes" (frequently combined in a derogatory sense by outsiders with the word "Hebes"); Sigma Alpha Mu members were "Sammys" or "Sammies," while Tau Epsilon Phi members were "TEPs." Fraternity members and officials, when communicating among themselves, frequently used the terms "brother," "sister," "frater" (sometimes spelled "fratre" or abbreviated as "Fra."), and "soror." In addition, they usually referred to chapters according to their Greek-letter designation, which most often indicated local seniority. For example, the Columbia chapter of Phi Epsilon Pi, the second to be founded within the national group, was called "Beta" while the New York University chapter, the tenth to be established, was called "Kappa." (The chapter at the City College of New York, as in the case of several other historically Jewish fraternities, was the "Alpha" chapter). In direct quotes using only Greek letter designations I have provided the name of the campus in brackets.

In referring to colleges and universities, I have followed the practice of writing the name out in full at its first occurrence and thereafter using its most common acronym or abbreviation: for example, "Penn" for the University of Pennsylvania, "Penn State" for Pennsylvania State College, "Carnegie Tech" for the Carnegie Institute of Technology, "Illinois" for the University of Illinois, and "NYU" for New York University.

Fraternities also used distinctive ceremonial names for their officers and national governing councils. The head officer in Zeta Beta Tau, for example, was originally known as the *Nasi,* a Hebrew term denoting "prince" or "president." Their governing council, also from the Hebrew, was at first called "the Supreme *Beth Din*" and later Anglicized to "the Supreme Council." Sigma Alpha Mu officers were known as "Priors," Phi Epsilon Pi's as "Superiors," Alpha Epsilon Phi's as "Deans," and so on. Phi Epsilon Pi's national officers met periodically in a Grand Council, while those of Alpha Epsilon Pi convened the Supreme Governing Board. I have usually maintained these usages.

As Jewish fraternities grew more affluent in the early 1920s, they followed the prevailing pattern by establishing central or national offices staffed by a professional secretary. It was through this "National" or "Central" office that reports were generated which investigated the potential for a new chapter or commented on the operation of one already in existence. What was known as "extension" or "field" work could be carried out by any authorized alumni official—a traveling or field secretary, an officer or alumnus who happened to live in the vicinity, a "province director," or a cooperative undergraduate. In cases where I do not specify in the text the status of the person writing the report, the simplest term, "investigator," is used.

I have also used simply "the administration" or "college officials" to denote whoever was responsible for allowing or prohibiting the presence of a Jewish fraternity on a campus. The individuals that fraternity investigators consulted upon arrival usually consisted of the president of the university and the Dean of Men or the Dean of Women. Both of these were nonacademic offices created by growing universities in the early twentieth century to supervise the manners, morals, living conditions, and extracurricular activities of the undergraduates. The deans, especially the Deans of Women, were frequently alumni or national officers in Gentile fraternities. This could add an aspect of either tension or sympathy in their interactions with Jewish fraternity officials. Fraternity investigators also commonly consulted with Jewish faculty, area alumni, Jewish families living in the town, and local rabbis. They often left behind fascinating portraits of these small communities whether or not a chapter was ever actually established at the college.

My sources were mainly contemporaneous written primary materials consisting of correspondence, meeting minutes, speeches, and fraternity publications and periodicals. Critical secondary historical literature on Jewish fraternities consists of fewer than a dozen articles and unpublished papers, which I have found helpful. The work of the late George S. Toll of Alpha Epsilon Pi deserves special mention. Jewish fraternities are discussed in passing in histories of college life and of discriminatory admissions policies. Two of the historically Jewish fraternities have sponsored in-house histories, which are also helpful, but these were geared mainly to the interests of members and alumni. A majority of the groups has disappeared and not all of those still in existence preserved their old correspondence, although all did maintain their minute books. Libraries, seeing no value in them, often discarded fraternity periodicals. In most cases, it was necessary to travel to the national offices of the surviving fraternities in order to gain access to these records. The national directors of Alpha Epsilon Phi, Alpha Epsilon Pi, Sigma Alpha Mu, Sigma Delta Tau, and Zeta Beta Tau all graciously allowed me access to their files. Those of Alpha Epsilon Phi Sorority headquarters were especially well preserved, with complete copies of correspondence going back almost to their founding in 1909.

I was also fortunate to discover two invaluable independent archival collections: the Irvin Fane Papers at the American Jewish

Archives in Cincinnati, Ohio, which contain extensive material related to the subject's role as midwestern regional director of Zeta Beta Tau from the early 1930s to the late 1950s, and the Phi Epsilon Pi collection at the American Jewish Historical Society now in New York, which consists of some seventy boxes of national and chapter correspondence, publications, photographs and memorabilia dating from 1914 to the early 1960s. Much of it contains material related not only to Phi Epsilon Pi, but to myriad other Jewish fraternities as well. Maurice Jacobs, who among his many accomplishments was at one time editor of the Jewish Publication Society and himself a book publisher, was an active member and national officer in Phi Epsilon Pi for over fifty years. As executive secretary he preserved every scrap of paper with loving care and donated it all to the American Jewish Historical Society when his fraternity ceased its independent existence and was absorbed by Zeta Beta Tau in 1970. I am much indebted to his foresight.

Many persons and institutions have contributed to the completion of this book, and I am grateful for the opportunity to thank some of them here. My sponsor, Arthur Aryeh Goren, first introduced me to American Jewish history during a year of study with him at the Hebrew University in Jerusalem. His guidance, patience and compassion through the process of writing the dissertation upon which this book is based were invaluable. Kenneth T. Jackson, my second reader, painstakingly reviewed every word of the text, and it was much improved by his editorial suggestions. Aside from providing valuable support and encouragement during the difficult writing process, he also allowed me to give early chapters their first public exposure at the monthly meetings of the George Washington Plunkitt Benevolent Association, a group of American history doctoral candidates who met each month under his aegis. During my years of graduate study at Columbia Yosef Hayim Yerushalmi insisted that I gain a thorough grounding in all areas of history and set before me a high standard of scholarship and professionalism which I shall always try to emulate. Michael F. Stanislawski has likewise served as a model of professionalism and academic integrity, and my work has benefited from his careful reading and extensive comments. Evyatar Friesel of Hebrew University and the Israel State Archives, with whom I began my study of Jewish history, always had faith in the topic and urged me to proceed with it despite many doubts. So too did Jonathan D. Sarna, whose advice, encouragement, and comments on earlier drafts were of enormous value. Throughout all my research on Jewish college fraternities, he was my most steadfast supporter and critic and was instrumental in having the manuscript published as part of Wayne State University Press's American Jewish Civilization Series. Ava F. Kahn gave ceaselessly of her time and energy to discuss the project with me and to orient me to the world of fraternities. I have been blessed with the friendship of Elisheva Carlebach, who helped to guide and encourage me through the dissertation process. My dear friends and then-fellow graduate students Nina Rothschild, Paul Radensky, and Beth Feinberg frequently served as sounding boards and consultants to the Jewish collegiate fraternity world. They also went far beyond the call of duty by cheerfully helping to organize and number by hand thousands of photocopied documents.

 This study could not have begun without the help and cooperation of numerous fraternity officials and members who appreciated the importance of my research, opened their records to me, and gave unstintingly of their time and insight. For extensive interviews as well as permission to consult their files, I am indebted to James E. Greer, Jr., the late Stanley I. Fishel, and Rabbi Matthew H. Simon of Zeta Beta Tau; William P. Schwartz and Paul Gearhart of Sigma Alpha Mu; Sidney Dunn and the late George S. Toll of Alpha Epsilon Pi; Patsy Lindeman and Ann Braly of Sigma Delta Tau; and Bonnie Rubinstein of Alpha Epsilon Phi.

 For archival work, I gratefully acknowledge the cooperation and assistance of Stanley Remsberg and Michael Feldberg of the American Jewish Historical Society in Waltham, Massachusetts; Abraham Peck, and Kevin Profitt of the American Jewish Archives in Cincinnati, Ohio; Cyma Horowitz and Michele J. Anish of the Blaustein Library, American Jewish Committee, in New York; and Susan Aprill and Gail Pietrzyk of the archives of New York University and the University of Pennsylvania, who thoughtfully answered my questions and provided me with information through phone and mail.

 Without a series of generous grants that allowed me precious time and freedom to work, this study could never have been done. Two vital years of travel, research, and voluminous photocopying were made possible by an unrestricted grant from the Zeta Beta Tau Foundation. Periods of research at the American Jewish Archives in Cincinnati were facilitated by the Rabbi Theodore S. Levy Tribute Fellowship, and at the American Jewish Historical Society by a grant from the Jewish Historical Society of New York. Doctoral grants from the Lucius N. Littauer Foundation, the National Foundation for Jewish Culture, and the

Memorial Foundation for Jewish Culture sustained me during the dissertation period. I would like especially to thank Pamela Ween Brumberg of the Littauer Foundation for her help and encouragement. None of these institutions, nor any of the individuals who aided me, bear any responsibility for any errors or misjudgments in this work.

The final writing of the dissertation was much improved for being completed amidst the incomparable beauty of the Pacific Northwest during a year as the Hazel D. Cole Fellow in Jewish Studies at the University of Washington in Seattle. Revisions on the manuscript were completed in Boca Raton, Florida, where I was fortunate enough to join the faculty of Florida Atlantic University. Thanks are especially due to my colleagues Henry M. Abramson, Carol Gould, and Mark R. Rose.

Last but not least, thanks are due to my family. My brother and sister-in-law David and Marjorie Rosenfeld Sanua and their children, Jacob Chaim and Julia Sallie provided cheer at every step. My parents, Victor D. Sanua and Stella Sardell Sanua, dedicated to permitting their daughter opportunities unknown in their own generation, supported and encouraged me through years of graduate school, urged me on when I faltered, and never ceased to believe in me even when I did not believe in myself. My dedication of this work to them is only the smallest way I can hope to repay them for everything they have done for me.

M.S.

Introduction

"Nonsense is nonsense, but the study of nonsense—is scholarship."
These words, reportedly spoken by the eminent Jewish Theological
Seminary Talmud and Rabbinics professor Saul Lieberman when in-
troducing one of Gershom Scholem's lectures on Kabbalah and Jewish mysticism in New York in 1947, might come to mind in scholarly
quarters when confronting the theme of Jewish college fraternities and
sororities. Certainly, at first glance, it might appear a more lighthearted
and frivolous topic than is usually found in the often "lachrymose" (to
borrow a well-known phrase from Salo Baron) annals of Jewish historical investigation.

And yet, what was and is known in the United States and Canada as the "Greek system" of national college fraternity and sorority
chapters was anything but nonsense. Secret societies as such go back to
the dawn of recorded human history. These modern American groups
and the life-long peer networks they created played an important role in
the lives of millions both during and after their college years. Some of
the most prominent, wealthy, and powerful individuals in North America are college fraternity graduates. Moreover, beginning with the
founding of Pi Lambda Phi and Zeta Beta Tau in 1895 and 1898, during the first two thirds of the century, an entire Jewish Greek subsystem
for undergraduates flourished throughout all of the United States and
Canada, consisting in the 1920s and 1930s of as much as one fourth
to one third of all young Jews attending universities outside the New
York City metropolitan area. As there were once clearly defined Jewish and Gentile law firms, town clubs, country clubs, summer camps,
and debutante balls, so too were there clearly defined Jewish and Gentile college fraternities. An additional "sub-subsystem" operated to serve

Jewish male and female students at professional schools in such areas as medicine, dentistry, law, and pharmacology. For undergraduates alone, at its height in the late 1920s this Jewish Greek subsystem consisted of at least seventeen separate multi-chapter national groups for men and at least five for women. Overall, this American Greek subsystem had initiated well over a quarter million male and female students by 1968.

Overcrowding, mediocre grades, Jewish quotas, and various techniques of "selective admissions" in the large and prestigious schools of the Northeast fed the expansion of the fraternities in the 1920s and 1930s. In a phenomenon known as "Jewish student migrancy" ambitious students (overwhelmingly male), encouraged by their families, ventured hundreds and even thousands of miles from their homes on the northeastern coast of the United States to the state schools and smaller private colleges of the South, Midwest, and West to attend any university or professional training program that would accept them. Wherever in the country these students went, chapters of Jewish fraternities followed.

Although close to a quarter of the original fraternities succumbed to the economic pressures of the Great Depression, the system as a whole survived and even flourished through the 1930s. While their commitment to maintaining a pleasant social life did not waver, Jewish fraternities in the 1930s also sheltered German Jewish refugee students, provided career guidance and job opportunities for graduates, and worked to better community relations and to fight antisemitism. Their campus activities had to come to a virtual halt during World War II as students entered the armed forces. Still, fraternity national offices served as clearing-houses and nerve centers, sending out packages, disseminating news and letters, and letting soldiers know of the whereabouts and fate of their comrades. After the war, when the GI Bill of Rights sent millions of veterans to college, their chapter homes helped to alleviate a critical housing shortage.

Although rabbis and Jewish communal leaders frequently expressed disapproval of these groups for their supposed neglect of religious matters, the fraternities were counted as part of the panoply both of general campus and of American Jewish organizational life. Homecoming parades included their floats, yearbooks and annuals listed and photographed them, articles and columns described their activities in the Anglo-Jewish press, communal leaders sought them out, and their social events were documented in the society pages of the nation's newspapers. After graduation, fraternity members filled the ranks and governing boards of American Jewish defense, fraternal, and communal organizations, donating large sums to Jewish causes and putting to good use the parliamentary procedure they had honed through years of attendance at mandatory Monday night chapter meetings.

Why the need for two separate Greek systems? Divisions began at first at the turn of the twentieth century because Jewish students, arriving in significant numbers at American colleges for the first time, were excluded from the existing framework. On isolated rural or semirural college campuses, or any campus where fraternities with the blessings of the local administration were the mainstays of student life, such exclusion, aside from causing discomfort and demoralization, could have disastrous consequences. Assuming they could be admitted to a school in the first place, young Jews could still be left with no place to eat and sleep in towns where landlords and landladies did not wish to rent them rooms and fellow Gentile students refused to share quarters with them. The elaborate student cafeterias and democratically priced living complexes so taken for granted in later years were yet to be built, and college dormitories if they existed at all were apt to be too small to accommodate every student. Such practical benefits of membership could continue throughout a member's life. The traditional networking and job contacts that the fraternity provided were invaluable to people seeking to earn their living in a world hostile to Jews, in days when simply getting a job posed a major challenge. Moreover, adult members could relax, knowing in advance that the troublesome problem of restrictions against Jews would not arise at the hotels, resorts, and clubs where fraternity social events took place.

Fraternal divisions between Jew and Gentile also began because students and their families truly believed it preferable and advantageous that members eat, live, prepare for their livelihood, network, socialize, and marry among their own people—or, as the half-humorous saying went, "M.O.T." (Members of the Tribe.) Not all members of the tribe were regarded as equal, however. Ironically, Jewish fraternities could be every bit as exclusive and discriminatory as their Gentile counterparts, with each fraternity occupying a distinct place within the social hierarchy. The rhetoric of "rush week," when fraternities selected their new members, reflected sub-ethnic conflicts between "Germans" and "Russians" or among Jews of different denominations, social classes, incomes, and length of residence in the United States.

Until 1941, for example, the membership applications of the most elite Jewish fraternities and sororities included blanks for the applicant's birthplace, mother's maiden name, and the birthplace of both parents—ironically, the very same information that was being used to exclude socially undesirable students from the nation's most elite undergraduate institutions. In the upper tiers of the Jewish fraternity hierarchy a name ending in "-sky," origins in Eastern Europe or the Middle East, residence in the wrong neighborhood, or an overly "Semitic" appearance severely compromised hopes of acceptance. Fraternity officers and members obsessed over the details of maintaining proper manners, acceptable dress and quiet speech in public, and demonstrating good "school spirit," believing that the performance of Jews in these areas would make or break the reputation of their individual fraternity and also serve as the best defense against external anti-Jewish discrimination. American Jews who did not conform to this "Best Behavior" syndrome, whether in or out of the fraternity, became objects of condemnation. The internalization of external anti-Jewish behavioral and aesthetic stereotypes almost to the point of self-hatred and the tendency to fling them back against their own people is one of the most striking, if disturbing, features of these fraternities' records.

Amity and not enmity, however, was a more common result of Jewish fraternity associations. Since it encouraged and even mandated dating and marriage, the Jewish Greek subsystem served as nothing less than a national ethnic matchmaking bureau, a factor that garnered it considerable support from segments of the larger American Jewish community. Even members of the majority who hardly gave the national organization another thought after their university commencement ceremonies, or who might recall their youthful fraternity days with embarrassment, often continued to live, work, socialize, and raise their children in the company of friends or spouses first encountered within the fraternity circle. The details of these early encounters illustrate specific techniques and provide important clues on how a scattered, relatively acculturated, and highly educated group never amounting to more than three percent of the nation's population managed to maintain relatively endogamous marriage patterns for as long as it did.

When unprecedented numbers of World War II veterans and other Americans began to attend college in the late 1940s, the Greek system as a whole geared up for an era of uninterrupted expansion and growth. It was not to be, for the U.S. had undergone an important transformation. From the end of World War II onward, the basis for the insularity of sectarian fraternities and, indeed, the dominance of the system as a whole had already been steadily eroding. Factors included the democratizing influence of people united in a world war and the subsequent GI Bill, post-war inflation, a housing shortage, ideological opposition to the Greek system as a whole, large-scale construction of alternative student room and board options, and most important of all, advances in civil rights legislation at all levels of government. Laws forbidding publicly supported educational institutions from discriminating based on race or religion were extended to include on-campus fraternity houses as well. There was also widespread communal distaste bordering on collective nausea that Jewish people after the war should be deliberately and actively discriminating against either Gentiles or other Jews in the traditional fraternity membership selection process. Instead, critics charged, it was both a duty and an enhancement of self-interest for Jewish people to surrender these antiquated organizations and lead the new peacetime battle of rooting out discrimination everywhere once and for all.

The issues of restrictive clauses, freedom in choosing members, and the ability of higher authorities to dictate the racial or religious make-up of these groups tore the American college fraternity world apart. Rabbis and communal leaders were no longer sure how they could formulate policy concerning such organizations. Jewish fraternity alumni officials did not know how to react when, at long last, Gentile fraternities began to accept Jewish students in significant numbers or, conversely, Jewish undergraduates began to demand the right to accept non-Jews into their houses. In many cases, it was not external interference that fraternity officials faced but opponents from within their own camp. Especially in Jewish groups, the younger and more progressive undergraduates, alumni, and particularly the new veterans of World War II pushed for changes in membership policy that older alumni leaders were reluctant to make.

Rebellion on the nation's campuses and the ascendance of the counterculture during the Vietnam War years of the 1960s and 1970s sealed the fate of the separate Jewish Greek subsystem. Attitudes of hostility or complete indifference replaced the earlier drive for fraternity reform. While the entire American college Greek system suffered during this period of upheaval, the Jewish groups, whose potential membership was well-represented among the ranks of the campus protesters, was particularly hard-hit. Despite its size and complexity it was still smaller in absolute membership as well as younger and less well endowed financially than the older Gentile fraternities. Consequently, the weakest Jewish fraternities were forced to merge with their older contemporaries or else cease operations altogether.

In the mid-1970s and 1980s, college fraternities in general enjoyed a modest revival, although they have never again reached the position of prominence and influence that they once enjoyed on the American college campus. The Jewish Greek subsystem itself never ceased
operations entirely. At the end of the twentieth century five of the original Jewish fraternities and four of the sororities were still in operation,
although not more than three placed strong emphasis on their historical
Jewish identity and all had a significant minority, and in some cases even
a majority, of non-Jewish members. The question of how they should,
or should not, relate to their religious and ethnic heritage continues to
be a cause of internal dissent.

Regardless of the outcome of these contemporary debates, the
records of the Jewish Greek subsystem in the heyday of its sectarian existence are a treasure trove of historical, sociological, and demographic
data. Among other factors, they allow us a peek into the often cruel
realities of American college life in days gone by, and the extensive anti-
Jewish discrimination which young people encountered before, during,
and after their graduation. Determined to live as happy and as normal
a life as possible despite the obstacles in their path, these young people nevertheless often made desperate efforts to remake themselves and
their fellows into the image of what they believed society was telling
them a good American ought to be.

We may speculate that these efforts met with some success,
given the remarkable socioeconomic rise of the American Jewish community within a relatively short period of time. And yet, we may also
wonder—at what cost to their inner life and peace of mind did that success come? Evidence of a ceaseless struggle comes through the records
of these men and women who went on to become the husbands, fathers,
wives, mothers, businessmen, lawyers, judges and all-around leaders of
the American Jewish community. We encounter them here in their most
formative years before World War II. These were the professionally educated people who passed well beyond the world of their parents and
grandparents and who set the agenda of the post-1945 world. As products of that relentless struggle they would have the power to shape their
society and their nation according to all the lessons they had learned.

Chapter 1

The Origins of Jewish Fraternities

The origins of the secret student society go back as far as the origins of the western university itself, to the great medieval European centers of Oxford, Paris, Bologna, Padua, and others. Some of the ancient student traditions, songs, drinking ceremonies, and rituals have been passed down to the present day, including hazing ordeals which had already developed into recognizable form by the fourteenth century. In addition to their social functions fraternities could also provide European students with quasi-citizenship along with some of the legal support and protection they sacrificed while living far from their homes.[1]

Central European Origins

Thus American Jewish students, when they formed their own college fraternity system, were hearkening back to a tradition that went back hundreds of years. They were also evoking the traditions of the lands from where many of their ancestors had emigrated. From the turn of the nineteenth century, student fraternities and dueling societies were especially popular in the German-speaking lands of Europe, where a prominent scar left from having one's cheek slashed in a staged foil fight was accepted as a sign of masculinity, physical courage, and honor.[2]

Jewish men attending Central European universities could participate fully in such groups until the early 1880s. At that point, however, an upsurge in Teutonic nationalism and antisemitism led to the shunning or expulsion of Jewish students. By 1890, Jewish male students at the University of Vienna were no longer even allowed to resort to the ancient method of dueling to defend their honor. Gentile fraternity leaders decreed that it was beneath their dignity to duel with them, since Jews had no honor and were thus incapable of "rendering satisfaction." Over the next three decades, Jewish students and their families were driven to maintain their own dormitories and cafeterias in order to escape verbal slurs, physical violence, and exclusion from existing student facilities.[3]

No less a figure than Theodor Herzl (1860–1904) regarded as the father of modern political Zionism, was a member of *Albia*, a pan-Germanic dueling fraternity at the University of Vienna. His student days there coincided precisely with the rise of antisemitism. When Herzl in the winter of 1881 joined the "Young Foxes," as neophytes of the fraternity were known, he proudly wore their blue pillbox hat, attended all its drinking parties, joined in the choruses of student songs, played cards and chess with his fellow members, participated in their daily fencing exercises and even took private lessons with a fencing master. In March 1883, however, *Albia* members sponsored an enthusiastic memorial demonstration in honor of Richard Wagner and endorsed the composer's antisemitic views. Herzl chose not to attend and sent in his letter of resignation.[4] That same year three other Jewish students at the University of Vienna decided to form their own separate student fraternity and dueling society, naming it *Kadimah* (Hebrew for "forward.") The young men of *Kadimah* later supplied Herzl with his most ardent supporters and volunteer workers as he laid plans for the first World Zionist Congress, and *Kadimah* was specifically cited as a precedent in the founding declaration of the American Jewish fraternity Zeta Beta Tau in 1898.[5]

Greek-Letter Societies in America

In the United States, the Greek system in general stretched back to the dawn of the Republic with the founding of Phi Beta Kappa at the College of William and Mary. "Phi Bete" began as a literary, debating and social group before evolving into an honor and scholarship fraternity.[6] The "Union Triad" of the social fraternities Kappa Alpha, Sigma Phi, and Delta Phi followed, so named because they were all formed by competing student groups at Union College in Schenectady, New York, throughout the 1810s and 1820s.[7] The customary two or three Greek letters represented the society's secret motto, which was to be known only to duly initiated members; the ideals and symbols of Freemasonry were borrowed to become the core of fraternity secret ritual; and the science of heraldry provided the basis for drawing up fraternity shields, pins, and coats-of-arms.

There were numerous aspects to this student fraternity subculture, including the ancient custom of "hazing" which was to become a leading source of criticism from lawmakers and the general public. The origins of hazing lay in medieval students' practices, the custom of "fagging" at British public schools, and most importantly, the usages of military camps and academies. In the United States, hazing was at one time part of a widespread general expression of student rivalry, with the upperclassmen of a school exerting their will on the new freshmen. College officials took steps to eliminate it in favor of such innovations as freshmen beanies and intramural athletic contests. However, the practice was maintained and refined by certain boys's preparatory schools and by the student members of American Greek-letter fraternities, particularly after the end of the Civil War in 1865. At that time, campuses filled with youth who had recently trained or fought in either the Union or the Confederate Army and had thus been exposed to hazing in their military lives. This last influence caused a notable rise in the intensity of fraternity hazing beginning in the late 1860s along with the first of many efforts by adult officials and university administrations to oppose the practice by edict.[8]

Typical hazing ordeals might include a probationary period of servitude to upperclassmen, humiliating games, "line-ups," punishing physical exercises, stunts, enforced sleep deprivation, forced consumption of large quantities of liquor or bizarre foodstuffs, the repeated assignment of apparently senseless and monotonous tasks, face-painting, the wearing of unusual costumes, and the regular administration of swats with a wooden paddle for infractions of rules. In extreme cases new fraternity members might be branded, either with silver nitrate or an actual red-hot metal implement, providing a mark that was roughly equivalent to the Teutonic slashed cheek as a sign of courage and devotion. The professed goals of these techniques were to make a "man" out of the newcomer by making him physically tough, to teach him his place, to test his courage and desire to join the group, and to build *esprit de corps* among the new members by imposing group suffering and the common memory of having survived it.

Whatever trials visited upon prospective members, the new student institution of fraternities proved popular. With few exceptions, they absorbed or drove into eclipse the literary and debating societies that had dominated American colleges from the colonial period. By 1840 the Greek-letter fraternity, both in the form of new organizations and additional chapters of older ones, had penetrated most of the colleges of New England and New York, and began to spread to the West and South.[9] A crucial difference separating fraternities from their collegiate predecessors—that unlike other student clubs, fraternity members pledged their loyalty and mutual aid in secret to a greater brotherhood meant to endure not just for the years at school but for the rest of one's life—may have been an important factor in this growth.

Although not more than two percent of the American population aged 18 through 21 attended college in 1800—a figure that rose to just over four percent in 1900[10]—fraternalism in general was becoming a strong value for much larger segments of the U.S. population. Such institutions were particularly well-suited to the United States with its large geographic area and highly mobile population. Fraternities in effect could create instant close family and business ties over long distances among large numbers of peers who were not related by blood or marriage and who had not dwelt in the same town for generations. Such conditions were common elsewhere in the world but unlikely to be encountered in much of nineteenth-century America. A historian of secret societies in Victorian America noted in fact that the last third of the nineteenth century became known as the "Golden Age of Fraternity." Out of a total adult male population of nineteen million in 1896, fraternal groups of some kind claimed more than five and a half million members, although many men joined more than one order. These included such groups as the Odd Fellows (810,000 members), Freemasons (750,000 members), Knights of Pythias (475,000 members), Red Men (165,000 members) and hundreds of other groups housed in the nation's 70,000 fraternal lodges. Their rituals consumed many hours and served as a major form of entertainment. Other popular organizations that stressed secret oaths and elaborate initiations included the Grand Army of the Republic (GAR), the Knights of Labor, the Grange, and mutual insurance societies.[11]

In such a conducive atmosphere, the college Greek system flourished, particularly after the Civil War ended in 1865. A reference work devoted entirely to them, Baird's *Manual of American College Fraternities*, (popularly known as the "bible" of fraternities) began publication in 1879 and went through fifteen updated editions before the U.S. entry into World War II.[12] Two periodicals, *Banta's Greek Exchange* and *Fraternity Month*, covered their activities and served as advertising forums for the many specialized companies that sprang up to supply college fraternities with robes, ritual paraphernalia, jewelry, trophies, accounting, and food services.[13] At least fifty national men's college fraternities were established by 1900. These were joined by at least twenty of their female counterparts as higher education became available to American women.

Like the men, women wished to enjoy the special benefits of belonging to a fraternal group. Early American female collegians also felt a special need to defend themselves by banding together in the face of unwanted attentions and the opposition of critics, particularly at co-educational schools, who still viewed higher education for women with hostility. The earliest women's college Greek-letter societies on record are the Adelphean Society, later renamed Alpha Delta Pi, founded at Wesleyan Female College at Macon, Georgia, in 1851, and its sister group, the Philomathean Society (later Phi Mu). Next came I. C. Sororis (renamed in 1888 as Pi Beta Phi), founded in 1867 at Monmouth College and Kappa Alpha Theta at Indiana Asbury University (now DePauw University) in 1870.

At first, no English word other than "fraternity" existed to describe these groups, and members simply referred to their societies as "women's fraternities." However, in 1882, the young women of the Gamma Phi Beta Society at Syracuse University (founded in 1874) began a trend by renaming themselves a "sorority" at the suggestion of their advisor, a male professor of Latin who considered the use of the words "fraternity" and "fraternity house" inappropriate for a group of young ladies. His opinion was shared by others in the men's fraternity world who either could not comprehend or did not appreciate the insistence of their female counterparts upon the use of a word that was identifiably male.[14] Thus the name "sorority" caught on, although many women's groups adopted the coinage only reluctantly and continued to use the term "women's fraternities" in official documents and when speaking among themselves.

Impact of the Fraternity House

The fraternity house, a building large enough for members to live, dine, and hold social events together, was an important innovation of the post-Civil War years that helped to legitimate the secret student fraternity in the eyes of college officials. Previously a student's quarters, a boarding-house parlor, the woods, or a room at a friendly inn could serve as a fraternity chapter's headquarters. After the Civil War however, the U.S. entered a new era of industrialization, urbanization, and scientific and technical development. Its university system expanded as well in size, sophistication, and degree of public support. The ideal of the university as a place to educate ministers and train gentlemen in the Greek and Latin classics did not disappear, but it faded in importance. The new status and wealth of college alumni was a by-product of this expansion. Now, alumni often became prosperous businessmen, enriched by the post-war economic boom and eager to direct their generosity toward the proper feeding and sheltering of their undergraduate brothers.[15] In time, the words "house" and "fraternity" became almost synonymous, although poorer fraternities could and did exist without one. "Fraternity Row" became a recognized part of American campus geography.

From the beginning, not every college president favored the presence of secret student societies on campus—nor, after the Civil War, did they favor surrendering authority to the quasi-independent fraternity house. However, the houses were too great a boon to be ignored, once it was demonstrated that they could be drawn into the web of college life to the administration's advantage. Not only did houses solve the problem of providing room and board for students but they also made the task of orienting and supervising post-adolescent male college students easier. Houses could take on collective responsibility for adherence to campus curfews and regulations. The threat of probation or expulsion of the entire house was a powerful deterrent to an individual member who contemplated breaking any rules. College officials felt less pressured knowing that, in the absence of parents, a mature fraternity alumni supervisor from the neighborhood or, if necessary, the national headquarters could be called in to come give the active members an appropriate lecture.[16] The introduction of periodic local and national rankings of all fraternity houses according to their collective grade-point averages stimulated competition and encouraged fraternity officers to incorporate some form of supervised studying into their programming. This could be accompanied by codified penalties and guidance procedures for any member whose bad grades were dragging down the average of the entire house. Indeed, some college administrations required a minimum grade-point average for freshmen before allowing them to be initiated into any fraternity. The fraternity house system also encouraged competition in the areas of school activities and athletics. Members who excelled achieved glory not only for themselves but also, by extension, for the entire fraternity and even the entire college.

Finally, college presidents soon discovered that there was nothing like a fraternity house for maintaining the continued interest of alumni. Fraternity houses were superb centers for such things as return visits to campus, football games, dances, and special meetings. Houses encouraged alumni to congregate around their school and channel toward it their political power—of particular importance to state-supported universities—and their practical support. That financially successful fraternity alumni blessed with happy memories came back to their campus more often and were far more generous in their financial contributions than non-fraternity alumni soon became evident to college presidents. Even where fraternity men were a minority of the school's graduates, they still donated to their alma maters far out of proportion to other graduates. The phenomenon remained constant through the twentieth century. In 1958, for example, the president of New York University noted that ninety percent of his school's alumni gifts came from the six percent of the graduates who had been affiliated with fraternities.[17]

Legitimacy and Guarantees of Official Support

Given all the advantages that the new system of Greek-letter fraternities could offer, college officials were more than willing to grant individual groups complete autonomy in their choice of members. From the 1890s onward college administrations increasingly turned from an attitude of indifference or opposition toward one of active support, offering land and guaranteeing mortgages and access to university services. The fraternities, in turn, were willing to submit to the administration's supervision and regulations in return for this recognition and help. The innovation of houses already had led to a shift in internal organizational priorities and membership criteria. Small, intimate chapters and individual initiations throughout the year gave way to the competitive practice of "rushing," or recruiting, incoming freshmen *en masse*, to keep fraternity houses as full as possible.[18] New students, after an appropriate background check, found themselves wooed by letters, promotional literature, and personal visits to make their fraternity selections even before arriving at school in the fall, and the round of parties and interviews that constituted "Rush Week" became one of the most important campus events of the entire year.

Although the spirit of competition was inherent in such a system, impulses toward cooperation existed as well. The leading fraternities preceived common interests and the desirability of standardizing and coordinating rules of recruitment and conduct. They also discerned a need to differentiate themselves from the hundreds of smaller American Greek-letter societies which were not truly collegiate or else did not merit the status of being "national." These forces led to the formation of two national "supra-fraternities," the National Panhellenic Congress (NPC) for the women's fraternities in 1902, and the National Interfraternity Conference (NIC) for the men's fraternities in 1909.

By the time these major interfraternal organizations were founded, Greek-letter societies had become an integral part of American higher education. On scores of campuses, they took on the qualities of exclusive social clubs that completely dominated student life and politics. On many campuses the majority of students did not want, could not afford, or just did not have the time to join a fraternity or sorority chapter. Yet it was the fraternity and sorority elites who set the campus tone, served disproportionately as class officers and leaders of extracurricular activities, and symbolized the collegiate ideals that others either accepted or rebelled against.[19] From the top of the campus social scale, they tended to look down among the non-Greeks, whom they termed "Barbs" (short for "barbarians"), "Independents," and sometimes "GDIs" (short for "Goddamned Independents").

Young men clamored to join the oldest and most prestigious fraternities not only for close college friendships, a home away from home, and a pleasant social life, but because access to the Greek system promised crucial training in social skills, leadership, and life-long access to a network of powerful political and business leaders. When critics attacked them for any reason—usually because of evidence of drunkenness, debauchery, dangerous hazing or public misbehavior—fraternity officials took great pride in pointing out all the presidents, cabinet members, and Supreme Court Justices who belonged to fraternities. According to the 1935 edition of *Baird's Manual,* every American president and vice-president born since 1825, including Franklin D. Roosevelt (of Alpha Delta Phi) was a fraternity member, with the exception of two presidents and two vice-presidents. Sixty-nine of the 141 members of presidential cabinets in the preceding fifty years were fraternity alumni, as well as more than two thirds of the Supreme Court justices appointed since the Civil War, 250 U.S. Senators, 275 state governors, 500 college and university presidents and 175 bishops—not to mention hundreds of leaders in industry and the professions.[20] During World War II, the fraternity Sigma Chi announced with pride that no fewer than twenty-eight U.S. Army generals could be counted within its ranks. Of late twentieth-century American presidents, Ronald Reagan was initiated into Tau Kappa Epsilon (the "Tekes") as a student at Eureka College and maintained close ties to the group throughout his life. Although Greek-letter fraternities did not exist at Yale University while he was in attendance there, George H. W. Bush was a member of the formidable secret society known as Skull and Bones.[21]

Exclusion

This Greek system, however, in its earliest years was closed to all but exceptional or hidden Jewish students, as it was to Black and Asian students and in many cases, Roman Catholics as well. Strict barriers of racial and religious discrimination were either spelled out in the group's constitutions or enforced by gentlemen's or ladies' agreements. The explicitly Christian content in the initiation rituals and insignia of many of the existing fraternities alone discouraged Jewish membership. Various forms of crosses, for example, were among the most common motifs. Customs such as a communal Grace before meals invoking the name of "Our Lord," required weekly or monthly attendance at church services of the appropriate denomination, and group celebrations of Christmas and Easter could make a young non-Christian student, particularly one away from the shelter of his own family and home for the first time, uncomfortable.

Traditional social barriers also remained in force. Joining a fraternity theoretically meant joining an extended family. The traditional rushing question, "Would you want your sister to marry him?" was not an idle inquiry. Being able to welcome a prospective member into one's own home was a common criterion within fraternity circles, as was the assumption that the siblings of fraternity or sorority members would be among the candidates of first choice for successful marriages. However, the prospect of Jewish and Christian students living under the same roof, sharing the same table, associating at parties together, dating one another, or being accepted at each other's parental homes as "brothers" or "sisters" was remote indeed.

Juridical barriers supplemented the old social barriers. From the 1870s and 1880s onward restrictive or sectarian clauses became common in college fraternity constitutions and by-laws. Membership could be limited to those belonging to a particular church or those who were "Caucasian," "White Christian," "born a Christian of two Christian

parents," or "of full Aryan blood."[22] In one Christian fraternity in the late
1920s, possession of one-eighth Jewish blood disqualified a student for
membership.[23] More than once naïve Jewish boys or girls were pledged
to such organizations, only to be asked to return their pins when the error was discovered. College officials rarely protested these exclusions. In
their view, fraternities were private social organizations and membership
selection was a private affair. Political and legal rights were one thing,
but the values of democracy and freedom of association were interpreted
to mean that no one had a right to dictate to Americans who they should
live, eat, and be close friends with.[24]

American Jews Confront Higher Education

Jews experienced the impact of collegiate discrimination with particular
acuteness in part because of a change in the character and volume of their
emigration to the United States and their greater tendency to seek out
higher education relative to other immigrant groups.[25] In 1880, there
were only approximately 250,000 Jews in the United States. Most of
these were German or of Germanic cultural background.[26] They were
geographically dispersed with concentrations in the Midwest in such
cities as Cincinnati and St. Louis. Precise statistics on the number of
Jews attending college before World War I are scarce, but there is no
doubt that only the merest handful attended a college or university, a
reflection of the low priority that higher education held for the general
population. Certainly before the Civil War, the ministry was the only
profession that required a higher education, with practical experience
and apprenticeship serving adequately for everything else.[27] Those Jews
who did attend a college or university tended to be highly acculturated,
well-to-do, and accustomed to living within a Christian framework.
They thus managed to blend into the student body without drawing
undue attention.

Between 1880 and 1920, however, the German Jews in the U.S.
were joined by almost two million Jews from Tsarist Russia and other
parts of Eastern Europe. In comparison to the relatively well-established
German Jews, the new "Russian" Jews appeared radically different in
language, dress, appearance, manners, politics, and religious loyalties.
They tended to concentrate most heavily in the cities of the eastern
seaboard, particularly in New York City's immigrant neighborhoods.[28]
The two immigrant blocs may have been separated by no more than
one, two, or three generations, yet a huge social gulf opened between
them which was almost as wide as that between Gentiles and Jews. For

many "German" Jews, the new "Russian" Jews were an embarrassment. Religious and civil duty decreed that they be aided in every way possible yet they were despised for their foreignness and for the possibility that they might jeopardize the already vulnerable position of those Jews who had been in the country for decades.[29] This perceived internal conflict in America between "German" and "Russian" Jews was destined to play a major role in the development of the Jewish Greek subsystem. Indeed, it was to color much of internal American Jewish history as a whole in the first half of the twentieth century.

The religious, social, and cultural struggles between Jew and Jew, as well as between Jew and Gentile, were played out on the expanding college campus as the Russian immigrants and their children took their places in America. Immigrant "Russian" Jews were upwardly mobile, career-oriented, ambitious, and hungry for all the educational opportunities that had been denied them in Europe. By 1918 the immigrant Jewish presence in American higher education, particularly in schools located in large urban areas, could no longer be ignored. By that year, according to statistics published in the *American Jewish Year Book*, they made up nearly ten percent of the total number of students in all of the United States receiving any kind of professional training.[30] The compilers of the statistics also took note of the high proportion of Jewish women, 14 percent, enrolled in law school, which was almost equal to the proportion of Jewish men—14.8 percent—and in great contrast to the proportion of 1.7 percent of non-Jewish women. Jewish women also accounted for 3.3 percent and 4.5 percent of dentistry students, compared with .9 percent and .5 percent for non-Jewish women.

Even as their numbers grew, reactions against them intensified. At every school where the Jewish enrollment rose after 1880, exclusion from existing social organizations grew pervasive, although official barriers to their admission did not surface until after the First World War. Prior to the war, City College's fraternities, Princeton's clubs, Yale's junior fraternities, and Columbia's literary and gymnastic societies began the practice of excluding Jewish students as a matter of principle.[31] Bernard Baruch, who entered City College in 1884, recalled in his memoirs the importance of the Greek-letter fraternities and their exclusion of Jews. "Although many Jews made their mark at the college," he wrote, "the line was drawn against them by these societies. Each year my name would be proposed and a row would ensue over my nomination, but I was never elected."[32]

The disproportionate presence of Jews in educational institutions of all kinds was most evident in New York City, where almost half of the nation's entire Jewish population resided. By 1918, Jews constituted between seventy-five and eighty-five percent of the enrollment of the City College of New York, depending upon whether one included night school sessions. The proportion was so great that students took to claiming that the acronym of the school's name, CCNY, stood for "College of the Circumcised Citizens of New York." ("Jewlane University" and "Sophie Jewcomb College" were similar nicknames used in New Orleans.) The percentage of Jews in Columbia College's entering class reached as high as forty percent in 1919; even after methods were introduced to limit their admission, Jews still made up more than one fifth of the College's first-year students.[33] Their proportion also rose markedly at other colleges. In the perception of non-immigrants and less-recent immigrants, cultivating social graces did not take adequate priority in the lives of Jewish immigrants and their children as they rushed to take advantage of America's educational opportunities. In the blunt words of one observer, "The Jew sends his children to college a generation or two sooner than other stocks, and as a result there are in fact more dirty Jews and tactless Jews in college than dirty and tactless Italians or Armenians or Slovaks."[34]

Denominationalism at U.S. Colleges and Universities

Perfect manners and behavior, however, would not have guaranteed acceptance either. The tendency to exclude or at least to limit Jews first from social institutions and later from admissions offices also reflected deep religious differences and the denominational heritage of most of the nation's private colleges. American Jewish immigrant parents and grandparents might imagine that U.S. higher education was a sort of neutral arena where nothing but hard work and intellectual merit mattered. Yet Harvard, for example, had been founded by Congregationalists, Columbia by Episcopalians, Brown by Baptists, Princeton by Presbyterians, Northwestern by Methodists, Fordham and Notre Dame by Catholics, and so on. Their presidents, either by constitution or by custom, were drawn from the ranks of the clergy. Although training for the ministry was no longer the core of the curriculum, until well into the twentieth century some form of required chapel was a fact of life at American institutions of higher education. (At Princeton University in the 1950s, students were able to discharge their monthly chapel obligation by signing in at the Hillel Foundation's Friday night services; hence the event was known to draw the occasional non-Jewish student who was reluctant to get up too early on Sunday morning). Colleges and universities continued to reflect what was to naive Jewish students an alien and, to them, hostile religious culture long after official ties with the church were broken. Even at public state schools, students were apt to be lectured on the necessity of maintaining Christian values when they asked to be excused from Saturday exams or requested that libraries, tennis courts, athletic fields, and gyms be opened on Sunday.[35] At Yale in the fall of 1914, freshman Louis B. Sachs approached the Dean of the College to make sure that his scholarship would not be canceled because of his absence from classes on the Jewish High Holy Days. "Young man," came a characteristic answer, "We don't run a Jewish institution here, nor a Mohammedan institution, nor a Buddhist institution. This is a Christian institution, and you'll take your chances. It's entirely up to you."[36]

Jewish students who managed to be admitted and who wished to join the college fraternity circle might slip through the cracks if they were particularly outstanding in some way, were products of suitably upper-class interfaith marriages (itself no guarantee of acceptance), had been raised as Christians, or somehow managed to keep their religious identity hidden from the other members. In one early systematic investigation of American social antisemitism, Heywood Broun and George Britt's *Christians Only* (1931), the authors described the conflicts caused by such incidents:

> Very often a college fraternity will select a young Jewish student for membership. Every college has the same story and it follows identical lines. The boy in most cases says when chosen, "would it have made any difference if you knew that I was Jewish?" Thereupon there is a scurrying of the members back to the Chapter House. The boys go into a huddle— and decide that it was courageous and frank on the part of the student to declare his religious affiliation in spite of the fact that it might tend to bar him. And in most cases, under the stress of a nascent liberalism, the Jewish boy becomes a brother, and I might add, a pet Jew.[37]

If prospective members were fortunate enough not to have any stereotypically Semitic features, they could sometimes conceal their identities by the simple device of changing their characteristically Jewish names, a subterfuge which occurs frequently in memoirs and autobiographical novels. An example of this which also illustrates fraternity antisemitism in action occurs in the autobiographical novel *Unquiet,* written by Joseph Gollomb, a Russian-born journalist for the *New York*

Evening Post and *Evening World* as well as a popular author. In the novel, he describes a basketball game between Columbia University and City College in which the Columbia crowd, aware of the overwhelmingly Jewish character of their competitors, taunts the City College students with antisemitic slogans and parodies of Yiddish accents. The Jewish protagonist, a City College student named David Levitt, is even more disheartened after the game when his group goes to a crowded local beer garden and has no choice but to sit next to four members of a Greek-letter fraternity at City College that considers itself "an oasis in a desert infested by Semites" and whose members "as a rule pointedly ignored Jews at the college." The Jewish City College men recognize only George Markham, the captain of the City College football team and a member of the Gentile group, as a student who has always been impartial to both Jews and Gentiles.[38]

Reluctantly, David and his Jewish friends sit down beside the Gentile fraternity members, and the situation deteriorates predictably as more and more alcohol is consumed. When Dan Baldwin, described as the "burly blond right tackle" of the City College football team, pointedly insults his Jewish tablemates, David Levitt, under the influence of three beers, responds with a loud toast in honor of the Jews. Baldwin's arm swings to punch Levitt but is stopped in mid-air by the placid Markham. Baldwin is stunned by this reaction, until he hears the popular football captain's revelation:

> Dan Baldwin drew off and eyed Markham. "Say," he demanded, "what the hell is Levitt to you?"
> "Nothing!"
> "Then what business————?"
> "My father's name was Markheim."
> Baldwin's red face showed confusion. "Why didn't you say so when you joined the frat?"
> "I'm saying it now. My father was part Jew. And just now I'm all Jew. . . . What do you want to do about it?"[39]

Indeed, what could have been done, and sometimes was, was to ask the Jew to hand back his pin, especially when his presence violated the constitution of the fraternity.[40] Few Jews, either through lack of desire or lack of ability to hide, were willing to take that chance.

Fear of the Blackball

Barriers against admitting Jews were further complicated by the system of "blackballing," a common electoral procedure for selective social organizations. Under a blackball system, any member could veto any candidate's application for membership by casting a single anonymous negative vote. The origins of the word lay in eighteenth and nineteenth century Britain, where exclusive clubs would vote on admission of candidates by giving each member two balls: one white for acceptance, and the other black for rejection. The balls were secretly dropped into an urn, or ballot box, and then the contents of the container were examined. If even one black ball was found in the urn or box, the candidate was rejected. This system served as a powerful deterrent and justification for keeping all but the most exceptional Jews out. (In later years the system came under debate in U.S. fraternities and in many cases was replaced by admission with a majority or two-thirds vote.) With the power of the blackball granted to every member, even those Jews who were accepted might be taken only upon promising that they would not allow any more of their kind in. The fear existed, according to Broun and Britt's report, that "if one Jew is taken in, he may refuse to pass anybody else until some of his Jewish friends are admitted. No fraternity wants the reputation of having a number of Jews as members."[41]

These types of fears would be repeated, documented, and analyzed many times, in sources both written and verbal. College fraternities were but the beginning of a pervasive system of social discrimination that extended to city, town, country clubs, and related institutions across the United States. In part galvanized by their experiences of World War II, in the 1950s the largest American Jewish defense organizations— among them the Anti-Defamation League of B'nai B'rith, the American Jewish Congress, and the American Jewish Committee—adopted an attitude of zero tolerance and mobilized to root it out of American society. In the 1910s and 1920s, however, these massive efforts, and the confluence of external conditions that would favor their success, still lay years in the future.

Fraternities of Their Own

Given their exclusion from such an important part of campus life and organization, Jews and other minorities had no choice but to form their own groups if they wished to be part of the overall system. Roman Catholic students attending non-Catholic colleges, the largest non-Protestant minority, were predictably the first to do so, although official church policies opposing affiliation with secret societies hampered expansion. The first fraternity for Catholic men was Phi Kappa Sigma, created in 1889 at Brown University; its initials stood for "Fraternity of Catholic

Students."[42] Later came Theta Kappa Phi, founded at Lehigh University in 1914. Alpha Delta Gamma, the third Catholic fraternity, was meant for male students at Catholic institutions.[43] A sorority for Catholic women, Theta Phi Alpha, was founded at the University of Michigan in 1912.[44] In 1916 a fraternity for Chinese students and alumni was founded at Cornell, calling itself Rho Psi.

An alternative fraternity system for African American college students came to match and, by the end of the twentieth century, even exceed the Jewish subsystem in size and complexity, initiating almost one and a half million men and women and creating an alumni network that became a major force in African American life. Indeed its most rapid growth took place in the late 1960s and 1970s, at precisely the point that the rest of the American Greek system was contracting. The first college fraternity for African American men, roughly equivalent to Zeta Beta Tau in the internal social order, was Alpha Phi Alpha, founded at Cornell in 1906. Kappa Alpha Psi at Indiana University and Omega Psi Phi at Howard University were both founded in 1911, while Phi Beta Sigma was also founded at Howard in 1914. The Black national sororities, in turn, were Alpha Kappa Alpha (1908) Delta Sigma Theta (1913) Zeta Phi Beta (1920) all founded at Howard, while Sigma Gamma Rho was founded in 1922 in Indianapolis. By 1930 all eight Black national collegiate fraternities and sororities had joined together in their own supra-fraternal organization, the National Pan-Hellenic Council (NPHC).[45] A ninth fraternity, Iota Phi Theta, joined the national Pan-Hellenic in 1997. In the 1910s, however, the years of greatest expansion for this remarkable system lay far in the future.

For young American Jews the birth and formation of their own, separate Greek college universe was destined to take place in the first two decades of the twentieth century. By that time the basic traditions, outlines and parameters of a college Greek-letter society had been set. They knew exactly what model they wished to follow. But in those days, for the most part, they could not have joined the Gentile fraternities even if they had wanted to. Important decisions now remained, as Jews proceeded to form their own fraternities, if and how they were going to be any different from those that excluded them.

Chapter 2

"Oh, Yes, That Nonsectarian Jewish Fraternity"

The Search for Identity, 1895–1906

No easy answer ever evolved to satisfy the obvious question of what was "Jewish" about Jewish college fraternities. From the dawn of their founding at the turn of the twentieth century, these organizations were embroiled in what the renowned psychoanalyst and author Erik H. Erikson would no doubt have diagnosed as a severe identity crisis.[1] What role should, or should not, Judaism play in the membership selection or programming choices of a supposedly secular, social, American-style organization never meant to resemble a religious congregation? Should membership be restricted to Jews only or theoretically open to everyone? And what about social distinctions between Jews of different background, income, denomination, and level of observance? By perpetuating such distinctions, weren't these fraternities violating the very values of brotherhood and solidarity they supposedly sought to embody and actually playing into the hands of the antisemites?

Each of the first three men's groups founded between 1895 and 1904 began with distinctive approaches to questions of Jewish identity that in turn led to tension and dissension within the ranks. The students who founded the very first fraternity in the subsystem, Pi Lambda Phi at Yale in 1895, were so revolted by what they saw as the religious prejudice of that era that they refused to acknowledge religious divisions of any kind. So thoroughly did they embrace the ideology of nonsectarianism and membership open to all faiths that they would not admit officially, or chose to forget, that all of their founders and the majority of their members until World War II were, in fact, Jewish.

Three years later fourteen young men pursuing studies simultaneously at the Jewish Theological Seminary and at secular colleges in the New York area took the exact opposite approach when they established the Z.B.T. Society in 1898, an organization which was destined to involve into the Zeta Beta Tau fraternity. Not standing for Greek letters at all, the acronym, suggested by the young men's Talmud instructor, stood for the popular Hebrew motto "Zion shall in judgment be redeemed"—*zion be-mishpat tipadeh*. At the beginning, ZBT's constitution and ritual were deeply Jewish, with emphasis on Zionist ideals. Until 1954, only Jewish men could become members.[2] The founders of Phi Epsilon Pi, established third at City College in 1904, at first embraced the militant nonsectarianism of their Yale predecessors. Soon, however, internal opposition led its officers to a compromise stance: acknowledgment of Jewish membership and activity but maintenance of a nonsectarian constitution, leaving expressions of Judaism up to each individual.

The extremes of Zeta Beta Tau and Pi Lambda Phi set the subsystem's parameters when it came to specific Jewish identification. All subsequent twenty-odd national college Jewish fraternities and sororities founded between 1895 and 1920 began with a stated identity somewhere between these two poles and through the years frequently shifted between one and the other. In the fraternity world, official sectarianism was expressed first mainly in two ways: by the organization's published constitution, denoting conditions for membership, and in its secret rituals, or the specific vows that a "pledge" had to make before becoming a full lifetime member. Some of the younger historically Jewish fraternities and sororities never placed either sectarian or nonsectarian clauses in their constitutions at all, believing that Jewish or non-Jewish membership would never become an issue. Therefore identity questions revolved around aspects such as programming, holiday observance and fraternity symbolism. In their periodicals, correspondence, and private conversation, members from both ends of the spectrum engaged in heated debate and soul-searching on exactly what the nature of their religious and social identity should or should not be.

The debate that raged was entirely an internal one. In the early years of their existence, whether they accepted the name "Jew" or struggled for the cause of true nonsectarianism, to the outside world, these Greek-letter societies without exception were perceived as "Jewish."

Pi Lambda Phi

On March 21, 1895, three German Jewish students at Yale University—Henry Mark Fisher '97, Louis Samter Levy '98, and Frederick Manfred Werner '98, rebelled against the social barriers of their school's Greek system by forming the first chapter of a national fraternity that would not raise any tests of race, religion, color or creed for membership. Leading their organization along lines "broader and more liberal than those employed at the present time," they stated their guiding principle as "non-sectarianism and the recognition of men on the basis of ability above all considerations."[3]

This notable innovation in collegiate fraternalism flourished, albeit with an overwhelmingly Jewish membership. Within two years of its founding at Yale, additional chapters of Pi Lambda Phi were established at Columbia, City College, Cornell, New York University, Harvard, the University of Pennsylvania, the Massachusetts Institute of Technology, and Union College. Founder and chapter president Henry Mark Fisher, who went on to receive his rabbinical ordination from Hebrew Union College in Cincinnati in 1903, found sufficient happiness during his undergraduate days to call Yale in his yearbook entry "the best college on earth."[4]

However, as often happened in transient undergraduate organizations, the founders graduated and left fraternity activities behind. None took their place and the first chapter at Yale ceased to exist. Soon after, all the other chapters except that at New York University succumbed as well, and Pi Lambda Phi added no new chapters until it suddenly emerged again at Columbia University in 1912.[5] The undergraduates who reorganized the society at that point somehow transformed the founders at Yale into a Protestant, a Catholic, and a Jew—or as all subsequent fraternity publicity and entries in *Baird's Manual of American College Fraternities* would have it, "undergraduates of different faiths."[6] Even the clerical denomination of Rabbi Mark Fisher, who after his ordination became a prominent congregational leader in Atlantic City and presumably paid little attention to his fraternity's progress, became transformed. In an article appearing in the *Jewish Daily Bulletin* of May 1929, during the protracted struggle of Pi Lambda Phi leaders to be accepted as a truly nonsectarian fraternity at Brown University, he was identified as "Rev. Henry Mark Fisher of Atlantic City, who is a Christian."[7] Rumor and collegiate folklore had somehow become a virtual fact. Such blurring of the lines of transmission could happen easily on any campus, after all, where the distance between three graduating classes could be infinity. Moreover, events leading to the founding of the original Pi Lambda Phi had occurred before some of the 1912 Columbia students had even been born.

Strong leadership, ideological purity, and no doubt the ultimate cachet of having been founded at Yale (as opposed to Jewish Theological Seminary, City College, Columbia, Cornell, or the University of Rochester) helped to fuel the new Pi Lambda Phi's rapid expansion across the United States and into Canada after 1912. Indeed, as the century progressed, and in particular after World War II, Pi Lambda Phi was able to enroll within its ranks more non-Jews than any of the other historically Jewish fraternities. In the process, it would appear that it became the fraternity of choice for the small number of relatively upper-class college men—such as Oscar Hammerstein II—who were products of interfaith marriages, particularly those between Jewish men and Episcopalian women.[8] However, between 1900 and 1912, Pi Lambda Phi enrolled few if any students, and the organization lay moribund.

Zeta Beta Tau

Zeta Beta Tau, which did not begin as a Greek-letter group at all, enjoyed far more success in the first decade of the twentieth century, although the ideological path it traveled was far from smooth. It was established on December 29, 1898 at the Jewish Theological Seminary under the leadership and inspiration of Professor Richard J.H. Gottheil. The Jewish identity of what he called "my ZBT boys" remained a preoccupation of Gottheil's until the end of his life, and his young charges found themselves struggling with his ideals even as they admired his personal qualities. Born in Manchester, England, in 1862, Gottheil moved to New York City at the age of eleven when his father Gustav was called to the pulpit of Temple Emanu-El, one of New York City's oldest and most prestigious Reform Jewish congregations. Gottheil received his BA from Columbia in 1881. One of his classmates, who graduated one year later, was Nicholas Murray Butler, the Nobel-Prize winning educator who gained fame as Columbia's president from 1901 to 1945, during which time he came to be known in some quarters as "Tsar Nicholas." While Butler's relationship with the Jewish communities of Columbia and of New York City was often complex and paradoxical, the two men enjoyed a life-long association which was cordial if not outright warm, and Butler came to serve as a valuable professional ally when Gottheil took up his teaching career at Columbia.[9]

After graduation from Columbia, Gottheil continued his studies abroad at the universities of Berlin, Tübingen, and Leipzig, where he
received his doctorate in Semitics in 1886. Upon his return to America
he was appointed as an instructor at his alma mater, and quickly rose to
the rank of full professor and chairman of the Department of Oriental
Languages, an unusual achievement at the time for a Jewish scholar. In
addition to his impressive academic credentials and remarkable erudi-
tion, Gottheil, in his first years of teaching enjoyed the advantage of a
position endowed by the members of the Temple Emanu-El congregation; it is not known what his professional fate would have been had
his funding been left up to Columbia alone.[10] His teaching career at
Columbia spanned forty-nine years. During that time, Gottheil became
the de facto advisor and advocate for Columbia's Jewish student body.
He and his Beirut-born and Paris-educated wife Emma Leon Gottheil
also opened their home as a gathering-place not only for Columbia men
but also for students from the Jewish Theological Seminary, City College, and New York University.[11]

Gottheil's interests were not limited to purely academic pursuits. With the encouragement of his father, he also embraced the cause
of political Zionism.[12] After attending the second World Zionist Congress in 1898, he was elected president of the FAZ (Federation of
American Zionists, a precursor to the ZOA—Zionist Organization of
America). His doctoral student at Columbia, the young Rabbi Stephen
Wise, served as Secretary. At the time, the Zionist movement was in its
infancy. Most Jewish immigrants to America were far too busy trying to
establish themselves in the country that in, practical terms, had become
their Promised Land. Any ideology that called for the establishment of
a Jewish state in an Ottoman province half a world away smacked of
wasteful dreaming at best and disloyalty at worst.[13]

The cause of Zionism was equally remote for the young, acculturated, well-to-do Jewish college men whom Gottheil encountered
daily back at Columbia. Yet it was precisely these young men who represented to him the best and brightest of their people, the most promising
potential leaders in the quest for a Hebrew renaissance. A Zionist student society modeled after similar groups recently formed in Central
Europe, Gottheil believed, might help convince these potential leaders of American Jewry that a Jewish homeland was worth fighting for.
More importantly, the adoption of Zionist ideals might bolster their
self-esteem, confidence, and pride in their heritage.[14] In acting upon
this idea, Gottheil had in mind a discussion which had taken place at
the annual conference of the Central Conference of American Rabbis

(CCAR) a U.S. Reform rabbinical group, in 1896. When they investigated the lot of Jewish collegians the rabbis discovered to their dismay that Jewish students were commonly ashamed of their background, going to great lengths to change their names and hide their identity.[15] If this was to be the path of the American Jewish educated elite, Gottheil and America's Reform rabbis wondered, then where could the community expect to look for its leaders in the future?

Gottheil was therefore eager to use any influence he had to encourage his student followers to form a collegiate Zionist fraternal organization. Those who were studying at the Jewish Theological Seminary in addition to Columbia were particularly quick to grasp the potential of such a group. There is in fact some evidence that Z.B.T. itself was a product of a small, preexisting organization, the Young American Zionists, founded independently by the students in 1897 immediately after the first World Zionist Congress.[16] Four of the original group—Aaron Eiseman, Herman Abramowitz, Bernard C. Ehrenreich, and David Liknaitz—were ordained and went onto prominent careers in the American and Canadian rabbinate and Jewish organizational life.[17]

In their founding statement, the young men of Z.B.T. specifically cited Vienna's *Kadimah* as their model. In addition to borrowing the Zionist symbols of a blue-and-white flag and the Star of David, they adopted Hebrew names for their officers and institutions. The *Nasi* (prince or president) was the head officer; *Segan Rishon* and *Segan Sheni* were the first and second vice-president: the *Sopher* (scribe) acted as secretary, while the positions of financial secretary, treasurer, and sergeant-at-arms were called the *Ro'eh Cheshbonoth*, the *Gizbar*, and the *Shomer Hasaph*. Presiding over the *Beth Din* (advisory and executive board) was the *Ab Beth Din*, a title going back to Talmudic times. The stated objectives of the organization according to its original constitution were "to promote the cause of Zionism and the welfare of Jews in general; and to unite fraternally all collegiate Zionists of the United States and Canada."[18] The name itself, Z.B.T., represented a Hebrew letter acronym for a motto that adorned the badges of delegates to the earliest World Zionist Congress convened by Theodore Herzl in Europe.

For two years, the original Z.B.T. flourished as a Zionist-oriented society, and the original fourteen members in New York City were joined by others who later became well-known public figures. These included Mordecai Kaplan, American Jewish leader and founder of Reconstructionism, U.S. Supreme Court Justice and Harvard Law Professor Felix Frankfurter, and Abraham Arden, NYU Class of 1901, better known as A.A. Brill, Austrian-born psychoanalyst and American translator and popularizer of Freud.[19] By 1900, the organization had chapters in New York, Baltimore, New Haven, and Cincinnati, and it represented eighteen different colleges and universities.

In its earliest years, ZBT would not have been recognized as a typical American college fraternity. Instead, it functioned more in the manner of German student clubs that operated in such places as Tübingen and Heidelberg. This development was not surprising, since the majority of the founders were either German Jews or from families which had embraced the dominant German Jewish culture and who might otherwise have sent their sons to Germany to pursue their higher education. There were no chapter houses or living quarters and they did not restrict membership to students from one particular school. All of the members of what came to be known within Zeta Beta Tau's history as "The Home Fraternity" came together from several schools and gathered at cafés and beer cellars in Manhattan, their favorite being the Café Logeling on Fifty-Seventh Street. There, at monthly meetings, they would listen to speakers—frequently Gottheil himself—and then discuss and debate various topics. These began with Zionism, antisemitism, the nature of Jewish identity, Jewish literature, and methods of furthering Jewish observance. Soon they progressed to burning political issues of the day including labor unrest, votes for women, and tariffs vs. free trade. They also drank beer, ate sandwiches and pretzels, smoked their pipes, and sang songs.[20]

Defending Jewish rights was high on the agenda of this original Z.B.T. (in its pre-Greek days, the custom was to place periods between the letters.) In the fall of 1899 for example, its Committee on Press and Propaganda published an open letter entitled "Stand for Your Faith" in the *American Hebrew* newspaper as part of an attempt to rally New York's Jews against the Columbia University practice of holding classes and entrance exams on Saturday. Classes on the Jewish Sabbath had already been, and for years continued to be, a regular feature of American college life. However, only at the end of 1898–1899 academic year did Columbia officials decide to schedule certain required college entrance examinations on that day as well. At that point, the consternation of Jewish parents who wished to send their sons to Columbia stirred Z.B.T. to action.

Committee president David Levine chided his readers for passively enduring this affront and taking the traditional religious attitude "that Israel is, after all, in 'Galuth' [Exile] and that we must reconcile ourselves to circumstances." By then, he pointed out to them, the number of Jewish students studying at Columbia was not small. "If we all show that we do not take kindly to instruction and examinations on the Sabbath," he declared, "such instruction and examinations will be prescribed for weekdays only. . . . If we are not tardy in giving this important matter the attention it deserves the schedule for next year will eliminate the undesirable hours. It is only of late that Sabbath sessions were introduced, and, as they are few in number, their abolition will not be a radical procedure."[21]

From Zionist Society to American Fraternity

Despite its early successes, the political and Zionist ardor of Z.B.T., following again a common collegiate pattern, faded after the original members graduated.[22] From 1900 to 1902, when the renowned scholar and rabbi Solomon Schechter arrived from England to complete the reorgnization of Jewish Theological Seminary, Z.B.T.'s focus shifted gradually away from the dual-curriculum rabbinical students and toward those pursuing secular studies only at City College, NYU, and Columbia full-time. The Seminary became less a part-time afternoon school and more of a full-fledged, full-time institution. It could no longer serve easily as a center for all of New York's Jewish university students. At the same time, the political and cultural background of Z.B.T.'s potential membership was broadening. By November 1901, less than three years after the organization's founding, its leaders resolved, as then-secretary Maurice L. Zellermayer recalled, to change the object of the fraternity to "the promotion of Judaism" since "it was found that as a Jewish College Fraternity we ought not to shut out those Jewish college men who were desirous of entering our Fraternity, but had not as yet taken any definite stand on the Zionist question."[23]

Other factors encouraged the transformation. Z.B.T. began to abandon the "Home Fraternity" model in favor of the more conventional multiple campus chapter form of organization when it absorbed Omicron Epsilon Phi, a local Greek-letter Jewish fraternity at City College. The Z.B.T. men themselves had already decided that their Hebrew initials could also represent the Greek letters of Zeta Beta Tau.[24] After the merger on February 2, 1903, the former local group, not the group at the Jewish Theological Seminary, was designated as Zeta Beta Tau's first or "Alpha" chapter. Subsequent chapters were designated with the customary Greek letters in the order of their founding.

The change was almost unavoidable as the Jewish fraternity idea spread across the country. Particularly on campuses outside large metropolitan areas, students were clamoring for an organization that would supply them with the room, board, social life, and a place within campus life that they could not find among the Gentile fraternities. Zeta Beta Tau's earliest entry in the national fraternity bible, *Baird's Manual,* stated the nature of the change explicitly: "It soon became apparent that Jewish college men in colleges other than those situated in New York were interested in any society which called itself a fraternity, because they were themselves not members of the fraternities existent at their colleges. The insistent demand for an exclusively Jewish Greek-letter college fraternity therefore changed ZBT into Zeta Beta Tau."[25]

In 1904 Bernard Bloch (who later anglicized his name to Block), one of the founders, articulated a further new mission for Zeta Beta Tau: the instruction of its members in the social graces and gentlemanly conduct, according to the standards of their surroundings, which would aid in professional, personal, and family success, ease the impact of antisemitism, and add to members's own enjoyment and happiness in life. A plethora of adult American Jewish organizations was even then in the process of formation. These organizations were already addressing every cause on the political spectrum, from the rescue of Jews everywhere else around the world, to the question of a Jewish homeland. Social training, however, would become the mission taken up with enthusiasm by the entire Jewish Greek subsystem. "The Jewish college man, like his Christian colleagues, seeks an outlet for social recreation," Bloch wrote. "He looks about him and sees college organizations, known as fraternities. He knocks for admission, but admission is denied him . . . We have banded together because we have recognized that a fraternity is a necessity. The Jewish student today is inferior to his colleagues in his social training. It is the purpose of our fraternity to train its members in a social way."[26]

Concern for social life and recreation did not mean that the evolving Zeta Beta Tau abandoned its Jewish educational programming. Lecturers on Jewish history and culture continued to address the members periodically. For decades, reading at least one Jewish book and answering basic questions on Jewish history were part of every pledge's preparation for admission. The charge to remember that one was representing "the highest type" of one's people and thus carried the burden of extra responsibility was written into ZBT's rituals in the 1920s. Until 1954 the final secret vows of an initiate included the words "I am a believer in God and the Brotherhood of Man; I am a Jew."[27]

On the American college campus, however, it was clear that the prevailing winds were blowing from Athens and not from Jerusalem. In 1906, after several years of discussion, planning, and informal use of Greek letters, Z.B.T. was officially reorganized and incorporated as Zeta Beta Tau, adopting all the constitutional and organizational features of a regular American college fraternity.[28] With the exception of the term *Nasi* to denote the highest leaders of the fraternity or of an individual chapter, the Hebrew names for officers and governing bodies were discontinued. (Even the Hebrew title *Nasi*, pronounced in those days "NOH-si," was jettisoned in the 1930s because members and especially German Jewish student refugees sheltered in ZBT houses did not feel comfortable using a title so close to the dreaded term "Nazi.") The "Supreme *Beth Din*," for example, became the "Supreme Council." The fraternity's crest and lapel pin, which identified it to the outside world, still included a small Star of David. The letters ZBT were still used. However, it was understood that the acronym—now to be written without periods between the letters—represented Greek and not Hebrew letters. In the new crest, designed by Herbert Lippman (Columbia '09) the traditional Star of David was still there, but it was now deemphasized in favor of more common symbols of fraternal life, including the censers of Justice, the lamp of Learning, the clasped hands of Friendship, a Greek Temple representing nobility of spirit, and the *memento mori*, a skull and bones—a powerful symbol which, among other things, was supposed to remind its viewers of their ultimate destination and the fate of a man left alone and without friends.[29]

For those who wished to enjoy conventional fraternity life without denying their origins in a theoretically nonsectarian organization such as Pi Lambda Phi, Zeta Beta Tau provided an alternative. In time, its seniority relative to other groups and its relative nobility of origin made ZBT the fraternity of choice for the American Jewish aristocracy. Most commonly, this meant affluent native-born Jews descended from German or French Jewish Reform families or those from a related Central or Western European culture, as opposed to more recent Yiddish-speaking immigrants from parts of Tsarist Russia or Poland. In part because of their exclusion of other types of Jews, ZBT unwittingly helped set into motion what would become the rapid proliferation of alternative Jewish fraternities from 1904 to 1920.

ZBT and the Fight for Jewish Identity

The long transformation from a Hebrew-letter to a Greek-letter organization could not and did not come about without tension. Debates about just how far Zeta Beta Tau should go in committing itself to Jewish education or social work activities remained a constant feature of the fraternity's internal life. Each issue of the *Zeta Beta Tau Quarterly*, a periodical whose first issue appeared in 1913, carried editorials urging members to participate in such organizations as the Young Men's Hebrew Association, the Jewish Big Brother movement, and most importantly, the local campus Menorah Societies, grouped under the Intercollegiate Menorah Association (IMA). No discussion of the history of Jews in American higher education in the early twentieth century could be complete without reference to these societies.

The first college Menorah Society, a Jewish cultural and literary club, had been established at Harvard University in 1906. Not unlike a national fraternity, the organization subsequently established chapters at schools across the country. As the largest, most vigorous, and in many ways the most competitive Jewish college movement outside the burgeoning Jewish fraternities, the Menorah Society, more than any other Jewish student organization, served as the indicator of the presence—or absence—of a strong Jewish identity within Zeta Beta Tau.[30] It was perhaps not surprising that Richard Gottheil, deeply disappointed by the Hellenistic turn that his beloved ZBT had taken, embraced the cause of Menorah and similar organizations and repeatedly urged the brothers of Zeta Beta Tau to join its ranks. "There is now hardly a college or a university that has not its society of students devoted to the care of Jewish interest—a Menorah, a Forum, or the like," Gottheil reminded his readers in April 1916 in an open letter published in the *Zeta Beta Tau Quarterly* entitled "Our Proper Position." "I trust I am wrong when I say that our Zeta Beta Tau members are conspicuous in their councils—by their absence. But that, at least, has been my experience."[31] Henry Hurwitz, the editor-in-chief of the Menorah Journal and later Chancellor of the organization, also urged Zeta Beta Tau men to join all Jewish students in the Menorah without regard for exclusivity or social divisions. Menorah, he declared should serve as a common forum for all, both "Greeks" and "Barbarians," where "the spirit of mutual understanding and friendship thwart all social and other cleavages" and members could move beyond their "narrower fraternity interests."[32]

However, a wide social gulf tended to separate adherents of the Menorah societies and adherents of the Jewish fraternity system. Menorah's leaders were largely the children or grandchildren of immigrants from Eastern Europe, usually with some traditional Jewish learning. The organization's leaders, in complete contrast to the fraternity ethos, actively discouraged holding purely social events, catered to the intellectual elite, and were by nature particularistic in their programming. Meanwhile, Jewish fraternity members sought to blend in and advance their collective Judaism, if at all, through conformity to Gentile manners and standards of excellence in mainstream campus activities. The very existence of the Menorah movement rendered Z.B.T.'s official participation questionable. By assuming the original cultural and educational goals of the former Z.B.T. society (although not, to the same extent, its strong Zionism), Menorah became what could easily be seen as the proper address for distinctively Jewish campus activities. The fraternities took care of the immediate needs and desires of a typical American college student.[33]

Though a scion of a rabbinical family, Gottheil should perhaps have realized that his high standards for Jewish observance and public activity could no longer be met by the new Zeta Beta Tau Fraternity. The young members had reason to believe that these old standards were unfair. More than a decade had passed since ZBT's membership ceased to be composed primarily of theological students. Yet membership was still limited to Jewish men, and pledging allegiance to the Jewish people was still an important part of the organization's rituals and training exercises for newcomers. Moreover, each young man had taken a significant step in choosing to affiliate with an openly Jewish fraternity and not choosing other nonsectarian alternatives. What more could Gottheil ask of them?

Still, the Zionist professor was not satisfied, and made a valiant effort to return ZBT to what he saw as the complete Jewish and Zionist spirit of its founders. After successfully running for the position of Supreme *Nasi* of the fraternity in December of 1911, Gottheil took every opportunity to exhort members to participate in the Menorah societies of their respective campuses and to take the lead in Jewish activities. He openly accused his charges of abandoning Jewish values altogether when, as their executive leader, he addressed the 1914 Zeta Beta Tau Convention in New York. There, delegates gathered from nineteen chapters across the United States and Canada, including students from

Cornell, the University of Pennsylvania, Boston University, Western Reserve, Ohio State, the University of Illinois, Tulane, and McGill, as Gottheil accused them of permitting "the social aspects of fraternity life to become all-absorbing." Among other criticism, he decried the lack of any Jewish works of art or books in ZBT chapter houses.[34] For that year's keynote speakers, he secured two of the best-known and most persuasive Jewish notables of the era, Israel Friedländer and Louis Brandeis, and made sure that the convention opened and closed with invocations and benedictions from prominent rabbis. Satisfied with these efforts, in a letter afterward to his friend Horace Kallen at the University of Wisconsin, a leading American intellectual who had embraced Zionism, Gottheil confided with obvious glee that at the convention "the boys had more Jewish material shot into them on that one day than they usually get during the whole year."[35]

Two years later, at the 1916 convention Gottheil again accused the members point-blank of not recognizing "the reciprocal duty" they had taken upon themselves by electing him Supreme *Nasi.* Once again he deplored the lack of Jewish books in chapter houses and the small number of ZBT members enrolled in university courses of Jewish interest.[36] Finally, in 1919, after Gottheil had stressed one too many times the importance of Zeta Beta Tau candidates being dedicated adherents to Judaism, the members of the McGill chapter dared to publish a plaintive letter in the *Zeta Beta Tau Quarterly* rejecting his criteria for membership and substituting their own.

"If a prospective pledgee is a good student and interested in Jewish affairs, but lacks good fellowship, i.e. the ability to get along with the fraters, he will not be initiated," they wrote, defending their selection process. "But if a man has the personality to make himself well liked by the fraters, he will be accepted whether he has the first two qualities or not. So, fellowship is the primary consideration. Of course, if he has the other qualities, all the better."[37]

That fall, Gottheil announced his decision to resign as Supreme *Nasi* of Zeta Beta Tau at the end of the 1920 academic year in order to pursue a sabbatical year at the University of Strasbourg and to conduct an extensive tour of post-war Europe.[38] Immediately editorials and letters from students began to appear in the *Quarterly,* indirectly criticizing their old *Nasi* and calling for the abandonment of all mandatory Jewish educational efforts. One group of youthful correspondents, writing in the last months of Gottheil's official stewardship, struck out at their adult targets in despair and confusion, denying both that they had failed to live up to ZBT's ideals and that the ideals propounded by the adult Convention speakers were truly those of their fraternity.

Despite all of the speeches stressing the need for "Jewishness," the young men pointed out, "no one seems to have more than a hazy idea of what that means." Living a "clean and upright life" and conducting themselves at all times in such a way as to prove equal to their non-Jewish fellows was their true ideal, not taking an active part in establishing centers for Jewish learning in the colleges. "How can we," they demanded,

> inexperienced and pressed for time, be expected to hold these weekly discussions on subjects of Jewish history and philosophy, when the Rabbis whose life work is to do that sort of thing are meeting with no marked degree of success? We would appreciate any practical suggestions from our honorary members as to how we can be of greater service to our religion. We would appreciate any constructive criticism on their part, and we believe that the fraternity would be grateful for any help that they might give. But let them not accuse us of having failed to live up to our ideals when they do not seem to even know what our ideals are.[39]

In May 1920 another strongly-worded editorial written by student editors outlined a new set of goals for the fraternity in the post-Gottheil years. It clearly stated principles that had first surfaced in 1901–1906 and had in all probability been the goal of the majority of Zeta Beta Tau's undergraduate members all along. "The prospective pledge," the editorial ran,

> ignorant of our *raison d'etre*, sees a group of Jewish college men who are the leaders of their classes in mentality, refinement, good fellowship, ability, and character, banded together by the closer bonds of fraternal intimacy . . . and *he joins the Organization, not because of its Jewishness, but because it is a successful collegiate organization which will help make his college life more interesting, profitable, and attractive.*

The writers continued:

> This, we maintain, is our real purpose. To demand a certain amount of Jewish learning as a requirement for admittance into our Fraternity is to misunderstand the ideals which a great majority of our members now profess. . . . *Our Fraternity is now frankly a collegiate organization striving to adjust the Jew to his collegiate environment.* . . . By so doing we present a united front of the best young blood of our race and make the best possible impression on the outside world. The average college man is apt to forget

that the successful Jew is a Jew. We label our men as Jews by the fact that he is a ZBT man. We say to the world, "Remember, all ZBT men are Jews. Wherein do they differ from you?" But we do not strive to emphasize our Jewishness in other ways. It is enough if we make them realize that we are Jews: we need not accentuate our Jewishness. [40]

The resignation of Richard Gottheil as Supreme *Nasi* sealed the ideological fate of Zeta Beta Tau fraternity. To the end of his life in 1936 and even after, he was revered as the founder and guiding spirit of the fraternity. As a professor at Columbia, he continued to welcome visits by the undergraduate fraternity leaders of the campus and to dispense advice and counsel. In the expression of his final wishes, written to Rabbi Stephen Wise in 1935, he requested that the brothers of Zeta Beta Tau—whom he referred to as "my boys"—line the aisle of Temple Emanu-El as his coffin was carried out after his funeral services there. [41] When he died his black-bordered portrait was displayed in every chapter house and all Zeta Beta Tau men were asked to observe a period of mourning. Zeta Beta Tau continued to graduate its share of rabbis and individuals active in Jewish social, educational and charitable affairs. But from the 1920s onward, the balance of ZBT's undergraduate membership was content to demonstrate its loyalty to Judaism by membership in a fraternity modeled along Greek collegiate lines.

Phi Epsilon Pi and the Struggle for Nonsectarianism

The first two fraternities, Pi Lambda Phi and Zeta Beta Tau, represented two ideological and religious extremes in the developing Jewish Greek subsystem. In contrast, later fraternities took the option of leaving matters of religion and culture up to the individual members, whether they specifically limited their membership to Jews, pursued the route of official nonsectarianism, or chose to ignore the entire question. The third group in the subsystem, Phi Epsilon Pi, was founded by a group of seven friends at City College in 1904. [42] While retaining some of the social cachet of Pi Lambda Phi and Zeta Beta Tau and striving to provide its members with the best features of a Gentile fraternity, Phi Epsilon Pi's officers considered themselves "the legitimate child of feelings of disapproval with the narrowing horizon of social ideals of the older fraternities." [43]

By constitution and ritual, in contrast to Zeta Beta Tau, Phi Epsilon Pi was to be ecumenical and nonsectarian. Theoretically, young men of any faith were welcome to join, and no mention of Judaism ap-

peared either in the constitution or in the initiation ritual. Phi Epsilon
Pi's officers stressed this repeatedly in their correspondence, although
it should not be thought that they ignored the subject of religion entirely. In fact, when drawing up the fraternity's identifying crest, these
City College students chose to include the symbols of the three great
monotheistic religions: a large central cross to represent Christianity,
flanked on either side by a small crescent to represent Islam and an even
smaller star to represent Judaism, although whether by error or by intention the star had five points rather than the traditional six.[44] A group
of transfer students formed the fraternity's second chapter at Columbia
University in 1905, followed by the third and first out-of-town chapter
established at Cornell in 1911.[45]

    Phi Epsilon Pi's forthright nonsectarianism in many ways was
similar to that of Yale's dormant Pi Lambda Phi. It reflected not only the
members's refusal to acknowledge the religious differences which barred
them from full participation in college society, but also their obvious
dislike and direct competition with Zeta Beta Tau. In the first twenty-
five years of its existence Phi Epsilon Pi tended to draw its membership
from the same socioeconomic pool as Zeta Beta Tau—that is, middle- or
upper-middle-class German Reform Jews of some affluence—who had
either been rejected by Zeta Beta Tau, preferred the company of the men
in one fraternity over another, or who were repelled by what they considered the overly Jewish emphasis of their fraternal predecessor. Competition developed along geographic lines as well. Some fraternities and
sororities, such as Phi Epsilon Pi, developed special dominance in the
South, while others might have a greater presence in the northeast and
Midwest. Also, as in the case of Pi Lambda Phi, stressing their nonsectarianism was an important tactic in combating the anti-Jewish barriers
placed in their way by college presidents and administrators who did
not want to attract any more Jews to their campuses by allowing Jewish
fraternities to establish a foothold there.

    However, as inevitably happened in the first two decades of the
twentieth century when a college fraternity was founded by Jewish students, translating the nonsectarian theory into fact proved to be virtually
impossible. Phi Epsilon Pi found the task of recruiting any more than
a handful of Gentile members fruitless. According to one calculation
made by the organization's national secretary, the non-Jewish members
never numbered more than fifty, and all them were no longer active by
1923.[46] In addition, college administrators, when dealing with Phi Epsilon Pi's requests to establish chapters at new schools, revealed that they

were not fooled by the fraternity's alleged nonsectarianism. That the officers nevertheless persevered and felt it necessary to go to almost comic lengths in their efforts illustrates just how religiously divided American social institutions were and just how desperately some American Jewish college students sought to deny it.

By 1916 Phi Epsilon Pi had grown to eleven chapters, including branches at the University of Rochester, the University of Pittsburgh, the University of Pennsylvania, Pennsylvania State College, Dickinson College, and Rutgers. The organization was eager to grow further. In strong competition with Zeta Beta Tau, it had established its preeminence in the American South by establishing two chapters at the University of Georgia and the University of Virginia, the former for a brief time providing the fraternity's most energetic national leadership. However, the desire to persuade non-Jews to join was a constant obstacle to growth. "You are sufficiently aware of the non-sectarian character of Phi Epsilon Pi and of the fact that its members are mostly Jewish," cautioned the fraternity's secretary, Jesse Acker, a graduate of City College, to a former classmate and medical school student attempting to form a chapter at the University of Michigan in 1916. "You will undoubtedly explain this part of it [to Philip Weisberg, their contact there] better than I can . . . You are also aware that the National Committee encourages the initiation of both sects into the fraternity and in acquiring new chapters always impresses upon them the necessity for maintaining the non-sectarian character."[47] The acquisition of non-Jewish members, Acker hinted, would also insure that the fraternity drew those men who truly wanted to be in it and not "men who merely want to come in to a fraternity for the sake of wearing a pin regardless of its significance"— i.e. Jewish students who could not have been accepted anywhere else. The warning was repeated throughout the year to anyone contemplating the formation of a new chapter.

Occasionally, the fraternity was successful in finding a Gentile to join it. Acker rejoiced a week later when he heard that a chapter at the Georgia Institute of Technology in Atlanta had been installed with eight men. One of them was a Roman Catholic. "With the nucleus we have down there, we certainly have a tremendous start," Acker wrote to Herman Kline (previously Klein) one of the fraternity's leading field organizers.[48] More typical, however, was the situation at the University of Michigan, where efforts to form a "mixed" group met with no success at all. Not a single Gentile name appeared on the list when Philip Weisberg, a Penn Phi Epsilon Pi graduate attending law school in Ann

Arbor, sent to New York City the names of the six young men he had found who were ready to form a new chapter. Acker was not pleased. "We would call to your attention the fact that Phi Epsilon Pi is non-sectarian and that the names appearing on the pledge list signify members of the Jewish descent only," Phi Epsilon Pi's leader sternly reminded his Ann Arbor associate. "This condition should be remedied at once, if possible." Weisberg, who despite a heavy load of legal studies had been putting great effort into setting up the new Michigan undergraduate chapter, defended his actions. "I have not included Gentiles among our numbers because we have not as yet come across any men of that faith, whom we would like to have as fraternity brothers, and who are not members of fraternities already," he wrote back. "However, we would gladly consider such a fellow, if the opportunity presents itself."[49]

By the end of the year, Acker was becoming impatient. In writing to A.N. Krieger of Baltimore, who was then attempting to form a chapter at Johns Hopkins University in November 1916, Phi Epsilon Pi's leader in New York warned:

> If I were you, I wouldn't try to make up a local of all Jewish men. We are always trying to boost the non-sectarian character of the Fraternity, but it seems that the Chapters insist upon getting only Jewish men. I admit that there is some difficulty in getting good gentile fellows, but there certainly seems to be lack of cooperation some place. I hope that if we start a chapter at Johns Hopkins, it will be done on a truly non-sectarian basis.[50]

Despite all these efforts Phi Epsilon Pi chapters out in the field became so thoroughly Jewish, with some actually joining the Menorah Society en masse and sponsoring prayer services on the Sabbath and other holidays, that a group of discontented students at the University of Alabama chapter in the spring of 1917 threatened to secede from the national fraternity union and join the older organization Pi Lambda Phi. By that year "Pi Lam," which had faded from the collegiate scene in 1903, was flourishing once more. Even though its membership was still virtually all Jewish, the older fraternity appeared to be far more faithful to the nonsectarian creed than the younger Phi Epsilon Pi.[51]

In hopes of averting Alabama's secession, the National Committee of Phi Epsilon Pi strove to collect sworn data that would prove to the discontented members the truthfulness of the fraternity's nonsectarian claim. Ralph Dubin, the secretary of the fraternity's "Alpha" chapter at CCNY, expressed surprise at the actions of his Alabama fraters and was pleased to report on his own chapter's relatively cosmopolitan nature.

City College's Phi Epsilon Pi alumni in fact included "50 Hebrews and 21 Gentiles," while the current undergraduate membership consisted of fourteen Hebrews and four Gentiles. In addition, Dubin cooperated by sending certified statements, signed by leaders of the Gentile fraternities, attesting to Phi Epsilon Pi's rank in City College as "a real non-sectarian fraternity."[52]

Eventually the Alabama chapter did refrain from leaving the fraternity over this issue. Others, however, were not so easy to convince, particularly college officials eager to maintain the Christian character of their institutions. Even Jewish college officials were skeptical of the possibility of any college fraternity being truly nonsectarian and fearful of the negative influence such a de facto Jewish group might bring. They refused to allow Phi Epsilon Pi to establish a foothold on their campuses. At the University of Missouri at Columbia, Dean of the Faculty Bernard Loeb—himself an American Jew of German origin—viewed consistent requests to form a separate fraternity as "inadvisable." The regretable restrictions against Jews in the existing fraternities were the policy of the national fraternity leadership, he insisted, and not the fault of local chapters. On the other hand, he pointed out, outside these social organizations Jewish students were admitted to all other university organizations and class honors, with "little if any evidence of racial and religious prejudice." To introduce a Jewish social fraternity on the campus would "promote rather than eliminate" this prejudice, and despite all claims to the contrary no one but Jews would join Phi Epsilon Pi anyway. "The fact that your fraternity does not restrict its membership to Jewish students is in its favor," he wrote in April 1916, "but of course the inevitable result would be the same, as if it had such a clause in its charter."[53]

Phi Epsilon Pi's officers in New York City at first refused to take no for an answer. Once more, they instructed their Missouri contact to emphasize their alleged nonsectarian character. "We, of course, have a great many Jewish Fratres; in fact, the vast majority are Jewish," they conceded to their agent in the field.

> At the same time, we do not want to dwell on this point, for the nonsectarian character of our organization can only be upheld by our insisting on fraternalism without religion. In case you correspond further with Dean Loeb, or in case you go to see him, we trust that you will make this point fully understood, and that if a Chapter is started at Missouri, it will be started with Gentile as well as Jewish fellows as Charter members.[54]

Dean Loeb, however, was still not convinced. Not wishing to deal further with the young men's persistent inquiries, he turned the matter over to a lower-ranking Jewish member of the Missouri administration—the secretary of the University's extension division, Norton J. Lustig. Lustig wrote back to New York in May 1916 rejecting Phi Epsilon Pi's petition on the grounds that he had interviewed prominent and "representative" Jewish students at Missouri and that "with a surprising unanimity of opinion," they were completely opposed to the project. In explaining their reasons, he was even more blunt than Dean Loeb had been. Any fraternity composed of both Jewish and non-Jewish students, he wrote, was "not a feasible idea"; fraternity lines were so strongly drawn at their college that "ultimately only the residue of desirable Christian students would affiliate themselves." Furthermore, what might be expected to work in "eastern universities" (such as in New York?) would not work in the "peculiar atmosphere" of Missouri, where the greater part of the student body came from agricultural backgrounds. Indeed, it was generally felt that a Jewish collegiate fraternity would "arouse a greater feeling of racial prejudice," not reduce it.[55]

Thus all the youthful optimism and energy which Jewish college men could muster in the Progressive Era was not successful in the formation of a truly nonsectarian fraternity. American society as it was organized at the time would apparently not allow it, and the attempt of Jewish college men to ignore this left them open to jokes and increasing ridicule. In the case of Phi Epsilon Pi, the final break with its idealistic origins came at the fraternity's December 1923 convention. Here, a single individual made a significant impact. Maurice Jacobs, a 1917 Phi Epsilon Pi from the University of Maine, led and won a campaign for the fraternity's Grand Council to remove the cross and the crescent from its crest, to stop apologizing for the Jewish background of their membership, and to cease from hobbling expansion by their constant search for elusive and ultimately unattainable Gentile fraternity brothers. Jacobs would go on to become the executive secretary of Phi Epsilon Pi, providing it with leadership for almost fifty years. He also became a prominent figure in the American Jewish communal, cultural world, and publishing world, among other activities heading the Jewish Publication Society of America.[56]

In the 1920s, one of Jacobs' strongest supporters toward the end of de-ecumenicizing the fraternity's crest was Ralph E. Cohn of the University of Michigan chapter. He helped to prepare the membership for the change by documenting in the pages of the *Phi Epsilon Pi Quar-*

terly the "considerable embarrassment" which the crescent and the large elongated cross were causing in the eyes of outsiders. "In regard to the world-at-large," he wrote,

> I am reminded of our former friend, Mr. Levy, as that gentleman covers his nose with one hand and presents the card of Mr. Abraham Murphy. Can Mr. Levy-Murphy ever expect to command the respect due either Mr. Levy or Mr. Murphy? If I were a statistician, I might make up tables of data showing the percentage of times that a sentence like this arose upon the mention of Phi Ep: "O, yes; that non-sectarian Jewish frat," or "Have you a little Goi in your chapter?" or "You mean the ones who pretend they're not Jewish."

The true Jewish identity of Phi Epsilon Pi, Cohn wrote, was no secret to anyone but the Jewish members themselves, and certainly not to the occasional deluded Gentile pledge who wandered their way:[57]

> The Mohammedan boys, of course, sing their praises to Allah in the broad inspiring spirit of Phi Epsilon Pi. Your loving son! The Christian boys soon find that religious differences are of little consequence compared to the racial differences manifested in the actions and thoughts of the Hebrews. They soon retire from the chapter house and from the fraternity. The Jewish frater, however, is the true ostrich with his head in the sand. The average Jewish boy of our colleges bothers very little about his ancestral theological doctrines, and his membership in a non-sectarian fraternity is a very convenient excuse for non-participation in Jewish groups or affairs. True, Phi Ep is not a Sunday School. On the other hand, it is not altogether proper for a group of Jewish men to dodge obligations which may present themselves to them.

Samuel M. Kootz, the influential editor of the *Phi Epsilon Pi Quarterly* and one of the oldest members of the fraternity, cast his vote along with Jacobson in favor of jettisoning both the old shield and the nonsectarian policy. In a personal article written under the title "Air Castles and Dissimulation," he declared: "Non-sectarianism is but a florid gesture at the moon. It is not practiced, it cannot be practiced. Held out as an enchanting democratic vista before the fledgling pledgee's eyes, it but gives way to derision and delusion, flagrant disciples of unfulfilled promises. It is not fair, it isn't playing the game."[58] In an editorial appearing just before the final vote at the 1923 convention he expressed the matter far more bluntly, invoking again the analogy of the ostrich hiding his head in the sand. "Ranging over a number of years," he wrote, "we have found that Phi Epsilon Pi today, in its active membership, is composed entirely of Jews, that its governing officers are all Jews, and that its predominating sentiment is away from non-sectarianism. It was inevitable."[59] When delegates from Phi Epsilon Pi's thirty-one active chapters gathered that month, the vote went in favor of abandoning the old shield, and thereafter the general stress of the fraternity upon Jewish programming and the fostering of Jewish leadership noticeably increased.

By 1933, even an officer of Pi Lambda Phi, which throughout its existence remained stubbornly faithful to the nonsectarian ideal, had to report regretfully, "So far as I know, there is in fact no non-sectarian fraternity."[60] Fraternity chapters with no restrictive clauses of any kind and with students of all faiths as members could not and would not become widespread until well after World War II had broken down the nation's rigid social barriers.

Until that day, the Progressive era myth of a nonsectarian fraternity might appeal to some Jews who wished to affiliate with an exclusive social organization while both maintaining a clear conscience and protesting their exclusion from fraternities limited only to Christians. The nonsectarian Jewish fraternities also might appeal to young, eager, fun-seeking Jewish collegiates who preferred to avoid the bothersome issue of religious divisions altogether. However, as the few Gentile members fell by the wayside and as quotas and anti-Jewish restrictions of various kinds became a fact of college life in the 1920s and 1930s, the Jewish nonsectarian fraternities for the most part had to face reluctantly the reality of their true Jewish identity, and to abandon what had become for most of them an embarrassing and hopeless charade.

Chapter 3

"Great Things on a Great Scale"

Expansion and Opposition, 1909–1919

For the first decade of the twentieth century, the officially Jewish Zeta Beta Tau and the then-officially un-Jewish Phi Epsilon Pi fraternities remained each other's only national competitors. Both tended to draw their members from the same applicant pool of the native born, German Jewish middle-to-upper middle class elite. Pi Lambda Phi, which lay dormant in those years, also had in the past, and would in the future, cater to the relative elite. A broader cross-section of the American Jewish population, however, was joining the subsystem's potential constituency. What might be called the "second stage" of the system's development began in 1909 with the founding at the City College of New York of Sigma Alpha Mu (pronounced "mew" as in "music.") The core of the "Sammies'" membership were products not of the well-established elite, but of the upward-bound children or grandchildren of Yiddish-speaking East European immigrants who had begun their stay in America in such neighborhoods as on the streets of New York's Lower East Side.

The advent of the "Sammies" signified three new phenomena in the Jewish college fraternity world. First, there was rapid proliferation and coast-to-coast expansion, with the formation of mature alumni networks and four new national fraternities founded in 1910 alone. Second, a distinct hierarchy developed, as social class, income, denominational, generational, ideological, and geographical differences led to separation and stratification between organizations designed to serve what was ostensibly the identical American religious and ethnic group. Confined within their own universe, each fraternity developed its own profile and style. Young Jews ended up seeking and finding room, board, friendship, recreation, and potential marriage partners from within many different fraternities and sororities.

Finally, Jewish fraternity organizers of all backgrounds began to face a storm of criticism not only from Gentiles but also from adults within their own communities. Rabbis and Jewish communal leaders charged that banding together in secret student societies wasted precious time, diverted energy and resources away from more traditional religious and cultural activity, encouraged assimilation, and divided Jew against Jew in a distasteful display of snobbery that their people could ill afford. In addition, the critics charged, fraternity students risked actually confirming the worst accusations of antisemites and increasing anti-Jewish feeling by encouraging campus clannishness and making unwanted Jews even more conspicuous than they already were in the eyes of fellow students, faculty, staff and townspeople.

The Origins of Sigma Alpha Mu

Sigma Alpha Mu's leaders at first took a distinctly casual approach toward such questions of communal concern. Unlike their predecessors, agonizing soul-searching or lengthy debates on the topic of sectarianism did not occupy a prominent place in their earliest records. According to the reminisces of the founders, originally twelve men, only nine of them Jewish, were invited to the first meeting at the home of Hyman Isaac Jacobson (CCNY '12) known as "Hij," on November 26, 1909, although only eight, all of them Jews, actually ended up coming. "We weren't any of us religious," reported "Hij" fourteen years later, confiding to an interviewer that his family had wanted him to be a rabbi, "and I was the worst of the bunch."[1] Clauses restricting SAM's membership to Jewish men only and specifications that fraternity business meetings should not be held on the Jewish Sabbath were not added until 1914, apparently without any major internal battle.

In a characteristic display of irreverence, the young men of Sigma Alpha Mu first considered calling their group the "Cosmic Fraternal Order" and using Hindu letters rather than Greek.[2] Because eight did attend the first meeting, an eight-sided figure or Octagon—devoid of any deep theological or philosophical implications—was chosen as the fraternity's symbol. SAM's governing council, for example, was called "the Octagon" while its publication was named *The Octagonian*. Their differences in dress and deportment from members of other fraternities as well as their relatively free-wheeling spirit was evident in a ditty sung about them in SAM's earliest years:[3]

> He's a son of City College and he founded S.A.M.
> He carries knives and pistols and he doesn't give a damn
> He dresses like a hobo, wears a khaki shirt of yeller
> But for all his sins we love him, he's a damn good feller!

SAM's first task was to secure its status as a legitimate student organization. While recognition from the College's administration was readily forthcoming, acceptance from fellow students was not. The fraternal newcomers had to fight for the ultimate sign of City College status—a wooden bench of their own among the many which stood next to the great pillars of the school's Lincoln Corridor. By custom, the school's fraternities and student organizations of all kinds gathered around these benches during lunch hour to hold their meetings. The physical plant of CCNY was too limited to permit quarters any more luxurious than that. When the men of SAM dared to stake out their own bench they had to endure, in another founder's words, "many a dirty look and worse comment," especially from the college's Zeta Beta Tau chapter, which met two benches away.[4] However, the Sammies held fast, and the meetings continued.

Within less than a decade Sigma Alpha Mu added twenty-one more chapters to its rolls including the Universities of Kentucky, Minnesota, Cincinnati, Yale, Harvard, MIT, Illinois, McGill, Alabama, Utah, and Toronto. This spread its bounds across the nation and made it numerically the largest Jewish fraternity after Zeta Beta Tau.[5] Yet the fraternal memories and sentiments attached to that humble piece of furniture were so strong that years later, when the Corridor was renovated and the benches scrapped, Sigma Alpha Mu's national officers arranged to have their own old meeting-bench removed. It was placed on display in the fraternity's national offices and remains there to this day.

How could Sigma Alpha Mu or any other fraternity, originating with a group of friends at one college, spread chapters across the land so quickly? In SAM's case, much of its expansive organizational energy came from the first meeting host, executive secretary, and fraternity editor "Hij" Jacobson. By academic training, he was a mathematics major and writer who joined the statistical department of the Metropolitan Life Insurance company after graduation. It helped that Jacobson was also an activist in social reform and political movements, including the fight to gain American women the vote. In the Spring of 1913, for example, along with three other Sigma Alpha Mu members, he marched in a demonstration of the Men's League for Women Suffrage, and made sure that all of his fraternity brothers were aware of this fact.[6] Much of his organizational drive in the 1910s, however, went into specific fraternity affairs, particularly the editing, writing, and production of the *Octagonian of Sigma Alpha Mu.*

A good fraternity publication, properly distributed, was one of the first steps toward national expansion and the creation of an alumni network. The *Octagonian* itself began as an amateur mimeographed newsletter in 1912 and progressed to professional printing, on par with that of other national college fraternities, by 1916. Through his editorial columns, Jacobson coaxed, cajoled, and preached to his fellow members, continuously reminding them not only of the high ideals of their fraternity but on practical details such as the proper use of pledges, oaths, and ritual books, distribution of shingles, and why it might be better to avoid the common college custom of giving away their fraternity pins to their girlfriends.[7] Techniques for recruiting new members, however, was the topic he stressed the most. An awareness of the size, power, influence and prestige of the Gentile fraternities and a longing to duplicate it in one's own Jewish group permeated Jacobson's expansionist rhetoric. Members' own siblings and friends were the first points of attack. "Who's Your Friend?" was his constant call, as he urged members to use every opportunity to enlist new brothers into their fraternity. "You went home during the holiday," Jacobson scolded his readers after what he termed their "Social Easter" vacation in April 1916.

> You met men from other schools. Did you talk Fraternity to them? How about that new Chapter? Now's the time! Get after them now! Write! But if you're too lazy to do it, drop a postal to the Executive Secretary and he'll do it! A two-cent stamp and two minutes will do more for the Fraternity than any amount of lamentation over the fact that only two chapters and only seventy-five men were initiated last year. . . . To be great Sigma Alpha Mu must do great things on a great scale, and the starting point is more Chapters. Do it now.[8]

When the editor announced the establishment of SAM's first chapter in Minnesota—remarkable news for many young members who had probably never been beyond the boundaries of the greater New York area in their lives—Jacobson wasted no time in urging them onward with typically competitive rhetoric. "As the click, click, click of the press keeps turning out these pages for your information and amusement, the dawning sun of Kappa Chapter lights up with glory the battlements and towers of the University of Minnesota. Next will come Lambda. How soon and where its birth will occur will be determined wholly by your interest and your effort."[9]

Methods of Expansion

Any single fraternity officer willing to accept the organization as an avocation and to pursue an aggressive campaign of letter writing, visits, negotiation, persuasion and recruitment could have a significant impact on the organization's growth in a short period of time. The same technique was used by SAM's predecessors in the optimistic and idealistic years immediately preceding the U.S. entry into World War I. Historians have observed that a burst of organizational and institutional formation took place across the American Jewish spectrum during this specific period, and moreover that organizations founded at this time have tended to endure to the present day.[10] "Phi Ep" added no fewer than twenty-four new chapters between 1911 and 1917, including the University of Georgia, the University of Virginia, Georgia Tech, and Auburn University. Zeta Beta Tau added as many plus five more in the same period. Phi Epsilon Pi's executive secretary Jesse Acker in New York City and traveling secretary Herman Kline were responsible for much of their fraternity's expansion. When not pursuing his professional studies at Harvard, Kline traveled constantly through New England and upstate New York in search of potential new chapters. He received no salary and slept at the homes of friends or relatives, although some of his transportation costs were covered.

"You know me, Jesse!" Kline wrote from Cambridge as he enthusiastically described his plans, most of them ultimately successful, to establish new chapters at Tufts, Harvard, MIT, Yale, Maine, Colgate, Union, and Syracuse Universities, in terms that would not have been unfamiliar to the organizer of a labor union. "My heart and soul are in the work!"[11] Wooing a potential group of friends away from the arms of another national fraternity and into one's own could be part of the job. Jesse Acker was himself not above urging another organizer in Philadelphia to "break up" the nucleus of a Zeta Beta Tau chapter, if their elimination was necessary in order for Phi Epsilon Pi to gain a foothold on a particular campus.[12]

Simpler and less aggressive expansion methods were also available. New chapters did not always need to be hunted down and then established from the ground up. The patterns of the collegiate Greek system were so well known that national fraternity officials often discovered that Jewish students on a particular campus had already banded together in a purely local Greek-letter fraternity. These "locals" could operate with their own customs, rituals, houses, and board plans for many years before deciding to "go national." At that point, the local fraternity could be the one that sought out one of more national fraternities to petition it for acceptance. Indeed, if fraternity investigators were unsure that a group of friends could handle fraternal financial and organizational responsibilities on a national level, they would encourage the undergraduates to form a Greek-letter local fraternity or colony first as a form of probation. If the local passed muster after a trial period, then it could be granted a full charter as a chapter of the national fraternity.

The older Phi Epsilon Pi was an example of growth by acquisition of pre-existing groups. Out of forty-five chapters founded between 1904 and 1945, twenty-six—more than half—were formed from preexisting Greek-letter locals.[13] At the University of Georgia, their chapter grew out of one of the oldest local Jewish fraternities on record, Eay Daleth Sigma (E.D.S.), which had been founded in the college town of Athens as early as 1895 and was courted by several Jewish national fraternities.[14] The majority of the group, most of them residents of Atlanta, eventually decided to accept membership in Phi Epsilon Pi in 1915. The University of Georgia provided the fraternity with an important southern base and thus helped Phi Epsilon Pi to become especially prominent in that region for decades afterward.

Transferring from one school to another with a desire to maintain or re-create a friendship network was another, relatively simple way for a fraternity to spread its bounds. The Columbia chapter of Phi Epsilon Pi, for example, was founded by "Alpha" men who had attended City College for one or two years and then transferred to their Ivy League neighbor on Morningside Heights. Transfers could occur for any number of reasons. Starting out at a relatively less prestigious and less expensive school and then switching remained a time-honored tactic for the impecunious but educationally ambitious. By this method a student could acquire the advanced academic training that he or she might have missed at an inadequate high school program and possibly save a year or two off tuition expenses. Students also might be forced to transfer because of the relocation of their families or for reasons of work or health. Medical factors were especially apparent in the early strength of Jewish fraternities at universities in the states of Arizona and Colorado. Both of these states contained cities and special medical facilities where doctors routinely sent patients suffering from tuberculosis or other serious diseases.

The earning of one's undergraduate degree followed by attendance at a professional school somewhere else in the country was another common method of expansion for the men's fraternities. A professional student who had enjoyed his undergraduate fraternity experiences and who received enough encouragement and support from the national officers might be glad to take time away from his studies and to start a chapter on his new campus. It was not necessary to secure huge numbers of men. Eight students were considered an excellent core for a new chapter, although a charter from the national organization could be extended with as few as five or even three students. SAM's Jacobson insisted that under optimum conditions twenty-five men were the maximum that any single chapter could hold comfortably. [15] In part because of the influence of active professional school members, undergraduate chapters of Jewish fraternities tended to spread most rapidly away from New York City and toward more southern, midwestern or western schools with large enrollments and prominent professional programs.

Expansion through the geographic mobility of graduate members from the East coast also could occur when the member, upon completing professional studies, moved out to the hinterland to set up a practice, pursue better vocational opportunities, or assume a faculty position at a college or university. Far fewer female than male college graduates had access to such opportunities. However, it was common among the sororities for a newlywed wife, having followed her husband to a new section of the country, to be called upon to try and establish or otherwise supervise a chapter in a nearby school.

Jobs and Professions

The acquisition of a profession and access to greater vocational opportunities were, after all, strong motives for young Jews and their families to seek out a college education in the first place. Professions in the traditional East European Jewish scale of values meant prestige, job satisfaction, a good income, flexibility, and geographic mobility, an important priority for a people accustomed to being forced to pull up stakes at a moment's notice. Education, once acquired, could not be taken away or revoked by hostile authorities; the "capital" imparted by education could easily be stored and transported in one's head and hands, and a practitioner was not physically bound to working a specific piece of land. Professions dangled the prospect that one might actually enjoy and find fulfillment through one's livelihood. This was a new and attractive alternative to toiling by the sweat of one's brow or spending years hunched over a machine, years standing behind a counter, years buying and selling merchandise, or any number of other uninspiring methods Jews had devised or been permitted throughout the generations of putting bread on the table. Above all, professions meant independence from corporations or bosses where a Jewish background or observance of holy days could limit one's upward mobility or indeed prevent a Jew from getting a job at all.

Not all professional positions were created equal, however. In fraternity records from the 1910s it is already possible to discern not only the movement of American Jewish men away from the proletariat and small business toward professions and white-collar occupations, but also how class background affected the type or level of profession a young Jewish man could aspire to. From the pages of Sigma Alpha Mu's *Octagonian,* it would appear that law, medicine, accountancy, actuarial science, municipal service and small business were the most popular occupations after graduation for its largely East European membership. One issue in 1916 noted with pride the role of one young alumnus in developing an entire new sewer system for Baltimore, a city previously notorious for its lack of a proper public sanitation system.[16]

"Sammies" seeking a career in medicine, however, faced serious challenges. The medical members of Sigma Alpha Mu in the 1910s, according to the fraternity's alumni news columns, were commonly able to find physician's jobs only within the New York City public welfare system (orphanages and Blackwell's Island employed a goodly share of them) public hospitals, smaller private hospitals of lesser prestige, or in institutions specifically established to service East European Jews. For example, a 1914 alumni news column reported appointments of Sigma Alpha Mu fraters at such places as Coney Island Hospital, Williamsburg and Bushwick Hospitals, and Sydenham Hospital. Exceptions to the rule were noted with special pride. "Columbia Medical's Frater Katz has made an internship at Dwight Memorial,[17] the seat of prejudice. 'Tis indeed a great victory," reported another column. "Landy and Natanson have succeeded in capturing high places at Mt. Sinai. . . . All our seniors are now well provided for, upholding SAM tradition."[18] Mt. Sinai was a Jewish hospital, but in general, it accepted only physicians of German Jewish name and background. Nor did Mt. Sinai cater to the religious or dietary needs of the traditional Jewish immigrant clientele. It was partly in response to this that a second Jewish hospital in New York City catering specifically to Russian Jews and Yiddish-speaking patients, Beth Israel, had been established in 1890.[19]

An East European slavic "sky" or "witz" at the end of one's name, rather than a more Germanic "son," "man," "feld," or "stein" (or an elegant "Rose" or "Rosen" at the beginning) could limit a Jew's progress even among other Jewish doctors. In all, whether for the sake of Gentiles or for other Jews, fraternity magazines of the 1910s and 1920s commonly served as a bulletin board to announce one's change of name. A typical example appeared in a 1913 issue of the *Octagonian* of Sigma Alpha Mu, informing readers that "Frater Sassulsky of Epsilon [Columbia Medical School] who becomes an Alumnus this week, is henceforth, by order of the Supreme Court of the State of New York, to be known as Irving J. Sands."[20]

Private practice, particularly among one's fellow Jews, was of course always an option upon the completion of one's medical training, as an article in the April 1914 *Octagonian* reported in a highly humorous vein. The item also illustrates the movement of thousands of Jews away from the Lower East Side of Manhattan and into new neighborhoods in the Bronx, the Upper West Side, and the neighborhood of Brownsville, Brooklyn, which in those days still contained plentiful farmland. There, Sammy doctors of the 1910s and 1920s regularly gathered for alumni reunions. This passage incidentally confirms and illustrates well the data of historian Moses Rischin in his classic study *The Promised City*: the percentage of New York City's Jews who lived on the Lower East Side declined markedly after 1910. By 1916 only twenty-three percent lived there, compared to fifty percent in 1903 and seventy-five percent in 1892:

> Many of our Alumni Fratres have already reached the end of the rugged path, have settled down and hung out their shingles in all parts of our great city including Brownsville, where a little community has congregated. We admit that Brownsville is incomplete unless a nucleus of Sigma Alpha Mu doctors is there. So that's why they are there—to make Brownsville complete. Not only that, but also to elevate medical ethics and may they make a smooth path of it! (No! not Brownsville—for the goats would have nothing to graze on.) Another obscure part of Brooklyn will be illuminated by Fra. Dr. Muller—Greenpoint. I tell you Brooklyn is going to be all light.

Others are Bronx Park and Central Park. Nothing like seeking a similar environment to the one you have been brought up in.[21]

By contrast, the columns and alumni reports of the *Zeta Beta Tau Quarterly* rarely acknowledged, in the 1910s or later, any discrimination against the fraternity's doctors. As affluent American-born German Jews, it would appear that ZBT men enjoyed easier access to the best schools, residencies, internships, prestigious European fellowships, and hospitals than their Russian Jewish compatriots did.

More Fraternities Follow

After Sigma Alpha Mu, the establishment of another Jewish fraternity at Columbia University, calling itself Phi Sigma Delta (1910), soon followed. Known as the "Phi Sigs," their secret Greek motto was *Philos Stegnon Dendron,* or "friendship is a flourishing tree," and the symbol of the Biblical Tree of Life was central to their initiation ritual. According to fraternity lore, Phi Sigma Delta began as an offshoot of Jewish students unable to coexist in the originally nonsectarian Columbia fraternity Delta Sigma Phi—hence the reversal of the letters and the founding of a new group.[22] Next came Tau Epsilon Phi (1910, Columbia School of Pharmacy, popularly named "Tep"), Tau Delta Phi (1910, City College, "Tau Delt") and Beta Sigma Rho at Cornell in 1910. Beta Sigma Rho began as a small local group and was significantly the first to be founded outside of New York City, although many of the Jewish students in attendance at Cornell came from the New York City area. At first it was known by the Greek-Hebrew letter combination Beta Samach, with, according to the founders, "the Greek Beta and the Hebrew Samach suggesting the application of the Greek society idea to the social and cultural life of the Jewish undergraduate."[23] However, as in the case of Z.B.T. the call of the Greek letters and the temptation to organize themselves on the same lines as the Gentile fraternities brought about the abandonment of this dual identification.

Kappa Nu, a relatively small fraternity founded by pre-medical and medical students, came next, established at the University of Rochester in 1911. Although the group adopted Greek letters as their name, their badge contained the Greek letters's Hebrew equivalents, kuf and nun, for *kesher neurim,* "the ties of youth." The constitution limited membership to Jews only, and Hebrew words and Biblical and liturgical references predominated in their secret initiation rituals.[24] Kappa Nu was followed in 1912 by Phi Beta Delta at Columbia. Omicron Alpha Tau, founded in 1912 at Cornell, was known as "the most Jewish" of them all and reportedly maintained strictly kosher kitchens for its members. Phi Alpha, founded in 1914 at George Washington University, had all its first chapters south of the Ohio River. At the same time Pi Lambda Phi was rejuvenating itself from its new base at Columbia University, adding six chapters to the rolls from 1914 to 1919—Penn State, University of Pittsburgh, Lehigh, Stevens Tech, Fordham, and the University of Chicago.[25] Overall, of the first eleven men's national Jewish college fraternities, seven were founded in the New York City area, where in 1914 almost half of Yiddish-speaking Jewish immigrants to America resided.[26]

The Third Stage: Night and Commuting Students

At first, the luxury of belonging to a college fraternity was limited to relatively affluent students who enjoyed the wherewithal to either live in residence at their colleges or at least be able to attend during the light of day. The bylaws of early chapters in New York City specifically limited membership to these "day school" rather than "night school" students who had to work for wages during daylight hours and had only their evenings free for study. Despite any admiration for their determination in pursuing such a potentially exhausting schedule, young night school students ranked low on the collegiate social scale, as did those who commuted long distances by subway to school. These students tended to be from lower-income families, closer to immigrant status, and not infrequently from more traditional religious backgrounds than day school students. They were also likely to have less time, energy, and funds to spare for engaging in collegiate-style social activities.

What might be called the "third stage" of Jewish college fraternities began with Alpha Epsilon Pi, which was founded at New York University in 1913 and known by the popular name AEPi or "Ay-ee-pie". AEPi originated from a group of friends who would meet at taverns and restaurants in the Washington Square area in order to eat dinner and enjoy each other's company before commencing their evening classes at New York University's School of Commerce. Their numbers included Charles C. Moskowitz, a talented basketball player who, according to AEPi's own annals, was asked to join the NYU chapter of a leading Jewish fraternity already in existence—on the condition that he not try to bring in any of his close friends.[27] Learning that they would not be welcome, legend has it, the athlete gathered ten of his friends around him at the Washington Square Arch on November 7, 1913, and declared them to be the "Alpha" chapter of the Alpha Epsilon Pi. By doing so, he thereby indicated his determination that theirs be only the first unit of a fraternity that would someday become national in scope. In its first years Alpha Epsilon Pi managed with little money, less recognition, no fraternity house, and not even a permanent meeting place.[28] In time, however, Alpha Epsilon Pi experienced spectacular growth, particularly in the post-World War II years, until it was almost equal in wealth and numbers to its older Jewish rivals.

The last multi-chapter Jewish men's fraternities to be formed included Alpha Mu Sigma (Cooper Union, New York City, 1914), Sigma Omega Psi (City College, 1914), Sigma Lambda Pi (NYU, 1915), and Sigma Tau Phi, formed by engineering and architectural students at the University of Pennsylvania in 1918. All of these were small and short-lived, eventually either becoming defunct or being absorbed into the larger and stronger Alpha Epsilon Pi.[29]

Women Students Organize

Jewish collegiate women matched the proliferation of men's collegiate organizations on a smaller scale. The first Jewish college sorority had in fact already been founded in 1903, one year before Phi Epsilon Pi, at New York City's Normal College, a teacher-training institute that later was transformed into Hunter College. Calling themselves at first by the initials J.A.P., the founders included Francine Zellermayer, the younger sister of Z.B.T. founder Maurice Zellermayer. She eventually married the brother of another founder, Rose Delson. Settlement house work on the Lower East Side and study sessions on women in the Bible were among J.A.P.'s earliest activities.[30] The women called themselves "Jay-ay-peez" and their publication *The J.A.P. Bulletin.* In a movement parallel to that of Z.B.T., the organization moved gradually closer toward the Greek-letter, multi-chapter model, and by 1913 had renamed itself Iota Alpha Pi.

Observers have wondered with justification if it is possible to assume that some of the earliest uses of the term "Jewish American Princess," came about in connection with this sorority. If it was used in connection with J.A.P., however, it would soon have become incongruous, for the group's seniority in the sorority hierarchy did not guarantee it a reputation for affluence or outstanding social prestige. The organization grew slowly and remained small. Normal College remained its only chapter until 1913, when a new chapter was founded at Brooklyn Law School. In the 1920s and 1930s other chapters established included New Jersey Law School (1922), Denver University (1927), University of Toronto (1929), and the University of Manitoba in Winnipeg (1932). In 1942, a young woman about to be initiated into Iota Alpha Pi at Brooklyn College eagerly awaited the moment when the true secret meaning of the initials "J.A.P." would be revealed to her. We are "Just a Plain Sorority," she was finally told—in other words, not for the especially popular, affluent, or snobbish, but just a group of good friends. J.A.P. chapters did not survive the upheavals of the late 1960s and the organization disbanded in 1971.[31]

Next among the Jewish sororities came Alpha Epsilon Phi, founded at Barnard College in 1909 and known by the popular name AEPhi or "Ay-ee-fie." AEPhi did in fact cater to the female collegiate Jewish elite and became in many ways a counterpart to Zeta Beta Tau. Phi Sigma Sigma, also founded at Hunter College in 1913, was a nonsectarian group that took the Egyptian sphinx as its symbol and the words "Aim High" as its motto. These were followed by Sigma Delta Tau, founded at Cornell in 1917, frequently AEPhi's closest competitor; and Delta Phi Epsilon, ("Dee-fie-ee") founded by a group of young women studying at New York University Law School. Even more so than Iota Alpha Pi, Delta Epsilon Phi became an important institution for the Jewish communities of Canada, and by the 1940s had established chapters at McGill University in Montreal, the University of Toronto, the University of Manitoba in Winnipeg, and the University of British Columbia in Vancouver.[32]

After World War I: Prosperity and Chapter Proliferation

The conclusion of World War I and its immediate aftermath in 1919 and 1920 brought the formative years of the national Jewish fraternity subsystem to an end. Excluding the purely professional fraternities, at least seventeen national organizations served college men and at least five served college women. Thereafter, growth came in the rapid expansion of membership rolls, not in the establishment of entirely new organizations. The war itself, which began in August 1914 and which the U.S. entered in April 1917, caused but a temporary lull in the fraternities's operation. Young fraternity men enlisted in the armed forces, and several lost their lives. The War Department in the fall of 1917 temporarily prohibited fraternity meetings or initiations as inimical to the war effort. Some college campuses were taken over by the military for training purposes through the SATC, or the Student Army Training Corps, a program derogatorily referred to by its detractors as "Saturday Afternoon Tea Club" or "Safe at the College." Fraternity houses were requisitioned for use as barracks, and furniture and ritual paraphernalia were put into storage for the duration.[33]

By 1919 the subsystem was on its feet again, however, and Phi Epsilon Pi, along with the other older and upper-tier fraternities, were able to hold their "Victory Conventions." By fraternity custom the annual conclave or convention was where the most important organizational business was transacted. It also ranked as one of the most important fraternity social events of the year. By comparing the location, length, and level of entertainment of conventions and social events of various fraternities, group class and income differences, as well as how these changed over time, become readily apparent. In the first half of the twentieth century, American college fraternities most often held their conventions in December, ideally on New Year's Eve, at the best hotel its members could afford. In the case of Jewish fraternities, an additional criterion was finding the best institution that would also admit Hebrews through its doors. In its first years, for example, the newer Alpha Epsilon Pi had to make do with a single night out in a restaurant to celebrate its annual convention. Not until the mid-1920s did it graduate to holding its convention at hotels.

For the relative elite of Phi Epsilon Pi, the 1919 gathering and first post-war reunion took place at the William Penn Hotel in Pittsburgh, "the newest and one of the best in Pennsylvania." The program began with a "smoker," a ubiquitous fraternity as well as a common professional form of sex-segregated relaxation where men would gather informally to chat and to smoke cigars, cigarettes, or pipes, all provided by the host. It went on to include a reception to introduce out-of-town members to their chosen dates, another reception at the University of Pittsburgh's chapter house, a night at the city's Davis Theatre, a formal banquet, and a formal dance held in the hotel's main ballroom on New Year's Eve. The entire event ran from Sunday through Tuesday and cost fifteen dollars, including the price of two theater tickets.[34]

The men of Phi Epsilon Pi in 1919 had reason to celebrate. In fifteen years their organization had grown from a group of seven men at City College to a national fraternity of twenty-six chapters and over one thousand members—four hundred undergraduates and six hundred alumni.[35] Despite the fraternity's relative youth at least fourteen chapters either rented or owned their own houses with room enough for all the undergraduate chapter members to live. Twenty-four active alumni who paid a pledged amount monthly supported the headquarters of the City College chapter, with six active members. The Dickinson College chapter in Carlisle, Pennsylvania, had just purchased a $10,000 home, almost entirely with alumni backing, while the Rutgers chapter was preparing to move into its own house, paid for and endowed with alumni bequests.[36]

Nor was Phi Epsilon Pi alone in the dedication and concrete support provided by its alumni. Whether out of pride, a desire to build a social center for themselves, or the wish to provide a safe and comfortable place for their children when they went to college, extensive building programs in the 1910s and 1920s raised the subsystem's prestige and desirability in the eyes of incoming Jewish college freshmen and their families.

Obstacles: Students, Administrations and Parents

The growth and expansion of the Jewish Greek subsystem did not proceed without hindrance, however. As had been the case at the University of Missouri, hostile college administrations were, and for many years remained, one significant obstacle. As the number and membership rolls of Jewish college fraternities grew, the issue of their official acceptance on individual American campuses became increasingly controversial. In 1916 for example, the same year that the campaign to win over Missouri failed, Brown University undergraduate Isaac Y. Olch, head of an illicit chapter of Phi Epsilon Pi at Brown, begged the national organization to keep their existence a secret and not to send him any mail addressed directly to the chapter house. William H. P. Faunce, the president of the university, had forbidden the formation of any Jewish fraternities on his campus and had threatened Olch and his friends with expulsion if they dared to form a fraternity chapter openly.[37]

Uncooperative student bodies represented, also in the 1910s and for years after, another obstacle to full acceptance for Jewish fraternity chapters. Jewish fraternities could find themselves shunned or ignored, denied entrance into the local interfraternity or Panhellenic councils that governed and regulated fraternity affairs, or relegated to some form of "Group B" or "Second Division" status on lists of campus organizations.[38] They could also be denied the right to be listed entirely,

as happened to the Zeta Beta Tau chapter at Columbia University in
1912. At that time the Class of 1914 editorial board of the *Columbian,*
the undergraduate yearbook meant to document all student activities,
refused to print any entries for any of the Jewish societies on campus.
When Professor Gottheil attempted at least to get his own fraternity
ZBT listed, drawing his opponent's attention to its relatively high social status, the result was a typed, two-page, single-spaced resolution,
passed unanimously, on why doing so would "not be in the best interests" of Columbia. The student writers went to almost comic lengths to
avoid using the actual word "Jew."[39]

By granting full recognition to the "organization in question,"
the resolution read, "the way would be thrown open to the recognition of
other such organizations, which would have the final effect of drawing
to the University an increasing number of a class of men, who as a class,
do very little for campus activities." The alumni, whose support was so
vital to Columbia, would also object to recognizing this "class of men,"
since their numbers in the alumni group were "almost negligible." The
resolution concluded: "Be it further resolved that as these ideas surely
point to the fact that we should not recognize the organizations of a class
of men who do practically nothing, as a class, for campus activities . . .
we cannot as a body. . . . make any exceptions, since the recognition of
one organization of this aforesaid class of men would lead to the recognition of all. Signed, the Board of Editors of the 1914 Columbian."

In reaction to this refusal to acknowledge a legitimate student
organization at Columbia College because it was Jewish, Gottheil decided to request the intervention of the president and his former classmate Nicholas Murray Butler. At first, the results were positive. Butler
promptly called in to his office the members of the editorial board—
one of whom happened to be Jewish—and persuaded the young men to
change their minds. However, as Gottheil later wrote to Felix Warburg
of the American Jewish Committee, reporting on the incident and including a copy of the resolution, the Christian fraternities at Columbia
reacted with such "agitation" that three weeks later the editorial board
voted to reverse itself. Moreover, when Gottheil suggested to the one
Jewish member of the board that he resign in protest over the whole
matter, the young man refused to do so.[40]

Gottheil declined with thanks Warburg's subsequent offer to
"bring in heavy artillery" from prominent Jewish leaders and the American Jewish Committee to fight for the right of Jewish student organizations to be listed in their own college's yearbook. "I am afraid there

is no use of doing so, as the battle is lost," he declared. He then felt compelled to express a seldom-voiced belief that the only cure for campus antisemitism would be to form a Jewish-sponsored university. This was an important issue in higher education that had and would continue to divide deeply different segments of the American Jewish communal leadership for decades to come. "There is, of course, only one solution to the difficulty which is felt more or less at all our institutions of higher learning," Gottheil wrote in November 1912, "but it is a solution which will never be envisaged by the Jews of this country. We need a Jewish University here—which, of course, need not be more Jewish than the University of Chicago is Baptist or Yale is Congregational. I am fully persuaded that this is the only solution. Of course, I shall never make any such a proposition in public. I should be a very small prophet in a very large wilderness."[41]

While lack of acceptance from Gentiles might trouble the vast majority of Jewish fraternity members and officers, lack of cooperation and obstacles to expansion that originated within the Jewish community itself could be even more disheartening. As the chapters proliferated it became evident that American Jews were themselves far from united on the wisdom of forming these organizations. Parents of potential members could be the first lines of support or opposition. Those of long residence in the country might well belong to a Jewish country club of some kind, have been exposed to American higher education themselves, or in some way at least understand that Greek-letter fraternities were the social centers of the universities and thus extremely important to the happiness and welfare of their offspring. For those with less formal education or of lower income or level of acculturation, however, the letter from the fraternity's officers advising them of their child's acceptance might be their first exposure to this strange American institution. They might not understand exactly what a fraternity was, why they should pay the extra bills for it, and why their children—whose college education might entail considerable sacrifice on their part—should waste time on anything beyond the serious business of studying.

In January 1916, for example, the national officers of Phi Epsilon Pi learned that "through parental objection or some cause of that nature," the initiation of a desirable pledge at Cornell had not materialized.[42] A few months later, when the national president demanded to know why only six men instead of the promised eight had paid their initiation dues at the new University of Michigan chapter, he was told by the local organizers, "We can only state that their families considered it inadvisable for them to become affiliated with any fraternity. Consequently, they had to withdraw from our club at the eleventh hour. We regret this fact more than you do, since they were very good men."[43]

As a result of these and similar incidents, in order to help forestall such potential criticism and the danger of last-minute drop-outs, Jewish fraternities realized that they had to send letters to the parents explaining exactly what their mysterious institution was all about and the benefits that the children could derive from them. If these explanatory letters were successful, then the enrollment of one Jewish student in a fraternity could set not only his feet but those of his entire family on the path toward acculturation. If not, then a valuable potential member would be lost. A joke long popular in the ranks of Phi Epsilon Pi illustrated well this type of bewilderment on the part of an apocryphal Jewish father who has just received a letter congratulating him on his son's acceptance into the Phi Epsilon Pi fraternity house. "After all I went through to send my boy to college," the father exclaims, "and he lives in a bakery!"[44]

The Importance of Being "Representative"

If a child were *not* accepted into a Jewish fraternity, then shock, resentment and disapproval from within the community could be even worse. Rejected students and their families, particularly where there were no ready opportunities to join other fraternities, could hardly be expected to experience feelings of warmth toward the Jewish Greek subsystem. Furthermore, the tendency of the fraternities to stress manners and acculturation to established American patterns of behavior could create a painful gap between young Jews who understood and strove to embody such behavior and their less enlightened comrades who, for whatever reason, seemed to miss the point and continued on in their stereotypically lower-class, ill-mannered ways. It was bad enough for newcomers to be looked down upon by Gentiles for their alleged uncouthness. To be looked down upon by one's fellow Jews as well doubled both the insult and the injury.

Jewish students eager to win acceptance from the wider community could all too quickly become acutely self-conscious, internalizing the external society's values and cringing when they saw fellow Jews violating them.[45] A common response was to seek total disassociation from such offenders or, in the case of fraternity expansion, to look upon a potential pool of applicants with especially critical and unforgiving eyes. In their investigations of possible new chapters, fraternity officers found themselves in constant debate whether one or the other group of Jewish students or a campus of lesser prestige was completely "hopeless," or whether there was some chance of salvaging enough usable "material" to make a chapter worthwhile. Miscalculation was risky, since too much emphasis on quantity at the expense of quality could cost any fraternity any reputation or standing it had hitherto managed to achieve. This pattern of thought and behavior appeared early in the formation of the Jewish Greek subsystem and it became increasingly pronounced in the decades leading up to World War II.

In one case in 1916, the officers of Phi Epsilon Pi, after overseeing their group's rapid expansion to nineteen college chapters, feared a drop in status and made a conscious decision to become more selective in their choice of new members. The days of Herman Kline signing up new chapters as quickly as he could find them, they decided, were over.[46] The communal key word most frequently used in such discussions was "representative"—i.e. the search for young Jews who would "represent" their people well, be American-born or close to it (a prized asset in an era of mass immigration) and not embody any anti-Jewish stereotypes. In February their president ordered negotiations with a local Jewish fraternity at Connecticut Agricultural College cut off because he considered the school of insufficiently high rank to merit a Phi Epsilon Pi chapter.[47] In addition, they called for the consolidation of the Harvard and MIT chapters because, in the opinion of their field investigator, "MIT alone isn't strong enough for a representative Phi Epsilon Pi chapter."[48] When it came to the development of an organization's public relations, it was not surprising that the expression of these similar views would arouse resentment on the part of students's families or the local Jewish community.

Concern with standard American or Anglo-Saxon manners and specific rules of etiquette became and remained almost an obsession in the publications of Jewish fraternities. A feature published in the *Phi Epsilon Pi Quarterly* informed fraternity leaders in harsh terms about the importance of enforcing good dress and good behavior. For example, the traditional Jewish custom of men keeping their heads covered at all times had no place in conventional western manners. Not to remove one's hat while indoors, whether for religious reasons or out of ignorance was considered a serious breach of etiquette. Table manners also came in for special scrutiny:

Don't sit in the windows looking out, with your hat on. You are only John Jones, not a millionaire member of the Union League Club. Passersby won't think it's a whim or carelessness. They'll merely conclude that your fraternity doesn't know any better. . . . Have the meals served rightly. Have clean table linen, keep the napkins clean, and (this may seem un-called for) *furnish napkins*. Remember, part of your job is to teach the hick how things are done by civilized people, and all these things are by no means included in classroom courses. Don't throw the food at the men in vats. At least three hours (one-eighth) of your day is spent in eating. Make those three hours an activity for men, not for animals.[49]

Communal Opponents

That fraternities as a whole promoted "snobbishness," lack of democracy, foolishness, and lack of sufficient attention to studies were general adult criticisms which anyone might make. So were condemnations of hazing, paddling, and roughhouse-initiations, which were an integral part of fraternity culture.

However, in addition to the usual adult suspicion and fear of the Greek system in general, Jewish leaders and rabbis in particular had special and sometimes contradictory fears regarding this new movement among their young people. On the one hand, college fraternities could be viewed as a "christianizing" and assimilatory movement that would destroy Jewish identity and prevent any organization of students along religious lines. The student leaders of campus religious and cultural organizations, such as the Menorah, Hillel, or student Zionist associations, resented the appeal fraternities held for college students and their tendency to divert student energy along nonreligious or noncultural channels, away from more conventional expressions of Jewish identity. On the other hand, at other times Jewish leaders voiced fears that Jewish fraternities promoted too *much* Jewish identity—that is, that secret societies formed of Jewish students would encourage clannishness, retard integration into the general society, and arouse fears of antisemites that Jews were banding together to conspire against them.

America's organized Reform rabbinate at first considered college fraternities as a serious obstacle to their plans. From 1897 onward the Union of American Hebrew Congregations (UAHC), the official organization of American Reform congregations, had begun to organize student worship and study groups through rabbis serving in congregations near college campuses. Jewish students, eager to blend in with the rest of the student population, too often responded to UAHC overtures with hostility and claimed that starting Jewish religious activities on their campuses would only inflame the very anti-Jewish hatred that had made formation of their fraternities necessary in the first place.[50] The related Central Conference of American Rabbis (CCAR), the umbrella group of Reform rabbis in the United States, responded in these early years by taking a strong stand against Jewish college fraternities. Ironically, their denomination probably included more individual fraternity members, chaplains, and advisors than any other did. During their student days at the Hebrew Union College in Cincinnati, the main seminary for American Reform Jewry, rabbinical students matriculated simultaneously at the University of Cincinnati, where several Jewish fraternity chapters existed.

To the rabbis of the CCAR, who had been discussing their concern for American Jewish college youth since their 1896 annual conclave, forming secret fraternities that aped Gentile ways and encouraged hostility to traditional religious figures was hardly the best way to preserve Jewish identity on the American campus. At the same time, they saw the existence of secret Jewish student societies as "un-American," undemocratic, separatist, and dangerously provocative. By their 1913 conclave, members of the CCAR sponsored a resolution opposing all secret fraternities. It was carried by an overwhelming majority.[51]

To Harold Riegelman (Cornell '14), soon to become the most powerful Executive *Nasi* in Zeta Beta Tau's history and himself a committed Reform Jew, the gathering of this "ignorant anti-fraternity sentiment. . . . among our own people," was the worst sting that their movement had to suffer. "There are those who attack on the ground that we are a fraternity, and hence objectionable," he complained, "and others who attack on the ground that we are a sectarian fraternity and hence doubly objectionable." The Jewish fraternity, it seemed, could not escape opposition on any front.[52]

Debate on Separatism: An American Dilemma

For most fraternity officials, exclusion and separation from mainstream campus organizations and activities was a constant thorn, and through the years much lobbying and campaigning would take place in an effort to eliminate it as an obstacle to full integration into campus life. A notable exception to this view, however, appeared in an editorial published in the *Octagonian of Sigma Alpha Mu* in April 1915, written by member Louis E. Levinthal (Penn '14). For him, separate Jewish fraternities were precisely the sort of agent whereby Jewish identity in the United States could be protected and preserved. Levinthal did not dispute that those barriers between Jews and non-Jews might someday fall. He did not agree with his fellow members, however, that such a goal was positive or desirable. Nor did he agree with CCAR opponents who believed that the separatism embodied in Jewish fraternity life would have a negative impact on the future of American Jews.

These unusual views for their time were perhaps the reflection of the author's intense Jewish and Zionist background. Levinthal came from a distinguished Orthodox Jewish family in Philadelphia (both his father and brother were prominent rabbis) and although he himself pursued a legal career, he was always active in Jewish affairs; he became president of the Zionist Organization of America in 1941.

In his caustic 1915 editorial in SAM's newsletter Levinthal praised the maintenance of religious separation, scoffed at the idea of universal brotherhood, and advocated that Jews continue to be as sympathetic and prejudiced in favor of their own people as Gentiles were prejudiced in favor of Gentiles. "So often we are told that the age of the Brotherhood of Man is shortly to be ushered in, that the hearts of all men are to beat as one, that racial and religious prejudice is to be relegated to the past, that I am quite willing to confess that I should dread such a condition of affairs," Levinthal wrote. "I have no apology to offer for the Jew-baiter. I am setting out to defend not the unnatural antipathy that has its source in ignorance and thrives in bigotry, but the natural, inherent and wholesome sympathy that every Jew should have for every other Jew, because all Jews are brothers." Discrimination could be a positive good, Levinthal continued, if through it Jews could prevent intermarriage and thus preserve their distinctive identity. "I am not at all sorry that this prejudice, so universal, exists," he admitted. "To be perfectly candid, I rejoice when I find that Jews are excluded from the ordinary college fraternity; I am glad to see the fashionable hotels advertise that they do not admit Jews. Why? Because I want nothing in the world so much as I want the Jewish people to continue to live as a people apart and distinct from the rest of the peoples of the world."[53]

The price would be the death of the Jewish people if separation were eliminated and Jews were accepted as true equals on the American college campus, Levinthal believed:

> How can we Jews hope to continue to be Jews if we mingle freely with the non-Jews? Where shall the line be drawn? If we eat and sleep with non-

Jews in fraternity houses and in hotels, why should we not marry their sisters and daughters? Isn't it a fact that those Jews who do mix freely with their non-Jewish neighbors drift away from the faith of their fathers into baptism and intermarriage? It is only by maintaining . . . as many separate factors as possible that we Jews can remain Jews amid non-Jewish surroundings. An exclusively Jewish fraternity, such as the Sigma Alpha Mu, with its ideals essentially Jewish, is a separative factor in the life of the American-Jewish college war. Long life to it!

Octagonian editor "Hij" Jacobson also saw the question of the internal Jewish attack on fraternities, and the charge that they might weaken Jewish unity and spread antisemitism, as subjects worthy of his personal attention and refutation. In the Passover edition of the *Octagonian* in May, 1913—which opened with the traditional greeting, "Le-Shono Haboah be-Jerusholaim," ("Next Year in Jerusalem"), Jacobson published a critical editorial by Jacob Turchinsky, a nonfraternity student at NYU who was deeply concerned with the growth and proliferation of fraternities that he saw all around him. In Turchinsky's views, no Jew who understood the full implications of these groups could possibly support this expansion.

"ARE YOU HELPING your Alma Mater, the citizens of your country, by being Fraternity men?" Turchinsky first asked his readers, and proceeded to give his own negative answer, invoking the name of millions of their fellow Jews overseas who were not blessed as they were with the freedoms and opportunities of American democracy. "WE ALL KNOW what the caste spirit has done," he wrote.

> Let us take an example with which you as young Jewish men are quite familiar. Take the Yichos of the Russian Jew. Because he happens to be a tailor, he will not permit his son to associate with the cobbler's family. Are you sure that you are not creating a caste spirit among us Jews? As it is, we are already divided into more than the proverbial 57 varieties. Are you Americans, upon whom the entire Jewish population of the world is looking with longing expectant eyes, are you going to disappoint them by creating artificial castes?[54]

The Turchinsky–Jacobson debate was one of the few times in the relatively optimistic 1910s when the anti-Jewish feeling which daily faced the readers at school was directly mentioned in the pages of the SAM newsletter. Turchinsky, as many others, believed that the formation of a separate Jewish-Greek subsystem in the end would increase antisemitism, not alleviate it, victimizing even those who did not choose to join such organizations. "IT IS TRUE that anti-Semitism exists in our schools," he admitted.

> The writer knows and has experienced it himself. He has fought back without avail. But will it be lessened by Jewish Fraternities? Will it not result in the lines being more sharply drawn than before? Will there not be clanning of the student body, and with it the inevitable result, the forcing out of a great number of Jewish students from our schools? I FULLY REALIZE that something must be done. I can see the time approaching when the spirit of anti-semitism will prevail over the entire country . . . Will not the creating of Jewish Fraternities only hasten the combining of all anti-semitic forces in the country, and with that bring the final encounter?

Turchinsky closed his letter by imploring his fellow Jews that if they persisted in forming their own fraternities, that they at least guard their conduct. "JEWISH FRATRES, be careful of your actions," he warned. "The entire Jewish population of the world will be judged by what you do. Your good actions will not be remembered; your bad ones will be exaggerated, spread over the face of the globe, and each of us will be liable for the action of any one of us. BE CAREFUL!"[55]

In his reply, Jacobson, in contrast, expressed the belief that Jewish fraternities that trained their members to compete on the same grounds as Gentile students could provide an important way for college students to fight antisemitism, not exacerbate it. "The world may not love a fighter, but it respects him," he wrote. "And we find that the Jewish Fraternity man, armed with the determination to be on an equal footing with the Gentile student, is more respected and has more opportunities in his college career than the non-frat men." The remedy to fraternity exclusiveness, he insisted, was not to abolish fraternities, but to make the system more pluralistic by forming enough groups so that everyone could enjoy the advantages of fraternity life. It was more Jewish fraternities, not fewer, wherein lay the true answer to fears of Jewish weakness in the face of antisemitism.

In his assertions, Jacobson did not hesitate to invoke the Russian pogroms that had motivated so many members' parents and grandparents to seek out life in the United States. "The writer's [Turchinsky's] attitude and ours are like the attitude of the Jew who reminds us that 'Israel's mission is peace,' and goes forth to soften the heart of the Czar with prayers, and that of the Jew who shoulders a gun to protect his home. And the odds are all in favor of the latter," he declared. "Jewish Fratres, be careful! Gladly we welcome the advice. But if what we are doing will bring anti-Semitism, let it come! We doubt whether the ill-feeling toward the Jew in American colleges can be much increased. But if it can, then all we can say is: 'If 'twere done, 'twere well 'twere done quickly!' "[56]

Despite all opposition, the Jewish Greek subsystem continued to expand. Chapters strove, and for the most part succeeded, in providing members with much of the normal college existence and peer companionship that students longed for. The fraternity chapter became almost a second or substitute family when social bonds began to weaken with parents and older relatives who had never attended college. Through the 1910s and afterward Jewish fraternities organized parties, dances, boat rides, theater trips, singing festivals, picnics, baseball games, banquets and anything else that could be done for their members's amusement. In their periodicals and meeting minutes, discussion of broader issues occupied but a small part. Members were far more likely to discuss such matters as where to buy pins and shingles, whether to print or continue mimeographing their publications, whether an $8.00 charge for annual dues was too high, and what kind of scavenger hunts, stunts, and gruesome initiation proceedings could be cooked up for the benefit of new members.[57]

By the beginning of the third decade of the twentieth century the structural similarities of the new Jewish Greek subsystem to its Gentile predecessors, to the outward eye at least, far outweighed the differences. For those young Jews who had the access, the desire, and the means to participate in their Greek system, this meant that for a short, precious time they might forget the trials of their ancestors. Society might not yet permit them full entrance, but they could still do their best to enjoy their lives as truly American college students.

Chapter 4

The Golden Age

College Fraternities in the "Roaring Twenties"

What might be called the "Golden Age" in the history of the American college Greek-letter fraternity came in the decade between the end of the First World War and the onset of the Great Depression. The Jewish Greek subsystem enjoyed its full share in that age. Fed by mass immigration, the American population and thus its pool of college-age youth had expanded. Postwar prosperity permitted more individuals and families to postpone their children's entry into the workforce. A growing network of public secondary schools was preparing more Americans for college-level work than ever before. Higher education became more desirable and necessary as training for new jobs openings in the fields of science, technology, finance, and the corporate world. The result was a veritable explosion in the number of young people and potential fraternity members making their way to the nation's campuses.

As late as 1910 there had been only approximately 150,000 undergraduates in the United States. By the end of 1929 there were well over a million and more than two-thirds of these were enrolled in co-educational residential colleges, precisely the type of campus where the Greek system was already strongest.[1] The existing collegiate infrastructures could hardly cope with this onslaught alone. The Greek system, however, was ready and waiting to provide large segments of the student body with food and shelter. The system also provided face-to-face contact and personal guidance now otherwise unavailable on campuses so large that no one person could ever hope to learn everyone else's name.

Leaders throughout the Greek system exulted in their popularity. Between 1912 and 1930, according to the latter year's edition of
Baird's Manual, the number of fraternity chapters in the country more
than doubled and the reported value of fraternity property increased
more than five fold. The number of national fraternities and sororities
reached had reached a high of seventy-seven organizations, with a total
initiated membership (including adult nonstudents) of over 740,000.
Furthermore, of the more than 2,700 chapters for undergraduates, over
1500 owned their own houses, which were valued all together at close to
seventy-five million dollars.[2] By the mid-1920s, an estimated thirty-five
percent of all the college students in the country belonged to chapters
of fraternities or sororities, while on some campuses the proportion ran
as high as forty to seventy percent.[3] The relative prestige of each group
served as an indicator of its members's status and popularity. Merely
being a college student was no longer automatically an indicator of high
social status. For access to the best social life, the best food and living
conditions, or the best chances for success in student politics, sports, and
most extracurricular activities, an ambitious student on a campus with a
strong fraternity system was considered lost if he or she did not "pledge
a good house."[4]

The influence of this youthful, frequently idealized, collegiate
fraternity culture also passed far beyond the college campus in the 1920s
through the new mass media. Even those Americans not attending college could listen to popular college fraternity songs broadcast coast-to-
coast on their radios. They could also view the alleged scandals of fraternity life portrayed on silent movie screens in such Hollywood films as
The Freshman (1925), starring Harold Lloyd, or *The Wild Party* (1929),
starring the decade's "It" Girl, Clara Bow. Collegiate life, clothing and
traditions in general and fraternity activities in particular were also an
increasingly popular subject for paperback novels, magazine articles, and
advertising.

The Triumph of Jewish College Fraternities

Along with the Gentile groups, the membership rolls of Jewish fraternities swelled as American Jews, who overall represented less than 3.5 percent of the U.S. population, fast approached the point of becoming ten
percent of the nation's entire college population. The proportions rose
much higher in schools located near large urban centers.[5] Moreover, it
was during the 1920s that Jewish Greek subsystem emerged triumphant

over other types of Jewish organizations such as the Menorah societies or Jewish religious congregations. When left behind, these groups therefore sometimes recapitulated their people's ancient history by forming an antagonistic attitude toward the Jewish "Greeks."[6] A 1927 survey published by the *American Jewish Yearbook* found, to the displeasure and dismay of many rabbis and communal synagogue leaders, that a minority of American Jewish college students chose to affiliate with a Jewish organization of any kind. Of those that did, over eighty percent chose affiliation with a chapter of a Jewish fraternity or sorority.[7]

Naturally, not every Jewish man or woman attending college in the 1920s either desired or could afford the "Jazz Age" collegiate lifestyle portrayed in the movies and popular magazines. Private bootleggers, elaborate parties, and all-night drunken revels were beyond the reach of the one-half to two-thirds of the student body who lived at home and rode the tram to school, or who held down demanding part-time jobs while struggling to maintain their grades.[8] Nevertheless, Jewish fraternity records indicate that a good number from this group were able to enjoy their college years by participating fully in all aspects of the new, popular collegiate culture in the 1920s, including "dating" (a new term), mixed dancing, necking, petting, drinking, smoking, listening to jazz music, traveling around the world, savoring the new mobility and privacy offered by automobiles, and displaying the same patterns of conspicuous consumption as their middle and upper-middle class Gentile counterparts.

The Ideal College Man

The members of Zeta Beta Tau, the oldest, largest, and still wealthiest of the Jewish fraternities, sought to epitomize the prosperity of the decade along with the new social and recreational opportunities it offered to American youth. The ideal "college man," according to one profile published in the *Zeta Beta Tau Quarterly* in 1928, could be identified by the following signs: "He disdains hats and garters; he plays the saxophone or banjo; he smokes a pipe or has a blind-fold cigarette technique; he knows at least one version of Frankie and Johnny; he wears jeweled badges on his vest or watch-chain [a reference to fraternity pins] and conversation always turns to football. . . . He also has a way of talking to a girl by phone, and a facile slang."[9] Coats made of raccoon or bearskin, the article reported, were a popular fashion item for collegiates of both sexes, particularly at the ubiquitous games of college football.

A University of Wisconsin 1924 ZBT graduate purportedly described the typical fraternity man's day in an article humorously entitled "Ulysses Universitatis, or Four and Twenty Hours from the Life of a College Youth." The author described a college man's experiences of waking up, washing and shaving in the communal bathroom, dressing, fighting with fellow members for the morning paper, enduring fraternity house breakfasts and dinners, and then professors, classes, exams, and the perennial "bull sessions" where students sat down together in the evenings and held heated discussions lasting hours on end.

The author also described the college man's continual search for new trysting places (unchaperoned young females officially were not permitted within the walls of the chapter house), carrying blankets out to the chosen spot, romancing one's girl by the strumming of a ukulele, and the ultimate joys of a "canoe date." The latter diversion, preferably undertaken at night under a full moon, was popular in the 1920s at any coeducational university located near a sizable body of water. Since the dates obviously took place without the wearing of flotation devices and in disregard of every principle of water safety, it may be assumed that the universities took steps to discontinue them at some point. However, until then a young fraternity man could enjoy placing a pile of pillows in the canoe, paddling with his date out into the middle of the lake, and passing a romantic interlude under the stars before paddling back and seeing his date to her front door.[10]

Prohibition

The popularity of alcoholic beverages among both sexes was also characteristic of college students in the 1920s, despite the existence of the Eighteenth Amendment to the U.S. Constitution, in force between January 1920 and December 1933, which prohibited the sale or transport of intoxicating liquors in the country. From numerous references in their publications and those of other groups, it is clear that Jewish college men and women participated in the underground "speakeasy" culture that came to replace legal drinking.[11] In one pseudonymous article covering the history of Prohibition at American colleges "John B. Quigley," a 1924 ZBT graduate of the University of Missouri who was himself a victim of the legally dry collegiate years, longingly recalled stories told by older fraternity brothers of all-night springtime revels in the country when chapter members, "filled with the spirit of brotherly love," would sing and drink around iced kegs. In those days before Prohibition, his elders told him, custom dictated that men drink in male company exclusively. Women would refuse to dance with a man if, "through a camouflaging clove," they detected liquor on his breath. [12]

Then came his own college days and Prohibition, the author continued, and a paradoxical escalation in college student drinking along with a severe decline in the quality of the alcohol consumed. At the very beginning of Prohibition in 1920–21, he recalled, students drank lemon extract, orange peel concoctions, patent medicine, or whatever was available at the local pharmacy. Then came back-alley bootleggers selling a poor grade of gin or white corn whiskey, which was "vile, stinking, and filled with pieces of charcoal"—but "it got results." Students would drink it at parties, killing the taste with gum, oranges, or grapefruit. Somehow, Prohibition also altered the males-only status of acceptable public drinking. By 1923 "bolder co-eds began taking a nip or two" and going out on late night dates; the phenomenon became so common that universities stopped expelling them for it.

By 1924, he recalled, "we entered a period more cosmically wet than any that had gone before." Students with the inclination and adequate funds could simply pick up the telephone and have their corn whiskey delivered. Its quality had even improved since the bootleggers had begun straining the charcoal out of it, and it now came in "fancy bottles with stamps on them." By 1929, guests were welcomed to drink at every party, including coeds "from the shyest families who wouldn't let their daughters drink coffee." "There she stands doing 'Bottoms Up' with the best of them," the author mourned. "The lips that touch liquor belong to both sexes." [13]

Some fraternity elders felt compelled to take care that younger members during the dry years in America were not deprived of an important part of their social and cultural education. The liquor available to United States college students in the 1920s might be limited to bathtub gin and corn whiskey, but once a Zeta Beta Tau gentleman traveled beyond the bounds of Prohibition, he was expected to know the correct beverage to order. A 1921 graduate of the University of California at Berkeley, "viewing with alarm the bootleg tastes being forced upon the younger drinking set by the ginger-ale manufacturers," proceeded in 1929 to write for the undergraduates a detailed treatise explaining the mysteries of different wines, the importance of matching them to different foods, proper serving procedures, and the merits of various kinds of Burgundies, Bordeaux, Champagnes, Sauternes, sherries, and liqueurs. The author concluded with the assurance that he could have gone on for much longer, but "I've said enough to last until Prohibition is modified. Or if you can't wait that long, clip this out and carry it with you the next time there's a ZBT meeting of some kind in Montreal. Or take it along when you win that European scholarship."[14]

German-Jewish Heritage

In the early years of the century, being a "gentleman" in the fullest American Jewish sense of the word usually meant being a member of the German Jewish aristocracy. It was not unheard of in the nineteenth and early twentieth centuries for Jews of Russian or East European Jewish background who could not or would not aspire to being Gentiles to change their recognizably Russian Jewish names to recognizably German Jewish ones. Zeta Beta Tau's membership in the 1920s was still largely German-Jewish, drawing heavily from the proverbial "Our Crowd," although wealthy East European Jews—particularly "Litvoks," the name for those whose families were originally from the Lithuanian lands—were beginning to make inroads. This is especially evident from the words of a humorous poem and toast recalling details of chapter life that was presented by Robert E. Segal (Ohio State '25) at the chapter's twenty-fifth anniversary celebration:[15]

> Late Monday and the chapter is in session down below,
> The Litvoks fight the Germans, they can give 'em blow for blow.
> The kid that came from Cleveland is one that's hard to beat;
> But golly me, he's blackballed; the reason is his street.
> We ought to go to Temple more; we're slipping bad, by gosh.
> Well Sunday next we'll send them half a dozen frosh . . .

Within the records of the fraternity from those years modern words—slang and phenomena of the Jazz Age—coexist with evidence of traditions dating from the much earlier era of members' parents and grandparents. These elders would have been products of the German-Jewish migration to the U.S. of the mid-nineteenth century. German phrases, expressions, and slang (including "n.f.k. beverages," a euphemism for liquor taken from the German words "nicht für Kinder"—not for children) and such terms as the "400 Verein" were still used occasionally in the *Quarterly's* pages. One parody that took aim at the mothers of ZBT men referred to a fictional "Vorschlag," or resolution, passed at a special meeting of the Hirsch Liska Sick, Benevolent, and Krankerunterschutzung Society. A bouquet of flowers was to be sent to the funeral of the group's recently departed Treasurer, Mrs. Hymie Benefsky (this a characteristically East European Jewish name—among ZBT-associated women the "Litvoks" were apparently penetrating also). The meeting itself was said to have taken place on January the thirty-first at the Harlem Palace, 25 West 115th Street, and was led by Mrs. Minnie Farfelzoop and Mrs. Henna Itzelfuss.[16]

The same author, a manufacturer of handkerchiefs who had graduated from Columbia in 1920 and was a frequent contributor of such humorous articles and parodies to the *Zeta Beta Tau Quarterly*, offered the following version of a rush letter from "the good old days" in a humorous feature entitled "Rushing as it Wunst Wuz." Filled as it was with insiders's jokes, it poked good-natured fun at "Our Crowd's" cultural markers. In those days, the author recalled, it was said that most men waited for bids from ZBT from the time they entered high school, that all girls were crazy about them, and that the fraternity could claim more Supreme Court Justices, Presidential candidates, and football captains than any other group:

> Dear Fraters: I am one of the charter members of the old Zeta Beta Melucha fraternity which in 1886 joined with the Free and Liberated Liederkranz out of which eventually grew the present splendid organization we now have. Sid Shepsel, Chaim Witzelfuss (now Warren) and I organized the first chapter at the Packer Soap School (no longer in existence) and we have never missed a convention since our first one was held at Max Schwarz's "Hanging Gardens" on First Avenue . . .
>
> The true reason for this letter is that Joe Hickelplatz, a cousin of ours, is planning to enter your college in the fall (provided he passes his Biology). Joe is one of the finest youngsters in the world and Wilkes-Barre, and I know you will find him fraternity material of the best caliber. He will surely be a valuable addition to your chapter.
>
> At high school he was the captain of the literary society and spoke first in all baseball wrangles. He got "A's" in his studies several times and was the most popular Jewish boy at the "Y."
>
> I trust you will show him the hospitality worthy of our loyal "K.K.P."
>
> Fraternally yours,
> BROTHER BIMBO HIRSCHORN,
> Old Alpha, 1889.[17]

Social Standards

Humor aside, within ZBT the process of choosing new members was carried out with utmost seriousness. The Committee on Standards of Membership in a September 1924 Supreme Council meeting specifically adjured evaluators always to ask the following question when considering an applicant: "Does his appearance show that he has the manners, culture, and necessary breeding which would compel us to feel that in him we find a truly representative specimen of young Jewish manhood?" Without such specific standards, terrible mistakes could be made. At the same meeting, the Supreme Council voted unanimously to expel Richard Loeb, a member of their University of Michigan chapter and recently indicted, along with Nathan Freudenthal Leopold of the University of Chicago, for the kidnap and murder in Chicago of 14-year-old Bobby Franks. After what became one of the most sensational murder trials yet seen in the United States, despite the best defense efforts of attorney Clarence Darrow, Leopold and Loeb were both convicted and sentenced to life imprisonment plus ninety-nine years. The two former college men put their education to good use by developing a successful correspondence school, which they ran from jail. Leopold lived long enough to be paroled to Puerto Rico in 1958 and to write a book about his experiences. Loeb met his death at the hands of a fellow prison inmate in 1936.[18]

After dispensing with the Leopold and Loeb matter in September 1924, ZBT's Supreme Council commenced planning that year's forthcoming convention, a luxurious affair which was to include a cruise from New York and Baltimore (presumably beyond Prohibition's three-mile limit) to the Hotel Monticello in Norfolk, Virginia, an oyster roast at Cape Henry in the evening, and both formal and informal dances at Norfolk's Ghent Club.[19] In general until World War II, if attendance at Jewish services were mentioned at all in connection with Zeta Beta Tau's programming, the day given for going to Temple was almost always Sunday, a clear indication of the group's classical Reform Jewish orientation.

With few exceptions, it was understood that the definition of "breeding" and "family" translated into acquired wealth, both individual and collective. It was understood that application and acceptance into the fraternity implied not only the ability to afford basic fees but to keep up with the standards of recreational activities, clothing, and entertainment set by the other members, along with any periodic assessments for parties and social events. Sorority women in particular from elite groups both Jewish and non-Jewish were expected to come from comfortably well-off families able to supply them with the necessary clothing and accoutrements to keep up with the rest of the chapter. Those without that financial ability did not apply or else sought out other fraternities—

and these did exist—where they knew the obligations would be lighter. The practical factor of variations in financial means alone was significant in the proliferation of Jewish fraternities. Seldom before or after the 1920s would there be as much substance to Zeta Beta Tau's tongue-in-cheek nickname of "Zion Bank and Trust" or "Zillions, Billions and Trillions." In the early 1970s, a series of crises and a contraction within the Jewish Greek subsystem brought about the merger of four formerly separate Jewish fraternities under the single Zeta Beta Tau umbrella. Senior alumni, by then mostly prosperous businessmen and professionals, were heard to react with wonder at their new membership status. "But we couldn't afford to belong to ZBT!" they exclaimed, recalling the leaner years of their youth.[20]

In the 1920s few fraternity houses anywhere could match the opulence of ZBT's University of Alabama chapter house in Tuscaloosa. The chapter photo of 1928 shows twenty-six men with their heads held high, all dressed in fine suits with stiff collars and ties. The chapter house, built in Georgian style with a sun-porch, featured a living room with heavy, elaborately carved mahogany furniture, upholstered sofas, a fireplace, a chandelier, and a foyer. The dining room, where a Zeta Beta Tau felt banner hung over a second fireplace, was pictured set with white tablecloths, china and crystal.[21]

Taking a "Grand Tour," or extensive foreign travel during summer and school vacations, was also a marked feature of the relative affluence and cultural sophistication of Zeta Beta Tau's membership. The prestigious Cunard Steamship Company acknowledged ZBT's potential volume of business as well as its social acceptability when it wrote to the fraternity in 1924 offering members traveling together shared staterooms in their ships at reduced rates. Such generosity incidentally also reduced the embarrassing possibilities of unwilling Gentiles being placed in the same ship quarters as Jews and having to ask to have their rooms changed.[22] "Where Have You Been?" was a typical topic for a bull session in each chapter house at the end of every summer.[23] Each issue contained news of members' travel to exotic lands. The fraternity quarterly's "Vacation Number," published in May 1929, remarked on the number of graduates who were about to depart "on that summer vacation trip to Europe, California, Hawaii and perhaps around the world."[24] The accounts of their adventures provide a fascinating portrait of life in Europe at the time as well as a poignant view of life in pre-World War II Germany, the land from which most of their ancestors had come as well as one of their most popular travel destinations.

The 1929 vacation issue included a particularly interesting travelogue, entitled "In the Land of Pretzels and Beer," written by a 1926 graduate of the University of California, Bernard S. Greensfeder, who was spending the year at the University of Berlin. Despite their distinctive culture, Germany, Greensfeder noted, was apparently overcome by a craze for Americanization, with cars, advertising, newspapers, translated books, foods (including chocolate malts, pork and beans, and Heinz ketchup) to be found everywhere, along with American films and music. To the author, writing barely twelve years before Germany declared war on the U.S., everyone seemed fascinated with everything American. All the students he spoke to expressed a longing to visit the country. In fact it appeared to him, in 1929, that Americans had completely taken over German industry, and that the entire country was dependent upon American money. "The finishing touch is yet to come," observed Greensfeder ironically. "That will be the arrival of a delegation of European ethnologists, seeking the remnants of German civilization in the city of Milwaukee."[25]

Greensfeder also provided his readers with a view of 1920s German university student life through an American's eyes. Most notable to him was the extreme poverty and complete lack of cars, for most of the university class, he observed, had lost everything in the post-war inflation. The German counterparts to American fraternities were known as *Corpsbrüdern*, where men with the same political beliefs were grouped together. Among them, dueling was "still in vogue" and a hacked face still a sign of manhood, although, as he pointed out, "many more Americans are killed in football than Germans in dueling" each year. They had no chapter houses, but met for lunch or dinner in designated public restaurants. The headwater would bring out a standard bearing the colors and crest of the fraternity and set it out on the table, surrounding it with beer mugs. Open drinking competitions were common. "They utterly can't understand our 18th amendment," Greensfeder observed. "Anecdotes of bootleggers, police raids, poison liquor, and pocket flask technique excite unbounded amusement, not unmixed with pity." On the question of whether German students were harmed by such indulgences, the author referred to illegal American drinking by writing "one must frankly compare a couple of harmless steins against a shot of paint-dissolver now and then."[26]

In addition to Germany and England, France was an especially popular destination for ZBTers as it was for most traveling Americans.

The traditional "stag" banquet at the twenty-first annual convention of Zeta Beta Tau, the Hotel Astor, New York City, Dec. 25, 1919. Banners from each chapter hang throughout the hall. (Zeta Beta Tau Archives)

First members of Zeta Beta Tau at the Massachusetts Institute of Technology in 1911. The chapter was declared "inactive" in 1927. *Left to right, front row:* Charles L. Gabriel '11, Isidore Spector '11, Ben Munch '11. *Top row:* Jacob S. Wise '12, A. J. "Buck" Freedman '12, Nathan Levy '11. (Zeta Beta Tau Archives)

Incoming pledge class at New York University's Zeta Beta Tau chapter in 1913. *Left to right, back row:* Unknown, Ned Marin, L. Levine, Samuel Sack, Cornelius Bregoff '17, unknown. *Front:* Victor House '14, J. Hern, Jacob Julian Brandt '14, Maurice Rashbaum '14, Abraham Blumberg '14. (Zeta Beta Tau Archives)

At McGill University in Montreal in 1913, members of the founding chapter of the Greek-letter Zeta Beta Tau fraternity pose with their mentor, Rabbi Herman Abramowitz (*with mustache, seated sixth from left*). Abramowitz, one of the founders of the original Zionist-oriented ZBT Society in New York in 1898, served as president of the United Synagogue of America and was honorary vice-president of the Zionist Organization of Canada. (Zeta Beta Tau Archives)

Members of Phi Epsilon Pi fraternity at the University of Maine pose on the porch of their chapter house in the late fall of 1919. Maurice Jacobs '17 of this chapter went on to become the executive head of the fraternity for over forty years, a part of his life as a major figure in the American Jewish communal and cultural world and head of the Jewish Publication Society. (Zeta Beta Tau Archives)

Ira N. Lind

Jacob Kaplan

Lester Cohen

Samuel Ginsburg

Hyman I. Jacobson

David D. Levinson

Abraham N. Kerner

Adolph I. Fabis

The eight of twelve invited City College friends who came to the home of Hyman "Hij" Jacobson in New York the night of November 26, 1909, and founded Sigma Alpha Mu. Seizing upon the symbolism of eight, the young men decided to call their governing body and their publication "the Octagon." (Sigma Alpha Mu Archives)

"The Founders' Bench" from City College of New York's Lincoln Corridor. Fraternities and student organizations of all kinds would gather at benches such as these during lunch hour to hold their meetings. SAM's earliest members gathered at this one from 1909 onward. It was a gift from the college on the occasion of the fraternity's fiftieth anniversary in 1959 and is now on permanent display at the SAM national office in Carmel, Indiana. (Sigma Alpha Mu Archives)

The founders and first pledge class of Phi Sigma Delta at the University of Denver in 1921. (Zeta Beta Tau Archives)

The founders of Sigma Delta Tau at Cornell University in 1917. *Counterclockwise from top right:* Regene Freund Cohane, Grace Srenco Grossman, Lenore Rubinow, Inez Dane Ross, Marian Gerber Greenberg, Dora Bloom Turteltaub, and Amy Apfel Tishman. (Sigma Delta Tau Archives)

Banquet to mark the installation of Zeta Beta Tau's new chapter at the University of California at Los Angeles, April 1, 1927. (Zeta Beta Tau Archives)

Stella Strauss   Ida Beck

Not Pictured
Lee Riess

Tina Hess

Helen Phillips   Rose Gerstein   Rose Salmowitz

The founders of Alpha Epsilon Phi at Barnard College in 1909. The group's first meeting was held in the dormitory room of Helen Phillips. Tina Hess, a history major, was elected the first president, with Ida Beck as treasurer and Stella Strauss as secretary. Rose Salmowitz, the Greek scholar of the group, proposed the name of the sorority, from the Greek *Aei Esto Philia:* "may friendship be everlasting." (Alpha Epsilon Phi Archives)

At the University of Washington in Seattle in 1921. Here the local Jewish fraternity Alpha Mu Sigma has just petitioned to join Zeta Beta Tau and is hosting the national representative at dinner. Many chapters of national Jewish fraternities were formed from such pre-existing "locals" that had already operated for years with their own houses and board plans. This group was accepted into ZBT the following year. *Pictured from left to right:* Harry Weinstein '24, unidentified, Herbert Shafer '25, Leon D. Dover '25, Hyman O. Solomon '23, Ben Z. Levin '21, Samuel L. Fendel '22, Arthur L. Sigmond '22, Milton S. Malakoff '23, unidentified, Norman M. Burnett. "Lee" Dover did not stay with this chapter. He moved from Seattle to Los Angeles and graduated from the University of Southern California, eventually moving to New York, where he served as ZBT's executive head for over thirty years. (Zeta Beta Tau Archives)

Chapter photo of Phi Sigma Delta at the University of Wisconsin, 1921–1922.
(Zeta Beta Tau Archives)

At the University of Michigan in 1927, nine of ten graduating seniors pose by the Zeta Beta Tau chapter house in Ann Arbor. Those pictured include, *far left,* Mentor A. Krauss; *second from left,* Henry P. Bitker; *far right,* Robert Ullman; *third from right,* Richard Weil. Also in that class were Normal Freehling, Harold Newman, Mark Rolfe Jr., Ray Rosengarten, Julius Weinberg, and Stanton N. Meyer, who saved and probably took this picture.

Phi Sigma Delta at the University of Pennsylvania in 1924. The yearbook lists the following names, but doesn't identify individual photos: Richard Liebman, Jack Polan, Maurice C. Kramer, Sol M. Hirsch, Mendel Silverman, Saul L. Kamin, Sidney Kavner, Irving Rosenberg, Morton Sanger, Edmund Kahn, Lester Gutterman, S. Milton Goldhame, Arnold Smith, Paul Dalsimer, Daniel Debrier, Melville Cheonis, Arthur Harry Maisner, Benjamin Wechsler, Edward Strauss, Rayme D. Grant, Nathan Margolis, Nathan Narman, Samuel Lavaur, Milton Miller, Carl Brukenfeld, Joseph Zable, Irvin Horwitz, Hyman E. Wine. (Zeta Beta Tau Archives)

At Western Reserve University in Cleveland in 1921, the founding chapter of Phi Sigma Delta fraternity. At center of bottom row sits Harry L. Wolpaw, the first chapter president, who became PSD's national president in October 1944. Harry's three brothers—Meyer, Benjamin, and Sidney—all attended Western Reserve and joined the fraternity also. The school federated with the Case Institute of Technology in 1967 to form today's Case Western Reserve University. (Zeta Beta Tau Archives)

Phi Epsilon Pi at Pennsylvania State University in the 1923–1924 academic year. *From left, top row:* William F. Adler, Morton M. Sladkin, Leon W. Shapiro, Bernard Cukerbaum, Janavitz. *Second row:* Israel April, Arthur H. Rosenfeld, Herbert H. Herskovitz, David S. Green, Jay H. Mervis, Harold V. Cohen. *Third row:* Theodor H. Schmidt, Morris Z. Kisseleff, Leon E. Spector, Jack Goldberg, Nathan Feldman, Irwin L. Bernstein, Simon R. Bloomfield. (Zeta Beta Tau Archives)

Sigma Alpha Mu at McGill University in 1920. *Top row, left to right:* Max I. Raphael '21, Newman B. Freedman '23, Nathan Fish '22, A. O. Freedman '20 (obviously added afterward), John M. Loebel '22, Gerald B. Fels '23, Harry I. Cohen '22, Leon H. Levinson '31. *Middle row:* Harry A. Coveler '24, Sol E. Goldman '22, Henry L. Echenberg '24, Sidney D. Pierce '25, Norman M. Vines '24, Barnett J. Cohen '21, and Lionel A. Sperber '24, who urged them all to keep up their pride during the Harvard quota scandal. *Bottom row:* Lewis K. Freedman '20, Joseph Cohen '21, Charles H. Goren '23, Lawrence Z. Cohen '24. (Sigma Alpha Mu Archives)

Not only intercollegiate but also intramural sports were a way for Jewish students to win glory on the playing fields of their schools. Here at Syracuse University in 1921 the Sigma Alpha Mu basketball team is ready to participate in the Interfraternity League championships. *Top row, left to right:* Walter Rose '22, manager; John S. Barsha '20, coach; Fuchs, substitute; S. Polk Waskowitz '21. *Bottom row:* William R. Weinrib '21, guard; Samuel C. Suisman '21, forward; Captain Robert H. Esken '22, forward; Harry Herbert '27, guard. (Sigma Alpha Mu Archives)

The Sigma Alpha Mu chapter at Harvard University in 1921, one year before President A. Lawrence Lowell openly announced the possibility of setting a ten percent quota on Jewish enrollment there. The resulting scandal, in the words of one SAM member, would become "the bomb that shook American colleges." *Top row, left to right:* Henry J. Friendly '23, Julius M. Collins '23, Meyer Kestenbaum '21 (he eventually became a member of the Harvard Board of Overseers). *Third row:* Manuel Weisbuch '23, Gustave P. Heller '21, Samuel J. Rose '23, Fletcher G. Cohn '23, Russell P. Kantor '24, S. David Coleman '21. *Second row:* Sol A. Rosenblatt '22, A. Martin Sonnabend '17, James M. Arnstine '22, Emanuel J. Rosenberg '22, Paul R. Harmel '24, Samuel H. Maslon '20, S. Leo Solomont '18. *Bottom row:* Lawrence E. Spivak '21. (Sigma Alpha Mu Archives)

Sigma Alpha Mu at the City College of New York in 1925. While this group and several others among the Jewish fraternities enjoyed a place of honor as the "Alpha" or mother chapter of the national organization, over time income and class differences tended to widen between undergraduates attending CCNY and members and alumni from other universities. In 1934, during the Great Depression, a group of SAM alumni had to take up a collection in order to pay the initiation fees of the four men accepted into the City College chapter that year; the young men would have unable to join otherwise. (Sigma Alpha Mu Archives)

Sigma Alpha Mu at the University of Michigan, 1925–1926. *Top row, left to right:* Herbert M. Segal '27, Melvin J. Kuttnauer '27, Jerome A. Spero '27, Samson Wiener '28, Howard A. Bloom '28, William H. Stern '27, Milton S. Solomon '25, William M. Mazer '28. *Second row:* Allan E. Levie '26, Arthur J. Levy '26, Milford J. Rush '26, David B. Simon '26, Bertram W. Amster '26, Emil T. Stern '28, Herbert Spitzer '26, R. Weiss, S. Robbins. *Bottom row:* Benjamin G. Friedman '27, Herbert H. Tenenbaum '29, Maurice J. Robinson '26, Alfred G. Krell '27, Martin J. Cohn '29, Stanley Friedman '29, Harvey W. Rosenblum '29, Robert B. Steinharter '28. (Sigma Alpha Mu Archives)

Members, friends, and relatives of Alpha Epsilon Pi's New York University
Washington Square campus chapter frolic at the beach in the summer of 1921.
(Alpha Epsilon Pi Archives)

Beginning in 1920 Alpha Epsilon Pi's New York University undergraduates and alumni pooled their resources to rent a summer bungalow at Beach 46th Street in the town of Edgemere in the Far Rockaway section of Long Island. Here members of the chapter are pictured in 1921 at the beach with their wives and girlfriends. Despite the casualness of the setting and the summer heat, most of the men have given no thought to removing their coats and ties. (Alpha Epsilon Pi Archives)

At first, the small and new Alpha Epsilon Pi fraternity was unable to afford lavish annual convention weekends at major hotels. They made do with no banquet at all or a single night at a restaurant. In time, however, AEPi moved up to the point that it, too, could hold its social events in hotels. Here the fraternity holds its convention dinner at the Hotel Martinique in New York, December 30, 1922. At the head table sit Milton Adler (Supreme Master), L. Siemon, L. Hamburger, Sidney Picker, Herman Rolnick, Maxwell Farber, Samuel Kahn, Philip Sohmer, Theodore R. Racoosin, Joseph Corin, and Jesse Safir. Also in the picture are Nathan Wolf and Isadore M. Glazer. (Alpha Epsilon Pi Archives)

Sigma Omega Psi Fraternity

INCORPORATED

by its

Grand Conclave

represented, reposing faith and confidence in the worthiness and good moral character of those whose names are herein inscribed, there is granted unto

Joseph A. Cohen   **Lawrence Oppenheim**
Henry Levy   **Benj. Arthur Trustman**
Lincoln Mekelburg   **Alexander Ulin**
Robert Ulin

their associates and successors

THIS CHARTER

constituting them as an active chapter of the aforesaid fraternity duly organized and initiated and to be styled the *Pi* Chapter of the Sigma Omega Psi Fraternity located at *Harvard University* Cambridge, Mass, so long as they shall conform to and obey the Constitution, By Laws and all other regulations now existing or hereafter enacted by the Grand Conclave and, or any other legally constituted body its or their officers and representatives giving and granting unto said *Pi* Chapter the right to perform all and severally the acts properly pertaining to the chapter as aforesaid.

Granted the twenty-sixth day of May One thousand nine hundred and twenty three in accordance with the Constitution and By Laws of the Sigma Omega Psi Fraternity, Incorporated by and with the consent and authority of the Grand Conclave.

In Witness Whereof — we have hereto affixed our signatures and the seal of the Fraternity, this 26th day of May 1923

Charter for the "Pi" or Harvard chapter of Sigma Omega Psi fraternity, signed by chapter president Frederick Katz on May 26, 1923. Charter members' names appearing on the certificate include Joseph A. Cohen, Henry Levy, Lincoln Mekelburg, Lawrence Oppenheim, Benjamin Arthur Trustman, Alexander Ulin, and Robert Ulin. Founded at CCNY in 1914, Sigma Omega Psi as a national organization did not survive the Depression and merged with Alpha Epsilon Pi in 1940. Frederick Katz went on to become the Supreme Master of national AEPi. (Alpha Epsilon Pi Archives)

Phi Epsilon Pi's chapter "Alpha Zeta," or Harvard University chapter, in 1926. (Zeta Beta Tau Archives)

Members of Phi Epsilon Pi's Pennsylvania State College chapter at an outdoor gathering in September 1922. When the fraternity began its chapter there in 1915 with only four men taking agricultural courses, a national officer referred to Penn State as a "rough, uncouth, back-woods school" which nevertheless "has splendid possibilities." By 1925 the College had welcomed over 100 Jewish students, a number that swelled to 350 young men and women by 1939. (Zeta Beta Tau Archives)

כ ש ר

Strictly Kosher--Must not
APPLY HERE.

SCURVY KIKES
ARE NOT WANTED

At New York University

if they knew

their place they would

not be here

Make New York

University a White

Man's College.

Antisemitic leaflet that appeared on the NYU uptown campus the morning of March 20, 1923, when Menorah Society president Mitchell Salem Fisher '23 challenged Gentile fraternity control of the Junior Prom that effectively barred Jews from attending. Two more years of political work and the intervention of national Jewish defense agencies was necessary before Jewish students were able to dance at the NYU Prom. (New York University Archives)

At Syracuse University in 1920, the members of the "Iota" chapter of the Alpha Epsilon Phi sorority. (Alpha Epsilon Phi Archives)

The first national convention of Alpha Epsilon Phi, held in Charlevoix, Michigan, July 1924. More than 250 women attended. (Alpha Epsilon Phi Archives)

"Yes, I've Been To France," another travelogue in the 1929 vacation issue of the *ZBT Quarterly*, written by Junior Henry J. Galland at the
University of North Carolina, urged ZBT men visiting that country to
go off the beaten path and to investigate Normandy, Brittany, the coast,
and the Basque country, in addition to Paris, which he referred to as
"The Paris of the floppy-trousered collegian," which was all most travelers ever saw. "It is Paris from one angle only," he warned, "the angle of
thousands of college men who come home happy in the belief that they
have seen all the Old World has to offer, and have tasted of the delights
of the complete traveled man."[27]

    The travel volume of Zeta Beta Tau's membership grew so large
that one member living in Kingston, Jamaica, complained in August of
1929 that too many ZBTs were traveling to the Continent or to England
every year for them to find one another if they wished it. Should not the
national fraternity establish some kind of central registry for traveling
fraternity brothers?[28] By the following summer, two bureaus had been
set up for the hundreds of ZBTs still traveling abroad eight months after the stock market crash—one at the office of the London *Times* in
England, and the other at that modern headquarters of Americans in
Paris, the American Express office at 11 Rue Scribe. ZBT's executive
head called upon members that summer to send in their names and
itineraries, and to prepare large ZBT parties to be held in both Paris
and London late in the summer.[29]

Professional Goals

In their discussions of professional training and work, an inevitable preoccupation of older college students, it is evident that, in comparison to
members of other Jewish fraternities at that time, ZBT members were
more likely to enjoy the cushion of family wealth. That wealth usually
came from fathers and grandfathers who had acquired it through storekeeping or some aspect of the garment trade. This class and financial
background, which assured that the professional student would not have
to work his way through school or suffer deprivation during long years
of training and certification, was a decided asset in the rush away from
mercantile pursuits and into the professions which began to characterize
American Jewry in the 1920s.[30] Success in business preceded and aided
success in the professions. "Ladies-skirts-wholesale is O.K. for the Old
Gent, if that's the sort of thing he likes," wrote Herbert Lippman, a 1909
graduate of Columbia, in an article about how to become an architect,

"but not for you. During the few years at college, you think about the offerings."[31]

Another work-related article entitled "Toward a Medical Career" by Dr. Clarence K. Weil, a 1920 University of Alabama graduate and practicing surgeon in Montgomery, suggested in 1927 that medically minded ZBT men study foreign languages, cultivate a sport and hobby to become physically fit and well-rounded, get an internship "in the biggest and best hospital that will take you," and then spend, with the help of letters of introduction from medical school professors, six months in Berlin, Amsterdam, Paris or Vienna to get tutoring in various areas of interest before going into private practice. For urinary diseases, he reported, "Paris is the place par excellence, and this is true in two ways"; a visit to Germany, he wrote, was best for learning about the diseases of children.[32] The author seemed to take it for granted in his writing that such aspirations would be within the reach of all ZBT men who desired to become medical men. European cities in those days were places of pilgrimage for physicians from all over the world, including the United States. Well-heeled specialists would flock there, sometimes with their families, to take advantage of short courses, workshops, or private teaching. It was not until the devastation of Europe in World War II brought the necessity of cramming fifty years's medical research into five that the U.S. achieved its eminence in the field of medicine and the general direction of these educational visits was reversed.

As the 1920s progressed, Zeta Beta Tau's national officers were gradually shaken from their customary complacency that theirs was the only Jewish fraternity worthy of any note. The rapid upward mobility and increased numerical strength of their collegiate coreligionists was becoming apparent. The change was reflected in the status and prestige of their fraternities. At a meeting of Zeta Beta Tau's Supreme Council in November 1924, held at the Wall Street law offices of Executive *Nasi* Harold Riegelman, General Secretary George Macy reported the unexpected news that there had been on college campuses "a fantastic increase in the number of worthwhile Jewish students." Before, he informed them, ZBT had had difficulty finding enough "fine Jews" to fill its ranks. Now, however, they could not accommodate all of the desirable candidates who were filling its rushing lists. Consequently, such candidates were streaming into the other fraternities, which "may well pass into the plane of what we have always considered ZBT caliber. . . . This is already evident at Pennsylvania. The chapters of Pi Lambda Phi, Phi Epsilon Pi and Phi Sigma Delta at that university would do credit to

ZBT at any university. We must therefore remember," Macy concluded, "that the time is probably coming when we will have the problem of social competition that has previously affected us only slightly."[33]

Much of ZBT's most immediate social competition came from Phi Epsilon Pi, a fraternity whose ranks included wealthy businessmen's sons studying both in college and on the job in the expectation that someday they would inherit their fathers's empires. Comrades followed their progress in awe and admiration. "Eta Man Works in German Plant: Son of American Millionaire Receives Fifty Cents a Day," a story published in a 1923 edition of the *Eta Egotist* of Phi Epsilon Pi's Eta, or University of Pennsylvania, chapter, gave the example of "Eddie" Bamberger, a recent graduate of the Wharton School and native of Cleveland, Ohio, whose closet at the fraternity house had reportedly contained fourteen suits and twenty-three pairs of shoes. "Eddie" had been directed by his father, president of the Bamberger-Reinthal Company of Cleveland, to forsake his accustomed life of luxury and to live the life of a German factory worker in the small town of Opolda, without heat, running water, a bathtub, or even proper wages, in order to study the German machines used in his father's plants in America. Eddie's duties included learning how to fix, oil, and even build the machines, as well as working under foremen in every department of the factory. He also served as an assistant salesman and, as a reward for his labors, accompanied the German head of the factory as an interpreter on trips to Belgium and England.[34]

1920s Social Life at Phi Epsilon Pi's Penn Chapter

While Eddie Bamberger labored in factories in a land from where his Jewish ancestors had emigrated only a few generations earlier, his comrades back at Penn's Phi Epsilon Pi house were preoccupied with other things. The same May 1923 issue that reported on Eddie's activities also described the fraternity chapter's two-day House Party in March, which included group attendance at the college's Senior Prom, a tea at the fraternity house and a dinner dance at Philadelphia's Ritz-Carlton Hotel. At such times, male fraternity members in Phi Ep, as in other fraternities, commonly vacated the entire house to turn it over to their female guests, who were guarded by a chaperone. "Girls, and what 'knockouts,' came from Smith, Wellesley, Vassar, Goucher, Chevy Chase, Bryn Mawr and other Eastern colleges," the paper reported. "All flocked to Penn to see Phiep put on the 'Ritz.' Come again girls; you sure are welcome."[35] The chapter's annual Spring Dance had recently been held at the Philmont Country Club, and on May 18th, Friday evening, the fraternity was to hold a "Daylite Savings Danse," [sic] planned by Fraters Dick Hano and Ernie Brav, and Julie Kobacker—"a novelty affair that will put to shame the far-famed 'South Sea Island Dance' that Eta gave a few years ago. Lest the name deceive you, the house will be lit up, but not with the inmates." Those who attended could expect member Hank Smith to have "charge of the intercollegiate champion necking balconies."[36]

In addition to reports of elaborate parties, the fraternity's society and gossip columns, including one called "Eta's Penn," lampooned the men's attraction to illegal gambling, listening to the radio at the expense of their studies, the massive sums recently spent to pay for the chapter house, and the men's tendency to come from families who had changed, anglicized, or possibly Germanized their Jewish names:

> Bridge is an expensive game in the Eta house. Ask the boys who played! One of them said that for an additional dollar on the levied fine, he could have bought the house.

> Someone said that any fraternity that buys a new house does not need wallpaper. All they need is a little paste and they could use the mortgages. Ask Eta—she knows!

> Phi Ep is the first one to install a radio in a fraternity house on the campus. (Install is the word to use, for that's the way it's being paid for, in installments). Owners are Frankie Weberman and Simp Mathis . . . but the way the fellows stream up to their room to listen, you'd think they were handing out diplomas free. It also has a wonderful effect on your scholastic standing, e.g., the writer caught Webby with the earphones on the other night, listening to a jazz concert, and at the same time "concentrating" on a Foreign Exchange problem.

> What's in a name—e.g. Hank Smith. He says his great-grandfather changed it from Schmidt to Smith for convenience. (Editor's note: We looked up the family tree and besides finding that Hank's the sap, we found that his great grand-pa's name was Schmidtsowitz. Sh-h-h-h-h!)[37]

Regardless of their class standing, the first requirement for fraternity social life was finding suitable members of the opposite sex to act as companions, or at least temporary partners, at parties and dances. The "ballroom" style of dancing that prevailed was designed for mixed couples. This could represent a constant challenge and source of anxiety for

both men and women, especially those not attending coeducational colleges. Members of Jewish sororities were one of the obvious first choices
as companions and potential dance partners for Jewish college men, but
that supply in the 1920s was still too small to meet the demand and
interfaith dating was frowned upon by all sides.

In the case of Phi Epsilon Pi's Eta chapter, approval of their
female guests, usually found and chosen by the social and auxiliary women's committees, was not universal. Although the customary rhetoric
in all men's fraternity publications would have it that every single woman
attending one of their functions was of movie-star quality, reality could
not always match fantasy. "If Congress ever regulates the tariff according
to quality, the boys who are doing the 'importing' at the house will have
to see to it that their dads get a raise or a better job," read one item in
the *Eta Egotist*'s gossip column. The term "import" was slang (still in
use in the late twentieth century) used by college men to refer to female
guests brought in for special events from outside the university, whether
the school in question was all-male or coeducational. Some members
of the chapter expressed their dissatisfaction with the females attending
the University of Pennsylvania with the following variation of a college
football cheer:

> Yen—Yen—Yen,
> Penn—Penn—Penn
> When will a good coed come to Penn?
> When?—When?—When?

Another item read, "The *Egotist* goes on record as a firm dis-
believer in spreading this sweet-convention-women stuff. If what was
seen at the last is sweet, I'll take quinine."[38]

Nowhere else was the men's preoccupation with finding women
more blatant than in their search for dates for the annual conventions, as
a typical announcement from a 1927 Phi Epsilon Pi convention flyer illustrates. The convention was slated to be held that year at the Waldorf-
Astoria in New York, with a New Year's Eve Dinner-Dance in the Main
Ball Room:

WHAT, NO WOMEN?
Yes, dear Fratres, plenty. By actual count there are about 3,692,741 members of the weaker sex in this fair city of ours, so you can imagine the task
it has been to pick, sort, and classify the eligibles. The committeeman

in charge of women has been playing the part of a combination George White and Flo Ziegfeld in his effort to cull nothing but the best, and take it from us, he's done a mighty good job of it.[39]

Those eligible women also had other options, however, and competition for their time was stiff. The ad continued:

Now New York women, despite their good looks, wicked line and amiable dispositions, have a peculiarity for which they can hardly be blamed. The New Year's weekend being the biggest of the year, dates are made months in advance. It has required heaps of tact, soft soap, oil and what not to induce the women on our lists to hold off until December 10th before making their engagements. So if you want a woman, and we'll vouch that you won't be stuck, shoot the coupon along NOW.

The coupon, of a type that was common among certain Jewish fraternity advertisements through the 1940s, read "I [do] [do not] want you to arrange for my convention partner" and asked for "General Measurements for My Partner" (approximate age, height, weight), "Color of Hair" (Blonde, Brunette, Black, Red, Titian, or What Have You), "Complexion" (Light, Fair, Medium, Dark, Peaches and Cream, Parlor) along with the member's name, chapter, and address.[40]

Even ZBT men, who in their rhetoric usually affected the attitude that any woman in their vicinity would simply swoon and fall into their arms, faced challenges when trying to establish relations with preferred members of the opposite sex. A 1923 graduate of the University of California noted the useful mystique and appeal of fraternity membership in this area when he mentioned the collegian "who first hooks his sparkling new frat badge center-vest in a move to break down the sales resistance of some alluring yearling damsel."[41] And a feature on how to improve one's wooing technique entitled "The Hindu Secrets of Love," published in 1923 in the same issue as news of the notorious Harvard quota controversy, showed that Jewish university men had far more on their minds than only the bothersome issue of collegiate antisemitism.[42]

1920s Social Life for Sigma Alpha Mu and Alpha Epsilon Pi

The rhetoric of men's fraternities whose members stood closer to the immigrant generation or were still relatively lower on the socioeconomic scale in the 1920s was noticeably more strained on the subject of women. Still, the subject clearly loomed as one of importance in their minds, and the possibility of actual marriage was mentioned more frequently. The monthly bulletin of Sigma Alpha Mu, which was celebrating its eighteenth (or "Chai") anniversary in 1928, urged readers to attend the upcoming convention at Pittsburgh's William Penn Hotel that year; in so doing, they invoked the best-known example of ancient Israelite concubinage when they promised: "They've got the girls: grade A-1, the very best in town, a regular beauty show, personality plus, trained to do what you tell them, wonderful dancers, enough beauty to make King Solomon look like a piker." Members who attended would enjoy Pittsburgh's finest jazz orchestra, terrific "eats"—"The William Penn Hotel doesn't serve hash"—and fifty percent discounts on taxis and rail fares. "If you have to rob your baby's dime bank to get the twenty-five dollars it'll be worth it to have the best time of your life," readers were told. The fee would include all banquets, dancing, comfortable rooms, great music, chic entertainment, real fraternalism, and best of all, "the girl you've always wanted to meet" and "Free marriage license for use at the convention."[43]

What came to be the Sammies' characteristic smooth confidence in their ultimate appeal to women, relative to their more genteel and perhaps more sophisticated Jewish brethren, grew swiftly through the years. With full recourse to the latest techniques from Madison Avenue, a full-page advertisement appearing in the Sigma Alpha Mu December 1929 *Bulletin* portrayed two flappers riding the New York City subway, breathless with anticipation at attending the upcoming Sammy convention in Detroit and ascending to the heights of hyperbole. The ad was headed, "My Dear, Don't Tell Me You Haven't Heard!" and read:

> The Sammies are planning a huge affair! Simply gigantic! One of those three day things with parties, and New Years Eve, and formals, and informals; and luncheons while the boys do their horrid business. . . . And Detroit! Don't you just love it?—with its big buildings—big doings—big everything!— . . . My dear, I'm simply thrilled beyond sensibility!—and the boys are so unusual! Don't tell me you've never dated a Sammy! Such dancing—and every one an Adonis—but their conventions are more— they're a riot!. . . . My blood just tingles—AM I GOING? MY DEAR! IT'S INSANE TO REFUSE![44]

Clearly a young Jewish woman with the requisite looks, connections, family approval, and sufficient supply of dresses (in contrast to the men, who could make do with one or two evening suits) could enjoy an active social life on the Jewish collegiate social circuit in the

1920s. For those not so blessed, however, the prospects were bleaker. A 1928 sketch in *The American Hebrew* entitled "A Party With Boys: A Penetrating Up-to-the-Minute Sketch of College Life," addressed this issue through the poignant story of a fictional Dorothea Brettmann, who was described as short and fat with flat yellow hair, round pale eyes, and tortoiseshell glasses. According to the sad tale, fellow student Ariadne Winkelberg, "a nosy little girl of Jewish extraction and Christian Science upbringing," whose father was president of the Winkelberg chain of dry goods stores and who was the richest girl in the sophomore class, was giving a party at a hotel during the Christmas holidays "with boys" and had invited Dorothea. "Whom shall I ask, Mama?" Dorothea implored in a letter to her mother. "Can you get me a boy?" The question prompts the following response:

> Mrs. Brettman sighed when she received the letter. She had sent Dorothea to college to meet a millionaire, perhaps—and yet every dance that came along resolved itself into the old problem. And Mrs. Brettmann would put on all her Wall Street diamonds and pay a round of calls to mothers of sons. They received her cordially, listened to how Dorothea was longing to go to the prom with a tall handsome boy like Charlie (or Willie) and then explained how Charlie would be out of town or Willie got an earache if he danced in a draft. Finally after much entertaining on the part of Mrs. Brettman, some mother would be cornered in such a position that she had to lend her son for the evening. But for Ariadne's party, Mrs. Brettman was stumped. Rack her brains as she might, Mrs. Brettman was unable to negotiate a boy for Dorothea. . . .[45]

Dorothea is overjoyed when she is finally fixed up for the party, through the efforts of her college roommate, with a Yale senior. Yet when they finally meet, he is described as short and frail with a wan and pimply face and "dark circles of over-study" surrounding his "weak, watery eyes"[46] and his date realizes that he stands hardly higher on the social scale than she.

In the case of Alpha Epsilon Pi's *The Scroll*, which began publishing in the fall of 1920, the crazed pursuit for female company was hardly mentioned. This was perhaps because the fraternity, limited as it was at the beginning largely to night school commerce students at New York University, was still young and poor relative to other fraternities. Members, busy with studies and daytime jobs, did not have the resources to enjoy dances, balls, and formal country club evenings requiring evening dress and suitably attired dancing partners. However, names of members's wives and "sweethearts," along with the women's extensive participation in such fraternity gatherings as theater parties, outings, picnics, boat rides, baseball games, basketball games, and sometimes tennis matches make an unusually frequent appearance in *The Scroll* in comparison to other fraternity publications of that era.

Vocational choices were also more limited for Alpha Epsilon Pi men than for members of the older Jewish fraternities. They could not so easily enter the fields of medicine or other professions. Selling insurance, working as IRS agents, teaching (in one case, an AEPi teacher married one of his former students at Bushwick High School in Brooklyn), small business, and becoming certified public accountants were the most common occupations for Alpha Epsilon Pi graduates in the early 1920s, with an occasional foray into the field of law—again, usually through the means of night school. Their conventions were also not as luxurious. Three-day hotel weekends were at first out of the question. It was all the fraternity could manage, for its fourth annual convention in December of 1920, to hire Delmonico's restaurant in New York City for one evening. The 1921 convention took place for one day at the Hotel Bossert in Brooklyn, not one of the city's premiere locations.

Upward Mobility

Nevertheless, within a short time Alpha Epsilon Pi was able to raise its aspirations. The locations and character of their annual conventions served as a clear barometer of rapid upward mobility, in some ways a microcosm for the American Jewish East European immigrant community itself. The seventh annual convention in December of 1923 included one New Year's Eve Dance at one of the smaller rooms of the Waldorf-Astoria. In 1924 the entire convention took place at the famed hotel, even though the given dates—December 27–28—did not include the popular New Year's Eve and thus the rates had to be lower than they otherwise would have been.

Another important rise in the fraternity's status was Alpha Epsilon Pi's expansion from three chapters in New York City to nineteen spread across the United States. These included NYU, Cornell, Penn, Illinois, Emory, Cincinnati, Georgia Tech, Ohio State, Penn State, Auburn, Ohio Northern, Illinois Tech, Virginia, Marquette, Delaware, Georgia, Wisconsin, Rhode Island, Washington University (Missouri), and Vanderbilt. At these colleges, members could pursue the liberal arts, and the relative social abyss of night school sessions did not exist. The

Supreme Master, Sigmund H. Steinberg, was able to report at their 1929 convention, by now held entirely at the Hotel McAlpin in Manhattan over a period of two days, "Year by year the chapters themselves have grown in affluence, acquiring houses, and even building palatial mansions."[47] If foreign travel was still beyond them, AEPi's living in New York City were able to rent a bungalow at Beach 46th St., Edgemere, L.I., for several summers beginning in 1920, and to spend their weekends together there. "'On to Edgemere!' is the cry these days," wrote the editor of the *Scroll of Alpha Epsilon Pi* in 1921. "The boys are getting impatient to get back to the seashore life. Is it the lull of the gentle waves, the stars shining upon the golden sand, or the beautiful girls?"[48]

As for the art of ballroom dancing, it did not take long for Alpha Epsilon Pi men to acquire that skill too. The report of the Cornell chapter in April 1920 mentioned that a "magnificent" new Victrola, a gift from the new members, was being worked "overtime" as dancing classes were conducted from eight A.M. to two A.M. Members Sam Schwartz, Jerry Gurwitz, and Ben Ozaroff were acting as instructors, while member Boris Bernard wanted to know "whether Chopin's 'Funeral March' is a fox-trot or a one-step."[49]

As Alpha Epsilon Pi spread beyond New York City, members previously confined to Greater New York discovered the opportunity to travel, to drive in an automobile, and to be hosted in areas of the country they had never seen before. One notable example of this was a house party given by the new Cornell chapter in 1920, to which members living in New York City were invited. As Alpha Epsilon Pi's "Beta" chapter, Cornell was the second to be established in 1917, and was referred to fondly in the fraternity's minutes as "our first born."[50] An obviously excited author described for the *Scroll* how members, wives, sweethearts, relatives and friends, almost all residents of Brooklyn, either took the train or "motored" up to Ithaca and the beautiful Land of the Finger Lakes.

This weekend in the country included a tour of the campus and its breathtaking scenery, a concert on Friday night, dancing at the fraternity house "until the wee hours of the morning," and a parade before the Yale–Cornell football game the next day. An "observation train" with five hundred other passengers took them to see crew races on Cayuga Lake, and on Sunday afternoon they viewed a baseball game between the Cornell chapter and the visitors. After Sunday dinner the group got into cars and visited Watkin's Glen, "one of nature's most beautiful spots." The trip clearly had as great an impact on the participants as if they had traveled across the seas. "No wonder the Cornell alumni have such a longing to go back and visit the scene of their collegiate life," wrote the author of the article, a student at New York University, with a touch of wistfulness.[51]

The Raising of the Gates

Despite these and other successes in the game of enjoying a normal collegiate social life, all was not well for young Jewish college students in the post-World War I era. The years of their higher education coincided with the years of jazz music and Coolidge Prosperity, but idealism had also given way to an era of relative intolerance in America. The Bolshevik Revolution in Russia in October 1917, the formation of the Third Communist International (Comintern) in 1919 to export that revolution around the world, and a series of radicalist bombings in the U.S. led to mass arrests and suspicion of all foreigners, especially those of Southern or Eastern European origins. In the canon of antisemitism, Jews were associated with the Communist Party. In addition, opponents of mass immigration to U.S. shores had been gathering strength for years, and at the end of the war, they had new ammunition supported by pseudo-scientific theories. The U.S. had already accepted more immigrants than it could possibly absorb without suffering the complete mongrelization of its culture, they charged. If the country did not put up the gates in the wake of the war then it would be flooded further with millions of refugees including Jews still left in Eastern Europe.

The nation's lawmakers agreed. After placing temporary restraints on immigration in 1921, the U.S. Congress effectively ended the era of mass immigration in 1924 with the National Origins Act. This placed a tight cap on the numbers allowed into the U.S. each year and parceled permits out according to a country-by-country quota system that was biased in favor of northern and western Europe and against the southern and eastern sectors of the continent. Jews already in the United States by then were well aware that their millions of relatives still in Europe would no longer be welcome in what they had once called in Yiddish "the golden land."

The land itself was not proving to be all that golden, if one looked closely enough. A newly invigorated Ku Klux Klan perpetrated violence against African Americans and those who aided them, and added Catholics and Jews to its hate list. The great industrialist Henry Ford, heeding the suggestions of his advisers, decided to run excerpts from *The Protocols of the Learned Elders of Zion*, a notorious antisemitic forgery, in the pages of his nationally distributed newspaper *The Dearborn Independent*. In addition, upwardly mobile Jews continued to find their way blocked at every turn. They were barred from certain hotels and resorts, neighborhoods, clubs, summer camps, and many white-collar or entry-level positions in non-Jewish firms.[52]

The raising of the gates that characterized U.S. immigration policy in the 1920s was played out in an almost identical fashion, if on a smaller scale, at the admissions offices of the nation's elite colleges. Until that point "social" antisemitism (such as name-calling, being beaten up by fellow students, remarks made in class by students or teachers, vandalism, exclusion from clubs, teams, or extracurricular activities) no matter how traumatic it might be, stopped short of actually preventing a determined student from seeking higher education. At the turn of the century so few students applied to college that even Harvard was bound to accept virtually any adequately prepared high school graduate who showed up, passed the battery of entrance exams and paid the appropriate fees.

After World War I, this changed. For the first time "selective admissions" systems developed to check the exploding number of applicants, and these systems included features that specifically targeted would-be Jewish college freshmen. Harvard itself, the oldest college in America and in many ways a symbol of Jewish immigrant parents's fondest dreams for their children, also became a symbol of these trends when in 1922 its president discussed openly the institution of a Jewish quota there. The resulting controversy cast a pall of fear, insecurity, and disillusionment among Jewish college students and their families.

In the face of external hostility and criticism, even the most communal-minded Jewish fraternity leaders tended to internalize the views of those who disparaged them collectively. Their writings in that era reveal how deeply anti-Jewish criticism touched their lives, and are couched in a rhetoric of intra-Jewish snobbery that all too often crossed the line into self-hatred. It would appear that many of the subjects of this inner communal wrath were motivated to modify their allegedly objectionable behavior all the faster. In all, increasing enmity from without and bitterness and despair from within could mitigate whatever happiness Jewish fraternity members managed to find during those brightest college years of the 1920s.

Chapter 5

"A Treacherous Alma Mater"

Facing College Antisemitism

That more Americans were rushing to receive a college education in the 1920s was not greeted with universal rejoicing. Long-time educators did not all feel comfortable with the changing values of the new university, with its new emphasis on practical and scientific education, elective courses, faculty research at the expense of teaching, and large, impersonal campuses. At the nation's most prestigious Eastern colleges, a counterrevolutionary group of faculty and administrators known as the "New Humanists," among them the president of Harvard looked back longingly to the values of gentlemanly leisure, a classical curriculum, and education of the "whole man" which they believed had once characterized their profession. They pressed for curricular and administrative reforms designed to restore the old collegiate flavor they felt was in danger of being lost.[1]

Accusations also surfaced among the general public, Jewish as well as non-Jewish, that too many unfit young people were crowding campuses and dragging down the level of instruction. In the unforgiving words of writer and editor H.L. Mencken in 1927, "everyone" was sending their children to college rather than those with particular intellectual, technological, or ministerial ambitions. This meant that colleges were now bursting at the seams and that "pedagogical ignoramuses" and "quacks" had to be called in to serve as professors.[2] "Today, entrance into a university is a matter merely of age and dollars," remarked one Zeta Beta Tau Wisconsin graduate in 1928, writing in a similar vein. "Everyone goes; it's hardly the thing for a parent even in moderate circumstances not to insist on a college education for his sometimes utterly unfit progeny."[3]

"Must Your Son Go to College?"

"Everyone," in a movement reminiscent of what had happened in nineteenth-century post-Emancipation Europe, included a disproportionate and conspicuous number of American Jews determined to better their position through certification and educational advancement.[4] This was especially the case at schools located in or near New York City, Boston, New Haven, and Providence. There, thousands of student children of immigrant parents could easily save money by living at home and riding the tram or subway to prestigious schools, or live in dormitories and boarding houses knowing that their families were nearby. Officials at such schools reacted not with admiration but with fear as they spoke of a "Jewish invasion" and devised steps to control it.[5]

Their concern, as we have seen, was not without some foundation. By 1920 Hunter College and City College of New York, both free municipal schools, had become 80–90 percent Jewish in their student-makeup.[6] Columbia University's Jewish student population, fed by the extension of the Broadway IRT subway to its uptown New York campus, reached 40 percent in the 1918 incoming class. Two years later, even after the quiet introductions of limitations, it remained at a considerable 22 percent. The affiliated Seth Low Junior College, which functioned in downtown Brooklyn from 1928 to 1938, was established by the Columbia authorities specifically to channel away from Morningside Heights undesirable students "of foreign parentage" as Russian-born alumnus Isaac Asimov recalled in his memoirs.[7] By the early 1920s, Jews comprised 15 percent of the student population at Syracuse University and, at Princeton, 9 percent. Harvard's Jewish student enrollment more than doubled in two years, going from 10 to 22 percent between 1920 and 1922.[8] The percentages were even more alarming in the nation's professional schools.

These statistics met with misgivings from inside and outside the Jewish community. Critics charged that families' unrealistic and misplaced social ambition, *not* the near-universal manifestation of intellectual brilliance among their children, was driving so many Jewish students to the universities. Since schools were already overcrowded, and since restrictions against Jews were a fact of life, the nation as a whole might presumably be better served if more Jews eschewed college and instead applied their energies toward some kind of trade. An example of this attitude was an article entitled "Must Your Son Go to College?" written by A. A. Roback, a professor of psychology at Harvard University, which appeared in the *Jewish Tribune* in 1925. The author (himself Jewish and an accomplished Yiddishist) remarked that at least in previous times, the preponderance of Jews in institutions of higher education was usually the result of the youth's own craving for learning. Now, however, the main impetus came from the parents. It was they, not their child, who feared that not sending their son to college immediately after completing high school would unjustifiably mark the family as "lower-class" and the son "mentally below par." Aside from fears for the family's standing, Dr. Roback continued, "there is the exaggerated notion of a college training as a universal need and the fond hope of seeing their son some day at the top of his profession, which is responsible for many parents scrimping in every possible way so as to make lawyers or doctors of their mediocre children."

Such hopes, in the psychologist's opinion, were often a waste of time and as ridiculous as expecting violin lessons to turn every Jewish boy into an "Elman or a Heifetz." Better to invest the four years and thousands of dollars in some sort of business, he advised, "and a good merchant would be the outcome, instead of the poor lawyer or physician who manages to raise his head financially largely on account of his business ability rather than his professional skill." His article ended with a call for the increased use of vocational guidance and psychological tests of Jewish youth's fitness for higher education, including one of the author's own invention. [9]

Presumably some of the *Jewish Tribune's* mature readers were convinced by these arguments, and might agree that more Jewish sons ought to forget about higher education and go into business instead—especially if they were someone else's sons. For the most part, however, throughout the 1920s and 1930s, Jewish parents refused to surrender. They kept sending their sons, and to a lesser extent their daughters, to college and professional schools in conspicuous numbers.

New Criteria for Selective Admissions

Despite the pervasiveness of American antisemitism in some form long before the end of World War I, college admissions officials had lagged behind other segments of society in taking concrete steps to limit the Jewish presence at their schools. The very real need, however, to limit acceptances to the number of places available served as a convenient framework to fulfill the desire of stopping Jews from swamping a college. This desire was fed by the continuing protests of wealthy alumni benefactors, especially of the elite predominantly Protestant schools. Among other factors, they objected to the idea of sending their offspring to once-beloved institutions now so filled with undesirable business and social contacts and unsuitable potential marriage partners for their own children.

By the early 1920s college officials had caught up with general trends, and formal or informal quotas for Jews and frequently Roman Catholics became a well-entrenched part of the admissions process. It was not necessary for a college to declare a *numerus clausus* openly or to refer to Jews by name in its written policies. Undesirable students could easily be identified and weeded out discreetly by techniques such as personal interviews, required photographs, psychological tests, physical exams, and forms which required the listing of color, church preference, the birthplace of both parents, or the mother's maiden name.[10]

Photographs and personal interviews in which an applicant's non-Anglo-Saxon appearance might be held against him or her became a point of particular anxiety, as illustrated in "Three Points for Beauty," a parody of the new admissions standards published in 1927 and written by Zeta Beta Tau's Arthur D. Schwarz (Columbia '20). Under the new admissions system, Schwarz informed his readers, studying was no longer the best way to prepare for college. "Not only have the requirements changed," he declared, "but the entire entrance examination board has been changed from a group of professors to a staff of civil and mechanical engineers with three or four artists thrown in and with an advisory council on the history of races and the Mendelian theory."[11] The meetings of college entrance boards could now be likened to bathing beauty contests, in which the evaluators measured the shape and size of applicant's noses and jaws with calipers and arranged classes according to hair and eye color. In keeping with these new requirements, Schwarz continued, he wished to suggest more appropriate procedures to be followed by college applicants.

These new procedures were 1. A complete series of treatments at Elizabeth Arden's Beauty Parlors: "He should have his hair slicked and if possible made blonde. The odds are still in favor of the Nordic at the universities." 2. A face lift. 3. The achievement of the necessary height: "He can't be too short for the Eastern universities. The quotas for coxswains are quickly filled from boys with great 'drag' and strangers under five feet five have little if any chance." 4. The educationally ambitious young man should choose a Madison Avenue tailor in New York to custom-make his interview clothes and seek out a skilled photographer who excelled in making "synthetic" portraits (i.e., using lights, "mist," special poses, and various other tricks of the trade to disguise or downplay a subject's large nose or other stereotypically Jewish facial features and coloring).

Finally, Schwarz concluded, the candidate should pay proper attention to molding his background, religion, and geographical origin to suit the tastes of the individual college. "If your mother was a Wolf," he wrote, "it may be necessary to change her to a Brady for college entrance purposes, and you may have to make a slight alteration in the name of your religion—to Jewish Lutheran or Catholic Scientist or some such more approved title. You will probably have to be psycho-analyzed, horoscoped, palm-read, fortune-told by gypsy and by cards, and the bumps on your head planed off." The writer would not be surprised, he concluded, if in the near future youth abandoned attendance at high school altogether as preparation for college in favor of "a complete beauty course, a series of lessons in charm and personality, and a stiff quiz session in where to have one's parents born and what religion to adopt."[12]

A President's Influence: The Harvard Affair of 1922–23

It was perhaps no surprise that the officials of Harvard University, having seen their own Jewish enrollment more than double in the first two years of the decade, would take steps in the direction of reducing it in 1922. Methods to do so quietly were already in place at other schools such as Columbia, Syracuse, Princeton and Rutgers. What was a surprise was the candor with which Harvard announced its intentions. An explosion of press coverage and controversy resulted when President A. Lawrence Lowell inadvertently allowed news to leak out that spring that Harvard was considering establishing an overt ten percent quota for Jewish applicants. People had whispered about this topic before but now it hit the front page of the *New York Times* on June 2, 1922 in the form of a scandal and it did not leave there for the rest of the month.

Lowell had already achieved some notoriety in the American Jewish community for his strong opposition of the appointment to the Supreme Court of Louis D. Brandeis in 1916 and his vice-presidency of the Immigration Restriction League, an organization that was playing a major role in barring the gates of the U.S. against further mass immigration. Lowell had to be aware that Harvard's influence and example in the matter of quotas would encourage other schools in the United States to follow his lead. Yet rather than denying it or apologizing for his words, he at first confirmed them and strongly defended his position in public. A quota would reduce race hatred and actually help to prevent antisemitism at Harvard from growing further, he insisted. Besides, as he pointed out to journalists, the proposed figure of ten percent was still more than three times the proportion of Jews in the general population.[13]

The resulting "Harvard Affair of 1922–1923" became, in the words of one editorial in the *Octagonian of Sigma Alpha Mu,* "the bomb that shook American colleges."[14] In the case of Harvard not only did the college president's attitudes become a part of the public record, but that of the Gentile student body as well. When an enterprising professor, Dr. Richard C. Cabot, took advantage of current events by asking his students as part of their final exam in Social Ethics to discuss if "race limitations" on Harvard's freshman class were justified, almost half the students, all of them Gentile, replied "yes." They assumed in their explanatory essays that increasing numbers of Jews were the focus of the question. The results became public in an article entitled "Harvard Student Opinion on the Jewish Question" appearing in the September 6, 1922 issue of *The Nation.* The piece attracted national attention.[15]

"Harvard should be the natural segregating place of the Anglo-Saxons," wrote one such student, for "they founded this country and this college. . . . The Jews tend to overrun the college, to spoil it for the native-born Anglo-Saxon young persons for whom it was built and whom it really wants." The specter of an alumni body that would be unwilling to send its sons to Harvard because its character had been destroyed loomed large. "Imagine having an alumni so strongly Jewish that they could elect their own president and officers! God forbid!" wrote another. Few objected to Jewish students because they were intellectually inferior; on the contrary, it was their tendency toward stellar academic performance and endless studying that helped to make them unpopular. Several accused Jewish students of taking all the scholarships, thus depriving "many worthy men of other races of a chance." "He does nothing but grind," complained one Gentile student. "Is it surprising that he should make better grades than those of us who have broader interests?" "They memorize their books!" wrote another student in exasperation, who himself reportedly received one of the lowest grades in the examination. "Thus they keep the average of scholarship so high that others with a high degree of common sense, but less parrot knowledge, are prevented from attaining a representative grade."

On this score, at least, Jewish students could object to the criticism, since Harvard was supposed to be an elite academic institution. "To tell a Cohen, whose average on the college board examination was 90, that he cannot enter because there are too many Jews already, while a grade of 68 will pass a Murphy, or one of 62 a Morgan, hardly seems in line with the real interests of the college," wrote one of the seven Jewish students taking the exam who objected to the idea of a quota. The student was alluding to another well-known technique of colleges wishing to favor the Protestant majority: requiring higher scores from Jewish and Catholic candidates.

More objectionable even than their over-studiousness, however, were the Harvard Jewish students' social characteristics and alleged lack of athletic prowess. These were serious drawbacks at an Ivy League college, where the intangible social atmosphere and the values imparted to students were considered as important as the acquisition of academic knowledge. "They do not mix. They destroy the unity of the college. They are distasteful to the men who have made Harvard what it is today," wrote one student. "Jews are an unassimilable race, as dangerous to a college as indigestible food to a man." "The Jewish race makes 'Take away' its motto, rather than 'Give and take.' They are governed by selfishness. They care nothing for the friends they make save as future business acquaintances; to them the social side of college life is only so much twaddle," wrote others. At least one student suggested that Jews follow the example of the Catholics, "who long ago saw the folly of forcing themselves on the American college, and built institutions of their own." Worst of all, Jewish students were accused of violating the college code by having no loyalty at all to their alma mater: "They go through college as cheaply as possible, and having acquired their education, depart to be heard from no more, not even at the most urgent solicitations of Loan Fund collectors."[16]

A similar collection of anti-Jewish feelings and stereotypes, ostensibly written by a Christian college student under the pseudonym "Cyrus McGinn Mulqueen," appeared in the *Zeta Beta Tau Quarterly* at the height of the Harvard controversy in December 1922 under the blatant title, "Why I Hate Jews." It is possible that in a fit of sardonic humor the feature was actually written by a Jewish ZBT member. Whatever the source of the article, it faithfully reflected the tone of anti-Jewish

prejudice which was common at the time and which, through the Harvard controversy, was now being openly debated in the nation's press. It
also documents faithfully the collection of impressions and stereotypes
Jewish college men of the upper strata were feeling pressure to disprove
every day by their own individual behaviors.

"Mulqueen'"s article began by noting that prejudice was a fun-
damental and universal trait and that recent anti-Jewish reactions, in
particular as they centered about "the recent events at Harvard," were
a natural response to the overcrowding of Jews in eastern universities
to the point that many had become "Semitic institutions, in fact if not
in name."[17] Gentiles at these institutions were thus unduly exposed to
the objectionable character traits of Jews, which the author proceeded
to enumerate. Many of these points, it should be noted, were identical to those voiced by Gentile Harvard students in the pages of *The
Nation*. Mulqueen's claims, however, were being published in a Jewish
periodical.

Jews, the author went on to charge, cared nothing for their institutions or for college traditions. They were ceaseless grinds, toiling
over their books day and night and neglecting friendships and extracurricular activities. Because they were "physically lazy" and lacked
"college spirit" they did not go out for teams. They were unsociable,
unattractive, unfriendly, hard to get along with, "morose," "sullen," "too
serious about themselves," and too clannish to reach out to non-Jews. In
civil society, they were the destroyers of governments and inevitably "the
leader in many of our radical political movements and labor upheavals."
In business they were hard bargainers, "sneaky," "underhanded," and
"untrustworthy," using any means short of illegal ones to better their
rivals and gain financial success.

The physical appearance of the Jew was also repugnant, "Mulqueen" continued. "The large curved nose; the coarse, curly, black hair;
the sallow greasy skin; the stout, phlegmatic body—these make him a
very unpleasant sight to look upon," the pseudonymous "Mulqueen" declared. "Besides, he is indifferent as to his bodily cleanliness and his
clothes are ill-kept, often dirty, frequently wrinkled, and always lacking in dignity." For those "newly-rich" who had only recently acquired
the means to buy good things, "Mulqueen" continued, the selection was
dominated by a desire to show off their wealth, rather than to appear
as attractive as possible: "Jewels in abundance bedeck the women's ear-
rings; ropes of pearls; diamonds of huge dimensions; rings of large size
and generally in large numbers. Diamond-studded combs adorn mi-

lady's hair, and we almost feel disappointed when we look in vain for anklets and nose-rings."

In society, the pseudonymous Mulqueen charged, the speech of Jews was unpleasant and "guttural": "His loud conversation—coarse and critical—and his even louder laugh are jarring to those of us accustomed to an environment of quiet and refinement." Their table manners were abominable: "they eat crudely with special emphasis on the mere act of eating. Their tables are set with rich foods in vast abundance—a marked contrast to the more simple diet of Christians. They fill up on these rich, highly seasoned foods and exercise so little that they grow fat and lazy." Only in the area of cultural life could "Mulqueen" find anything positive to say about Jews, and even here he denied that Jews possessed any "true appreciation" of the arts, since they bought paintings and prints and concert tickets more for the sake of "showing off" than out of love for beauty: "The emotions of the Jews are too stilted to allow him to appreciate any but the tragic type of music—music resembling his own mournful melodies," he wrote. "True, the Jews compose a large percentage of the patrons of concerts. These are refined Jews, the exception that proves the rule. In drama . . . most of their plays display a great deal of wealth but little taste or else are of the girl and music type. The real dramatic gems are beyond the understanding of the Jew."

The Jews's biggest mistake, in the author's opinion, was that they did not allow sufficient time to unlearn their objectionable traits before trying to climb the social and economic ladder. "He tries to *push* his way into the best society—to *buy* his way in," wrote Mulqueen. "In a few years, he hopes to acquire what other families have taken years to attain. . . . Perhaps the grandchildren of the newly-rich immigrant Jew may attain the desired social prestige, but for the present generation it is impossible, and to try to push or buy oneself into society can only bring a storm of criticism upon one's shoulders." At the conclusion of this diatribe "Mulqueen" conceded that this writing was not meant to include "all" Jews, and certainly not the "best" ones, but it did fairly represent the "average" Jews, consisting "in actual numbers, of at least 80 per cent of the whole number, and representing in New York perhaps 95 per cent. A group is judged, not by a few outstanding men, but by the rank and file of the great majority."[18]

The public airing of these types of attitudes in the 1922–1923 academic year raised equally blatant cries of outrage from concerned prominent citizens and the general public. Harvard was turned upside-down that year as the president, the admissions committee, the faculty, and Massachusetts politicians struggled over the implementation of the college's admissions policy. The governor of the state appointed a legislative committee to investigate charges that Harvard discrimination against Jews violated state laws assuring all residents equal opportunity in Massachusetts colleges. Harold Riegelman of ZBT was heard to say at one point during the scandal that the university's actions were hurting Harvard more than they were hurting the Jews.[19] Former Harvard president Charles W. Eliot, under whose sympathetic aegis the first Menorah Society had been founded in 1906, led a vigorous opposition from his position on the Harvard Board of Overseers. Eliot had opposed Lowell's appointment to replace him as president of Harvard in 1909, and for him the quota controversy was just further evidence of a wide gap between the principles and worldviews of the two men. He and the anti-Lowell forces appeared to have won when in April 1923 the Harvard admissions committee renounced the idea of any discrimination based on race or religion and officially rejected the overt imposition of a ten percent quota.

Any celebration on their part, however, was premature. The admissions committee, in addition to its announcement, also soon put forth a thirty-two-page report supplemented with eighteen pages of charts, graphs, and proposed formulae. This turned out to be an equally effective alternative to a flat Jewish quota. Henceforth the number of students in Harvard's freshman class would be capped at one thousand. Students would be chosen according to a complex policy of "geographical distribution," wherein fewer students from the Boston area and more students from beyond the Mississippi would be admitted. Theoretically, the committee argued, a university of national standing ought not to have a student body too lopsided in the direction of any single geographic, religious, ethnic, or racial group. Presumably, the campus atmosphere and the educational experience of all would be enhanced by the chance to interact with students from all across the United States. By 1928, under this system Harvard's official Jewish enrollment had fallen to precisely ten percent. It did not rise from that level until the retirement of President Lowell in 1933 and the new presidency of James B. Conant, under whose watch the proportion rose gradually back up to twenty-five percent.[20]

Other schools that had not yet taken steps to limit Jewish enrollment and wished to do so, including Yale, took the lesson of Harvard to heart and through the 1920s and 1930s adopted similarly indirect methods that would achieve the desired result without attracting undesirable publicity.[21] These compromises, ironically, were similar in character to those made by the U.S. Congress to achieve the long-sought goal of restricting immigration to the U.S. in 1924. It would have been a violation of deeply-held American principles as well as public relations suicide for American lawmakers to declare openly that they wished to halt immigration from southern and eastern Europe, areas with particularly large concentrations of Jews and Italians. However, the complicated formula, charts and graphs of the National Origins Act, which limited immigration according to a quota system based on the proportion of nationalities in the American population as recorded in the 1890 census, had exactly the same effect.

In time, the bywords "geographical distribution" were widely adopted at other colleges and professional schools as a defensible and acceptable method of limiting Jewish and/or urban enrollment and thus maintaining the prestige and social cohesiveness of a school. Jewish applicants living in major northeast U.S. metropolitan areas could attempt to circumvent the policy by falsely claiming the home addresses of cooperative relatives living in Houston, Des Moines, Cedar Rapids, Seattle, or any other city in America where the Jewish population was comparatively smaller and the level of Jewish acculturation to the surroundings presumably higher. However, few students felt comfortable with such subterfuges, and the ruse was too easily discovered to be widely effective.

The Impact of Anti-Jewish Attitudes on Fraternities

The techniques and widespread anti-Jewish attitudes so clearly illustrated by the Harvard affair could not help but influence the world of college fraternities. After the institution of "selective admissions," the resulting drop in Jewish enrollment at some colleges had an immediate impact. Without a sufficient number of potential members entering a school, chapters already established might need to close down. Those chapters that were left might be forced to compete more aggressively for fewer students. The worst such damage to a campus Jewish Greek system in the 1920s occurred at Columbia University where the Jewish enrollment fell by half in less than two years. In general, Alpha Epsilon Pi and the younger fraternities, which had arrived on campuses later than the others, were particularly hard hit. For example, in June 1921 the faculty at Georgia Institute of Technology in Atlanta ruled that the number of Jewish students there did not warrant the existence of three Jewish fraternities and that Alpha Epsilon Pi's Zeta chapter, the last to be inducted on the campus the previous year, had to go. The fraternity had no choice but to close the chapter. A wave of cutbacks in Jewish enrollment was destined to have a similar impact on Jewish fraternity chapters during the years of the Great Depression.

The leaders of the senior fraternities Phi Epsilon Pi and Pi Lambda Phi had already discovered in the 1910s that unfavorable views of Jews could determine whether a chapter would be allowed on a campus at all. From the late nineteenth century no fraternity could be officially established or recognized on a campus without the permission of the college. This was usually granted only through the agency of the Dean of Men, the Dean of Women, or the college president. Failure to obtain this permission could—and did—result in expulsion from the school. As the Jewish Greek subsystem expanded permission to set up chapters was not always forthcoming, especially in the well-established schools of the northeast where limitations on Jewish enrollment were most likely to be in place. The administrations of Bowdoin, Williams, Amherst, and Wesleyan, for example, never permitted any openly Jewish fraternities to organize on their campuses, despite numerous entreaties.[22]

The official reasons given by university officials for nonrecognition of Jewish fraternities were usually that they did not wish to segregate their students along racial, religious, or sectarian lines. This of course ignored the discriminating practices of the Gentile fraternities. The real reasons, as suggested in the correspondence of Jewish leaders and the deliberations of fraternity officials during that time, may have included blatant antisemitism, terror of a Jewish secret society aroused by reading the forged *Protocols of the Learned Elders of Zion,* a desire not to acknowledge to the world the presence of Jewish students on campus, or, if they were already there, a desire not to provide conditions that would encourage any more of them to come.[23]

At the December 1927 annual meeting of the National Interfraternity Conference (NIC) in New York City, the representative of a Gentile fraternity defended the reluctance of non-Jewish students or administrators to recognize or fully accept chapters of Jewish fraternities in words that were excerpted and passed on to the president of a major American Jewish defense organization. The remarks were considered especially insulting since it was this same annual meeting where Harold Riegelman of Zeta Beta Tau was elected by his peers as the first Jewish man ever to serve as Chairman of the NIC:

In this growth of fraternities there is one very real difficulty which I would like to refer to quite frankly because it is a difficulty to be met and solved. I refer to the chapters of Jewish students, which are multiplying with great rapidity. I feel that I at least can touch upon this delicate topic, because I have very many warm friends who belong to that gifted race. Now, regardless of the merits of the case, or the reason therefore, this feeling of prejudice, what you will, is a fact to be reckoned with. It may be theoretically true that there should be no lack of complete sympathy between the Jewish and other races, and that in an ideal democracy there would not be—that racial and religious distinctions and an age-long alienation would disappear. . . . But it is too much to expect of our students that they shall be immune to the threefold and cumulative effect of racial, religious, and, broadly speaking, social differences that have profoundly moved the masses of men for centuries. No doubt our Hebrew friends realize this and will make allowances for it. We are entitled to ask them to look facts in the face as well as being under obligation to do so ourselves. Things being as they are and not as we would have them, we must find some practical way of mutual adjustment, not always insisting upon attaining the full measure of our ideal. . . . American democracy is evolutionary and is content to take a step at a time.[24]

Non-Recognition of Jewish Fraternities at Brown University

One of the longest and certainly the best-known instances of opposition to the establishment of Jewish fraternities occurred at Brown University in Providence, Rhode Island, whose bylaws in the 1920s still required that its president be a Baptist minister. The number of Jewish students at Bowdoin, Williams, and Amherst then was too small for the lack of Jewish fraternities there to have a major impact. Brown University, by contrast, was located in a major metropolitan area, and student activities and social life at the all-male school were governed by its fraternity system. Yet for almost twenty-five years William Herbert Perry Faunce, president of Brown from 1899 to 1929, forbade the legal establishment of a single chapter of any Jewish fraternity on his campus. That he avoided openly and specifically declaring his intentions only contributed to the problem. It took years for the veiled excuses and discreet manipulations of the president's office, along with the experiences of isolated generations of teenaged college students and national fraternity leaders, to add up to a clear pattern of discrimination.

Phi Epsilon Pi's energetic traveling secretary Herman Kline, while traversing New England and upstate New York in January 1916 on an otherwise successful mission to establish new chapters, was as yet blissfully ignorant of the nature of their opponent. He was still full of

optimism, as his letters that year to the fraternity's national secretary in
New York Jesse Acker reveal:

> Now Jesse, I want a little quick diplomatic work from you, it must be
> quick and fine to win the day and I think we can put it over. If we do,
> Phi Epsilon Pi in New England is assured of a stronghold stronger than
> Gibraltar. I have a bunch already at Brown—but there's one drawback.
> There are already 20 frats at Brown and three years ago the President said
> that he'd have no new frats. Two years ago Z.B.T. tried to get into Brown
> but the Prexy sat on it. Now if we can get the Prexy's permission we'd be
> the only Jewish non-sectarian frat. At Brown and with 150 Jews to draw
> from, can you imagine how great we'd be! Now I want you to sit right
> down and write to the President of Brown, give him a good line about the
> need of a non-sectarian frat., no Jews can be represented, etc., our ideals,
> our record etc., and you feel that both we and Brown will be benefited.
> Use the flowery language tactfully, diplomatically, and freely. Give him a
> list of our great men—Viereck, Townsend, Otis, Finchberg, etc.; and I
> think we can slip it over.[25]

Kline and others refused to believe that Faunce's ban on new
college fraternities had any anti-Jewish sentiment behind it. Ironically,
in naming the few non-Jewish alumni of Phi Epsilon Pi, Kline included the name of George Sylvester Viereck (City College '06), a German American author, publisher, and pro-German propagandist during
World War I. Earlier, Viereck had shared cultural values and friendship
with the fraternity's German-Jewish founders at City College. By 1920
however, Viereck would resign in disgust and protest at the Jewish character of his allegedly nonsectarian fraternity. Even worse, in the 1930s
he was destined to become a prominent Nazi as well as a secretary and
spokesman for the German-American Bund.[26] As for Faunce, it became
apparent only over a long period to Phi Epsilon Pi and similar groups
that it was their Jewishness, and not the thought of more fraternities on
campus, which disturbed the Brown University president.

The extant transcript of one of many meetings where representatives of Jewish fraternities at Brown presented their case to the president or his representatives shows the difficulties which Jews encountered
and the subtle nature of their opposition. In the spring of 1921 three
young alumni—Walter Adler, Herman M. Davis, and Arthur J. Levy—
met with Dean Otis E. Randall of the college, in this case a spokesman
for President Faunce, to see once again if there was any possibility of establishing a chapter of Phi Epsilon Pi there. The report of the meeting,
which included virtually verbatim notes taken down by Arthur J. Levy,

reveals the remarkable skill and unctuously genteel manner in which the Dean deflected the requests of these naïve petitioners. Over a period of several hours, Dean Randall not only managed to hold firm to his claim that Brown simply could not tolerate the presence of any more fraternities, much less sectarian ones; he also tried to convince the petitioners that in fact their main problems were caused by other ill-behaved Jews on campus who did not even deserve to be admitted to Brown:

> For several hours there was a full and frank discussion of the fraternity situation at Brown, with the Dean telling us just what his problems were, and with us trying to be as helpful as possible. He declared that the first and dominating policy of the administration was to have no more fraternities, and that if he could have his way, the present nineteen would be reduced by about five.
>
> He volunteered the statement that one of the most pressing problems in connection with the fraternity situation was that Jewish men every bit as fine as any other men on the campus were not invited to join the fraternities with very rare exceptions and that the matter had been troubling him for some years. He said he would do anything that he could to see that the finest type of Jews who come to the college received better consideration at the hands of the fraternal-social structure of the college.[27]

In Dean Randall's view, however, not enough of the "finest type of Jews," such as the petitioners from Phi Epsilon Pi now before him, were coming to Brown. He thereupon launched into a general criticism of Jewish student behavior on the campus, repeating many of the common anti-Jewish charges of the day. In the process, he managed to place blame on the Jewish students themselves for their lack of acceptance and to make his listeners grateful that they themselves had been privileged to become Brown students at all:

> On the other hand he frankly said that there is another type of Jewish men who come to the college, which the entire university would prefer to stay away. He mentioned as reasons, that they came to get everything they could out of the college, without giving anything to it, that they did not enter into the spirit of things at Brown, that they came up to the Hill to study, and left it behind with not a further thought, that they were dirty and unkempt, that they flatly and absolutely lied to the university in applying for scholarships, etc. He said that letters had been received by alumni stating that they would send no more men to Brown unless the enrollment of Jews was kept down.
>
> This last, Dean Randall said, would absolutely not be done in any particular. He said that Brown University was glad to welcome Jews just as it

was glad to welcome everyone, who can come to Brown and enter wholly into the Brown spirit, giving and taking, and measuring up to the high standards of American college life. He mentioned a number of men who had come to Brown, and who had made good on the Hill in the eyes of the administration, and said that more of their type were welcome. He included his hearers in this class, and said that if more of the same kind came to Brown, there would be no present problem . . .

The representatives of Phi Epsilon Pi continued to try the Dean's patience by pointing out that Brown did indeed have at least one sectarian fraternity, Phi Kappa Sigma, a group restricted to Catholic students which had been founded there in 1889 and that Phi Epsilon Pi itself was not truly a sectarian fraternity, since their chapter at Dartmouth actually had one Chinese member. Dean Randall simply replied that the general exclusion of Chinese students from fraternities was regrettable, that the existence of Phi Kappa was equally regrettable, and that if he had been Dean at the time no such sectarian fraternity would ever have been founded, and none ever would as long as he was Dean of the College. Finally Dean Randall, perhaps observing with some anxiety Arthur Levy's detailed scribbling, brought an end to what had been from the beginning a fruitless discussion by once again hinting that the blame for exclusion lay on the Jewish students themselves:

> The Dean repeated several times that he wished he could do something to solve the problem whereby some of the really fine, the wanted Jewish men, could be in the fraternity circle, and said he would be ready to do anything to urge the present chapters to aid in this movement, but he said too that the administration made it a point never to interfere in the slightest with the selection of men. . . . He finally made the statement that he would even be willing to break his policy of no more fraternities if an organization could be formed general enough to include Jew and non-Jew alike, but which would take only the finest type of Jewish men, men who would measure fully up to the members of the other fraternities at Brown. He stated, however, that he could not be sure the President would agree with this view, and was not sure even whether he could finally agree to it.

The Phi Epsilon Pi representatives finally departed without coming close to achieving their goal, just after giving Dean Randall the assurance he demanded that there was not now nor had there ever been a secret chapter of their Jewish fraternity at Brown University.

As the years passed and word about the peculiar situation at Brown spread through the greater American Jewish community, it became apparent that anti-sectarianism and the alleged bad behavior and nonparticipation of Brown's Jewish students were not the main obstacles there. By the late 1920s observers could note that the Jewish student body at Brown was not only large—numbering almost one-fifth of the student body—but also well-represented in campus activities. This active group included varsity football stars (the most famous being Al C. Cornsweet '29, captain of the team), basketball stars, soccer players, swimmers, bandleaders, the president and manager of the orchestra, publication editors, and others in every conceivable activity. [28] Ironically, President Faunce, in a rejection letter to Louis S. Lebenthal of Tau Epsilon Phi written in January 1928, invoked this extensive participation as an excuse that Jewish fraternities were not needed at Brown, since Jewish students were obviously so happy and productive without them. To change the status quo would, as he put it, only "kindle the fires of racial antagonism. . . . I do not believe that you and your friends would desire to inject an unwanted fraternity into a community where all is now peaceful and kind feeling prevails." [29]

By then several Jewish fraternity officials as well as Brown University students and alumni were writing to describe their experiences and to appeal to the American Jewish Committee, a leading Jewish defense organization, and to its prominent president Louis Marshall, to see if something could finally be done. "You may ask," wrote Samuel Klivansky, who had belonged to a sub-rosa Jewish fraternity chapter at Brown in 1918,

> why this glorification of such a frail and meaningless institution as the college fraternity. Brown is essentially a fraternity college. Every conceivable activity at Brown is dominated and controlled by the fraternities. A non-fraternity man is a non-entity at Brown. It is a most miserable and disheartening experience for the young Jewish freshman at Brown to find that with the advent of the rushing season, he is shunted into the questionable category of the unwanted, the ignored, the despised—perhaps to be tolerated, but not to be associated with.

The establishment of Jewish fraternities, in his opinion, would in and of itself help Jewish students to achieve more and to refute critics by helping them feel more loyalty to the university. "As it is," Klivansky explained, "the Jewish student at Brown is embittered and sullen while at school because of this galling discrimination, and retains this animus when he graduates." [30]

Another such letter was received from senior Louis Pomiansky, Class of 1928. In it he vividly described the lot of the Jewish student at Brown and implored the American Jewish Committee to do something about it. "We Jewish men have always wanted our frats," he wrote to Marshall. "The Goy has his and more than enough to satisfy him. And since we are as good or as bad as he is, and since we are an integral part of the university, we have every right to have ours. We have our pathetic Menorah, and to us Jews who want our frats, it is like a decapitated rag doll, without an arm and a leg. . . . And as students, we can do nothing. They will not listen to the idle chatter of babes. But you and your associates have power. You can bring pressure to bear. You can force them to come out in the open somehow, make them lay out all their trumps and spades. We ought to have not one, but several frats here. It is owing us like a long-overdue bill . . ."[31]

In his long and anguished letter, Pomiansky pointed out that the old charges and criticisms Gentiles had for so long made against Jews were now falling by the wayside.

> Now, Mr. Marshall, you have in some measure heard my heart throbs as it were, heard what every loyal Jewish man must feel deep, deep down in his heart. They once said that we were vulgar, loud, uncouth, ill-bred. They cannot say that of us now, for even the classic Jew has gone. . . . And after that came the greasy grind era. And that has gone by the board. Here at Brown Jewish men are playing leading parts in both the classroom and the athletic field. Well, what will they say next?. . . . I know one thing. Brown is my alma mater. To me she was and still is life. To me she is opportunity, and I owe her much, and I trust I will owe her more with the departing years. For this I will always be grateful. But in another way she has left me cold; she will never, never win my deepest love.

These and other impassioned words of Brown students and alumni had been prompted by the decision of Louis Marshall, after years of scattered reports, that it was time for the American Jewish Committee to take public action. A review of the abovementioned Gentile fraternity president's remarks at the 1927 NIC conference, passed on to him by the national president of the Jewish fraternity Tau Epsilon Phi, was the final straw. Marshall's motivation was apparently not any great affection for the idea of Jewish Greek-letter societies themselves, but rather a sense of injustice that Jewish students as a group should be denied the right to organize them while other groups were not. Privately, as he confessed to the Jewish fraternity president who sought his aid,

Marshall despised the entire institution of college fraternities and saw no value in them whatsoever:

> The only phase of the subject which interests me is that of discrimination. To my mind they are an absurd exhibition of infantilism. They involve a criminal waste of time. For grown men to make them the center of thought and activity seems to me to be inexpressibly silly. . . . I am filled with disgust and contempt at the mental attitude exhibited. There is a total lack of a sense of propriety and of moral values. Booze and sex and their concomitants seem to constitute the be-all and end-all of their mental lucubrations. Any movement which would forbid secret fraternities in our colleges and universities would have my whole-hearted support. Personally I think it would be a blessing in disguise if our Jewish students were deprived of this great boon. They could form organizations in which serious work requiring thought and industry could be accomplished.[32]

Despite these negative views, however, Marshall, a distinguished and accomplished attorney, had become convinced that Jewish rights were being violated at Brown University and that it was the place of his organization to defend them. As he wrote, "From the standpoint of an unjust and unreasonable discrimination, the action of President Faunce stirs my fighting blood." His response was a long and eloquent letter to President Faunce pleading for the case of Jewish fraternities at Brown. Both this letter and President Faunce's answer were published in full in several Anglo-Jewish newspapers, in the *American Jewish Year Book* of 1929–1930, and in excerpts in the Nov. 12, 1928 *New York Times*, where they were eagerly read by Jewish Brown students and alumni.

In his letter, Marshall wrote of the exclusion that Jewish students suffered on the campus, the unjust segregation that already existed, the vital role that fraternities had come to play in college life, and the harmlessness of Jewish fraternities elsewhere. "The Jews are in a minority," he wrote, "and as such are placed under a ban. Is it sportsmanlike to increase these artificial disadvantages by withholding from them the right of associating among themselves? Are they dimming the light of learning, or muddying the stream of knowledge, or interfering with the flow of goodwill, by seeking a more limited brotherhood because a broader spirit of fraternity is denied them?"[33]

Once again, the appeal was to no avail. President Faunce wrote back that the establishment of any fraternity along racial or religious lines at Brown was out of the question. To do so would constitute "a confession of failure on the part of the American democracy." He continued:[34]

Some of the fraternities undoubtedly have clauses in their constitutions which prevent the admission of any but white Protestants. I trust such narrowness will soon be outgrown. But we can hardly expect the immature minds of American college students to share the broader views which you and I have attained by long experience in living. We must have patience with them and seek to lift them out of all exclusiveness and littleness into the true democracy of emancipated spirits. . . . If some limitations on true democracy still remain among certain fraternities, we can only hope and believe that by the slow processes of education reforms may be achieved which are impossible through revolution.

Open Jewish fraternities never did gain a strong foothold at Brown. A chapter of Pi Lambda Phi, one of the officially and militantly nonsectarian "Jewish" fraternities, was established the next year, in 1929, but only after continued pressure from the American Jewish Committee, major media controversy, threats of prosecution from the fraternity's officers, and the timely retirement—closely followed by the death—of an ailing President Faunce at the end of that school year.[35]

The "Fight Against the Prom" at New York University

Encounters with these and other types of anti-Jewish attitudes could leave deep scars. Under such circumstances it is not difficult to comprehend why some Jewish students might truly be guilty of the charge of Harvard's students and Brown's Dean and so many others that they were insufficiently loyal to their schools. After graduation, they truly might not wish to donate a penny back or step foot on the campus ever again. An especially bitter and detailed memoir along these lines, sarcastically entitled "For Love of Alma Mater" was published in the *Brandeis Avukah Volume of 1936*, a publication of the American Student Zionist Federation.[36] The memoir is notable because the events described took place in New York City, rather than on the campus of an elite New England school. They illustrate well the character of the discrimination faced by Jewish students in the 1920s, as well as the important role that the Gentile Greek system played in it.

Mitchell Salem Fisher, the child of Russian Jewish immigrants and a 1923 graduate of New York University's uptown campus, served as president of NYU's Menorah Society, majored in Greek and Latin classics, graduated *magna cum laude,* and went on to earn both rabbinical ordination and editorship of the *Columbia Law Review.* Yet, as he himself stated, he could not feel any ardor for the place of his undergraduate education, which had done so much to make these achievements possible. In writing publicly about his negative experiences, he gave his campus the pseudonym "Da-Da University" and thinly disguised the names of NYU professors and administrators. Nevertheless, a review of NYU's archives verifies his story in every detail.

Fisher, a champion college debater, began his memoir by recalling his joy when he was chosen as one of the three representatives of NYU to travel to Great Britain to debate at several universities there. However, a few weeks before his departure, rumors began to circulate that he was not to go. "The debating coach, in answer to inquiry, stated that the Oxford University Union had sent Da-Da University a letter saying that since Da-Da was a 'metropolitan' university, it should be very careful of the social character of the men sent," he wrote, "and to my 'liberal' university friends, that signified but one thing—Jews!" Fisher had to fight to go in the face of the coach's attempt to dissuade him and attempts by a faculty committee to have him removed from the team.

More humiliation was in store. Upon his arrival in England, the American Rhodes scholar who headed the Oxford Student Union confirmed that the letter had indeed been referring to Fisher's probable identity as a Jew. He politely requested Fisher to withdraw as one of the principal speakers, and to confine his participation to remarks from the floor. Once again, the reaction of Fisher's university fellows was less than sympathetic. Neither fellow team members nor the University's representative in London considered refusing to debate under those restrictions, and Fisher himself thought the whole matter "too stupid and picayune over which to fuss." Furthermore, upon the team's arrival in Oxford, there was mysteriously not enough room to house Fisher at Magdalene or the other colleges where his Gentile companions were staying. Instead, the one Jewish member of the team was lodged at an inn in town, "whose charm measurably compensated for the embarrassment."[37]

Back at NYU, in his junior year, 1923, Fisher came to realize that because of rigid control wielded by the Gentile fraternities, no Jewish student had ever been able to attend one of the central events of any university's social life—the Junior Prom. In great anger, he described both the form of the discrimination practiced by the fraternities and the acquiescence to it of NYU's president and other members of the administration:

> Jews might be officers of the junior class, might captain the football team and wade in the gore for alma mater, but established tradition had it that

the sacred portals of the Prom were closed. The manner of our exclusion
was simple. The President of the Junior class (always a Gentile fraternity man since Jewish students were subject to an unofficial but rigorous
quota) would appoint as Prom committeemen only the representatives of
accredited Gentile fraternities. The Prom, therefore, was entirely a Gentile fraternity affair, from which even long-recognized Jewish fraternities
were barred. In my own junior year, the Jewish boys did not know when
the Prom was to be given. None of us could buy a ticket. The whole floor
of the ballroom was divided at the side into fraternity booths, so that if
by some freak of chance a bold Semite might actually procure a ticket and
venture in, there would be no chairs for his use, he could not go into the
booths, and his girl would have to stand up all night! Just a pleasant little
system![38]

Fisher decided to take to the road of political activism to protest
this situation. For the Jewish boys at the University, he wrote, the exclusion represented a "brazen insult," not so much because they truly
wanted to go to the Prom—which they did—but because the discrimination "was an open slap in the faces of every Jewish student and every
Jewish alumnus," with the full cooperation of the University's administration. Chancellor "Black," Fisher pointed out, "might coddle Jewish millionaires over a teacup in order to get money; he was Honorary
Chairman and regularly led the grand march at the Prom."[39]

Fisher began by sending a strong letter of protest to the chancellor, to the deans, and to the NYU daily student newspaper. He stressed
that if Gentile fraternities wished to hold an interfraternity ball it was
their privilege, but they should not call it "the Prom of the Junior
Class."[40] The newspaper's student editors, on their part, at first refused
to print or even to acknowledge receipt of the letter, while the university's chancellor called Fisher to his home in an attempt to dissuade him
verbally from his rebellious course. Only when Fisher refused to back
down and threatened to release his letter to the general media did the
student editors relent and print it in the March 15, 1923 issue. The resulting publicity exposed Fisher and his backers to expressions of hatred
from both faculty and students. Dean "White" of the College of Engineering sought him out for an additional administrative confrontation
as he walked through the halls from his classes:

> "You're Mr. Fisher?"
> "Yes."
> "What are you trying to do? Start a fight around here?"

"Why, no, Dean, I just wrote what I thought was right and in the interests of the University itself."

He suggested that I visit at his office. The conversation ran so close
to the proverbial, classic conversation with the cultured and yet bigoted
Gentile that its occurrence is almost entirely unbelievable.

"You know, Mr. Fisher, my fathers came over here in the Mayflower.
They came here for religious freedom. Your people came here to make
money."

I answered that the May Laws of Russia probably had as much to do
with my parents' coming to this country.

"Well, uhduh, there may be exceptions. But most of you Jews come
here to make money."[41]

Members of the Gentile fraternities, not taking his protests
lightly, threatened bodily harm, and rumors spread that one group in
particular would beat up Fisher and dunk him in the college's fountain.
The assault continued with the sudden appearance of large antisemitic
posters plastered on the walls of Fisher's dormitory and other buildings
on and around the campus, declaring "Kosher . . . Strictly Kosher . . .
Must not apply here. SCURVY KIKES ARE NOT WANTED at New York
University. If they knew their place they would not be here. Make New
York University a White Man's College."[42] Fisher mobilized the Jewish
fraternities and as a group they immediately tore down the posters and
organized for self-defense even as the University threatened to punish
the perpetrators:

> We swarmed over the campus tearing down, pulling down, scratching
> away the placards. A campus war was threatened. At the noon day chapel,
> Dean Rawton of the College of Arts excoriated the perpetrators of the
> libel. The University would expel the men who printed and put those
> posters up! The University was a great and liberal university! The Associ-
> ated Press carried his words to all parts of the country. The Yiddish press
> which flamed with headlines concerning the affair, wrote editorials prais-
> ing him. The Anglo-Jewish weeklies expressed appreciative satisfaction.
> The culprits would be expelled! At the mass meeting of the Jewish stu-
> dents which followed chapel, a resolution was passed expressing our confi-
> dence in the ability of the university authorities to deal with the situation.
> We arranged that the Jewish students would not congregate on going to
> or from classes in order to avoid the physical conflict which seemed in-
> evitable. With good maneuvering and patience, trouble was averted. . . .[43]

Two days after the Dean's chapel address, Fisher received a letter
signed by the Ku Klux Klan, warning him "to leave the campus or else

I would meet with bodily inflicted violence." From that moment on, he recalled, "several Jewish huskies were constantly with me." Fortunately, the personal threats soon subsided. But the rage remained when detailed detective work by Jewish students revealed the unmistakable identity of the poster's distributors by tracing the butcher shop where they had obtained the stencil of the Hebrew word for "kosher." The Jewish students passed on the information, but neither Dean "Rawton" nor any official of the University did anything of any substance and the perpetrators graduated with their class.

Two more years of political work, including the formation of a coalition of Jewish students and Gentile nonfraternity men in order to capture the presidency of the Junior class, were necessary before the fraternities's control over the Prom was broken. Even then, according to Fisher, many of the customary Gentile patrons and patronesses whose financial contributions were essential to the Prom's operation refused to extend their aid. The American Jewish Congress, one of the leading American Jewish defense agencies, had to be called in to intervene. Finally, the Prom took place as promised, and Fisher triumphantly described his delayed attendance there:

> I invited the "girl" of my college years to come to the Prom. We were among the first couples on the floor, the first Jewish couple at the Prom in its over three-quarters of a century of history! At the end of the dance, we walked over to the booth for the patrons' committee. Dean Rawton was there. He looked up as I entered. Few alumni ever attend the undergraduate Prom. But the embarrassed expression in his eyes indicated that he knew why I had come. With curious surprise, he surveyed my companion's Park Avenue fashioned dress and listened to her perfect English speech. We bowed away, and waltzed. . . .[44]

In the end Fisher could not help but disown the college he had wanted so badly to love. To express such sentiments was nothing short of treasonous in the 1920s when loyalty to one's school was an integral part of American collegiate culture. And yet, by 1936 there was an alternative on the horizon. In keeping with the author's strong Zionist ideology and the appearance of his memoir in a Zionist youth publication, Fisher's emphatic negation of NYU was coupled with an allusion to another university—the Hebrew University, which had just been built on Mount Scopus in Jerusalem. Speaking perhaps rhetorically and with more than a touch of bitterness, the author declared that only in a homeland of his own and in a university of his own could he and his people ever hope to find the true happiness and acceptance they longed for:[45]

> I have no alma mater. The love that I had for the campus, its lilacs and chrysanthemums, its shaded walks and the moon riding high over the library . . . both are long dead. Like hundreds of others, I have no college mother. To her Jewish sons she was no alma mater, but a treacherous mother. What she gave us, we achieved by the piling up of index cards, the scribbling of themes, the sheer strength of our intellectual might and the genius of the unyielding labor of many nights. I have but one university. . . . It is on the hills of Scopus.

The two-year battle at New York University to break the control of the Gentile fraternities over one of school's major social events of the year, and the participation of American Jewish defense agencies in the process, illustrates the importance of these events in the lives of the students. It made little sense to claim that young Jewish students had truly equal access to institutions of higher education in New York City or in the U.S. if they could not even dance at their own prom.

Fisher and his associates had the strength to challenge this exclusion, to fight against it for years, and to achieve ultimate victory. If less hardy and more sensitive Jewish youth were exposed to these attitudes, manipulations, and exclusionary practices long enough, however, they might just accept that what their critics said about their people was all true. Blows from the surrounding non-Jewish powers might have been more violent, but they also might have hurt less in days and places where Jews as individuals had fewer hopes of participating in those societies. In the United States of America, where expectations and hopes were so much higher, we can only imagine what psychic scars they were left with for the rest of their lives from campus experiences such as these.

Chapter 6

"What Have I Done?"

Intra-Jewish Hostility and the Internalization of Antisemitism

Not just the virulence of the Harvard affair and similar cases, but the unexpected source of the infection caught American Jews off guard. It did not fit in their hierarchy of values. Henry Ford, after all, was just a businessman. But the President of Harvard University? Somehow they had expected better treatment from the world of American higher education. As McGill student and Sigma Alpha Mu member Lionel A. Sperber observed in December 1923, the anti-Jewish edicts being issued in Cambridge and other college towns were not the work of "ignorant peasants or religious fanatics" as might be expected in the Old Country. "Why this pernicious actor of our present-day civilization should choose a milieu of learning and enlightenment in which to breed and fester seems a rather difficult situation to comprehend," Sperber observed. "Hitherto we have been accustomed to regard anti-Semitism and ignorance in complementary terms. . . . Superficially it would seem that the case for Semitism were much worse as not only the ignorant but the learned as well share the noxious prejudice."[1]

Reactions and Responses

By the 1920s, as the product of the east European mass migration found itself poised to enter mainstream American society, social, educational, institutional, employment, and residential anti-Jewish restrictions were a fact of life. This prejudice alone, however, would not determine the

143

course of their progress in the United States. Rather, American Jewish life for the next fifty years would be determined by the ways segments of the Jewish community chose to *react and respond* to the challenge of antisemitism.

The responses were many and varied. Within fraternity circles, these included bewilderment, despair, anger, denial, humor, humility, drives to collect scientific data, fleeing to more welcoming schools, stressing an organization's Jewish identity more, and stressing an organization's Jewish identity less. They also included a marked tendency toward self-blame—that is, an internalization of the external charges. This in turn resulted in desperate attempts to erase their own allegedly objectionable characteristics, camouflage, overwhelming emphasis on good behavior and manners to the point of self-policing, and disgust and fear directed against those fellow Jews and potential fraternity members who would or could not adhere to these elevated standards.

Response: Scientific Analysis

To Harold Riegelman, executive head of Zeta Beta Tau, when the anti-Jewish attitudes exposed by the Harvard affair first hit the presses, his first order of business was to obtain hard scientific data on the question. In the 1922–1923 academic year he commissioned a nation-wide survey on campus anti-Jewish feeling, directed by Bernard A. Bergman, a ZBT graduate (Ohio State '16) and editor of the *Jewish Tribune*. Questionnaires were distributed to 1500 undergraduate fraternity men located on sixty-seven campuses. Subjects were also invited to submit their own comments and suggestions on how best to deal with "race prejudice" on the American campus. (Before World War II in the U.S., both Jews and non-Jews routinely referred to Jews as a "race.")

Of the sixty-seven colleges reporting, the survey revealed, Jews were not admitted at all to Gentile fraternities and sororities on fifty-two campuses, while on fifteen a few might be admitted "occasionally." It also revealed to no one's surprise that Jews were disproportionately represented in the groves of academe. Though only three percent of the U.S. population as a whole, Jews composed approximately ten percent of the total undergraduate student body in the nation—eleven percent of the men, and eight percent of the women. "Slight to moderate" prejudice by students against Jews could be found on forty-one percent of the campuses surveyed, and "severe prejudice" by both student and faculty on eighteen percent. The most common form of student prejudice reported was keeping Jewish students out of public or honorary offices; for faculty, it was holding Jewish students up to special ridicule in class.[2]

As for possible solutions, the University of Virginia representative suggested "Discontinue loudness and congregation in public places—abide by university customs." "Personal intercourse and acquaintance," was the recommendation of the University of Texas respondent. Several claimed that the fraternity itself was the best solution: "Fraternities and sororities minimize prejudice by trying to correct loudness and other faults," contributed the students at Western Reserve; another at Johns Hopkins claimed that fraternities minimized prejudice because "they make men go out for activities and thus gain respect of Gentiles." The representative of Georgia Tech was more optimistic. "Do nothing to abolish prejudice," he wrote. "It will work itself out."

The survey also included questions on the extent of Jewish participation in athletics and extracurricular activities. Those, including Riegelman himself, who saw athletic prowess as the fastest ticket to acceptance in the U.S. were cheered to discover that Jewish students composed a respectable, even disproportionate, seven percent of the nation's varsity teams. However, to his displeasure, the statistic paled before a much greater disproportion in campus publications (20 percent), debating clubs and teams (23 percent), and worst of all, team managerships. The last was viewed as a refuge for Jewish boys blessed with intelligence and love of sports, but lacking the brawn (or, as often, parental encouragement) to participate directly.[3]

Response: Denial, Out-Marriage, and Conversion

In order to avoid the handicaps of Jewish name or birth, attempts to "pass" or to seek deliberate out-marriage or formal conversion were the first and most obvious, though not the easiest, avenues of escape. Ethical Culture, Christian Science, and the Unitarian Church are most often mentioned in fraternity records as havens for lapsed Jews, particularly for women who changed their names automatically upon marriage. ZBT humorist A.D. Schwarz noted this phenomenon in a brief 1923 essay entitled "Why I Hate Jewesses," a non-pseudonymous companion piece to "Cyrus McGinn Mulqueen's" earlier article "Why I Hate Jews."

Ever since they started mixing up the Van Schmyck's dinner parties with the engagement notices of the Bashky Felzensteins and the Guedalia

Schickers in the society columns of the newspapers, my hatred for Jewesses has rapidly increased. The advent of the 400 Verein and the new
type of Unitarian-Christian Science Jewess now manages to sneak one
over too easily. You pick up a paper and read: "Boyle-O'Reilly: Mr. and
Mrs. Abe Boyle announce the marriage of their daughter, Iris Becky, to
Mr. Ike O'Reilly of the Bronx. Rabbi Mashlansky performed the ceremony." Only the sturdy and loyal rabbi . . . can serve to give one a clue
as to whether the bride was or was not Jewish, and instead of scanning
hastily down the column to see if one's friends are dropping off, a fellow
has to read every notice carefully, and then he isn't sure. . . .[4]

Response: State Schools and Jewish
Student Migrancy in the 1920s and 1930s

When facing college admissions quotas or barriers of any kind at schools
near their homes, individuals from the northeast could also respond by
taking to the roads and applying to colleges and professional schools
across the country that *would* accept them. The U.S. was blessed with
hundreds, if not thousands of institutions of higher learning spread
across all forty-eight states. Many were public institutions that officially
could not discriminate against Jews. They also charged low tuition, a
blessing to families of limited means who had to scrape together the
resources to give their offspring every advantage. Although bound to
grant preferential admission and lower fees to in-state residents, out-
of-state Jewish students could still be admitted, and if they wished the
students could achieve the status of state residents within six months to
a year. A less affluent Jewish undergraduate from an urban area might
arrive at a state school far from home with few clothes, less spending
money, the need to work part-time for his keep, and the inability to
purchase a railroad ticket home more than once or twice a year. He also
might find himself in debt upon his graduation. Nevertheless, if both he
and his family were willing to make the necessary sacrifices, the option
of becoming a student migrant was there.

From the viewpoint of the Jewish fraternities, the migration of
the more well-to-do academic refugees from the northeast was in fact a
boon and major factor in their 1920s expansion. These students swelled
the local Jewish population and helped create a basis for larger and better
chapters. The large state universities and smaller rural or semi-rural colleges of the South, Midwest and West, where so many migrant students
sought haven, were precisely the places where the Jewish Greek system

was strongest and where students relied most heavily on their chapter houses to supply room, board, and social life. Membership was also important because acceptance into certain fraternity chapters within these schools could carry as much weight in social status as acceptance into Ivy League institutions back on the east coast.

By 1929 the momentum of Jewish students toward public state colleges rather than private institutions was so pronounced that even the elite Zeta Beta Tau had nineteen out of thirty-three chapters located there. The advantage of state schools, in the words of Ted Goldsmith '30 of ZBT's Ohio State chapter, was "an air of democracy because of cheap tuition and low entrance requirements." Most importantly, he noted, "state universities have dispensed as much as possible with entrance exams and nose-measuring psychology tests. . . . A state university with its open-door policy can't very well resort to stratagems of the schools with selective examinations in halting the Semitic invasions."[5]

The colleges and universities of the American South proved to be an especially important outlet for wandering collegiate Jews until the early 1950s. Some went so far as to recruit Jewish students through public invitations and requests that their fraternities establish new chapters there. At Alpha Epsilon Pi's 1920 annual convention, for example, Supreme Master Milton Adler noted with pleasure that their third southern chapter and the first in the state of Alabama had just been established at Auburn University—at the specific invitation of the University's president and with the approval of the school's faculty. It was the Auburn president's hope, Adler noted, that "through us many more promising young Jewish men can be attracted to the institution."[6] In 1926, *The State*, a newspaper published in Columbia, South Carolina, ran an advertisement for Jewish students. The same issue included an editorial claiming that if Jews would only look beyond northern schools like Harvard and seek out smaller state institutions like the University of South Carolina, both they and the universities would benefit.[7]

The University of Alabama at Tuscaloosa, which had sixty-eight Jewish students enrolled in 1926, more than half from out-of-state, proved to be an especially welcoming admissions haven in the late 1920s and early 1930s. This was so despite unfamiliarity of northeastern "Yankee" Jews with the geography and customs of the area. Regional prejudice could go both ways, as illustrated by the following uncomplimentary parody of a semi-literate Alabama farmer entitled "Squire Perkins' Remarks on Colleges in General," penned by a New York City native and member of Alabama's Sigma Alpha Mu chapter in December 1922:

> Yea, colleges is great institooshunns—course I aint never been to none, but lots of my family has. Now there's my son Henry, which went up to the University last Christmas. Wel, he aint been there long and he ain learnt much YET, but maybe he'll know all about Weinstein's theory of relationship and then he'll be able to milk them cows a hole lot faster. . . . My brother, Ab, went to college by sellin' his intres' in the farm—he staid thar four years and he's been working for me ever since. He wears swallowtail coats and I betcher fo-bits he aint never said "aint" since he's been to college, but then again I reckon he aint never HAD fo-bits debt free since then either . . .[8]

Response: A Jewish Woman at Vassar

While the fraternities' periodicals confined themselves largely to an analysis of problems faced specifically by men, the May 1923 issue of the *Zeta Beta Tau Quarterly*, entitled "The Prejudice Number," included information for Jewish collegiate women as well. How should a Jewish woman at an elite Seven Sisters institution conduct herself when faced with evidence of discrimination because of her background? Writer Dorothy Linder (most likely the sister, girlfriend, or other associate of a ZBT) described how her journey to Vassar College began with advice to leave blank or else to write "none" the space on the application form requesting her religious affiliation. For the required photograph and three letters of reference, she wrote, the Jewish applicant "must go to an expensive photographer and have her picture taken full-face-in-mist, to hide her nose and make her generally unrecognizable." As for the requisite three letters of reference, the distracted mother tries her best to recall some non-Jewish acquaintances who would "lend their names to such a worthy cause as putting the Committee on Admissions off the scent."[9]

Arrival on campus forced the decision whether to attend Vassar's "beautiful chapel services" and aroused anxiety that her adviser, classmates, and neighbors would guess by her absence that she was a Jewess. However, as it happened, religious affiliations soon became a matter of public record. They were posted on the bulletin board next to each freshman's name for all the college to see, ostensibly so that upperclassmen could escort the young women on the first Sunday of each month to appropriate church services in town. After that, the writer

wondered, should she or should she not join the YWCA (Young Women's Christian Association) as the majority of her classmates did? Most
of their activities, she observed, did appear to be entirely nonreligious.

Despite these and other questions facing her, Linder denied
that antisemitism was the governing factor of a Jewish student's life at
Vassar. Prejudice, she insisted, was a universal trait and Jews were not
its only victims. "To ignore race distinctions" and "to be accepted for
your own worth and value" were still possible. In fact, she noted, Jewish
women "invariably" took Vassar's highest scholastic honors and excelled
in dramatics, politics, debating and publications, areas where cleverness,
efficiency and individual efforts—rather than group work, where she believed Jewish women had less training—counted most. Jewish women's
true "inferiority in sports" and not religion was to blame for their general
absence from athletic teams. Jewesses, in her opinion, even those blessed
with the advantages of summer camp experience, were still handicapped
by their "short stature" in comparison to the "five-foot-six" of the Vassar athlete and their general lack of precollege training relative to the
"Christian boarding school type of athlete."

Appearance was also a legitimate handicap for a Jewish woman,
Linder observed. "She doesn't make Daisy Chain, that group of the
twenty prettiest sophomores who carry the chain at Class Day," the Vassar student noted.

> And the one and only reason why she doesn't is not because she is Jewish,
> but because she (the Jewish student) isn't sufficiently good-looking. You
> may protest violently and maintain that there are beautiful Jewesses, but
> they simply do not meet the modern standard of beauty. They are not tall
> enough. Their darkness, which is so attractive by candlelight, turns yellow
> looking next to the blonde fairness of the American girl. And Jewesses are
> frequently too fat, and look out of place in sport clothes, the only costumes
> in which students ever see one another. Nor will it do to protest that the
> standard is a Christian one, since our leading designers and dressmakers
> are Jewish. Our standard of beauty being what it is, the Jewish student
> seldom meets it, and therefore, and not because of prejudice, does not
> make Daisy Chain.

In all, Linder suggested, the best thing Jewish students of both
genders could do for themselves was to avoid hurt by scaling down their
expectations. "The absurd megalomania of the average Jew in college,
the probable reaction to years of oppression, makes him or her aspire
too much," she concluded.[10]

Response: Humility and Patience

Dr. Louis E. Wise, a professor of chemistry at Syracuse University and an associate member of the Phi Epsilon Pi chapter there, counseled similar advice to undergraduate members in June 1923, invoking the example of Jesus of Nazareth. His message came four months after Syracuse's Student Council called for open admissions restrictions against Jews on the grounds that they did not contribute sufficiently to school athletic teams.[11] The faculty overturned the vote, but the Syracuse Jewish student body was shaken nonetheless. "I feel that if a large group of Jews forget their 'persecution complex' (as their detractors have named the Jewish reaction under the lash of anti-Semitism) and work with these same detractors in every constructive effort for the common good, the problem will become less and less acute," Wise wrote. Bigotry, in his view, was as likely a result of ignorance, not wickedness, and thus it could be remedied through education and example. "The Jew must respect the laws of his city, his nation, and his university as no one else respects them," Wise wrote. "He must work unceasingly, but always quietly, with a deep sense of humility and forgetfulness of self . . . He must labor for humanity, handicapped by the insults of the men with whom and for whom he works. The task is not easy, but it can be done. A great Jew did it nineteen centuries ago. Individual Jews are doing it today, and more Jews must join with them in the days to come."[12]

Rabbi Edward N. Calisch, a pulpit rabbi in Richmond, Virginia, an honorary member of Phi Epsilon Pi, and the president of the Central Conference of American Rabbis, (the national umbrella group for Reform rabbis in the U.S.) counseled similar advice to his followers that same month. American justice was bound to triumph over bigotry eventually, he believed. At present collegiate Jews should accept their position and play the game as best and as bravely as they could without "fretting" over the inevitable disappointments and defeats they would suffer. "This attitude will do far more to destroy the discrimination than all the vocal protests that may be made," the Rabbi concluded. "The present wave of accentuated anti-Semitism, both within and out of college life, will subside. Let none of us do anything now in anger or resentment which may later give cause for regret."[13]

Response: Intensify Jewish Identity

For some Jewish fraternity officers, including those who came from a more traditional background, the times demanded a more assertive and

separatist philosophy. Alpha Epsilon Pi, for example, from the beginning had pledged itself to promoting Jewish communal leadership, and
included national officers who observed the traditional dietary laws and
Sabbath.[14] Nathan Wolf, elected the Supreme Master of the fraternity
in 1919, exhorted members at the 1920 national convention that they
"must be interested in everything Jewish" and should fight antisemitism
actively anywhere and anyhow they could. In doing so, they should pay
particular attention to the "dastardly, mean, unscrupulous, skulking, underhanded, and unintelligent work" of Henry Ford and his associates
who were fomenting fears of an international Jewish conspiracy by running excerpts from the *Protocols of the Elders of Zion* in Ford's *Dearborn
Independent* newspaper.[15]

As for Sigma Alpha Mu, which did not hold business meetings on Friday nights or Saturday mornings, Jewish education was a
subject for special comment. Benjamin Schwartz (Cornell '18), himself secretary of the Board of Jewish Education in Baltimore, called in
the pages of the fraternity's bulletin in December 1922 for the mod-
ernization and upgrading of afternoon Hebrew schools for children, so
that "the ideals and purposes of the Jewish people" would be better preserved for future generations. Philip D. Sang, another SAM at the Armour Institute of Technology in Chicago, similarly cautioned his fellow
young adults not to forget their origins, for someday soon their people would call upon them. "If the future leaders of American Jewry are
weighed in the balance and found wanting Israel's great calamity would
be obvious," Sang observed. "It falls upon the shoulders of the Fraternity to prevent any such catastrophe."[16] He concluded with a call for
mandatory study of Jewish history for Sigma Alpha Mu's pledges, regular chapter attendance at synagogue services, libraries of Jewish books
and magazines in each chapter house, monthly lectures on Jewish topics, participation in Jewish communal affairs, and an increase in Jewish
rituals for such events as the Passover seder and memorial services for
departed fraters.

Other SAM commentators writing at the time of the Harvard
affair in 1922–1923 advocated work to close the denominational gaps
between Orthodox, Conservative, and Reform Jews in America. David
I. Arbuse in June 1923 warned his fellow members about the increasing
dangers of exogamous marriage. "It is nothing unusual nowadays to read
names of pledges, which sound anything but Jewish—or to hear that
many of our own Fraternity are intermarrying," he wrote. "Neither is
this peculiar to our Fraternity alone, but to all Jewish Fraternities—in
fact to our entire Jewish people." This phenomenon, he warned, might

lead America's three million Jews to disappear in the course of two or three centuries.[17]

In "Zionism: The Solution of the Jewish Problem" by Emmanuel Abrahamson of SAM's Columbia chapter, the author went so far as to suggest in December 1922 that the voluntary departure of U.S. Jews to their own homeland might provide the ultimate answer to their difficulties. Referring to Torquemada of the Spanish Inquisition in Spain and the Black Hundreds in Russia, Abrahamson sardonically warned his readers of some of the historical alternatives used to eliminate an unwanted Jewish presence. "I should not like, for obvious reasons, to recommend this method of solving the American Jewish problem," he wrote, "though I feel that we should reckon with it as a future possibility."[18]

Response: Best Behavior and the Mission of Manners

The vast majority of American Jewish college students, however, did not see the path of religious observance or emigration to another land as the solution to their problems. Instead, they either believed or had been taught by their families and peer groups that anti-Jewish feelings and stereotypes were based on real foundations, and that the good name of all Jews could be either enhanced or harmed by the behavior of a single Jew. It was therefore their responsibility to behave correctly at all times, both for their own sakes and for the sake of their people.

This mentality, which might be called "the best behavior syndrome" or the "mission of manners" was in part an expression of solidarity, a modern extension of the old rabbinic dictum that all of the House of Israel are responsible one for the other. Though the American-born students may not have been conscious of it, it also echoed through the generations the medieval fear that to bring harm or threat of death to one's fellow Jews at the hands of outsiders constituted the sin of *chilul hashem*—the desecration of God's name. Conversely, to behave in public in such a manner as would enhance their people's safety was a sanctification of God's name. However, in modern times such attitudes, if they existed, could easily backfire and lead to the internalization of external hatred along with an intense desire to disassociate oneself from ill-behaved Jews. This force was itself destructive to the maintenance of the community. Within the Jewish Greek subsystem, this conflict could express itself through intra-Jewish resentment directed against independents, lower-ranking fraternities, or applicants for admission who did not meet an exaggerated set of standards set by a Gentile world that actually excluded all Jews without exception.

"On the subject of prejudice it is worthy of note that most of the writers point out that the Jew does not come into court with clean hands," noted Harry S. Winer (Ohio State '23) of Sigma Alpha Mu. "How often at college does one hear the aggravating expression, 'greasy Jew,' and worse epithets, applied by one Jew to another. Surely each one of us must be convinced that we dare not hope to minimize the prejudice of non-Jew against Jew before we eliminate the prejudice of Jew against Jew."[19] The editors of the *Indiana Jewish Chronicle* made the same point with even greater emphasis in an editorial published in the mid-1920s. Jewish fraternities, the editor wrote, which had begun as a necessity, "are now degenerating into a cesspool of Jewish hatreds."[20]

Such attitudes were common even among the men of Sigma Alpha Mu, who, along with calls for greater Jewish consciousness, were also called on to guard their behavior scrupulously in response to antisemitism in general and the Harvard controversy in particular. "The boisterous, garrulous, obnoxiously self-assertive Jew is so common, that we are all, deplorably, judged from that viewpoint. Let us be more modest and we will command greater respect and tolerance," suggested Charles I. Stoloff, a graduate of City College, in June 1922.[21] Lionel A. Sperber of McGill recommended that members of the fraternity and all Jews be ready "to remedy any of their repulsive defects." As he exhorted his fellow Sammies to have pride in their "race" and in their heritage, and to spread like missionaries the example of their goodness, William C. Kranowitz (Columbia '18) also accused those Jewish students who by their conduct were unworthy of the privilege of a college education. "Shall that precious privilege be demeaned by uncouth behavior, by unmannerly conduct?" he wrote. "Begone, then, the Jewish student, who by such conduct, misses his opportunity, wrecks his privilege, and blasphemes the fair name of his race! Let him not even shadow college portals!"[22]

For the oldest and most elite Jewish fraternities and sororities, every rushing season brought the fear that their group might "slip" both in their own eyes and in the eyes of Gentiles if socially unacceptable men and women managed to slide through the blackball barrier. In the view of one observer of Zeta Beta Tau, writing anonymously in September 1922, the oldest Jewish fraternity had already failed in its mission of producing a fraternity aristocracy that could "rival in airs, manners, and tradition the Dekes, the Sigma Chis, or the Betas." In its early years, the author wrote, ZBT "had to discriminate against the greasy, objectionable type, popularly known as the 'kike.' Zeta Beta Tau has never said this in so many words, but this is exactly what it had to do."[23] To reach that goal, it was necessary for at least one man in each chapter to "do his duty for both the fraternity and for the Jewish race by wielding the blackball unmercifully." He regretted that because of the lowering of social barriers and the need to acquire paying boarders during World War I, ZBT's standards had fallen. The fraternity, in his opinion, was now filled with too many members of the "mob" who were not true "ZBT material." Even worse, ZBT now faced competition from "a host of mediocre imitators." "Other Jews, stung by the discrimination of ZBT, reacted to ZBT like ZBT reacted to the Christian fraternities," the author wrote, describing in part the reasons behind the rapid growth of the Jewish Greek subsystem. "Ten or twelve other Jewish fraternities set out to prove that all Jews were as good as ZBT Jews. As ZBT now stands, they have won their point."[24]

Response: The Philosophy of "Pro-Semitism"

For Harold Riegelman of Zeta Beta Tau, the work that his Jewish fraternity did in fostering acceptable social behavior in public and encouraging success in varsity athletics was not just a necessity; it was a positive good. If during the college years future leaders of the world could observe his men smashing anti-Jewish stereotypes, in the end the benefits would accrue to the entire Jewish people. Riegelman termed this philosophy "Pro-Semitism" and throughout the 1920s advocated it often in speeches and in articles for the Anglo-Jewish press. As an attorney and World War I veteran who was achieving prominence in both Jewish communal and U.S. public affairs (Riegelman would run for Mayor of New York City on the Republican ticket in 1953) his words carried weight.[25] He also defended his own and other Jewish fraternities against the charge, made by a Harvard professor in Spring 1923 during the height of the Harvard affair, that Jews were by nature "clannish" and that it was unfair of them to be asked to be treated as individuals as long as they always insisted on forming separate groups.[26] In doing so, the professor was unwittingly echoing charges made on the floor of the French National Assembly in the late eighteenth century by critics who did not believe that the revolution required granting the Jews of France full emancipation.

In his response, Riegelman claimed once again that the banding together of individual Jews into groups was necessary if they were ever to surmount the prejudice against them:

> It is entirely proper, it is more than proper—it is necessary, so long as certain predispositions with respect to Jews exist—that Jewish men should associate themselves as Jews, and as Jews steadily, continuously and persistently, by their sportsmanship on the athletic field, their reserve and decency of deportment, their generous support of movements looking toward relief and communal betterment and solidarity, demonstrate day in and day out on the campus and off the campus the inherent fineness of their character as men among men and the inherent, blatant, stupid falsity of predispositions to the contrary. This is the field of the Jewish fraternity. And this is the watchword of Jewish fraternity men.
>
> "They ask to be treated as individuals, but they form a group." They form a group, if you please, for one purpose only—to demonstrate their right to be treated as individuals.[27]

Paul Yawitz of the University of Missouri, in an essay entitled "Well, ZBT Men *Are* Different," agreed with Riegelman's philosophy and went so far as to claim that their exclusiveness and insistence on high breeding was "the death knell to anti-Semitism in American colleges."(The title was a play on a common remark of that era made by Gentiles to Jews that could compliment, disarm, or infuriate them when the subject of anti-Jewish behavior entered the conversation: "but *you* are different.") Ruthless selectivity and shunning of any Jews who might jeopardize their cause had helped ZBT ingratiate itself "into the favor and cordiality of the hostile gentile" and to attain finally the goal that a "maligned and persecuted race" had been dreaming of for centuries.

"Zeta Beta Tau men set out to make themselves as much like their Gentile neighbors as was possible," Yawitz claimed.

> First they elected new men to their ranks, men who came nearest to the criterion they had established. These men possessed the full appreciation of things American, harbored the ideals of their associates, and offered an appearance that was immaculately that of their best neighbors. . . . Their habits and manners, their polish and breeding, were beyond reproach. In the home their conduct was pleasing; on the campus their courtesy was patent. Only such were chosen!

Gradually, Christians came to believe that some Jews really were better than others:

These men of Zeta Beta Tau were of the flesh and blood he never imag-ined them to be. They spoke in well-modulated tones, no longer the "loudmouth Jew" of Gentile tradition; they ate their food with the table manners of royalty, no longer the ill-bred, earth-born; they were gener-ous and considerate, no longer the common, grasping pinchfist; they were clean, kempt, and natty, no longer the careless, slattern immigrant with the grime of generations.[28]

As a result, Yawitz concluded, Zeta Beta Tau had produced the "accept-able" Jew, one who was "so like the Gentile" that he was indeed a new entity. "Zeta Beta Tau men need never feel the poisons of prejudice that imperil Judaism," Yawitz insisted. "Zeta Beta Tau men are different."

In Search of the Right Material

Maintaining these high standards in the pre-World War II United States however, required almost the same level of vigilance as that dis-played by the admissions officers of elite northeastern colleges. When a student applied to Zeta Beta Tau fraternity or the Alpha Epsilon Phi sorority, until 1941 the required form included questions on the birth-places of both parents as well as the mother's maiden name. There was no quicker way to determine what the officers referred to as the "cul-tural background" of the applicant, or a quicker way for the unsuitable applicant to see that he or she did not belong in this organization. Such questions, ironically, were also being used on college application forms to weed out socially undesirable Jews and others that were viewed as unfit for admission.

Among Jews themselves, origins from the wrong part of Eu-rope, a name ending in "-sky," residence in what was considered an undesirable neighborhood, insufficient wealth, a father with a hum-ble occupation—such as butchering or tailoring—and membership in a non-Reform Jewish synagogue could automatically exclude an appli-cant from joining one of the elite groups. (Such factors did not, how-ever, exclude membership in Sigma Alpha Mu, Alpha Epsilon Pi, Phi Sigma Sigma, Delta Phi Epsilon, or other fraternities further down in the hierarchy). The terms "kike" or "yid" and, especially for women, "greasy grind," were commonly used in rushing sessions. Investigation rhetoric also included such terms as "representative," "unrepresentative," "desirable," "undesirable," "n.g." (for "no good") "type"—as in "not from the better class or type of Jew"—and "rating," as in "her family simply doesn't rate in Baltimore."

Other class divisions apparent in records of rushing and investigation reports of potential chapters included the superiority of origins
in Manhattan vs. the Bronx or Brooklyn, rural or suburban areas anywhere vs. New York City, and Southern Jews vs. Northern Jews. Even
among Southerners, important distinctions were drawn between those
who came from Atlanta and those who came from other parts of the
South. In the case of the University of Washington in Seattle, a city with
a considerable Sephardic (Judeo-Spanish) Jewish population with roots
going back to the Expulsion of 1492 and origins from Turkey and the
island of Rhodes, intra-Jewish discrimination went three ways. In the
1920s and 1930s Zeta Beta Tau was mainly for the German Jews, while
Sigma Alpha Mu accepted primarily Russian Jews. By custom neither
accepted Sephardic Jews, who were considered an alien entity. Alpha
Epsilon Pi, however, whose chapter was established at the University
of Washington in 1947, welcomed Sephardic Jews, as well as military
veterans who did not wish to go through the customary roughhouse initiation proceedings of the other fraternities. The chapter list of that first
year reveals at least a half-dozen characteristic Judeo-Spanish names.[29]
     The internalization of anti-Jewish discrimination could also af-
fect the relationships between Jewish men and women. Access to women
was a major reason for freshman college men of any background to join
a fraternity in the first place. For the most part, Jewish fraternity men
in the 1920s and later went out of their way to seek out Jewish women
for both dating and marriage. However, a young Jewish fraternity man
might well come to accept the stereotype of Jewish females as dark,
unattractive, loud, socially inept, and fat. Furthermore, he might resent
that the most desirable Gentile women considered it beneath themselves
to date him and were thus "out of his league." In such a case the Jewish
male might easily direct, in turn, the distaste of the external world upon
the Jewish females of his own circle, while considering it a great triumph
to woo and win the heart of a Gentile female through lavish expenditures
of money for dates accompanied with his best fraternity-bred displays
of charm and gallantry.

Elite Jewish Sororities

The upper-level Jewish sororities, which were battling the negative attitudes of Gentile women and both Gentile and Jewish men, thus felt
pressured to be triply careful of the appearance, manners, and class
background of their initiates. Applicants originating from the Greater

Metropolitan New York area were particularly suspect, since the size and anonymity of the city made the customary background checks on their families so difficult. In the case of Alpha Epsilon Phi, the sorority's national officers were scrupulous in their investigations of candidates and their evaluations of both the college and the surrounding Jewish community when planning sites for new chapters.

"Theta [Penn State] must be considered—it needs help and it needs it badly . . . It's the 'thorn' in the East and is doing more damage all the time," visiting Northwestern undergraduate Beatrice Feingold reported to the national office in 1929. At the time, Penn State was becoming a popular destination for dozens and later hundreds of Jewish women from the New York City area, not all of whom were considered proper "AEPhi material." The chapter's officers in any case were for several years known to have "too strong a Jewish consciousness" to mingle sufficiently with Gentiles on the campus. They also, campus visitors alleged, tended to disregard family background when choosing their pledges. [30] In another case, an Alpha Epsilon Phi member at Hunter College—a free-tuition women's institution in New York—sought to transfer to the sorority's chapter at the University of California at Los Angeles. Members at UCLA were reluctant to accept her transfer to their chapter without knowing more about her family. A typical Western Union telegram was immediately dispatched: "HAVE SOME DISCRIMINATING PERSON TRACE FAMILY RUTH COWAN HUNTER TRANSFER AT PHI AND WIRE INFORMATION TO ELIZABETH ELDRIDGE SIX NAUGHT THREE NORTH STANLEY AVENUE LOS ANGELES . . ." "Very difficult to trace anyone in New York," came the reply. "The information I gathered Father a doctor, family nice nothing outstanding . . ." [31]

Similarly, because of the small size of the New York State Normal School at Albany, its questionable status as a teacher-training and not a liberal arts college, and the doubtful family background of its members, Alpha Epsilon Phi continually debated jettisoning a chapter established there in 1917. (The school later evolved into the State University of New York at Albany). As Field Secretary Dorothea Slepyan wrote to the National Council in 1927:

> As a whole the girls are refined in a quiet, reserved manner, but lacking real polish. They are decidedly provincial, but sincere in their endeavors. They lack social contacts with men while at school, but claim that they do not feel such a need although recently they have taken to inviting men from Union College to Sunday afternoon at-homes. . . . With the excep-

tion of their dean and four other girls in the group I feel that Eta does not represent the finest type of American Jewish girl. This is particularly true of all the Albany girls with one exception. They are essentially Jewish in mannerisms, but not obnoxiously so, in that there is a quietness of manner. . . .[32]

Residence in the wrong neighborhood, or even on the wrong street, could seal a potential pledge's fate. Anyone originating from the South Side of Chicago was for many years *verboten* among the higher-ranking Jewish fraternities. In one case, the visiting Feingold, herself an undergraduate with limited experience in such matters, in 1929 recommended two young women in Chicago to aid in the season's rushing, advising that they had "good appearance, good family." Seeing their addresses, Alpha Epsilon Phi's National Dean, while reviewing the report in New Orleans, underlined their names and wrote in large letters in the margin: "NO! Kill S. Side rushing!"[33]

No One Who Would Want to Join Our Club

While careful to maintain the highest standards in choosing their Jewish members, the national officers of Alpha Epsilon Phi did not hesitate to rally in dignity and solidarity when their ranks were challenged either by non-Jews or Jews who shunned them in the hope that they might be accepted by a Gentile sorority. A highly illustrative case of the national officers's attitudes in this area took place in 1926, when one of Alpha Epsilon Phi's undergraduate chapters sought permission to initiate a Protestant woman faculty member. It was, in the words of National Scribe Ruth I. Wien, "the first problem of its kind to come before us," and the sorority's Executive Board wished to hear the opinion of all eight National Council members before rendering its decision.[34]

Wien herself referred to the faculty member simply as "the woman in question" and firmly opposed her admission. Additional debate over the matter dragged on with exchanges of correspondence cross-country for five months until the sorority's executive board finally handed down its refusal. The responses portray the delicate balance of social prestige that Alpha Epsilon Phi was trying to maintain and the psychological and cultural gulf that made it impossible in those days for Jews and Christians to co-exist in the same sorority. It also demonstrated that while upper middle-class Jews themselves might not wish to join any organization that might accept them as members, they in turn were not willing to accept just any Gentile who wanted to join *them*.

Freda M. Rosenthal, the national president of Alpha Epsilon Phi, stressed the threat to social ease and intimacy when she wrote briefly, "I am not in favor of installing other than members of our faith as A.E.Phi. . . . while our constitution is non-sectarian I believe it is setting a dangerous precedent to permit the installation of any person not of our faith. I do not believe such a person could be wholly in sympathy with us or at all times enjoy her affiliation with us. She could never become heart and soul A.E.Phi."[35] In a similar vein, National Ritualist Stella Caplan Bloom wrote, "I have always felt that the introduction of Christian members would always make for disruption in the Chapter and for the loss of that freedom of speech and ease that should exist in each chapter. All my experience with 'Christian Scientists' etc. in the Sorority has been *most* unsuccessful. That is why I am so against it."[36] It was Alpha Epsilon Phi's National Historian Bertha W. Feitel, however, who most strongly invoked the need not to break ranks over the issue:

> I am inclined to think. . . . that the type of faculty member who wishes to be affiliated with A.E.Phi, is not likely to be influential enough to make us take the first step toward breaking our solidarity.
>
> I realize that our Constitution is non-sectarian, but I am not so sure; our Ritual speaks of "our people," etc. Its tone and that of other expressions of ours . . . are not non-sectarian. Either changes or much tact and stalling will be necessary if the faculty lady becomes a "good sister" who attends meetings. . . . She might, too, try to influence the chapter to admit Christian girls on the campus—which would be absolutely logical and fair of her to do—and my, oh my, where would we stand?
>
> I am afraid I should rather A.E.Phi to be a first-rate Jewish fraternity, even though never acceptable to NPC [the National Panhellenic Congress, later Conference, which at the time refused to grant membership to Jewish sororities] than a mixed group of no particular standing. You know how little prestige could be added by the few Christians who would accept A.E.Phi bids, in the eyes of outsiders or ourselves. We could not hope to attract the best (as per recognized standards) and so would have little or nothing to gain, perhaps much to lose.
>
> You called for an opinion. You have it. If it is a vote you want, with no more facts offered than have been, I vote NO.[37]

The women of Alpha Epsilon Phi continued to display their characteristic attitude of bitter dignity and self-respect in a section of one of their rushing booklets from the 1920s entitled, "What to Tell the Girl Who Hesitates to Align Herself with a Jewish House." In it they explained to their members the need for a potential pledge to be open and proud about her Jewish identity, for practical as well as ethical reasons:

> It is a known fact that Christian fraternities are either definitely closed to Jewish girls or the girl who is taken in is asked to deny her religion, etc. (If the girl chooses to pursue this policy, it is just as well not to rush her further). It is not true that a girl who pledges a Jewish house is stamped as such any more certainly than the girl who does not. It soon becomes known to the curious that the girl did not make a house because of her religion. Because of the Policy that the best fraternities follow of taking out only fraternity women, the unaffiliated Jewish girl cannot hope to break through into the charmed circle. As a member of your organization she acquires prestige with the desirable Jewish men on campus and if it is Christian dates she wants, they are still open to her as much as if she were unaffiliated. . . . Stress the fact that the name Alpha Epsilon Phi carries dignity and respect on your campus, show how it has not handicapped your position. Indicate how lost you would be without it and what few contacts you would have with the inside workings of the college world that are controlled almost entirely by the Greek Letter world. The Jewish girl who will not be Jewish is an anomaly. It is unfailingly true that she loses the very respect she covets, for no one values a girl who values herself so cheaply as to deny her origin.[38]

Not "Up to Standard": Fraternity Chapter Purges

To refuse to pledge a man or woman because they supposedly did not live up to a fraternity's established criteria was standard operating procedure throughout the collegiate Greek-letter world. Rush weeks everywhere were dedicated toward that specific purpose. However, to expel on those grounds an entire chapter that had already been in operation for several years was more serious. The early 1920s, the same period as the Harvard quota scandal, saw a rash of suspensions, charter revocations, and the appointment of "supervisory committees" of alumni in order to raise the prestige of the organization as a whole and to ensure that the group's social standards would be uniform throughout the country. New York City colleges, where most of the Jewish fraternities had been founded in the first place, were the most susceptible to this trend.

In the case of Phi Epsilon Pi, the election of Atlanta native Eugene B. Oberdorfer Jr. to the post of National Superior in 1920 (a graduate of a military preparatory school and the University of Georgia who, like Riegelman, had served as an officer in the U.S. Army during World War I) was followed by nothing less than a fraternity-wide purge. Casualties of this era included Phi Epsilon Pi's chapters at New York

University's Washington Square Campus, Rhode Island State in Providence, and Carnegie Tech in Pittsburgh, all of which had their charters revoked. The fraternity's Columbia University chapter was cushioned by greater wealth, but it too succumbed in 1928. What all these chapters had in common was their location in urban areas and their tendency to draw the poorer sons of comparatively recent Jewish immigrants to their campuses.

Andrew Carnegie, a Scotsman who had arrived in America virtually penniless and who had worked his way up to be a multi-millionaire, had specifically endowed Carnegie Tech as a low-tuition school to train poor, deserving young men in the practical arts of engineering and technology. The program attracted large numbers of upwardly mobile and ambitious Jewish students, and a Phi Epsilon Pi chapter—first established in 1916—thrived there, even though most of the members were working their way through school. At that point a typical class-based national fraternity chapter problem surfaced. A chapter of the same fraternity had also been established in 1913 at the nearby University of Pittsburgh [Zeta], a private school that drew the wealthy Jewish sons of Pittsburgh's oldest Jewish families. Most of the members were well-to-do and planned to enter either the professions or their father's businesses. Coming from such different backgrounds, members of the two chapters located in the same city ended up despising one another. In addition, at national gatherings the rest of the fraternity did not approve of Carnegie Tech's members and refused to accept them as fraternity brothers.

As a result, members attending the 1921 annual convention voted to suspend Phi Epsilon Pi's Carnegie Tech chapter from the fraternity for not being "up to standard." (Ironically, the school later became the renowned Carnegie-Mellon University, eventually ranking higher in selectivity and prestige than the University of Pittsburgh). The insistence of Percy Pachtman, an alumnus of the Penn State chapter and a regional officer, that under the earlier standards chapters were still capable of doing wonders with less-than-perfect incoming material, did no good:

> Permit me to explain Theta's [Penn State] method of taking in new men. Theta is also a poor man's school, and when we admit new men, we attempt to teach them etiquette, etc. for we are not so fortunate to obtain the wealthy high-bred class, such as Nu [University of Virginia]. We seat

initiates at the different tables, with Seniors in charge, to give the proper
correction, and let me tell you, that we boast a set of alumni as good
as those of any chapter in our fraternity. . . . We are, I honestly believe,
more broadminded, and are seeking character and quality of our material, irrespective of what group he associates with, and irrespective of his
being poor, or having a nose with a "hook," or having a name ending in
"sky."[39]

Phi Epsilon Pi's executive secretary, Maurice Jacobs, answering
from the fraternity's national headquarters in Philadelphia, insisted on
defending the suspension and the maintenance of the fraternity's new
standards. "If I am going to reside in Boston," he informed Pachtman,
"you can just bet your life that I will have something to say as to who
gets into Tufts or Harvard, and if they are not the type desirable for our
fraternity, they will not get in regardless of their unimpeachable character. There is such a thing as fraternity material, Perc, and there is no
sense avoiding the point."[40]

In the case of Phi Epsilon Pi's New York University, or "Kappa"
chapter, objections came because most of the members were poverty-
stricken evening Law School students, unable or unwilling to conduct
a proper residential collegiate life. Furthermore, they were located in
NYU's "Downtown," or Washington Square, campus, which had first
opened in 1900 as the School of Commerce, Accounts, and Finance.
The most desirable undergraduate students were thought to be attending NYU's "Uptown" or University Heights campus in the Bronx, first
opened in 1894, where the School of Arts and Pure Science was located.
NYU did not sell this campus and move all undergraduate operations to
Washington Square until 1973. Efforts in the 1920s to force the chapter
to pledge men from "the Heights" were to no avail.

Naturally, the men of Kappa were highly insulted and resentful
when, in 1921, a "supervisory committee" was placed over them with
the power to veto their choice of members. "What is there that is lacking in Kappa that makes the Grand Council deem it necessary to appoint a supervisory committee over us?" demanded their corresponding
secretary. "Has the personnel of Kappa made such an abominable impression at the convention . . . so that now the Grand Council feels that
Kappa is going astray in its choice of men and requires a committee who
knows little or nothing of its internal affairs to pick its men for it?"[41] A
last-minute circulation by Kappa of a petition pleading for the national
membership to prevent this "unjust excommunication" did no good.[42]

At the fraternity's annual convention held in late December 1921, the charter of Phi Epsilon Pi's New York University chapter was revoked, and the members were ousted from the fraternity.

The Menorah Associations

Lest it be thought that negative intra-Jewish rhetoric and the Best Behavior syndrome were limited in the 1920s only to the Jewish fraternities, the records of the Intercollegiate Menorah Associations, their earliest organizational rivals, reveal similar tendencies to criticize and police collective Jewish behavior. Officers of the Menorah societies might criticize what they saw as the snobbishness of the Jewish Greeks, but they were equally capable of delivering sharp reprimands to their fellows. In one instance, Hyman S. Mayerson, president of Brown's Menorah Society in 1922, after recounting a successful year of lectures and Jewish study circles, also reported with pride the role Menorah had played in molding raucous and uncouth new Jewish students along more acceptable lines. "Another branch of work that we have stressed," Mayerson wrote, "has been what we call 'social service amongst the students.' We early realized that with the growing influx of Jewish men into the college, something had to be done if the Jewish man was to retain his position on the campus." He wrote:

> From the first day, we hammered the fact that every man must do his best to get into college activities, to meet the college man on his own ground, to command the respect of the student body in general. Good appearance, neatness, and restraint were stressed. The "pool-room nuisance," [a euphemism for lower-class vulgarity] common in many colleges and much more conspicuous at Brown, was first attacked. The men were not coerced or threatened, but at one of our open meetings to which every Jewish man was invited, we frankly discussed the matter. Several prominent graduates were present and the matter was settled to the satisfaction of all concerned. Every man was constituted a vigilance committee to see that no Jewish man could be accused of acting wrongly, etc. [43]

In a similar fashion, Marcus H. Rabinowitz, president of the Menorah Society at the University of Minnesota in 1921, reported a comparable menace that had surfaced at his school. "During the past three years the number of Jewish students on the campus has grown quite rapidly," Rabinowitz wrote.

The influx brought with it an element of Jewish men who were not as careful about their conduct on the campus as they might have been; an element which showed no interest in Menorah nor any other worthwhile influence on the campus. Their conduct especially at the Men's Union has brought forth criticism from the management of the union as well as from the office of the Dean of Student Affairs. In short they were jeopardizing the reputation of the entire Jewish community on the campus.

After two years of discussion, Rabinowitz reported, the threat was "neutralized" by a coalition of students, alumni, and one of the few Jewish faculty members, an assistant professor at the medical school who agreed to give an appropriate lecture to all incoming Jewish students. These leaders called a mass meeting and extended a special invitation to the objectionable students. Few came, but nevertheless the word spread that these students had best be on their guard:

> We had about 40 men present from the student body and about fifteen older graduates. About 35 men whose names the committee got in various ways were personally asked to come to the meeting but suspecting the purpose only about three were there, that is from that group. Nevertheless the meeting was successful and I thought very much worthwhile in that it took a definite step toward correcting a serious situation. Dr. [Moses] Barron took upon himself the duty of communicating with all Jewish students as soon as they matriculate and in that way we hope to not only eradicate the existing evil but prevent its recurrence. I felt that the problem was a serious one and I hope I was within the sphere of the Menorah idea in acting upon it.[44]

In her semiannual report of September 1923, Menorah national secretary Julietta Kahn, a recent graduate of the University of Oklahoma, complained of the "deterioration" of the Menorah societies and how, wherever they coexisted with the Jewish fraternities and sororities, Menorah inevitably became an organization of "low caste." In the same report, she noted that while fifty-one societies across the country were still active, in the past six months it had been necessary to suspend the Menorah Societies at the Universities of Chicago and Pennsylvania, "as the work done by these groups was not up to the standard required by the Intercollegiate, nor were the groups representative of the Jewish student body as a whole."[45] The terms "up to standard," and "representative" were of course also the bywords commonly used by officers to describe a successful Jewish fraternity chapter.

Response: Self-Defense Through Humor

For the members of college fraternities, doses of humor in their period-icals, heavily laced with parody, irony, and cynicism, provided members with some relief from the heavy communal responsibilities being placed upon their shoulders. They also served as an indirect method of criticiz-ing from the inside what they perceived as perverse fraternity rushing values. Arthur Donald (a.k.a. "Aidee") Schwarz (ZBT Columbia '20) in a typical parody, portrayed the Supreme Council officers' instant ac-ceptance of a candidate sight unseen because someone had learned that he was "having his tonsils repaired at one of the fashionable hospitals in his home town."[46] In a similar March 1922 column entitled "Sans Rhyme or Reason," George J. Hirsch of Sigma Alpha Mu declared that building up the fraternity's social standing was the supreme goal and that the best technique for doing so was to continually impress "the weaker sex," by first going "wild" over the most popular—as well as the most talkative—girl on the campus.

An adjustment of academic attitudes was also part of this for-mula for a chapter's success. Classes, quizzes, and finals should best be ignored as much as possible, Hirsch advised. "The girls hate 'grinds,' so for pity's sake, don't answer in class if called on, particularly if the question is in any way difficult. It's much easier to get over a zip on the record book, than the sneers of the better set in college" he wrote. "One should never hurry to class; 'ten thousand times better be late' than to give the impression that you actually wanted to be there." In addition, it was advisable to "shun the college library" and not even consider joining Phi Beta Kappa, because the men who were in it were too prone to study.

In addition to winning prestige for one's chapter through the campus dating and mating game, Hirsch also had several other con-crete suggestions on clothes, liquor consumption, and attitudes toward money. "Devote as much of your time as possible to clothes," he in-sisted. "You can't be too Brooksy. Sometimes it is worth your while to sit down at your study table and put in three or four hours in thinking up a new style to be worn on your campus. Think what it will mean to your chapter!" He also suggested having liquor in one's room, so that "some of the real big guns" could be invited to partake; "Unlim-ited prestige may be gained thus." It was also crucial to spend as much money as possible, with no regard for cost. "This cannot be overem-phasized," he wrote. "Even if your father has to sweat blood for each extra two bits you throw away, it's far better to have the old boy (always refer to him thus) do a little sweating than to have his son be classed as a piker."[47]

In a similar parody published in September 1923, Phi Epsilon Pi's David Paull of the Syracuse chapter, who later became a national officer, poked fun at what he saw as the fraternity's superficial criteria for membership along with its recent tendency to shun or expel anyone who did not live up to its "ideal model." This model could actually be mail-ordered from their national office and should be set up in the chapter house living room to make comparisons during Rush Week:

> Place the victim beside the model. The test must be fair, but thorough. Everything is cut and dried. Nothing must be left to snap judgment. Give your man the casual "once over." This is to enable you to focus properly and get the general impression of the specimen. Having arrived at the lower extremities, pause—is it a Rank Bros.' shoe he is wearing? Well, perhaps it is a P & G. Any other would put the candidate out of the running. We follow the natural upward trend to the suit—that graveyard of so many aspirants. Be very careful about the suit, frater, examine the label— Dukes Brothers, nothing else will do. Look for the four buttons—"that well-groomed look" you know. Should he appear in knickers, no further examination is necessary; but if he wear plebeian trousers, then direct this question at the candidate, "Have you or have you not knickerbockers; answer yes or no." Do not take an evasive answer. Remember, the future of the fraternity is at stake. . . .

Once satisfied that the candidate was wearing the proper clothing, members were required to judge personal appearance, financial solvency, popularity, political outlook, and to assure themselves of the candidate's lack of intellect. Facial blemishes and freckles barred the applicant immediately. A knock on the victim's skull should elicit the same hollow sound obtained by knocking on the head of the model mannequin. Meanwhile, the treasurer should be consulting either *Dun's* or *Bradstreet* to check the family's financial standing: "Dear old dad must be well rated," Paull wrote, "or how can the acorn hope to grow into a sturdy oak!" In the required oral examination, the candidate should be asked how much liquor he could hold, what was his record for eighteen holes, was he "100 percent American," and was he "at least distantly related to a department store."

The final "catch" question was to ascertain that the candidate was dyed-in-the wool political conservative and never laid eyes on the leading liberal magazine of the day: "Very quickly, ask him if he reads the *Nation*," Paull directed. "If he answers 'yes,' and is not willing to reform, then very politely kick him out of the house. If he answers 'what nation,' or simply 'no,'—then lock the doors, and rivet a pledge pin upon his lapel! For he is the true type, the salt of the earth, the comfort of your old age . . . Gird your loins, men of Phi Epsilon Pi! Go forth into your colleges with that vision of the true type ever before you."[48]

"What Have I Done?"

Not all Jewish fraternity members and spokesmen participated in the orgy of self-blame, group criticism, and deflective humor in the wake of the Harvard controversy or other attempts to limit or discourage the presence of Jewish students in American colleges. Considerable numbers wrote to defend their people, to voice their doubts on the success of the "pro-Semitism" philosophy, and to express their discomfort at the necessity of wielding the blackball against fellow Jews.

In the fall of 1927, ZBT Kalman R. Plessner (Missouri '20) openly criticized his fellow members for what he saw as the fraternity's "snobbery and conformism"—the tendency of members to copy and judge one another, and to dismiss men of "the poorer dorms" because they were not "our type" or in some ways refused to follow the crowd. "The individualist is probably disturbing at times, and we don't want to be disturbed," Plessner observed with bitterness:

> He is probably careless of some of the social conventions; and, above all else, our men must be social successes. His bridge game is likely to be poor, his dancing inadequate, his after dinner conversation forced. He didn't go to the right prep school, or summer camp, or dancing class; and, most objectionable of all, his parents didn't come from the right part of Europe. He's hardly the sort of fellow we'd like to take home for the holidays.[49]

Another ZBT in the fall of 1925 tried to explain with dispassion the dilemmas caused by applying external social criteria to their own people. "Because we have attempted to simplify our membership problem in drawing a racial line," he wrote, "we have opened up our selective system to a much more complicated problem than most fraternities face, for we find that in our race social lines are still distinctly thin and transparent, and, day in and day out, we are faced with the necessity of defining what sort of social fraternity a Jewish social fraternity can be." He continued:

> Our chapters disagree in their definitions. Some have decided that in order to be eligible for membership, a candidate must come of a family

which is beyond reproach, but, usually, Jewish "good families" owe their possession of this sobriquet to the presence of wealth and the ability of that commodity to purchase comforts, prestige and sleekness; and in a great majority of these cases that wealth is so recently acquired that is simply denotes the fact that the possessor's ancestors emigrated to this country just one generation sooner. Upon such a flimsy claim to social prestige can be based no definition of social worth which cannot be quite justly laughed at; yet there are other points of departure to social worth which our chapters have made use of. A candidate is not considered worthy unless his parents are of a definite original nationality; and there we run afoul of the flimsy demarcations that are drawn between the Portuguese Jew and the German Jew, the German Jew and the Polish Jew. A candidate is not considered worthy unless he worships in the proper places; and here we run afoul of the flimsy demarcation between the reformed Jew and the orthodox Jew.[50]

Another seventeen-year-old member of Zeta Beta Tau, writing pseudonymously in the fall of 1929, expressed his agony and disillusionment at the recent rushing season, upon realizing that he had virtually ruined a fellow sixteen-year-old Jew's life when he had refused him entrance into the fraternity. "What have I done, with my wildly wielded weapon of the blackball, swung in my 17-year-old wisdom with the vehemence of a Cossack's thong?" he lamented. "And for what? I did not like the cut of his coat or the part of his hair or his handclasp or his manner of speech. . . . I have blackballed a man who is of flesh and blood and bone and human sinew as much as I am, whose family is as decent and worthy as mine if not as refined and educated, for after all the step back to steerage is hardly more than two generations."[51]

Bernard A. Bergman, an Ohio State '16 Zeta Beta Tau graduate who as managing editor of the *Jewish Tribune* had directed the fraternity's survey of antisemitism on sixty-seven college campuses, warned that undergraduates were "merely falling into the attitude of the anti-Semite" when, in their long answers, they expressed views echoing the anti-Jewish writings of the day. "Loud Jews, vulgar Jews, Jews who haven't gotten on to American ways, Jews whose mannerisms are offensive, who don't know how to act, even 'typical Jews,' these and nothing else are the cause of anti-Semitism in our higher seats of learning," he observed in his write-up of the survey published in March 1923. How could these students direct such attitudes toward their "Jewish brothers" who, through accident of birth and no fault of their own, did not find themselves in the same fortunate position as their critics?

"Most of us, I suppose all of us, were born in America," Bergman observed. "Many of our fathers are also native-born. But when we indict the newly arrived immigrant, or the boy who hasn't grown up in the social environment in which we were lucky enough to land, are we playing fair? How did our fathers or our grandfathers disport themselves when they came to America? I doubt if they were any more polished than the loud and vulgar college students we now condemn." It was precisely those Jews and their families whose culture might be far greater than their own, who had "fought and faced death" for the sake of their religion and race and some of whom were even now "building up Palestine with their raw, bleeding hands, the most glorious adventure in idealism the world has ever witnessed." Should they not be willing to extend the helping hand of brotherhood to these people, "rather than spit upon them?"[52]

Bergman also went so far as to express direct criticism of national leader Harold Riegelman's philosophy of "pro-Semitism." "[He] hopes, through Zeta Beta Tau, to show the non-Jewish world just what the Jew is, and thus gradually eliminate anti-Semitism. And now the Jew turns out to be an anti-Semite!" he charged. Jews should not give in to such general excuses for anti-Jewish hatred, he advised, for they were only a pretext; in reality, the same hatred was directed toward all of them. "Can't we be big enough and broad enough to break away from this narrowness of vision, which is so common among those of our people who have lost their vision and their soul, who will stop at no humiliation in order to gain a Gentile smile or a Gentile pat on the back, when in reality their servility wins them in time only a Gentile kick in the pants?"

Similar objections to internal antisemitism were voiced by Benjamin D. Salinger (Columbia '21) in May 1923. The theme of his article was the use of the term "too Jewish," apparently an epithet of scorn and resentment often used against one's fellow Jews. In fact "Jewish jokes" and the expression "Kike," according to his observations, were far more widely used in Jewish circles than in Gentile.[53] What was it that Gentiles and some Jews found so "obnoxious" about these "too-Jewish" Jews? If there was such a thing as "the Ghetto type," then collegians should remember that the ghetto, along with the undesirable characteristics it fostered, had been forced upon the Jews by non-Jews. If many of them fit the generalization of the "Semitic type of features"—a dark complexion, curly hair, and a prominent nose—would any Jew have scorned those features three thousand years ago when they were a "proud and independent people"? And what of Jews who spoke with accents and resorted to foreign words and phrases? So indeed did anyone who emigrated to a country late in life. And what of charges that the Jew was "unsociable, unmannerly, ill-bred, miserly, clannish, ostentatious, cowardly"? These, and every vice known to man could justly be ascribed to some Jews—and, in Salinger's opinion, to many Gentiles. The Jew simply served as the Gentile's convenient personification of human faults.

As to sneering at Orthodox Jewish practices, Salinger denounced such attitudes that would deny to any group of people the cherished American freedom to worship in any way they chose. Indeed, the "Ghetto Jew" with beard and sidelocks whose pride and faith were central to his life might be superior to the German Jewish upper classes, or those Americans who sought to escape their identity. Certain truly Jewish characteristics, Salinger insisted, would always outlive the ghetto—namely, superior intellect, intuition, earnestness, a sense of real values, and personal intensity. After listing some of the major Jewish prophets, intellectuals, and philanthropists throughout the centuries, in a stirring peroration, he warned that Jews who sought to assimilate would still be labeled as Jews and would also forfeit the characteristics that made them a superior people:

> If the Jew cannot be inspired by these examples, if the term "Jew" is repulsive to him, then let him cease to be a Jew. Let him straighten out his curly locks and his curved nose, let him become a Christian Scientist, or an Ethical Culturist, or a Unitarian, or a Protestant, or a Catholic, or a Mohammedan, or a Parsee—let him so completely assimilate himself that he will not wince when his friends tell him the story of an ugly, miserly Jew—and then, above all, let him guard his actions and his words so that he may not commit an indiscretion and be labeled as a "damned Jew."
>
> And he *will* be a "damned Jew"—self-damned, for he has lost the truly Jewish traits as well as those Gentile-given Ghetto characteristics. . . . Had he kept his sense of moral values he would have seen that he was, ostrich-like, hiding his nose, selling his tradition, his heritage, for the outward acceptance of himself socially by the Gentile world. . . .
>
> Damned Jew!
>
> The Jew is damned only in so far as he damns himself—he will be blessed when "too Jewish" is an inspiration to him rather than a slur.[54]

Despite Salinger's stirring words, an era where the term "Jew" would become more of a blessing than a curse was nowhere imminent among the masses of the American Jewish population in the 1920s.

Somehow, in the face of all obstacles in their path, American Jews struggled through the barriers, polished their accents, behavior, and dress, got their educations at any institution that would take them, established themselves economically, and climbed steadily up the ladder of social mobility.

And yet, as the prosperity of the decade collapsed in the New York stock market crash of October 1929 and the ominous signs of Fascism and life-threatening antisemitism appeared in Europe, the prospect that young people would be able to view their Jewish identity as a blessing appeared bleak. So too did the prospect that Jews could ever win group security by improving their manners and educating their fellow citizens. Indeed, the 1930s gave American Jews reason to fear that despite individual achievement and a constant striving to become part of the American mainstream, both they and their entire people would be damned no matter what they did.

Chapter 7

"The Idea of Quitting Is Abhorrent"

Challenges during the Great Depression

The golden age of the American college fraternity was followed all too soon by some of the system's most precarious years. For thousands of young Americans the chance to attend or to finish college was jeopardized by the spiraling economic disaster set into motion with the New York stock market crash of October 1929. For seniors or recent graduates, the insecure situation of their fraternity houses was among the least of their worries. The sight of millions of able-bodied Americans out of work and the fear that school did not guarantee them any job caused bewilderment, despair, disillusionment, and demoralization.

Faith in the value of a college education inculcated from childhood could be shattered. One recent ZBT graduate in 1931 referred to it all as a "four-year loaf." College, he wrote in the fraternity's quarterly, was a useless enterprise, and did nothing to train students to take on real jobs. All it promised was a four-year break before being flung out into the world to compete with others for survival.[1] Others accused their contemporaries of not making the most of a precious education. "At this writing 8 million young people in the U.S. are unemployed, and 35 percent of college graduates between 25 and 29 have no jobs," wrote Missouri undergraduate Kalman B. Druck in the spring of 1936. "Yet too many students in college are there just for the ride, interested only in movies and social affairs. . . . Is it any wonder that graduates need diplomas to drive trucks or to get ten-dollar-a-week jobs?"[2]

The bitterness and disillusionment of the Depression years, along with the formative experiences of its college-age youth, were especially well documented in an impressionistic autobiography entitled "We Grow Up, 1915–1938." Jerome L. Schwartz, a 1937 Ohio State ZBT graduate, recalled as a toddler in 1917 being told that his papa and older brother were "going away across the sea to make the world safe for democracy so that when you grow up there won't be any more wars for you to face." In 1918, the boy played at being a soldier, watched the Armistice Day parades from his perch atop the shoulders of adults, and, thought happily, "everything was going to be fine now. The war was over. The reign of evil was past." In 1919, the little boy played with mud pies while others talked about Progressivism. In 1920, while "white-hooded men burned crosses in the South," he and his friends munched popcorn and watched the "magical movies." Next came memories of the Roaring Twenties, the awkward entrance into adolescence, and the call to success.

Following the stock market crash, however, the teenager came to fear that all his elders had been telling him all these years was nothing but lies:

> 1929—The great American balloon burst. Suicides, bankruptcies. But this is still the land of milk and honey! Punch harder. . . . 1931—No, the high school officials said, your class can't have dances, you can't have an annual. People are starving they said . . . You can't dance when people need bread. . . . 1932—Was this never going to stop? We heard all about the glories of the last generation. But you and your generation must bury your heads in your pillows . . . you must drink in the darkness. 1933—a pounding in our veins, a longing in our hearts, but the world was cold. . . . 1934—The bank failed. No big Eastern University for you, son. Go to the State University. You're lucky. Many boys are starving. 1935—Crawling into a warm, academic cloister, feeling the soft touch of books, a desire to lull yourself into forgetfulness of the world outside. . . . 1936—Moonlit nights and a girl. . . . 1937—the firm clasp of friendly hands, and the desire never to let go. . . .[3]

Upon graduation, Schwartz found himself facing a life for which he had been neither prepared in college nor reared for by his family. "1938—You had been a success in college. . . . They patted you on the back, gave you honors, handed you a Phi Beta Kappa key that was excellent to clean your fingernails. They poured more success down your throat. They fashioned you in the image of a lost generation. Then they shoved you into a world that had changed. So pound the pavements, fellow! Slave away! You and your generation have been kicked in the face."[4]

Hard Times and the "House" Plan

For the executive secretaries and officers of the Jewish fraternities in the early years of the Great Depression, the outlook for their organizations and their dependent institutions at first appeared bleak. Even the academic giants Northwestern University and the University of Chicago were seriously considering consolidation into a single "Chicago Northwestern University" in the fall of 1933 as a means of remaining solvent.[5] Fewer men could now enter college because of restricted family budgets, fewer jobs were available for students who needed to work, and fewer students who made it to campus could afford the relative luxury of membership in a fraternity.[6] Many of those who were already members faced the prospect of being forced to drop out and go to work in the hope that they could save up enough to resume their education later.[7]

Membership and real estate were the most urgent problems facing all college Greek-letter groups, as payments became due for large houses purchased in more prosperous times. At the University of Michigan, one of the most important fraternity schools in the country, the problem was acute. With sixty national fraternities represented on the campus, at least 1,150 new pledges were needed just to fill the existing houses. However, in the fall of 1933, only 400 applied during the customary rush week, and the top ranking twenty fraternities snapped up more than half of these.[8]

Bad economic times also led, directly and indirectly, to other changes in higher education that were to the detriment of college fraternities. For example, during the formative years of the subsystem in the 1910s, it had been possible to enter certain professional schools directly from secondary school. Long Island Medical College had thus supported active chapters of both Zeta Beta Tau and Sigma Alpha Mu, while the Columbia School of Pharmacy, and not Columbia College, was technically the founding place of the Jewish college fraternity Tau Epsilon Phi. By 1934 however, professional schools were both reducing their Jewish enrollments and requiring a BA for admission. These changes brought about the extinction of SAM's Long Island Medical Chapter. Those fraternity-minded students able to get in either already belonged to another undergraduate social fraternity or else joined one of the several Jewish medical fraternities upon their matriculation. They did not join SAM.[9]

An additional Depression-era peril for all fraternities was the growing unpopularity of the Greek system among college officials, even those who had themselves joined fraternities as undergraduates. The forces that denounced fraternities as agents of class and religious divisions, a detriment to the development of academic life, an endangerment to life and limb because of hazing practices, and a loss of room and board income that might better be paid directly to their institutions, were gaining ground. In a pathbreaking speech before the twenty-third annual session of the National Interfraternity Conference in New York in November, 1931, Henry Suzzallo, then president of the prestigious Carnegie Foundation for the Advancement of Teaching, warned the assembled Greek officials of this new development. Unless fraternities became more "intellectual," raised their cultural and academic standards, and cooperated with their colleges more, he declared, the "house" or residential college system that had long marked English universities would soon replace the collegiate Greek system across America.[10]

Indeed, from the late 1920s and through the rest of the century the predominant trend in American higher education was to discourage or weaken the power of Greek-letter fraternities. This could be done by building dormitories and house plans, feeding students in common halls, and requiring that students who wished to join chapters defer for either a term or an entire year. The American educational elite took the lead in this process at Harvard and Yale where, as ZBT's Lee Dover noted in 1936, "the introduction of the House Plan at these universities has practically eliminated the fraternities and most of the clubs."[11] Jewish fraternity officials expressed their displeasure that Jewish philanthropy sometimes played a major role in making this abolishment of fraternities possible. In a discussion between Maurice Jacobs and the president of Phi Epsilon Pi's Chicago Alumni Club, both agreed that "Chicago was a good fraternity school in the past until Julius Rosenwald [president of Sears, Roebuck, and Company] foolishly gave them money for these new dormitories."[12]

Making Do

Jewish fraternities were, and would remain, more vulnerable to such external challenges than the non-Jewish fraternities. At the time of the stock market crash, all but one group in the Jewish Greek subsystem were less than thirty years old. The size of their endowments and membership rolls, as well as the quality of their housing, could not approach that of the older Gentile groups. For example, the leading Gentile college fraternities Beta Theta Pi (founded 1839), Phi Delta Theta (1848),

Sigma Chi (1855), Sigma Alpha Epsilon (1856), and Alpha Tau Omega (1865) all enjoyed endowments approaching or surpassing three million dollars. Their membership rolls ranged from 25,000 to 40,000 members, many of them individually more than that of all the Jewish fraternities combined. By contrast, of the fourteen national Jewish men's fraternities that were members of the National Interfraternity Conference in 1933 only Zeta Beta Tau's endowment reached seven figures ($1,800,000). Three (Pi Lambda Phi, Sigma Alpha Mu, and Tau Epsilon Phi) were worth between half and one million, while the remaining ten were worth half a million or less. Two of the youngest ones, Alpha Mu Sigma and Sigma Lambda Pi (neither would survive the Depression) had initiated fewer than a thousand members.[13]

Consequently, chapters of Jewish fraternities were especially susceptible to dissolution or the need for mergers or absorption by stronger groups in order to survive. At the beginning of the 1930–1931 academic year, for example, twenty percent of Zeta Beta Tau's original chapters and twenty-five percent of Phi Epsilon Pi's were listed as "inactive."[14] By 1934, Phi Sigma Delta had had to withdraw from Boston University, the University of Vermont, and Lehigh University. It was also on the verge of losing its Columbia chapter, where the institution of selective admissions had sharply decreased the number of Jewish students. In the same year, Phi Beta Delta had closed its chapter at the University of Colorado, while officers of their University of Denver chapter were planning to surrender their charter.

Tau Delta Phi, itself a small and relatively young Jewish fraternity founded in 1910 at City College, absorbed most of the remnants of the even smaller and younger Omicron Alpha Tau, a fraternity known for its adherence to traditional Jewish dietary laws in its houses. The remaining OAT chapters absorbed into Tau Delta Phi included Rutgers, NYU, Marquette University, and Cornell, while chapters at Syracuse and University of Pennsylvania were absorbed by Phi Epsilon Pi and Phi Beta Delta. Zeta Beta Tau, after some struggle, finally gave up on its "Alpha" chapter at City College, while Alpha Epsilon Pi was discontinuing its University of Virginia chapter. Also in 1934, the tiny University of Rochester-based Kappa Nu, with over a quarter of its original chapters gone, was dropped from the NIC for its failure to pay a $35 bill due since 1932.[15]

For those chapters of modest means that did remain, economizing became the order of the day. Having members wait on their own tables, do laundry, and keep the house and yard clean was one way to "make do." At the Sigma Alpha Mu chapter at Indiana University in Bloomington in April 1935, for example, the president dismissed all employees except "Mrs. Barton, a Jewess," who received $27 per week as their cook. One outside student received free meals for dishwashing, two members got rebates for waiting tables and pledges and freshmen made beds and cleaned the rooms. Twenty-seven boys lived with inadequate shower facilities in what was meant to be a private family dwelling, and the basement served as their dining room. The members bore their burdens with few complaints, the chapter president reported to the national office. In addition, he voiced his gratitude for the tax exemption on fraternity property granted by the State of Indiana as well as the university's insistence that fraternity bills be paid if members wanted to avoid having their grades held up.[16]

Other Jewish local fraternities during the Depression never even considered "going national" and were content to render service to their members within the confines of one campus. On these lower levels of the Greek-letter hierarchy, members lived on the edge of physical survival. A member of Kappa Beta, a Jewish local at New York State College for Teachers in Albany, recalled in the early 1930s riding up to school the evening after Yom Kippur in a friend's chicken truck, with only $25 in his pocket. Only the fellowship of Kappa Beta, he recalled, allowed him to stay for four years. Members pooled their resources and lived together in a rented house on Western Avenue in Albany, where they maintained a kosher kitchen. A Jewish woman from the town cooked a kosher dinner for them each day, while the sisterhoods of the local synagogues donated old furniture. Members made it through the Depression by finding jobs for one another, whether as shoe salesmen, waiters, day laborers, or anything else available. Kappa Beta continued as a Jewish fraternity until after the end of World War II, when it dissolved. Its alumni, however, continued to gather for reunions for decades afterward.[17]

Mad Rush

The problem of too many Jewish fraternities chasing too few potential members caused the old techniques of "rushing," or recruiting new members, to reach new levels of intensity during the Great Depression. At the University of Illinois for example, Sigma Alpha Mu's chapter appealed to the national organization for help in the spring and summer of 1939 when it discovered that only 14 upperclassmen would be returning in the fall—half the number required to maintain their house. Declaring that the outlook was "serious but not hopeless," the national officers responded with a series of Illinois alumni rushing parties held in June around the country. These included events at the Mt. Vernon Country Club sponsored by the fraternity's Westchester and North Shore of Long Island Alumni Clubs. This location indicated the importance of the New York metropolitan area as a source for Jewish students at Champaign-Urbana. At these gatherings, SAM officers directed outstanding candidates toward Illinois with the understanding that the fraternity would accept them once they got there. With these extra efforts, SAM's Illinois chapter was saved for another year.[18]

Also at the University of Illinois, in 1937 Phi Epsilon Pi chapter members reported keeping lists of boys from "feeder" areas who would not be ready for college for another ten years. At the University of Pennsylvania, members reported getting one of their numbers to date the secretary of the admissions office in order to obtain unofficial information on the Jewish students of the incoming freshman class.[19] The Penn chapter officer's manual of 1938 called upon members to mobilize their prep school, city club, country club, and Jewish summer camp contacts. Freshmen from such backgrounds would fit the fraternity's social profile and presumably be able to assume its financial obligations. Young men who had been counselors in Jewish summer camps were considered especially good material.[20] As soon as the new class was sent its acceptance letters, a list of the new students was obtained either directly from the registrar's office or through the good offices of a sympathetic Gentile dean. Thereupon, alumni and undergraduate members combed it for Jewish names.[21] If investigation revealed that these men were of "fraternity caliber," then they would be sent the organization's literature and invited for local rushing parties and house visits.

If a suitable candidate did not agree to join the fraternity at that point, then the window of opportunity was still open during his first day of arrival at a new school. The Phi Epsilon Pi national Rushing Manuals for 1937 and 1941 suggested that as many rushees as possible be brought to school by active members and alumni and assisted through the red tape of registration. To ferry students back and forth from the train station and also to make a good impression, Phi Epsilon Pi's University of Illinois Rush Chairman in 1937 stressed the importance of members begging, borrowing, or stealing cars to be used during rush week. "*Get that car*—somewhere, somehow," he wrote. "If your car doesn't have an engine in it, we can at least set it out in front of the house for appearances' sake."[22] If candidates needed a place to stay, the Manual warned, under no circumstances should a good prospect be allowed to sign a rooming house lease. If he later joined the fraternity, it would cost too much for the chapter to take the lease over and besides, as one sample letter put it, "there are always plenty of good rooms these days."[23]

Jewish sororities used similar tactics, although since there were many more young women eager to join (often at the urging of their families) and far fewer places for them within the Greek system, the intensity of the courtship of prospective members was far less and the necessity of having a personal recommendation by a member, preferably a mother, aunt, or sister, much greater. There were never more than four truly national Jewish sororities in the entire United States and Canada, and by long campus custom and National Panhellenic rules chapters were smaller and thus had to be more selective in their membership. Rushing for the Jewish sororities was more a matter of eager young women donning their best dresses and attending a weeklong course of teas and dinners. Those who did not pass muster would be cut from consideration.

Economic crisis or no, the national sororities still had their pick. In its own rushing manual for 1937, for example, Sigma Delta Tau suggested a coding system of three different flowers to be drawn on the rushees' name tags pinned to their dresses: a rose was for girls who were definitely wanted, a violet was for those whose desirability was doubtful, and a jonquil meant that they knew almost nothing about the girl and that all active members should do what they could to find out as much about her as possible.[24] Still the competition between sororities for the most desirable candidates, especially between Alpha Epsilon Phi and Sigma Delta Tau (whom the former referred to as "Cedars"), could become heated in the 1930s.

In Alpha Epsilon Phi sorority, national officers considered the technique of "colonization" as a way of beating their competitors to a particular campus. The national sorority would pay a young woman's tuition and fees on the condition that she attend or transfer to a certain school and gather members of a new chapter around her. In one such case, Elizabeth Eldridge, National Dean (or President) of Alpha Epsilon Phi urged in April 1935 that a paid colonizer be sent to the University of Alabama before a rival chapter of Sigma Delta Tau could take root.[25] In June 1936, she similarly recommended paying a colonizer as well as using alumnae to divert southern women toward Louisiana State University at Baton Rouge. LSU, she reported, had recently enjoyed spectacular growth under the legislative support of "Kingfish" Senator Huey P. Long as part of his plan to get revenge against New Orleans's

Tulane University, an elite bastion of political opposition that he despised. LSU, she pointed out, was a logical haven for young Jewish women who wished to join Alpha Epsilon Phi at Sophie Newcomb College, Tulane's sister institution, but who had little hope of finding a place there. Even through the darkest years of the Depression AEPhi's Newcomb chapter was so selective and drew so many legacies—that is, daughters, sisters, and other relatives of older members—that it constantly turned applicants away.[26]

The oversupply of suitable young women at Newcomb College was also a factor in the suggestion of Eleanor G. Reinach of St. Paul in 1938 that someone be sent to colonize the University of Minnesota. As director of the sorority's midwestern province, she knew of a member at Newcomb who was originally from Minnesota and might be persuaded to leave and to return to her home state. In addition, she knew of another Alpha Epsilon Phi student at the University of Illinois who might be willing to transfer to Minnesota to finish her education if the sorority were willing to give her financial aid for doing so.[27]

Quotas and Anti-Jewish Discrimination: Dartmouth, Syracuse, McGill, Lehigh, Duke, and Purdue

In all, despite the need for belt-tightening everywhere, the Great Depression did not cause immediate harm to the overall structure of the Jewish Greek subsystem. Both Jewish/Jewish and Jewish/Gentile discrimination continued to feed its expansion and maintenance throughout the 1930s. Exclusion from a normal campus life and the need for Jews to have their own portal of access to the Greek system was as great as ever, if not greater. In a 1932 survey of campuses with more than five Jews where Phi Epsilon Pi did not yet have a chapter, Maurice Jacobs reported that out of seventy colleges responding, fifty-one did not admit them to "general" fraternities under any circumstances. In eight schools—Alabama Polytechnic, Brown, Kansas, Kentucky, Purdue, Washington State, and Williams—Jews were accepted "seldom" or "occasionally." In only nine cases was the answer an unqualified "yes"—Amherst, Buffalo, Colgate, University of Chicago, University of Denver, Marquette, Nebraska, UCLA, and the University of Washington.[28]

On individual campuses, the introduction or arbitrary intensification of Jewish quotas and admissions restrictions did not help the subsystem expand and, as they had in the 1920s, could cause havoc when the number of potential fraternity initiates was reduced suddenly and unexpectedly. Jewish officials in the early 1930s reacted with special alarm in the case of Dartmouth College, an important and prestigious fraternity school. In the past it had supported three national Jewish fraternities (Phi Epsilon Pi, Pi Lambda Phi, and Sigma Alpha Mu) and had 186 Jewish men in its student body in 1932. However, in the fall of 1934 its Dean of Freshmen, perhaps wishing to reassure Dartmouth's Gentile alumni, stated in the Dartmouth alumni magazine that the unusually large "Jewish delegation" of 75 men who had entered in the fall of 1930 was now "back to normal." "Back to normal," as it turned out, meant cut in half to 37 freshmen, a number further reduced in 1935 to thirty.[29] By that point, with all its upperclassmen graduating, Sigma Alpha Mu was no longer able to compete with Pi Lambda Phi, and the "Sammies" were forced to close their Dartmouth chapter.[30]

The rushing outlook at Dartmouth was also complicated, ironically, by the unusual willingness of the Gentile fraternities to accept some half-dozen of the Jews' most outstanding Greek-letter candidates. These included football team captain Philip Julian Glazar '34, who was accepted into Alpha Delta Phi, and star ice hockey player John Benjamin Wolff Jr. '32 of Hempstead, New York, who was offered membership in the well-known "Dekes," or Delta Kappa Epsilon.[31]

In 1937, the Jewish enrollment at Syracuse University, another strong fraternity school with a sizable New York area contingent, was also being drastically reduced. There the SAM chapter was so entrenched, enjoying such loyal alumni backing along with free and clear alumni ownership of the house, that it was able to persevere in the face of competition.[32] Other chapters were not as fortunate. At McGill University in Montreal, where five Jewish fraternity chapters—Zeta Beta Tau, Pi Lambda Phi, Sigma Alpha Mu, Tau Epsilon Phi, and Omicron Alpha Tau—had flourished in the 1920s, the authorities reduced Jewish enrollment to twenty-five students per year. ZBT desperately fought to stay on campus by abandoning its customary selectivity and pledging every available Jewish male. At the University of Toronto, fortunately, fraternity officials were relieved to report that the Jewish enrollment was undiminished. Even so, the high cost of coal was too much for the members of Toronto's Sigma Alpha Mu chapter to bear. National alumni officers criticized the younger members for their weakness in surrendering their house and meeting in local members' homes rather than enduring the discomfort of gathering in an unheated building during the winter.[33]

In another such case of sudden reduction, Lehigh University in Bethlehem, Pennsylvania, which had formerly supported five Jewish fraternities, so limited the number of entering Jewish freshmen in 1934 that two chapters were forced to close their doors. At Duke University, where in 1932 Maurice Jacobs reported the Jewish enrollment was being restricted to three percent, the faculty assembly actually voted to allow no more than one Jewish fraternity on campus.[34] At Purdue University in Lafayette, Indiana, the Sigma Alpha Mu chapter faced a fight for its existence. Only fifteen Jewish men were entering in the fall of 1935, and their competitor Tau Epsilon Phi (the "Teps") would be rushing the same incoming students. At Purdue direct quotas were not as much of an obstacle as the perception that engineering, the school's specialty, had become a hopeless profession for Jewish men.[35]

Despite these difficulties, SAM Purdue alumni in the Lafayette, Indianapolis, and Dayton, Ohio, areas eagerly agreed to do what they could to support the dying chapter. "The idea of quitting at Purdue is abhorrent to them," reported James C. Hammerstein, SAM's executive secretary, in May 1935. "Only five years ago there were eighty-five Jews at that university and Sigma Eta [their Greek-letter name for the chapter] was sitting on top of the world."[36] As in the case of Phi Epsilon Pi's Illinois alumni, the loyal Sammies alumni of Purdue contributed funds and threw rushing parties throughout the area, encouraging good candidates to apply to the school with the promise of membership to Sigma Alpha Mu if they got in. Through these efforts, the chapter was saved for another year.

Presidential Refusal at the College of William and Mary

Aside from declining numbers, presidential or senior administrative opposition, as had been the case at Brown University, could still prevent Jewish chapters from establishing themselves on a campus at all. The "small Ivy" was as resistant as ever. Twenty-five Jewish students at Bowdoin College in 1932, for example, were reportedly eager to form a chapter of Phi Epsilon Pi. However, as Maurice Jacobs reported with regret in his December 1932 survey, President Kenneth C. M. Sills of that campus "at the present time does not care to have a Jewish group on his campus." Amherst and Trinity Colleges, he observed, also "have made it quite plain that they will not harbor Jewish fraternities," and the officially nonsectarian Pi Lambda Phi reportedly had not been successful in its efforts to maintain even clandestine chapters at Amherst and Bowdoin.[37]

Another small and eminent institution, the College of William and Mary in Williamsburg, Virginia, had a student body of 3,000 in

1933, including one hundred Jewish men divided between two fraternities and twenty unorganized Jewish women. The campus was ripe for the formation of a national Jewish sorority chapter, and when the president did not raise any major objections, Alpha Epsilon Phi moved in to help the young women form one. Yet they and the sorority's national officers were in for a grave disappointment that year when President Julian A.C. Chandler unexpectedly withdrew his support.

The relative autocracy that President Chandler enjoyed at William and Mary presented a special problem when protesting his decision. There was no recourse to a Board of Overseers, an alumni association, or some other body that could serve as a counterweight to his authority. Much of the campus was Chandler's personal property and he ruled it with an iron hand, coming down with special severity on the women students, who had been admitted only since 1918. His authority extended to every aspect of college life. In her 1933 investigation of William and Mary, Elizabeth Eldridge noted with surprise that conventional dates and even visits between male and female students were either forbidden outright or strictly regulated by the president himself. With rare exceptions women students could walk with men students only along two specified paths that led not more than one block from the campus.[38]

With only one theater, no dances, no business district beyond the "first block," and dormitory curfew at ten, the sorority houses, in Eldridge's opinion, were the only things that kept the young women of William and Mary from "dying of boredom."[39] At least, as she observed, the rule of William and Mary's personal "Mussolini," as she described him, had some advantages for the students' religious development. A visit to Sabbath services at the local Reform Temple revealed every Jewish female student there, most with dates. The cause, Eldridge surmised, was not overwhelming piety but the chance to escape the suffocating confines of the campus and to interact with members of the opposite sex. "It is something to do, it is an excuse to walk past the 'first block,' it is a chance to date," she reported to her fellow officers. "Unpopular rabbis, consult Dr. Chandler!"[40]

At first the college president had granted his verbal approval to the sorority—on condition that he also have final approval of its housing arrangements. Lucille Fritz, the William and Mary undergraduate slated to become the AEPhi chapter president, thereupon inspected the home Chandler offered them and requested two improvements: first, an outside paint job and second, an additional shower, since the building had only one bathroom. The President's reaction revealed that his earlier verbal agreement had been deceptive. His college was financially unable to provide these "numerous repairs and additional equipment," he insisted, nor could it provide the young women with another, better-equipped house. Furthermore, he could not "dream" of making "the Jewish sorority" so unhappy and discontent as to deny them physical quarters when all the other women's groups had houses. Therefore, Alpha Epsilon Phi could not come to the William and Mary campus at all. [41]

Protests that they did not need an actual house to begin operations at William and Mary only increased the firmness of his refusal. "I am not willing that you should organize a group at the College, because there is no house available for them," President Chandler wrote. "I do not mean to assume an unfriendly attitude in this matter, but I know conditions so well here, and I feel that you would see the wisdom of my decision if you knew conditions as I do." [42] Lucille Fritz expressed her discouragement and anger to her national officers and confirmed their suspicions that prejudice, and not finances, were at issue. "The demands made were not numerous nor unjust, as you know," she wrote in May 1933. "The fact that the college is not 'well off' financially has nothing to do with the house, for it is Chandler's personal property. It seems that he just won't tolerate a Jewish sorority on campus—he could have said so immediately without getting us so excited. What steps are to be taken next?" [43]

President James L. McConaughy of Wesleyan University

Wesleyan University located in Middletown, Connecticut, was another venue where the force of presidential opposition to Jewish fraternities and the distress that it caused was especially notable. It was, as Maurice Jacobs noted in a report to Phi Epsilon Pi's national governing body in December 1932, "in every sense a fraternity school, with the independent man out of the running." More than eighty percent of its all-male student body lived in some of the most spacious fraternity homes in the country. Yet the Gentile fraternities categorically excluded Jews, while the administration forbade the establishment of any Jewish Greek-letter organizations or clubs. Maurice Jacobs recalled his own student days when he was president of his Phi Epsilon Pi chapter at the University of Maine in 1917. A group of boys attempting to form a Jewish fraternity chapter at Methodist-sponsored Wesleyan were promptly "paddled by vigilantes" and told that Wesleyan was a Protestant college. In all the time since then the only permissible organized Jewish activity on campus was a weekly Sunday meeting in place of the required chapel service.[44]

Simmering discontent erupted in mid-February of 1932 when Austin M. Fisher '32, a senior, submitted a column to the biweekly *Wesleyan Argus* entitled "Is Wesleyan Fair to the Jews?" He protested the fraternity exclusion and called for Wesleyan to exercise "greater honesty" in its admissions practices. Officials, he insisted, should frankly inform Jewish applicants either verbally or in the college catalogue that they would find no admittance to the fraternities and virtually no social life on campus once they matriculated.[45] Austin himself, it developed, was Jewish on his father's side only and had suffered the indignity of being depledged from the Gentile fraternity Alpha Delta Phi in his freshman year when his origins became known. He had finally been accepted by another well-known Gentile fraternity, Sigma Chi, and had spent most of his years at Wesleyan not associating with the Jewish students. However, in his senior year, about to leave the school behind, he felt compelled to take a public stand on the issue.[46]

Such blatant accusations by a student on a subject most often treated in a hush-hush manner invited media attention, and the story spread quickly to the Hartford and New York City newspapers. Ever alert to any opportunity to organize at Wesleyan, Phi Epsilon Pi's Connecticut alumni read the stories and determined that the time was ripe for another attempt. They gambled that in the face of such adverse publicity, Wesleyan's administration would not dare to take a public stand and bar all Jewish groups. The following Sunday, the fraternity's local alumni association openly invited the entire Wesleyan Jewish student body for a meeting in the basement of Middletown's YMCA to discuss the formation of a chapter. Eighteen potential new members showed up.[47] Possibly the alumni had already begun quiet, renewed organizational activity that term, and Fisher's letter was prompted by it.

In public the controversy continued, drawing immediate administrative reaction from President James L. McConaughy, who served as the head of Wesleyan from 1925 to 1943. Replying to Fisher's letter in both the campus and local newspapers, he insisted that the student was exaggerating his university's responsibilities. Wesleyan could neither pledge boys to fraternities nor regulate student social life. Moreover, the president himself had "often intimated to prospective students of the Jewish faith, or to their parents, that the boys are not likely to find satisfactory social contacts in Wesleyan fraternities." Three-quarters of

Wesleyan's Jewish students in 1932 lived at home, he pointed out, either in Middletown or its surrounding cities, and thus were "scarcely in a position to be affected by the conditions of which Mr. Fisher speaks." "The remainder," McConaughy wrote, "I believe are well acquainted with the facts as they exist here, and do not come here with any expectations of entering fraternity life." His statement concluded with a reference to Wesleyan's significant concession in exempting Jewish students from Sunday Chapel services.[48]

On the campus itself, not all Wesleyan's Jewish students were happy with Austin Fisher's outspokenness. M. M. Resnikoff '34, who had attended the Phi Epsilon Pi alumni organizational meeting, condemned Fisher in the pages of the *Argus* as a "a false prophet who tries to cleanse his own soul without remembering the welfare of his campus brethren" and who "stirred up the forces of prejudice and flung Wesleyan Jewish hearts into the flames." More public advertisement of Jewish woes was the last thing they needed when their woes were already public enough, he wrote. Resnikoff claimed that he spoke for the majority of his fellow Jewish students when he counseled patience and a spirit of reconciliation. "The constitutions of some fraternities are not fair," Resnikoff agreed. "Remember, though, both Jew and Gentile have clannish prejudices of their own. Give time a chance. In the meantime, we shall be patient, and we shall forgive those, real or imaginary, who wound us."[49] Ultimately, he concluded, both Jew and Gentile must "learn to laugh at the prejudices of each other so heartily that the heavens will fall in shame and the common Apostle of Peace shall come forth, bearing the scroll of Tolerance." "This is no occasion for War," he observed. "This is an occasion to learn how to laugh!"[50]

President McConaughy, however, was in no mood to laugh. Following publication of Resnikoff's letter, he invited the writer for a personal interview, having in the meantime gotten word of the Wesleyan Jewish students' attempts to organize a fraternity chapter on his campus. According to Resnikoff's account of the meeting in March 1932, McConaughy stated that Jews were at Wesleyan only by tolerance and that his university would not permit the establishment of any distinct Jewish group. Any attempt to establish a fraternity or club under any guise, he warned, would result in Wesleyan cutting down the number of Jewish students admitted. Furthermore, McConaughy claimed that while he was willing to meet with rabbis or Jewish representatives to discuss the general situation, "Wesleyan did not need any outside advice or suggestions as to how to treat or handle their individual problems."[51]

According to another student's report on the president's ire, Herman E. Colitz '34 (a Phi Epsilon Pi transfer from Miami University in Ohio), McConaughy allegedly threatened not only reduction but outright expulsion of the Jewish students if external interference did not cease immediately.[52]

The student members of the abortive Phi Epsilon Pi chapter, fearing the possible consequences of their actions, fled for protection and counsel to Phi Epsilon Pi alumnus and Hartford attorney Louis B. Rosenfeld. Along with his associates, Rosenfeld agreed to intervene on their behalf and to confront Wesleyan's president on his alleged threats. At the resulting meeting, Rosenfeld reported to his fraternity's executive secretary, McConaughy tried to mollify these Jewish communal representatives with a promise that at the university's upcoming 1932 commencement an honorary degree would be bestowed "on some outstanding national Jew to show that we have absolutely no ill feeling against members of the Jewish race." The president also reminded his critics that at least one Jew sat on Wesleyan's Board of Trustees—"although," as the Hartford Jewish attorney confessed, "I am not familiar with the name of the person who holds that distinction." Afterward, having reassured the Jewish students that their college careers were not in jeopardy, Rosenfeld concluded that it would be too dangerous to go directly contrary to the president's wishes and to continue organizing any fraternity activity at Wesleyan.[53]

Almost two years later, in November 1933, Herman E. Colitz '34, one of the original eighteen men, made another attempt to aid Phi Epsilon Pi by calling for a student referendum on the issue of admitting Jewish fraternities. McConaughy responded by calling a meeting of all the fraternity chapter presidents—Colitz himself was not invited—in order to discourage them from such a vote. Shortly thereafter the Wesleyan student government "flatly refused" the call for a referendum.[54] "To attempt anything at your Alma Mater seems to be an impossible task," responded Maurice Jacobs, upon hearing Colitz's description of the incident. "Time and time again, Jewish students have been rebuffed in the same manner. Wesleyan definitely does not want our boys to have equal rights and will not move from its position. The University is in the saddle and what can be done?"[55] The experiences of Jewish students at Wesleyan would change significantly with the new administration of President Herbert Butterfield, who served from 1943 to 1967.

Responding to criticism and controversy, as well as an honest desire to serve the unaffiliated and socially rejected, college administrations such as Wesleyan's that did not permit Jewish fraternities began to establish alternative university dining facilities. At the time of the original controversy in the spring of 1932, Wesleyan had recently set aside a furnished building known as the "Ivy Club" for non-fraternity men who wished to have a place to live and to eat. Practically all the men, according to reports, were Jewish or Catholic.[56] In the case of Amherst, the college established a "Commons Club" with fraternity privileges for the non-affiliated students; again, this included virtually all the Jewish men.[57] Similar institutions existed at other schools, including Williams and Harvard. None, however, provided the sense of first-class citizenship that membership in one of the dominant selective student societies could provide.

Interfraternity Council (IFC) Recognition: Maryland, Penn, and Berkeley

Even when administrations accepted the presence of Jewish fraternities at a particular college, the hurdle of full corporate recognition remained. In the world of the Greek system the local interfraternity councils (IFC's) and their female counterparts, the Panhellenic associations, made up of delegates from each of the member organizations, set rules and regulations for rushing and fraternity activities. Through their influence, they also ended up governing much of campus life. Exclusion from these de facto organs of student government meant exclusion from the campus corridors of student power. The fight for full IFC or Panhellenic recognition was often, therefore, in the 1920s and 1930s the second item on the agenda once a Jewish fraternity established itself anywhere.

For example, at the University of Maryland, where Jewish Greek organizers in the 1930s noted unusually strong anti-Jewish prejudice from both students and faculty, repeated attempts by the Jewish fraternities and sororities for equal representation were to no avail. According to reports filed by Alpha Epsilon Phi investigators Marion Diamond and Florence Orringer in 1939, Maryland President H. C. Byrd met complaints with the suggestion that "Jewish students could form their own councils."[58] At times, a local IFC might offer membership to one Jewish fraternity while denying it to another one of allegedly lower social status. In that case, Jewish students faced a painful choice — submit to the rule of "divide and conquer" or else deny themselves for the sake of ethnic and religious solidarity.

The men of Sigma Alpha Mu at Maryland in 1935 had faced
such a choice. Approximately one hundred Jewish men and women
attended the university that year and they supported three men's fraternities — Sigma Alpha Mu, Tau Epsilon Phi, and Phi Alpha. The
Maryland IFC then offered full membership to Sigma Alpha Mu while
declining to offer it to the two other groups, which they considered to be
of lower caste. After some deliberation, the Sigma Alpha Mu chapter
voted to reject the offer. Although at the time and on that particular
campus TEP and Phi Alpha indeed were smaller, younger, and ranked
lower in the internal Jewish Greek hierarchy, the Sammies did not wish
to break ranks with their fellow Jewish students over the issue—nor did
they wish the disadvantage of being subject to restrictive official IFC
rushing rules and regulations while their competitors were not.[59]

At the University of Pennsylvania, another administrative tactic
theoretically granted Jewish students "separate-but-equal" status while
keeping them a safe distance from the Gentile fraternities. There were
no apparent restrictions on Jewish enrollment there in 1935, and no
fewer than thirteen Jewish men's fraternities and two sororities flourished on the Philadelphia campus. On the other hand, there was no
equal IFC representation either. Gentile fraternities were organized
into a "Group A" while the Jewish fraternities were organized into
"Group B."[60]

The granting of "associate" membership status, where a Jewish
fraternity or sorority's delegates might attend the main meetings but
not vote or hold office, was another possible concession that Gentile
groups might grant. Still, when such status was offered to the chapter of Alpha Epsilon Phi at the University of California at Berkeley in
1934, the national officers considered the offer unacceptable and sent
in their leader Elizabeth Eldridge to confront the situation.[61] Eldridge
described for her sister officers her introductory meeting with Mary B.
Davidson, Associate Dean of Women. The Dean insisted to this Jewish
woman's face that the decision to exclude her sorority from full admission to Panhellenic on both the local and national levels had been a
"wise one" and that she "emphatically" would not recommend any of
the other Jewish sororities (including Sigma Delta Tau, Delta Phi Epsilon, and Phi Sigma Sigma) for admission. The reason? "She told me
that if they granted the privilege to us they would have to grant the same
privilege to the Japanese, Chinese, and Negro sororities if they wanted
it," wrote Eldridge. "I thought several things, but I told her that they
were not considering petitioning and at the time they did, they could be

handled as a separate problem . . . but if it was a state university, everyone should have equal rights in an organization under the university's jurisdiction."[62]

At Berkeley in the winter of 1934, powerful outside contacts, Jewish philanthropy, and good relations with the university's president in the end effectively counteracted the Dean's influence. Eldridge described enlisting the aid of an unnamed but "prominent" male member of the local Jewish community as a witness and dropping in unannounced to repeat the entire episode to Berkeley's acting president, Dr. Monroe E. Deutsch. He listened to the story without comment and then asked her to come back a few days later. When she did, Eldridge reported, a chastened Associate Dean Davidson was also there. She meekly nodded her assent to the president's claim that he could not tolerate even the "suspicion of injustice" while he was president of the institution. The Dean also promised that she would "do her very best" to ensure that the young women of Berkeley's local Panhellenic council saw things "President Deutsch's way." She then departed without a backward glance.

Surprised and pleased at the result of this meeting, Eldridge stayed behind to speak to the president. What assurances could they have, she asked, that Mary Davidson would continue to behave in so cooperative a fashion once she was no longer within earshot of her boss's office? "I spoke to her much more emphatically before you came in," President Deutsch replied, as he invoked the family name of some of the most prominent Jewish philanthropists on the West Coast. "I told her that Fleishhacker money and Fleishhacker generosity had built this university and kept it open, were even now paying her salary and that if the Jews were discriminated against, it would be a sorry state of affairs."[63] By the beginning of the Spring 1935 semester Alpha Epsilon Phi sorority had been admitted to full membership in Berkeley's Panhellenic association.

Jewish Sororities and the National Panhellenic Congress

Beyond the local level, the most important achievements for an aspiring national college fraternity or sorority included admission into the umbrella or suprafraternal National Interfraternity Conference (NIC), founded in 1909, or its female counterpart, the National Panhellenic Congress (NPC), founded in 1902.[64] Here also Jewish groups faced obstacles to full recognition, although at this level the battle waged by the

women's groups was far more serious and took far longer to win than
the battle waged by men.

For the men's NIC, official criteria for admission were straight-
forward and relatively simple—a minimum number of chapters and a
majority or two-thirds vote of assembled delegates. The body's president was similarly elected annually by majority vote. As they grew, the
largest national Jewish men's college fraternities were admitted in due
course to the NIC beginning with Zeta Beta Tau in 1913. In addition,
a Jewish man—ZBT's Harold Riegelman, Cornell '11 — was actually
elected by his fellow delegates, albeit not without some comment, to
wield the gavel at the annual December assembly in New York City as
the NIC's president for 1927–28.[65]

In comparison to the men's group, however, the women's National Panhellenic Congress (NPC) in the 1930s was still not able to
take the first step in admitting the national Jewish sororities to its membership. Smaller (less than one quarter the size of the NIC) and more
socially exclusive in its membership criteria and governing structure,
the NPC still operated under the blackball system. A single negative
anonymous vote from any delegate could bar a candidate's admission.
In addition, National Panhellenic officers were not elected; instead, each
delegate served in turn through a set system of rotating chairs. Thus, the
right of equal admission for Jewish women also meant their automatic
right to serve in positions of power over the non-Jewish women. Under
these conditions, from Alpha Epsilon Phi's first application in 1917 until after World War II the four Jewish national college sororities waged
a losing battle to be accepted into the National Panhellenic Congress.
"Associate" membership came only in 1946, and full membership not
until 1952.[66]

The usual official explanation for refusing to admit the Jewish
sororities to the National Panhellenic was that they did not rank as truly
national sororities because of their "restricted" or "limited" membership.
This criticism apparently did not apply, as AEPhi's officers pointed out
repeatedly, to such Gentile sororities as Phi Mu or Chi Omega. The former required candidates to be "professing Christians born of two Christian parents," while the motto of the latter was "Hellenic Culture and
Christian Ideals."[67] A second explanation, usually unwritten but often
expressed in conversation, was that if the NPC lowered its barriers to
Jewish women it would have to also accept the sororities of Catholics,
Blacks, Japanese, Chinese, and so on. Hence, the essential character of
the organization would be endangered. Other objections came from in-

dividual National Panhellenic Congress delegates who claimed to represent strictly Christian organizations. If Jewish people were admitted to the NPC, they said, then they themselves would feel compelled to withdraw from the organization.[68]

The ladies of Alpha Epsilon Phi refused to take no for an answer. Elizabeth Eldridge, who from 1929 to 1937 traveled from one end of the country to the other as the sorority's field secretary and then its national leader, was also designated as its "Panhellenic Chairman." A San Antonio native and professional writer whose German-born grandfather had fought in the Civil War, she was responsible for writing the applications, soliciting letters of recommendation and endorsement, lobbying for support at official sorority functions, forming alliances, and in general coordinating the campaign for admission into the NPC.[69]

Gradually, these efforts brought success. By April 1936, at an NPC regional conference reception in Columbus, Ohio, Eldridge discovered from helpful and sympathetic delegates that the ballot to admit them at the last national meeting had failed by only two votes. Eight Gentile national sorority delegates had come out strongly in favor of the measure and two had made persuasive speeches from the convention floor. It was only AEPhi's "restricted membership," confided Phi Mu delegate Cora Rader (an ally who had voted for them) that had kept the vote from being unanimous. Eldridge began to sputter in anger that the supposedly "restricted" Alpha Epsilon Phi was no more restricted than Phi Mu, which only admitted born Christians. At that point, as she reported the scene for her sister national officers, L. Pearle Green of Kappa Alpha Theta (who had also voted in AEPhi's favor) appeared. The resulting exchange of words at this most genteel of gatherings revealed the depth of the attitudes Eldridge was confronting:

At this moment, Pearle Green joined our conversation. Mrs. Rader said "I've been talking to Miss Eldridge about Alpha Epsilon Phi's admission to NPC and she wonders if there is prejudice. I say no. What do you think? Pearle?" And Miss Green replied: "Well, no, unless you'd call that argument of that one sorority, Cora, prejudice. You know, the one that says that if we admit the Jews, we'll have to take the niggers." I laughed and said, "Well for purposes of argument, we'll call that prejudice." And Mrs. Rader, meaning to salve my feelings, I'm sure, said: "You know how fond we've all been of you at this meeting. You know, too, how much we have in common. You and I could go off for a weekend together and enjoy ourselves thoroughly. It's just too bad that all people are not so broadminded!"

"So, in the last analysis," concluded Eldridge in her report of the Columbus, Ohio, National Panhellenic regional meeting, "I'm afraid that it is still a matter of 'some of my best friends are Jews,' though I'm sure she meant it kindly."[70]

In October 1938, more than two years later, Elizabeth Eldridge was able to obtain a luncheon meeting with the influential and sympathetic Harriet Williamson Tuft, national president of the Gentile sorority Beta Phi Alpha and the immediate past president of the entire National Panhellenic Congress. For two hours, she pleaded her case before her. "Suppose you were in the Panhellenic, theoretically," came the cautious answer from the NPC leader. "What would your attitude be toward the other Jewish sororities? Would you press their admittance? Would you vote for them?"[71]

Here, subtly phrased, came once again the choice being presented to select American Jewish men and women as they approached the gates of exclusive social institutions, clubs, and neighborhoods across the United States: if we accept you, will you promise not to bring in any more? "Reading between the lines," Eldridge reported to her sorority sisters, "I believe that Phi Sigma Sigma (another Jewish college sorority that had been founded by women of predominantly East European origin) is one reason among others that we are not in NPC and that if Panhellenic could see its way to letting us in and excluding others, our chances would be better."[72]

The temptation to say "yes" to such a question was powerful. Eldridge was as capable as anyone in her social class of voicing contempt for other Jewish women whom she considered beneath her own and her sorority's standards. Nevertheless, at that moment and afterward, she could never bring herself to make that promise. She could not accept the idea of admission for Alpha Epsilon Phi only at the cost of betraying the other national Jewish sororities. Here lay a line she would not cross, then or later. Alpha Epsilon Phi would not take up its place as a full member of the National Panhellenic until the other three major national Jewish sororities did as well in the early 1950s.

At that moment in October 1938, however, hearing Eldridge's refusal, the NPC past president advised her Jewish colleague to embark on yet another goodwill tour among all the Congress' delegates. Eldridge thereupon lobbied one last time for NPC acceptance of Alpha Epsilon Phi during receptions at the Congress's December 1939 meeting. She did not succeed. A rejection letter came back the following week, this time announcing "with real regret" that their petition had not received the necessary unanimous vote.[73] Alpha Epsilon Phi's secretary was directed to send out a letter acknowledging the nonacceptance, which she did on January 3, 1940. By then, the Second World War had broken out and had been raging for four months. It would be long over before Alpha Epsilon Phi and the other Jewish sororities received the full NPC recognition they longed for.

By then, it would be a hollow victory, coming so delayed and after such a cataclysm. It also came at a time when the United States was poised to undergo a series of social, political, civil, and legal changes far beyond anything that Eldridge, Harriet Tufts, or anyone at that December 1939 NPC gathering could have envisioned. The foundations that supported a system of separate Jewish and Gentile fraternities and sororities in the first place would already be starting to crumble. In the 1930s, however, with or without full social acceptance, young Jewish Greeks continued to work hard within the system to get their educations and achieve success and happiness in the face of whatever obstacles stood in their way.

Chapter 8

Fighting Back and Keeping Up Standards

With the onset of the Great Depression displays of the previous "rah-rah" collegiate culture, as contemporaries referred to it, declined in popularity. When Adolf Hitler became Chancellor of all Germany in January 1933, the event added an edge of external anxiety to politically aware American Jewish college students. In the 1930s, in addition to economic concerns, anti-Jewish demagoguery filled the radio waves, and isolationists accused Jews of fomenting war. A lack of faith in the elder generation that had permitted both the Depression and the rise of Fascism to happen led formerly quiescent young people to embrace radical ideologies. At the same time the divisiveness of radical politics ruptured friendships and sowed fear in the hearts of the more conservative segments of the Jewish community that they would all be branded as revolutionaries and traitors because of the affiliations and actions of a portion of their people. The German annexation of Austria and the Czechoslovakian crisis caused grave apprehension and left the more politically aware students and their families glued to their radios for much of 1938 and 1939. Soon the military draft would be revived and male U.S. college students would be facing the interruption of their studies for the sake of a second world war that was already consuming the rest of the globe.

Business as Usual—Wealth and Social Life

Fears that hard times might destroy Jewish fraternity life, however, proved to be unfounded. Officers everywhere reported, to their surprise, that the loss of students who could not afford tuition or fraternity fees was soon balanced by others who decided to begin or to prolong their schooling. In normal times, such students might have managed well without college or departed without their degree. Now it made sense to ride out the economic storm in the relative shelter of academia rather than form businesses or face bleak employment prospects. The value of degrees and formal credentials was also rising in a tight employment marketplace. Contrary to expectations, surveys revealed that the number of students doing undergraduate, graduate, or professional work in the United States actually increased during the Depression. After the initial shock of the Crash, both Lee Dover of Zeta Beta Tau and Elizabeth Eldridge of Alpha Epsilon Phi noted that their pledge classes of 1931 were equal or larger than they had been in 1929.[1]

Life went on. Although they lived in the shadow of economic difficulties and international instability, the average member of Zeta Beta Tau in 1938 was probably more preoccupied with the cheering example of one of their own, William S. Paley (University of Pennsylvania '22.) A former president of his chapter who had entered the infant radio business right out of college, Paley made the cover of *Time* magazine in September of that year as president and principal owner of the Columbia Broadcasting System (CBS).[2] (ZBT's star quarterback Sid Luckman, Columbia '39, made the cover of *Life* magazine in October). ZBT men also thrilled to the example of Leslie Alan Epstein '35 (he later changed his name to Falk), former president of the University of Illinois chapter and a second-year student at the Washington University School of Medicine in St. Louis, Missouri. In 1937 he became the second of their number and one of the few Jews ever to win a coveted Rhodes Scholarship for two years of study at Oxford University. Among the first had been James Goodfriend, Jr. '34, of ZBT's University of Missouri chapter.[3] Phi Sigma Delta members in those years also enjoyed reading about the successes of their own alumni, including movie producer Joseph Mankiewicz, composer Lorenz Hart, and the industrialist Walter Annenberg.

The men of Sigma Alpha Mu thrilled to the exploits of track star Marty Glickman, Syracuse '39, who made the Olympic track team and traveled to participate in the 1936 games in Berlin. In his autobiography *The Fastest Kid on the Block,* Glickman, who also excelled in football, basketball, and baseball, recalled how five Sigma Alpha Mu Syracuse alumni had offered to pay his first year's tuition and all of his house fees if he would come to their school. More Jewish athletes

at Syracuse would loosen quotas and make it easier for other Jewish
students to be admitted, they told him. Unfortunately, Glickman and
his Jewish teammate Sam Stoller never got the chance the run in their
Olympic event, the relay race, which was scheduled after Jesse Owens
had already shredded the myth of Aryan racial superiority by winning
three gold medals. The American coach and Olympic officials, perhaps
thinking that the almost certain victory of these athletes on the track
would be too much of an insult to their Nazi hosts after the previous
display, pulled them off the team and substituted two other runners. [4]

Not all in the upper tiers lost their funds or had to drop out of
college. Alpha Epsilon Phi members from 1930 through 1934 traveled
to Europe, attended finishing school, studied French at the Sorbonne,
summered on the Jersey shore, and took part in yachting parties. [5] Fewer
ships were crossing the Atlantic, but the traditional Grand Tour of Europe continued for fortunate ZBT men. [6] "When Better Times are Had,
ZBT's Will Have Them" became a fraternity slogan. Their June 1935
magazine alumni news columns carried the evocative engagement notice
of Arnold G. Buchsbaum (a graduate of the University of Pennsylvania
chapter) to a Miss Isabelle Hecht of New York City, a graduate of the
Alquin School and Les Allières of Lausanne, Switzerland. They were to
be married in the fall and would continue living in New York where the
husband was "in the bond business at 25 Broad St." At the same time,
Edward Lasker of Chicago and Yale announced his recent marriage to a
Miss Carol G. Gimbel, daughter of Mr. and Mrs. Bernard F. Gimbel of
Port Chester, NY (of department store fame). The ceremony took place
at the Chieftains, the Port Chester estate of the bride's parents. [7]

Zeta Beta Tau may have lost five chapters during the decade,
but it added twelve, and the University of Pennsylvania and the University of Missouri were able to build new houses through a combination of
endowments, member assessments, and alumni contributions. The final
list of furnishings at the house in Columbia, Missouri in 1938 included
red damask draperies, French doors, and Chippendale sofas. [8] The ZBT
chapter at Washington and Lee University in Lexington, Virginia was
renovated during the summer of 1937 under the direction of the house
mother and her staff of servants. Also in 1937, the University of Nebraska chapter in Lincoln issued an invitation for visitors to stop by and
enjoy a meal in their newly furnished dining room equipped with a complete set of ZBT-crested china. [9]

Concern for social life did not waver. When the men of ZBT's
University of Alabama chapter in 1935 longed for a congenial group of

Jewish women on the campus to keep them company, they personally invited Alpha Epsilon Phi sorority's Elizabeth Eldridge to visit them at their house in Tuscaloosa. Presenting her with a list of young women they wanted to see attending the university (presumably high school juniors, seniors, or first-year college students from Jewish communities in Alabama or from other adjacent states throughout the South), they promised to help the sorority with their rushing if Alpha Epsilon Phi would establish a chapter there. "This list caused amusement in New Orleans," (at the time the sorority's national headquarters) Eldridge later reported, "for it read like a dance list or a house party of a debutante gathering. The Zebes know cute girls, if nothing else. . . . They will rush for us during the summer and when they make a rushing tour of the state for their own fall rushing, they will interview girls for us, persuading them to come to Alabama. They will guarantee the chapter that does transfer the best time any girls have ever had at Alabama."[10]

The amenities were not limited to the oldest, upper-tier fraternities. The passage of time and intracommunal associations were doing their work in the acculturation and homogenization of American Jewry, as was the Depression itself, which tended to have a leveling effect. Times being what they were, the accident of having money left was more important than the accident of having old blood. The world of banking and high finance that had produced the legendary "Our Crowd" of German Jews had now been discredited in the wake of the Crash and no longer commanded the same automatic deference that it once did. In time, social, class, and ethnic differences between the different Jewish fraternities were destined to fade if not to disappear altogether.

Sigma Alpha Mu, the highest-ranking fraternity founded by "Russian" Jews, had displayed a relatively informal and low-key fraternal persona during the 1910s and 1920s. In the 1930s, however, the terms "desirable" and "undesirable," previously almost unknown in their records, began to make a frequent appearance. By 1931 the fraternity was rejecting as many petitioning chapters as it accepted.[11] In addition, a review of advertisements, invitations, brochures, and reports of their social events indicates that the quality of the hotels and country clubs that they frequented reached a level not far below that of Zeta Beta Tau or Phi Epsilon Pi. Full evening dress became *de rigeur* for their formal affairs, a fact evident both in the invitations issued for the events and the fraternities' own photo files from the period. In 1932, even Alpha Epsilon Pi for the first time held a convention dance at the Standard Club in Atlanta, previously an unbreachable stronghold of the German Jews.

It is possible that had it not been for the prevailing economic conditions either the operators of the club would not have permitted it or the group could not have afforded the usual fees. Whatever the reasons, the event represented a giant step forward socially, and afterward there was no turning back. The report of the dance in Alpha Epsilon Pi's minutes read: "a most beautiful place—but the corn liquor was terrible."[12]

The annual conventions and conclaves of the men's fraternities continued throughout the Depression, along with the organized search for eligible Jewish women with the cooperation of mothers, family friends, members of the extended Jewish communal network, and the fraternity's own social chairmen and committees. Fraternity documents in general did not record what the women thought about their blind dates. The men were apparently not always satisfied and might be tempted to skip the process altogether, as is clear from a short promotional piece entitled "Blinding Dates" that appeared in a 1934 Phi Epsilon Pi convention newsletter. It also reveals, incidentally, how prized a place on that date list could be in those days and how it could be used as a form of ingratiation in extended family relations and in the business world:

> Inmates of the House of Good Shepherd, daughters of clients and customers, hideous hags and toothless crones, sisters, nieces and cousins will not this year grace the date list for visiting fraters. Chicago Convention Committee stands ready to defend its contention that these individuals are not necessary to the success of the Convention. Too often in past years have visiting men been subjected to needless pain. This year, unbounded pleasure, instead.[13]

Another advertisement for Phi Epsilon Pi's 1937 convention headed "Come to Cleveland!" tried to motivate readers to register promptly with photographs of movie stars and the famous "Goldwyn Girls" on the borders of the page. Those who wanted dates had to supply their age and height. This was no time to economize, the ad writers claimed. A small investment in the convention and the feminine companionship they might find there was just the antidote for low spirits caused by the Depression:

> COME TO CLEVELAND! For here in the Convention City we have the epitome of your desires, the balm for your rejuvenation, the tonic for your jaded senses. We have GIRLS—femininity, pulchritude, naivete, sophistication—girls, girls, girls. At this writing they are stacked four deep outside

the door, breathless with anticipation, each tiny heart apitty-pat with eagerness. Can we disappoint them? No! Will they disappoint you? No! So why delay? Let's put all three of our minds at rest and make certain that every moment of your stay in Cleveland will be perfect.[14]

As a semiofficial social service agency and matchmaking bureau, a Jewish fraternity conducted its activities the entire year, not just at convention time. The work was multigenerational. In one instance Mrs. S. F. Kiely of Kansas City, Missouri, wrote to the Midwest regional director of ZBT in the same city to request the names of all the young, unmarried Zeta Beta Tau alumni in the vicinity. The director immediately obliged by sending her the names of seventeen men.[15]

In 1935, Lee Dover remarked to an observer on his work with "old-timer" ZBTs who graduated and then had no contact with their fraternity for years. They would then resurface, seeking to reestablish themselves in the organization's good graces by letters, phone calls, volunteer work, belated dues-paying, or donations. The cause was inevitably a young marriageable daughter or a son coming up for membership in some chapter. "Eventually," observed Dover, "Every ZBT comes back."[16]

Student Migrants to State Universities: Illinois, Massachusetts, Penn State, and Others

The search for a college education in the face of all odds, which had become such a marked feature of American Jewish life in the post-World War I period, only intensified during the Great Depression. The bad economy did nothing to dampen their ardor. In their own version of the "geographical distribution" maxim that limited their numbers in elite eastern institutions, young Jews, primarily men, were willing to "redistribute" themselves geographically over vast distances in order to go to school. With the blessing and support of their families, they sought academic and professional opportunities that would be as high in quality and as low in cost as possible. Their sons and their grandsons and granddaughters might someday storm the gates of the nation's most elite colleges and professional schools back east and amass tuition bills running well into six figures. At this stage in the American Jewish journey, however, such schools were beyond their reach.

The destinations of these migrant students included land-grant colleges that were just beginning to outgrow their status as purely technical and agricultural institutes along with geographically isolated schools of lesser prestige and doubtful accreditation. Wherever these students went Jewish fraternities of all backgrounds and income levels had to follow, taking up anywhere from a quarter to half the Jewish students. Through this movement, new concentrations of Jewish students developed, and with them the rudiments of a traditional communal Jewish life.

The large state schools of the Midwest continued to admit thousands of Jewish students, some from nearby and others from hundreds of miles away, particularly from the overcrowded New York City metropolitan area. A 1937 B'nai B'rith Hillel report estimated that the number of students migrating from the New York area was reaching approximately 5,000 each year.[17] As in the 1920s the largest populations were centered at the University of Illinois at Champaign-Urbana, Ohio State University at Columbus, the University of Michigan at Ann Arbor, the University of Minnesota in Minneapolis-St. Paul, and the University of Wisconsin at Madison. Some of these schools in the 1930s claimed a thousand or more Jewish men and women among their students.[18]

It was at the University of Illinois in 1923 that the first Hillel Foundation to serve the religious needs of Jewish college students was established, led by recent Hebrew Union College graduate and Phi Epsilon Pi alumnus Rabbi Benjamin M. Frankel. Illinois history professor Abram L. Sachar continued the tradition after Frankel's premature death. By April 1940, Hillel had become a major American Jewish organization with foundations serving college students at campuses across the country. Still at the University of Illinois, where he had served as Hillel's National Director since 1933, Sachar led a first night Passover seder for over 150 Jewish students. While purported tensions between the Hillel foundations and the Jewish fraternities would remain a theme on American campuses for generations to come, relations were apparently quite good at Illinois in April 1940. The national Hillel publication for the following month, which reported mass seders at colleges across the country for students who could not go home for the holiday, reported that the second night seder at Illinois had been conducted by the leaders of the Jewish fraternities.[19]

Closer to the northeast, sharp growth in the number of Jewish students took place at the Massachusetts State College in Amherst and at Pennsylvania State College in State College, Pennsylvania. Massachusetts State had begun as the Massachusetts Agricultural College in 1863, under the provisions of the Morrill Land Grant Act of 1862.

In 1931 it was renamed Massachusetts State College, becoming the University of Massachusetts only in 1947. "The Jewish enrollment has grown by leaps and bounds," wrote Maurice Jacobs of Phi Epsilon Pi in his report on the campus in 1932, just two years after it ceased being an agricultural school. "There are approximately 75 men on this campus and but this one [local] fraternity to handle them. . . . In the matter of a very few years, this group can be developed into a strong organization as there is no question that with the liberalizing of the curriculum, will come a very much larger Jewish student body."[20] Sigma Alpha Mu's executive secretary Jimmy Hammerstein was similarly optimistic about Massachusetts in 1937. It was growing rapidly, he noted, and would soon be able to grant the Bachelor's degree. By that time, the total student population consisted of 800 men and 200 women. Fully ten percent were Jews, with forty-one having entered in the freshman class of 1936 alone. With eleven national fraternities represented on the campus and with 65 percent of the students affiliated with them, the college represented a fertile Jewish fraternity field.[21]

The rapid growth of Pennsylvania State College as a center for Jewish student life was even more notable. When Phi Epsilon Pi began sponsoring a new chapter of only four active men taking agricultural courses there in 1915, Penn State was considered, in the words of one officer, "a rough, uncouth, back-woods school" which nevertheless "has splendid possibilities."[22] By 1925, when a Sigma Alpha Mu representative visited the campus, he noted that State College now had well over one hundred Jewish students along with two Jewish fraternities. In 1927, Phi Epsilon Pi officers noted with pleasure how their chapter house at Penn State was being filled by a sudden and large influx of "good New York and Brooklyn men."[23] Seven years later, along with the burgeoning of the total student population, the number of Jewish students at Penn State had more than doubled to 250 and was still growing.[24] Penn State was an especially popular destination for young Jewish women, as Alpha Epsilon Phi investigators noted when they visited the campus in 1935. The Dean of Women informed them that the college was doing everything it could to increase the female student registration by building new dormitories as well as taking other measures to encourage them to come.[25]

For Pascal A. Greenberg, Phi Epsilon Pi's executive secretary in 1939 and himself a 1935 graduate of the school, the devotion and loyalty of their Penn chapter was nothing short of remarkable, as he observed at the celebration of their twenty-fifth anniversary in April of that year. Present were 112 alumni and their wives along with fifteen past chapter presidents—even though only four of the alumni were "town" men and most others, as he noted, had to travel "hundreds of miles to get to State College."[26] Maurice Jacobs had earlier observed that an unusually strong level of Jewish identification and cooperation with the Hillel Foundation matched strong fraternity consciousness at Penn. Possible factors, in his view, were the personal popularity of Hillel director Rabbi Ephraim Fischoff, the campus's isolated location, the religious background of the men and women who went there, and the willingness of the Penn State administration to excuse Jewish students from classes falling on their holidays. In 1936, the Phi Epsilon Pi chapter voluntarily turned its house over to Hillel to be used as a synagogue for the High Holy Day services. Jacobs reported proudly that a standing-room only crowd of 150 students had attended for the Jewish New Year services and over 200 for Yom Kippur. For any college this was an excellent turnout, and he and his fellow officers considered it especially good at Penn State since the Jewish student population totaled 350, and many of these had gone home for the holiday.[27]

Penn State's Phi Epsilon Pi furthermore was responsible for building in October 1939 what was billed by Hillel journalists as "probably the first *Succah* in Jewish collegiate fraternity history." The actual design and construction of the Feast of Tabernacles ritual booth, which measured twenty feet long, eight feet high and eight feet wide, was done by Ralph Madway and Arthur Jaffe. In keeping with the agricultural nature of the holiday festival, students decorated the booth with appropriately collegiate drapings of ivy, along with chinese red peppers, apples, deep green fir branches, carrots, turnips and other fruits and vegetables. The Hebrew biblical inscription "How goodly are thy tents, O Jacob, thy dwelling places, O Israel," greeted visitors as they walked in, and on one wall hung a solid blue Star of David, trimmed in white, flanked by two tapestries. The *sukkah* reportedly became a place of pilgrimage not only for Jewish fraternity members but also for students, faculty, and townspeople for miles around.[28]

Other state colleges also showed sharp rises in their Jewish student population. According to a survey of 120 universities conducted by Maurice Jacobs of Phi Epsilon Pi in Fall 1932 these included the University of Arkansas at Fayetteville, which showed a Jewish male student population in 1932 of 75, up from an average of 30; Louisiana State, 40, up from an average of 28; the University of New Hampshire, 30, up from an average of 20; Indiana University, 70, up from an average of 50; and the University of North Carolina at Chapel Hill, 200 Jewish men, up from an average of 140.[29] The Jewish student population at the University of Florida in Gainesville was also "consistently growing," according to Jacobs. There were already 139 Jews in attendance there in 1935 and chapters of two Jewish fraternities and he was convinced that a Florida chapter of Phi Epsilon Pi might attract a number of men who did not wish to join the chapters of Tau Epsilon Phi or Phi Beta Delta already there. "This would be an ideal place for us and will tie in our Miami chapter with another group in the State," Jacobs noted in his 1935 investigation report. "The University of Florida has changed tremendously in the past five years and is a good school. Any opinions we formerly held on this score should be forgotten and the decision should be based on the evidence submitted."[30]

The South as Haven: Mississippi, Georgia, and Alabama

In a pattern startlingly similar to the age-old Jewish Diaspora experience, expulsions or restrictions in one area of the United States were often followed by invitations to settle elsewhere. For potential Jewish college students and their fraternities, the welcoming arms of large state schools were nowhere wider or warmer than in the American South. The contrast with other areas of the country was so great that after Hitler came to power in Germany in 1933 at least one national officer of Alpha Epsilon Phi sorority seriously wondered if within fifteen years the South might be the only region in the United States where Jews could attend college freely. This possibility might justify their acceptance of petitioning southern chapters that normally would not make their grade. "For the sake of the future growth of the fraternity in southern fields, which to my mind are going to be the fastest growing ones as the restrictions in the number of Jewish students allowed is more rigidly enforced in the eastern colleges, are we going to establish chapters of *material we know* to be of lower standard than we desire?" wrote Louise W. Wolf to Elizabeth Eldridge in November 1933, "Or are we going to abandon these fields to other Jewish sororities altogether? . . . Now we are forced with Hitlerism and it is surely going to have its influence on this country, believe it or not, and we have therefore, a problem to look out for."[31]

Maurice Jacobs had no such qualms when he attended the installation banquet for the new Phi Epsilon Pi chapter at the University of Mississippi in Oxford in 1936, headed by undergraduate president

Moses Wander. He was stunned and proud at the top brass sent to welcome his organization. The University administration was represented there by no less than the Chancellor himself, several Deans, prominent members of the faculty, and the heads of all sixteen Gentile fraternities already on the campus. "At no university in the past," Jacobs wrote, "have we been greeted as royally as has been our greeting at 'Ole Miss.'"[32]

Nor was "Ole Miss" the only school in Mississippi that actively extended hospitality to Jewish students. In 1938, Sigma Alpha Mu officials found themselves in the odd position of actually being courted by the Dean of Men at Mississippi State University in the town of Starkville. Primarily an engineering and agricultural school located in a remote area, the school drew very few Jewish students. Those who wished legal or pre-medical training in their own state much preferred to attend school in Oxford, which was more than 100 miles away. Otherwise, young Jewish men from the area tended to go to the University of Alabama, Vanderbilt University in Tennessee, or Washington University in St. Louis, Missouri. SAM's Sigma Psi chapter, the single Jewish group at Mississippi State, was established in Starkville that year with only seven active students. The school's Dean of Men expressed his delight at their presence to SAM's traveling secretary and promised that as soon as the boys were ready for a house of their own, he would see that they got one.[33]

The University of Georgia in Athens was another possibility for Jews seeking higher education in the 1930s, although it was not as popular a destination as others for northerners and its reputation as a campus prejudiced against "Yankees" was particularly strong. The Phi Epsilon Pi chapter there apparently participated in this prejudice. Maurice Jacobs sharply criticized the group in 1932 for flatly refusing to take in any Jewish men originating from north of the Mason-Dixon line. Such men, according to the campus social code, were restricted to the more plebeian Alpha Epsilon Pi. Jacobs also criticized them for their consistent snobbery in preferring residents of Atlanta to residents of Savannah or any other part of the state of Georgia. On the other hand, he noted in his report, the strength of their Jewish identity was to be commended. It was a pleasant surprise to discover that without any external compulsion the chapter had joined the local Jewish congregation in Athens *en masse.* "This is the first example I have found of this interest throughout the country," Jacobs announced at the fraternity's December 1932 convention, "and I heartily recommend Mu [University of Georgia] for its acceptance of its Jewish responsibility."[34]

As in the previous decade, it was the state of Alabama, however, which provided the most noticeable southern shelter for beleaguered Jewish university students in the 1930s, with Tuscaloosa a most popular destination for both men and women.[35] By 1935, when Elizabeth Eldridge of Alpha Epsilon Phi visited the campus at ZBT's request, she found 43 Jewish women in attendance and hundreds of Jewish men. In expressing her hesitation to establish a chapter there, Eldridge revealed clearly what a haven Alabama had become for Jewish students unable to attend school anywhere else. "The Jewish student body is a conglomerate one," she reported to her fellow officers. "Alabama raises no barriers and has no restrictions. It is also known as a campus with little Jewish prejudice. Accordingly, it attracts to it many Jewish students from New York who cannot get into schools elsewhere and who are 'undesirable.'"[36]

In time the University of Alabama became so saturated with Jewish fraternity activity that when Maurice Jacobs of Phi Epsilon Pi scouted the state in 1937, he was able to recommend the reactivation of an old chapter at the Alabama Polytechnic Institute (soon to be Auburn University), but he had to conclude that his fraternity had missed the boat at Tuscaloosa. "There is no possibility of a chapter at the University of Alabama," he reported to his fellow national officers, "because the ghetto of American colleges has more Jewish fraternities than it has any right to have."[37]

Small Colleges: Pennsylvania, Ohio, and New York State

Large state schools were not the only institutions that welcomed Jewish students and Jewish fraternities. Especially in Pennsylvania and Ohio, small private colleges sometimes went out of their way to attract Jews. As was sometimes the case in larger schools as well, the attitude of a single president or dean could make a significant difference one way or the other. Dickinson College in Carlisle, PA, which was expanding and building up its law school in the 1930s, enjoyed a favorable reputation for its treatment of Jewish students and hosted what Maurice Jacobs considered one of Phi Epsilon Pi's better chapters. In 1934, along with five men from the Dickinson chapter, he investigated Gettysburg College, in the southern part of the state, which then had an enrollment of 12 Jewish men and had just seen the formation of a small Jewish local society. "The college has openly stated that it is anxious to have Jewish students there," Jacobs reported, "and contacts have been made with some of the better high schools in the northern cities." The college administration promised immediate recognition of any Jewish national fraternity that would have them.[38] Muhlenberg College, a Lutheran-sponsored institution in Allentown, PA, also welcomed Jewish students, and Phi Epsilon Pi established a chapter there in 1932.[39]

Other relatively friendly spots for Jewish students and Jewish fraternities to help feed, house, and supervise them during the years of the Great Depression included St. John's College in Annapolis, Maryland, where in 1934 fully ten percent of the enrollment of 250 men were Jews from Maryland, New Jersey, and New York.[40] At Colby College in Waterville, Maine, Maurice Jacobs of Phi Epsilon Pi found more than 50 Jewish male students in 1932, and the administration appeared happy to have more. Half of these belonged to a local Jewish fraternity. Colby was then in the process of relocating to a new campus, expanding to a total student population of 1,000, and building uniform fraternity houses, with one reserved specifically for the Jewish fraternity.[41]

Ohio University in Athens, Ohio, which had a strong fraternity tradition, became through word-of-mouth a popular destination. The Jewish student body at the relatively small and obscure school jumped from "next to nothing" in 1927 to more than 150 Jewish men in 1932. Miami University at Oxford, Ohio, also had a rapidly growing Jewish student population of 55 in 1931, and the administration there made it clear that it welcomed chapters of Jewish fraternities in order to encourage Jewish students to come.[42] Wherever Jewish fraternities went, sororities followed. In 1932 an investigator from Alpha Epsilon Phi sorority noted that the number of Jewish women at Miami had doubled in the past year "due to the Depression and the fact that one is spreading the good news about it to the next and there is no question about it being a first-rate school. . . . The number of men no doubt attract the girls there."[43]

During this same period, the Jewish student population of Bucknell College in Lewisburg, PA, doubled to 50 and Sigma Alpha Mu established a chapter there.[44] Union College in Schenectady in 1932 had a growing Jewish student population of 81 and chapters of no fewer than four national Jewish fraternities—Zeta Beta Tau, Kappa Nu, Alpha Mu Sigma, and Phi Sigma Delta. Other private colleges showing significant gains in Jewish student population included Clark University in Worcester, MA, Lafayette University in Easton, PA, Franklin and Marshall in Lancaster, PA, and Alfred University in upstate Alfred,

NY, where more than 60 Jewish men in 1932 made up one fifth of the school's enrollment.[45]

The Unwanted: "Depression-Product" Commuter Schools: Butler, Newark, Akron

Despite or even because of hard times, the value of "keeping up standards" remained strong for fraternity officers eyeing potential material. No one wanted to fall into the trap of grabbing every potential member or chapter that came along. The student migrancy movement was an advantage because residential colleges away from urban centers had always been the main targets for chapter expansion anyway. But what of the opposite geographical case, also a frequent occurrence in Depression times? Groups of desirable students who normally might have left home for college were being forced to attend comparatively poor urban commuter schools near their homes and were applying for Greek membership from there. Their dues, initiation fees, and infusion of good blood would be welcome. But in the view of the national officers of the elite groups, adding such chapters to the permanent fraternity roll was risky. Some day the Depression would end, they reasoned, and this superior material at nonsuperior schools would be gone. If they admitted these chapters now, they might sully their rolls forever in the future.

In one such example of avoiding a "Depression-product school," Alpha Epsilon Phi's national council, after eight months of consideration, finally refused to consider pledging a group of young women at Butler University in Indianapolis. The social acceptability and desirability of the women was not an issue. Investigators rated several of the potential members "A-1" by the highest sorority standards. A chapter at Butler, they believed, would go far to challenge the traditional strength of Sigma Delta Tau in the Midwest, while AEPhi was confident of its prestige in the American South. The school itself, however, was a source of concern, as were the reasons why such high-ranking young Jewish women were attending it in the first place.

As Lillian Newman of Chicago described it in 1932, Butler University in Indianapolis was a "second or third rate school" which "would lend no prestige."[46] Others observed that it was "4th rate scholastically," a Presbyterian school "with not a Jewish member on the faculty and therefore very prejudiced," and "that it is only because of the depression that the Jewish girls of A-1 material are probably at Butler."[47] From 1500 students, not more than 24 were Jewish, and the women outnumbered men two to one. Most importantly, interviews revealed that the most desirable girls in attendance there had either transferred from Wellesley College in Massachusetts for financial reasons, or were attending Butler hoping to go on to Wellesley once their families' financial conditions improved.[48] (There was no hope of ever having a chapter at Wellesley or any other Seven Sisters school, since these schools had long ago abolished all college sororities on principle). It was the final opinion of investigator Roz J. Silver in October, 1932, that the group would not continue to draw the best material after potential members from the "better-connected families" were able to realize their dream of going away to school.[49] In the end, the young Jewish women of Butler University did not make it onto AEPhi's chapter roll, although some probably did make it to Wellesley eventually.

In 1938 Alpha Epsilon Phi's National Council made a similar decision to reject a desirable petitioning Jewish local sorority at the University of Newark, New Jersey, which they saw as another urban "Depression product" school.[50] Similarly, in 1939 Phi Epsilon Pi decided to reject the petition of the Phi Kappa Rho local Jewish fraternity at the University of Akron in Ohio. The Akron group was a substantial one by local fraternity standards. With twenty-one active members and sixty-five alumni, it had been in operation for sixteen years and maintained its own small house, where the commuting students could gather for lunch and for meetings. And yet, diligent though the Akron students might be in their studies and dedicated though they might be to their fraternity, the chapter apparently had not and was not drawing members from the upper brackets of the American Jewish hierarchy. As the Phi Epsilon Pi investigator reported, "The boys attending Akron University come from low income bracket families and practically all are forced to work while attending school in order to help defray expenses." This made them unsuitable as a potential Phi Epsilon Pi chapter.[51] They were, however, acceptable to the national fraternity Alpha Epsilon Pi, which placed the University of Akron on its rolls in early 1941.[52]

The informal rule that chapters within driving distance of one another ought to be roughly of the same class and income level also continued to hold despite the bad economy. Here the New Orleans Sophie Newcomb chapter of AEPhi, though it was the pride of the national sorority, actually hampered expansion in the area because it was so difficult to find enough Jewish college women of equivalent status and appearance in any other school nearby. Similarly, in 1934 Maurice Jacobs of Phi Epsilon Pi expressed his desire to pledge an "excellent" petitioning Jewish local at Temple University in Philadelphia. However, he concluded with regret, it was "an utter impossibility" to establish a chapter at Temple "as long as we have a good chapter at the University of Pennsylvania."[53] The problem was similar to the tension that had existed in the 1920s between Carnegie Tech and the University of Pittsburgh. Both the Ivy League Penn and the more plebeian Temple University offered their students an excellent higher education. For purposes of socializing, however, the gap between the two schools and the class of students in attendance was too great for fraternal peace to prevail between them.

Rejection Rhetoric

The old lessons equating desirability with long residence in the U.S., "Gentile" appearance, wealth, and attendance at campuses of established status, were not lost on the officers of Alpha Epsilon Phi sorority. If anything, against the background of economic and world events in the 1930s, they began to apply these criteria even more stringently in their investigation reports. If a state school was poorly funded or drew too many students of undesirable background, other fraternities or sororities might be interested; but for the elite they were relegated to a thick folder of reports labeled "Petitioning Groups Not Accepted." The reasons given for rejection paint a vivid picture of Jewish class, religious, cultural, and geographic divisions, Jewish absorption of general social standards of the period, and an acute anxiety of what the Gentile world would think of their organization's members.

These reports, usually labeled "confidential," had to be written in detail and mimeographed for distribution. The feelings they reveal could not be relegated, as they might be in later generations, to whispered face-to-face conversations behind closed doors or furtive home telephone conversations. The sorority's national officers lived scattered throughout the country. The parameters of these discussions in those days were considered a legitimate part of any sorority's rushing business, Jewish or Gentile. The cost of long distance telephone calls in the 1930s was prohibitive, and all business and discussion had to be conducted by post. Thus, every nuance of attitude was committed to paper. There was little reason to hesitate in any event. As every Jew had reason to know who had ever applied for entrance to a college, a club, or a job in a competitive company, this was an era when letters of reference written by Gentiles routinely made reference to a person's religion, general appearance, race, ethnic background, mannerisms, anatomical features, and semitic or nonsemitic appearance. Neither law nor custom dictated otherwise.

For example, in recommending that they reject a petitioning Jewish local at the University of Maine in Orono in late 1930, the sorority's field secretary reported that the girls were good scholastically, "rated" in activities, were accepted socially, were charming hostesses, and were "beautifully organized." However, the university, the state, and the social class and finances of the girls it drew were not acceptable, and the group would never be considered "AEPhi material" by any other chapter. The school itself, with 1700 students including 500 women (25 of them Jewish) was small and geographically isolated, and for the past two years had been supported only by a millage tax from the state. With only two cities of any importance in Maine and no industrial centers, the girls had "no particular money or social ranking," and were also too close for comfort to poverty, immigrant origins, and Orthodox Judaism:

> The cities are Portland, with 75,000 people and one Reform congregation; the smaller is Bangor, which has three Orthodox congregations and no Reform one, although the Reform Jews there import a rabbi for the holidays. Having the opportunity of meeting the parents of several girls, I found that with the exception of one family, most of the parents were foreign born and spoke with an accent, some Russian, the majority of German descent. . . . The girls live in these old-fashioned houses, chromos, tin types, seashells, ugly, non-descript old-fashioned furniture, etc. They, themselves, reflect a small provincial atmosphere—as a group they don't know how to dress and probably don't need it. There are some Jewish types among them—but while being Jewish, they are NOT the loud, cheap, Jewish type—they reflect . . . probably the community, certainly the best of Maine—they are countrified, provincial, and as Jewish as such a background would suggest.[54]

In the end, Alpha Epsilon Phi did not accept the group, although their competitors Sigma Delta Tau did.

Elizabeth Eldridge, who served as the national head of Alpha Epsilon Phi in 1931–1937, was capable of expressing the most merciless anti-Jewish judgments against young women who failed to meet her standards. This could occur even while she was pouring her energy into defending her people and trying to convince the Gentile sororities to admit Alpha Epsilon Phi into the National Panhellenic Congress. The two phenomena, while seemingly paradoxical, may not have been unrelated. As part of her job as Panhellenic Chairman, Eldridge, then in her mid-twenties, was being exposed year after year to the prejudices of Gentile representatives and to their smooth excuses that only the bad behavior of other Jews was ruining AEPhi's chances for full acceptance. In one of her earliest visits to their George Washington University chapter in Washington D.C. in 1933, her comments were favorable with one exception: "Only one of the girls fits the description 'greasy' (forgive me the use of the adjective). She is a Phi Sigma Sigma transfer from Iota [Syracuse University] and their pledge problem. I was left to lecture her, etc. but I could do it only half-heartedly, for I hope she depledges . . . Such a girl should have been blackballed emphatically."[55] The following year she described the members of a petitioning local at the University of Iowa as "ill at ease. . . . small town girls, no poise, complete lack of background and a bit pathetic," and that they would be good material for "Fleishigmaigma, ha ha!" (her derogatory term for competitor Phi Sigma Sigma, based on the Yiddish word for "meat.")[56]

However, Eldridge's strongest words were for a local at Indiana University at Bloomington, which she visited two days later on March 9, 1933. To her horror, the group had already been officially pledged to Alpha Epsilon Phi while she herself was away visiting the West Coast. Apparently a nervous national officer, upon hearing that competitor Sigma Delta Tau was after the group and had issued them with an ultimatum, telephoned the leader of the local and pledged them to Alpha Epsilon Phi without doing the customary background check (the campus at the time had 180 Jewish students, 140 men and 30 women). "Indiana has no place in AEPhi," Eldridge protested, "and the problem now is not how we got it but what shall we do with it?"[57]

According to her evaluation, most of the members of the local were lower-middle-class Jews from traditional or immigrant backgrounds. The group was furthermore burdened by several New York City women who were out of the question as AEPhi material, as Eldridge pointed out in her confidential individual evaluations. (The full names were used in the original source; these are omitted and the initials changed here.)

> *U:* is the dean and most unattractive. No family background, a gross personality, would not be pledged AEPhi at any other chapter . . . *V: (Gary):* Absolutely impossible. In appearance a typical fat largehipped, heavy breasted, greasy-haired Jewish mama with offensive mannerisms and a slight suggestion of a foreigner in her speech. Apparently had money. I simply cannot see her wearing an AEPhi pin. Forgot to say she wears tight-knitted suits and loose brassieres to complete the picture. *W:* I understand she has a presentable mother. Father a jeweler in Richmond,

Ind. Passable in appearance. *X:* Originally from N.Y.—typical ghetto personality. Impossible! Phi Sig material. I absolutely refuse to put a pin on her. *Y:* Add to description of V.—gold teeth. Edited high school paper. Pledged because she makes A's. Impossible! *Z:* My impression of her is a bad case of eczema. Country hick, also impossible.[58]

As a group, Eldridge continued, the Indiana women failed every possible standard, including the religious one:

They are not physically an attractive-looking group of girls. Some are unpleasantly semitic in features. They are not collegiate. They dress poorly. They are not worldly but represent the product of Indiana farms . . . They are not a wealthy group of girls. They do not come from homes of much background. They are still superstitious. They would not let me sit on the floor because one sits so for the dead, or mend clothes on myself without chewing a piece of bread, etc. They are not socially desirable by any standards of judging Jewish communities by the European countries from which they came.

Finally, the house was unlivably dirty and cluttered, and their food inedible. Eldridge's vote was to depledge the group, refund their money, "and then I want a one-way ticket to Siam."[59]

In succeeding investigations, the investigator showed a tendency to focus on candidates' "Jewish" or "Semitic" features when presenting evaluations. Even in Eldridge's highly positive report of the ill-fated William and Mary chapter later that month, the terms intruded: "*Alberta Alperin:* Junior . . . very popular with gentile girls . . . Petite, cute, not Semitic looking . . ." and "*Hannah Steinhardt:* Freshman in charter group—very good-looking in Semitic way, extremely refined."[60] Signs of traditional Jewish observance were also considered a drawback. In May 1933 Eldridge strongly advised against taking the petitioning local at the University of West Virginia at Morgantown, saying that the only reason the girls were there was that they could not afford to go to Ohio State, where most of the "best" material from that part of the country went (the total student population at the time was 2500, including 120 Jewish men and 25 Jewish women). Besides, she and Reba B. Cohen had found "only eight girls at the most who are presentable and possible material," and it would not be possible to separate out this desirable material for the following reason:

The difficulty lies in the fact that the group could not be split because Goldie somebody-or-other's mother runs a kosher boarding house for the girls and they could not think of leaving her for a house. Goldie is quite impossible; and a look at her foretells the worst about the boarding house. In conversation with the Dean of Women, she mentioned conflict about the dietary laws as a reason the girls could not live together happily in a sorority house. Do not misunderstand me; I am not writing a brief against orthodox Judaism or stating that a girl is undesirable because she lives according to the dietary laws. However, in a small-town state like West Virginia, Iowa, Indiana, etc. you are apt to find that the orthodox Jews are the unassimilated element in the population. It is a poor beginning for a charter group.[61]

In this case, as Eldridge pointed out, the attitude of their main competitor Sigma Delta Tau was the same: apparently a representative from that sorority had already visited the campus "and offended the girls by discussing desirability and letting them know that they were not interested in families who spoke Yiddish." Her own overall impressions was that "they would make an excellent chapter of Phi Sigma Sigma . . . and in ten years might develop into a borderline AEPhi chapter" but for now, she "emphatically" recommended against rushing them.[62]

When Ruth Eldridge followed in her older sister's footsteps as a national Alpha Epsilon Phi officer, perceptions of Jewish appearance as a detriment similarly colored her report on a Jewish local sorority at the University of Arizona in Tucson in 1936. There, the student population totaled 2000, and 50 of 900 women students were Jewish. Arizona was booming at the time because of the growing popularity of Tucson as a health resort, and increasing numbers of Jews were settling there, either temporarily or permanently, for the sake of a sick member of the family.[63] In her individual evaluations, she made the following observations:

> *Lillian Brill:* She doesn't look particularly Jewish to me . . . *Juliette Kruger:* Vivacious personality, attractive. . . . a great favorite with everyone. Has four very popular brothers, all of whom are Zebes. . . . She's a dance major and her family is Orthodox, interestingly enough. *Irene Marion Rosenblatt:* Helen F's first cousin, same age. Not as pretty as Helen, small, more Jewish looking but quite refined. Nice personality . . . *Tillie Farber (El Paso Texas):* . . . She has a very nice personality but is quite Jewish looking . . . Has a brother who is SAM at Yale, a brother-in-law who is a Zebe at Arizona, and her sister's husband owns Levy's, one of Tucson's department stores . . .[64]

While women from department store-owning families were considered highly desirable, those who belonged to the small business or merchant class were not. The evaluation of Marion Diamond, in reporting on a small Jewish local at Penn State in 1935, was that it decidedly did "not rate" socially, financially, in campus activities, or in any other way.[65] A major source of the trouble seemed to be the economic position of the girls' families, who were mostly engaged in storekeeping and who violated the middle-class value that a married woman should not work outside her home:

> The largest percentage of the girls come from small Pennsylvania mining towns, and their families own small merchandise stores. I say "families" because the entire family works in the stores and consequently have time for nothing else. Lack of outside interests and culture are noticeable and affects the interests in college. Main topic of conversation among the girls is the happenings in the stores. I enlarge upon this because the presence of the mothers in the business rather than the homes has produced in the girls an absolute lack of knowledge as to how to run a home, of how to plan a social event, no charm—no interests outside their small world. A few of them know how to meet and converse with outsiders but most of them cannot carry on a conversation and are always ill at ease. All of this was evident at a tea given by them for me. Many of their remarks were ill chosen and tactless and would, if I had been a visiting officer of AEPhi to a chapter, have embarrassed me considerably and caused a lecture at a later meeting.[66]

The latter part of this passage suggests, incidentally, why the social education in upper-middle-class American Anglo-Saxon manners and mores within the Jewish fraternity system was so effective. Outside the intimate circle, it might be considered the height of rudeness to draw a person's shortcomings to their attention. Within a fraternity chapter however, and certainly among a semifamilial group of young Jews, no such reservations existed. Perceived errors received immediate admonishment from officers or older members. This type of learning could be painful, but it was swift, and it was unlikely that pupils would soon repeat their mistakes.

During investigations to evaluate potential members for the sorority, the Gentile Dean of Women on each campus was an important potential partner. When contacted, she could be rude or dismissive, as was the Dean at the University of Oklahoma at Norman in January 1932, who scoffed at the idea of there being any difference between Alpha Epsilon Phi and Sigma Delta Tau. All Jews were alike, she insisted, including all 30 young women then attending the University of Oklahoma, and "one sorority is good enough for them."[67] Or, the Dean of Women could be a cooperative ally. In the case of Alpha Epsilon Phi's investigation of the petitioning local at the University of Maine, their field secretary was able to write with obvious pleasure in November 1930: "The Dean understands Jewish problems very well. She told me frankly that she had eliminated the offensive Jewish type by personal interview and that the 25 girls on campus were all acceptable. Only one, H., in the local, was disliked because of her pugnacity about grades."[68] At Randolph-Macon College in 1932 investigator Virginia D. Frolichstein reported

> Miss Whiteside, the Dean of Women, was very cordial and quite frank. . . . She's eager to have the right type of Jewish student and seems completely without prejudice. . . . The townspeople of Lynchburg send their offspring to R-M but they are not, in the words of Miss Whiteside, what we would want. There is one family, the Guggenheimers, who are outstanding. They have nothing to do with the other Jews and are the family to sponsor AEPhi.[69]

Similarly, Aline Lazard Roos, the sorority's National Ritualist and investigator of a Jewish local sorority at the newly-built Duke University in North Carolina, was pleased but cautious when she reported in January 1934, "The Dean of Women, Miss Baldwin, had only good to say of them. She interviews practically every Jewish or Eastern or Northern person who applies to Duke, therefore ruling out undesirables, but am afraid her standard is just so they aren't flagrantly unrefined and do have good scholarship records. They want the university to retain its southern flavor."[70]

The New York Jewish Problem

When it came to social distinctions and the elimination of "undesirables," few Jews suffered more both at the hands of Gentiles and of other Jews than the denizens of New York City and its environs. The reluctance of the best Jewish fraternities to pledge Jews from the New York area presented a significant problem, since they represented easily one-third to one-half of the American Jewish population. However, if one feared loud, pushy, vulgar, unrefined Jews, then with few exceptions, Jews from New York were considered the epitome of loudness, pushiness, vulgarity and coarseness.[71] The big city had an unfortunate tendency to breed college students with a taste for radical politics and ignorance of or disrespect for the preferred local norms of behavior.

It was also widely acknowledged that New Yorkers did not make the best fraternity material. The Greek system as a whole had never flourished in greater New York City. Its natural environment had long been the small college towns of the South, Midwest, and West, where college students were completelyW dependent upon it. In states and cities with a relatively small Jewish population, as in Alabama, Mississippi, and Louisiana, Jewish fraternity houses could easily become a focus of Jewish communal activity and financial contributions. In New York City, however, with its millions of Jews and thousands of Jewish institutions, fraternities were a leisure-time club at best and a curiosity at worst. Too many other attractions competed for time and attention. In addition, as in any large urban area, in New York too many students could live at home and thus avoid the communal discipline and correction that was the ideal of fraternity life. Furthermore, the price of real estate in Manhattan made maintaining a house, clubrooms, or guestrooms for out-of-towners difficult for the wealthy fraternities and impossible for those less well off.[72]

Consequently, although all but two of the original twenty-five Jewish national fraternities and sororities had been founded in New York State, by the late 1920s the focus of Jewish fraternity life had shifted in other directions. One might call this phenomenon the "de-Newyorkization" of the Jewish fraternities, and it was illustrated well by statistics compiled for the 1932 directory of Zeta Beta Tau. By that year, less than one quarter of the fraternity's 4,452 living members resided in New York City. A significant number of these had not been born or raised in New York, but had migrated there after college graduation for the employment opportunities it offered.[73]

An additional challenge to maintaining strong fraternity organizations in New York City was also what might be called the "Alpha Problem" ("Alpha" being the first, or founding, chapter of a fraternity). In the case of the Jewish groups, this was most likely to be City College, Columbia, New York University, Barnard, or Hunter. At the turn of the twentieth century, the City College of New York still maintained an aristocratic tone, and Greek and Latin were an important part of the curriculum. Within a decade, however, the tuition-free school was becoming the proverbial "Harvard of the poor." Hours of classes, a long subway commute, and work at outside jobs left little time for fraternity activities and the cultivation of gentility. Intellectually and academically, by the 1930s City College men felt themselves to be far superior to their Jewish student counterparts across the country, and indeed CCNY was distinguished by its high admissions standards and demanding academic program. However, serious class and cultural differences became

painfully obvious when members from across the land gathered in New
York City for annual conventions and rubbed shoulders with men from
City College.

New York University in Washington Square did charge some
tuition, but the social and economic position of most of its male students
was perceived as being as low if not lower than their City College counterparts. City College at least put its students through a rigorous training
in sciences and the liberal arts, whereas students at NYU's downtown
campus for the most part studied business administration. This unfortunate development had resulted in the virtual excommunication of Phi
Epsilon Pi's downtown NYU chapter in 1922. Phi Epsilon Pi was willing to consider establishing a chapter at NYU's uptown or "Heights"
liberal arts campus, located in an attractive, semisuburban section of the
Bronx, but no more than one or two potential student members ever
materialized there before the end of World War II. National fraternity officers outside the metropolitan area also became aware of the vast
rivers that separated the actual island of Manhattan from the boroughs
of the Bronx and Brooklyn. "I am absolutely not interested in any group
of students at NYU downtown," wrote Philadelphian Grand Secretary
Charles H. Fleishman of Phi Epsilon Pi in the summer of 1930, when
other officers suggested that Depression-time economics dictated taking
another look at the downtown school. "It is in the mercantile section of
the city where the students have as their campus the business section
of the city without the possibility of any campus activity or fraternity
life. You can also well imagine the nature of the students who attend
such a school. About eighty percent of the group with whom we are
negotiating reside in Brooklyn. Such a fact is extremely unfavorable."[74]

As for finances, the situation reached its nadir during the Depression, when the majority of City College or NYU students could
barely afford their carfare, much less fraternity dues and fees. In fall
1932, for example, when the initiation fee at Phi Epsilon Pi's "Mother"
chapter at City College was $85.00, the chapter's Superior Morton
Francis Bickart found himself forced to write to the national office that
of seven men initiated only two had been able to pay in full. The office responded by lowering the fee down to $50.00 and again down
to $30.00, but it was still too much for "the chapter which gave birth
to Phi Epsilon Pi" to pay.[75] In the case of Sigma Alpha Mu in 1934,
not one of the four pledges was able to pay his fees in full, and none
could be initiated until a group of alumni had taken up a collection for
them.[76]

On the evening of their June graduation dinner in 1935, members of Phi Sigma Delta chapter at New York University's "uptown" or semi-suburban University Heights campus in the Bronx are photographed outside their chapter house. (Zeta Beta Tau Archives)

While other schools were tightening their restrictions on Jewish enrollment in the 1930s, the administration of Miami University in Oxford, Ohio, was encouraging Jewish students, along with chapters of their fraternities, to come. Here the charter members of Zeta Beta Tau at Miami University gather on the day of their chapter's installation into the national fraternity by a visiting alumni team, Feb. 22, 1936. *Front row, left to right:* Arnold D. Swartz '37, Seymour Weisberger, Samuel E. Mendelson '36, , David K. Leshner '37, Irving D. Robinson '37. *Back row:* Arthur B. Aurbach '36, Sanford R. Katz '37, Robert W. Reis '38, Benjamin J.Weiss '38, and Morton W. Weingart '36. (Zeta Beta Tau Archives)

The interior of the Alpha Epsilon Pi chapter house at Emory University in Atlanta in the 1930s. (Alpha Epsilon Pi Archives)

Billed as "The First *Succah* ever built in an American Jewish fraternity house," this Feast of Tabernacles ritual booth, designed and constructed by class of 1942 Phi Epsilon Pi chapter members Arthur H. Jaffe and Ralph Madway (pictured here), attracted students, faculty, and townspeople for miles around when it was erected at Penn State in October 1939. (Zeta Beta Tau Archives)

Sigma Alpha Mu regional conclave held in Bloomington, Indiana, 1935. (Sigma Alpha Mu Archives)

At the University of Iowa, Sigma Delta Tau sorority members and their housemother gather on the steps of the library to be photographed during the 1934–1935 academic year, the second of the chapter's existence. (Sigma Delta Tau Archives)

At the University of Iowa in 1933, the first chapter of Sigma Delta Tau. (Sigma Delta Tau Archives)

The 1934 national convention of Alpha Epsilon Phi in Colorado Springs. Elizabeth Eldridge (in dark dress) is seated in the center front row. She served as traveling secretary and then national head of the sorority from 1929 to 1937. (Alpha Epsilon Phi Archives)

Members of Sigma Delta Tau sorority from across the country gather for their seventh biennial convention in December 1934 at the Hotel Statler in Buffalo, New York. (Sigma Delta Tau Archives)

Sigma Delta Tau sorority at Indiana University in Bloomington, Indiana, in 1940. (Sigma Delta Tau Archives)

Alpha Epsilon Pi's national convention Dec. 31, 1940, held at the Hermitage Hotel in Nashville, TN. *Standing in the back row, from left:* Arthur Pick, Sidney Steinberg, O. C. Carmichael (Chancellor of Vanderbilt University), I. E. Goldberg, Morris Davis, Rabbi Julius Mark, and Leon Traub. (Alpha Epsilon Pi Archives)

At the University of Connecticut at Storrs in 1942, Joseph Kruger (holding book), the executive head of Phi Sigma Delta, formally pledges a local group of Jewish students to the national fraternity. (Zeta Beta Tau Archives)

At the University of Michigan, c. 1940s. Outside Stockwell Hall, then the women's dormitory, men give their dates a goodnight kiss on a snowy winter's evening as the 12 A.M. curfew and school regulations force them to separate at the door (the curfew could be extended to 1 A.M. on Saturday nights). Housemothers were known to stand guard outside dormitories and sorority houses, blinking the lights or otherwise making sure that the farewells were not too prolonged. On a typical American residential college campus before the late 1960s, two married couples were supposed to serve as chaperones at official university social events and visits between male and female students in their rooms were either forbidden or regulated. The most common rules called for limited visiting hours with "both feet on the floor and the door open at least a book's width." (Zeta Beta Tau Archives)

Sigma Delta Tau sorority at the University of Nebraska at Lincoln in the 1940s. *Top row, left to right:* Annette Jacobs, Miriam Krulick, Rodine Isodofsky, Sylvia Guravick, Tootie Monowitz, Jackie Gordon, Doris Belzer, Darlene Marcus, Lorraine Davidson, Marcia Lee Civin. *Second row:* Arlene Cooper, Arlene Swartz, Beulah Hatloff, Dorthea Rosenberg, Selma Lou Mandelberg, Sarah Bernstein, Maurine Ewen, Flo Pred, Lenore Simon, Beverlee Meriam, Phyllis Freed, Lorraine Steinberg. *Third row:* Beverly Marcus, Eileen Darkovsky, Jean Bernstein, Estelle Mazer, Ethel Miller, "Aunt" Jean Israel (housemother), Glita Hill, Marilyn Adler, Charlotte Hill, Shirley Grossman, Lorraine Abramson. *First row:* Bernice Papeney, Betty Kuklin, Mildred Zuker, Pearl Brick, Charlotte Musin, Ethelyn Lashinsky, Ruth Goldberg, Anna Lee Strauss. (Sigma Delta Tau Archives)

The Sigma Delta Tau sorority at the University of Iowa at Iowa City in front of their chapter house in 1942. Members pictured here include Susan Cohen, Marilyn Shapiro, Denny Menzer, Reva Brody, Delores Sklar, Marilyn Glassman, Louise Nathanson, Edythe Bubb, Helyne Wohlnen, B. R. Kubby, Harriette Smuleson, Eilene Rosenthal, Pauline Fishbein, Corrine Gould, Miriam Katz, Evelyn Rasen, Bea Rosenberg, Lillian Sherman, and Mrs. Chapman, a.k.a. "Aunt Vi," housemother. (Sigma Delta Tau Archives)

The Sigma Delta Tau pledge class at Penn State in 1942. (Sigma Delta Tau Archives)

The founding chapter of Sigma Delta Tau sorority at Pennsylvania State University in 1943. *Top row, left to right:* Betty Berman, Eileen Ershler, Ruth Constad, Roz Dulberg, Jeanne Eisenberg, Ruth Cohen Freed, Mimi Kraungold Robinson, Flo Marcus, Libby Peters. *Second row from top:* Teddy Weenoff Rappaport, Jacquie Stiefel Spritzler, Sydelle Buckwalter, Til Bronstein, Flo Krieger, Carol Finklestein, Harriet Finklestein, Jane Metzendorf. *Third row:* Nina Rabinowitz, Dottie Leibowitz, Mae Schultz Leuchuer, Melba David, Dotty Robinson, Raisa Robinson Poser, Norma Poster, Irene Klein, Joan Miller, Lucille Rosenblum, Clavie Kahn, Bobbie Grosshart, Arlene Freedman Rabinowitz, Sybil Peskin, Jean Labell. *Bottom row:* Ruth Kahn Posner, Cecile Pichel Henschel, Bernice Alpert, Evie Sherman Jackson, Shirley Beth Feldman Levine, Flip Lawenbaum Grossman, Terry Rosenthal, Arlene Crystal, Florence Kraster. (Sigma Delta Tau Archives)

Mrs. Margaret Rossiter, for decades the administrator of Zeta Beta Tau's national office in New York City, works at her desk during World War II next to the fraternity's service flag. The numeral "2024" indicates the number of the organization's members serving in the armed forces. Gold stars at top indicate those killed in action. (Zeta Beta Tau Archives)

As the alumni of Zeta Beta Tau celebrate the end of World War II in the fall of 1945, a large banner on the wall announces their "Victory Convention" to be held in Los Angeles the following summer. The customary annual gathering had not been held since 1941. Approximately one-third of the living membership of ZBT served in the armed forces during World War II, and 121 lost their lives. (Zeta Beta Tau Archives)

Hasty snapshot of a bouquet of flowers lying at the foot of a Star of David in a field of crosses at a military cemetery in Margraten/Maashricht, Holland, in 1945. Pvt. Jerome C. Cantor, NYU and Phi Sigma Delta Class of 1941, age 25, fought in the infantry in the Battle of the Bulge. He died in a German prison camp on March 15, 1945 and was buried in this grave on June 6. He was survived by his parents, Dr. and Mrs. Jacob A. Cantor of 21 West 86th Street, New York City. (Zeta Beta Tau Archives)

Annual formal dinner dance of the Marquette University chapter of Alpha Epsilon Pi fraternity in Milwaukee, WI, 1947. The chapter's new officers that year included Harry Katz, Elliot Shafton, Seymour Solomon (Master), Laury Spitzer, Jay Werner, and Herb Wischnia. (Alpha Epsilon Pi Archives)

A song leader leads Phi Epsilon Pi members in the traditional singing of "Alouette" at the formal dance of the University of Pittsburgh chapter held October 10, 1948, at the Jackson Hotel. (Zeta Beta Tau Archives)

"Parisian Night" at the Wayne State University chapter of Alpha Epsilon Pi, c.
1952. This photograph was taken and saved by Mitchell Tendler of Detroit.
(Zeta Beta Tau Archives)

Formal dance night at the Vanderbilt University chapter of Zeta Beta Tau in June
1940 in Nashville, Tennessee. *Men seated front row, left to right:* George J. Fox
'41, Jack A. Bernard '40, Frank, Harris S. Abrahams '40, Leonard C. Ghertner
'40, Clifford Tillman '42, Louis Levy '40, Gerald Winokur '40. *Middle row, right
to left:* Richard L. Goldberg '43, Stanley W. Gross '43, Edward Baloff '41, Alfred
I. Rosenbaum '42, Everett H. Erlick '42, Eugene Greener Jr. '42, Joel W.
Solomon '42, Asher Rosenblatt '44, Henry L. Reitler '42, Leon May '43. *Back
row, left to right:* Gilbert S. Fox '42, Louis H. Brooks '43, Samuel J. Simon '42,
Hal Gerber '43, Allen S. Eskind '43, Charles Cohen '41, Gus D. Kuhn, Jr. '43,
William J. Ziv '42, Maxwell Rasman '42. (Zeta Beta Tau Archives)

Formal initiation dinner dance at the Hotel Syracuse, April 6, 1940. (Zeta Beta Tau Archives)

Junior Prom weekend at Rutgers University, Phi Epsilon Pi chapter house, March 1962. (The housemother is seated at the center.) Within a few short years campuses such as this would be convulsed with riots and student unrest; proms, fraternities, and related student rituals would be branded as "irrelevant." At Columbia University in 1968, the Phi Epsilon Pi house was abandoned and turned over to the SDS (Students for a Democratic Society). The national fraternity itself could no longer function independently and had to merge with an older and larger organization in 1970. (Zeta Beta Tau Archives)

Meet Some of the Girls . . .

ANITA NOODLEMAN   MARLENE GREEN   MABLE RUTENBERG   MARCY SINYKIN   RENE BECHTER

. . . They're Your Convention Dates!

The girls here, plus Margie Album on the front page, are just a dozen of the beautiful, fun-loving girls the convention date committee, under the chairmanship of Dick Firestone, has rounded up exclusively for you Paul Bunyan Convention-goers.

IRENE NEWMAN

NANCY WOLFSON

And when will you meet them? Before your first date, of course!

Those of you arriving in time for the pre-convention open house at Alpha Delta Chapter may find your date there. If not, you'll meet the girls at a special cocktail party and reception held following the first day's business sessions in the Garden Room of the Dyckman Hotel.

BETTY SILVERMAN   RENE MILSTEIN   LOIS KLUGMAN   ESTHER BERMAN

So Get Your Date Request In Now!

Advertisement in the October 1950 Phi Epsilon Pi convention newsletter urging unattached members to send in both their reservations and their "date requests" for the upcoming annual December convention in Minneapolis, hosted by the University of Minnesota chapter. The young women pictured here and others have been chosen by the fraternity's "date committee," assisted by the sororities and the local Jewish community, to be matched up with visiting convention-goers. The traditional social and matchmaking functions of the Jewish Greek sub-system had been powerful motives for the support of parents, rabbis, and communal leaders against the many who opposed college fraternities. With the end of legal sectarianism in the 1950s and 1960s, that support waned or disappeared. (American Jewish Historical Society)

As time went on, the "Alpha" chapters became more and more of a financial drain and a social embarrassment to the fraternities' names, and thus reluctance to support them increased. By 1937, the Phi Epsilon Pi City College chapter was down to only two active members.[77] Zeta Beta Tau, which had not truly been founded at City College and was less troubled by sentiment toward it, had already jettisoned their chapter there in 1936.

For the Jewish fraternities, New York Jews posed an even greater problem outside the Big Apple than inside it. When quotas, admissions restrictions, limited finances, family pressure and undistinguished grades sent thousands of them into America's hinterland, officers were pleased to see the beds in their houses being filled. Yet they were not pleased with the unpopular reputation that New York Jews always seemed to garner for themselves. "This boy seemed to be excellent material," wrote a Kansas City alumni officer in explaining why a certain student should not become affiliated with the Zeta Beta Tau chapter there. "My only objection to him was that he is from New York. I do not say that facetiously; most of the boys who come out here from the east do not make good fraternity men."[78]

Maurice Jacobs, as a graduate of the University of Maine and a Philadelphian, made the same observation in 1932 when he reported on the health of Phi Epsilon Pi's chapter at Cornell University. "At Cornell we have always had two different elements in the chapter, which for the sake of a better name I shall call the Brooklynites and the non-Brooklynites," he wrote. "These elements . . . seem to represent two distinct types of men in that institution. I want to be entirely fair in the matter and say from my own observation that the men who have come from places other than Brooklyn have been a much better element in our chapter."[79] In 1937, Samuel J. Sherman, a close friend and fellow national officer from Chicago, wrote to Jacobs asking him to comment on a new "menace" that his Midwestern fraternity associates kept mentioning. "Since my school days, a dread spectre seems to have descended on campuses—N.Y. Jews," he wrote. "What's it all about, and what does it mean? . . . They're beginning to appear at Northwestern, and other campuses where they were formerly unknown. If you have time, could you enlighten me?"[80] Jacobs wrote back:

> The matter of the problem of New York Jews is one which I would rather not discuss with you in a letter, but when I see you next time, I will give you a real harangue on the matter. That is a very serious problem and one

which I have talked about privately before many groups. It is the biggest
problem we have in our American colleges today and one which will not
be solved in five minutes. The New York Jewish men can't get along by
themselves in a Chapter composed only of their own men, and they can't
get along in a mixed chapter since they take that very supercilious attitude
that the Hinterland begins where the subway ends. They are the typical
wise guys, are the product of America's worst environment, and just don't
fit into the picture in most places.[81]

Without a doubt New York Jews had an impact on a fraternity chapter's status and social standing. In general, in the large state
universities and most certainly in the South, the more local area Jews
a chapter could draw, the more prestige accrued to it, and the stigma
of not attracting local Jews could be felt keenly. In 1937, for example,
the undergraduate officers of Sigma Alpha Mu's University of Kansas
Chapter in Lawrence, Kansas, lamented that all ten of them were "east-
erners," and that their chapter did not seem to attract any of the Kansas
or Missouri students.[82] At the University of Georgia, it was already a
long-established pattern that only true southerners (preferably from Atlanta) were accepted at the upper-tier Phi Epsilon Pi, while middle-
and lower-tier Tau Epsilon Phi and Alpha Epsilon Pi took in the New
Yorkers.[83]

New York's size and social anonymity also detracted from its
suitability as a source for good Greek material. Fraternity and sorority leaders were accustomed to shooting telegrams and telephone calls
across the country and instantly receiving the full family background of
a prospective member. But they could never get used to a city so large
that no one could keep track of the status of various addresses, and even
among the Jewish community no one seemed to know anyone else.

Lee Dover of Zeta Beta Tau's New York City national office
was completely bewildered when the Irvin Fane, the Midwestern regional director in Kansas City, wrote to request a background check on
several New York City area men who were up for membership at their
University of Missouri chapter. Since Dover had grown up in western
Canada and Seattle, the social and physical geography of New York City
was a mystery to him, as his reply to the request indicates:

With reference to the three men who live in New York City (including
Brooklyn) I also must score a goose egg. Some parts of Brooklyn are nice,
and others are ghetto. I cannot even find anybody that ever heard of Dahill
Street or Avenue. The chap that lives on Schenectady Avenue lives in

close to downtown Brooklyn. East Fourth Street in Manhattan is down in Greenwich Village—some homes are extremely nice and others are shanty. We have about 2,000,000 Jews in New York City, as you know, and it is extremely difficult to get a line on any family, including some that may live the same apartment building as a ZBT. Omega [University of Missouri Chapter] will have to judge these boys on their own impressions, and use the pledge period as one of probation.[84]

The officers of Alpha Epsilon Phi faced similar challenges when investigating the ill-fated Jewish local sorority at the College of William and Mary in Williamsburg, Virginia, in 1933. Of the twenty young women in the petitioning group, ten were from the greater New York area, including Manhattan, Brooklyn, Queens, the town of Lawrence, and Newark, New Jersey. Of the others, eight were from various towns or cities in the state of Virginia, one was from West Virginia, and one was from Baltimore. The requisite background and family checks went with far greater ease for the non-New Yorkers. "You will, of course, appreciate that it is difficult to check Newark, Brooklyn, and New York girls," Elizabeth Eldridge wrote to the members of the National Council, apologizing that their information was so incomplete. "My checking was done by wire and phone calls to Alpha Gamma [George Washington University chapter] and by wire to Alice Greene [a resident of Manhattan]." Eldridge included the text of Greene's return wire, which read: "Leona Kanangeiser of Iota [Syracuse] Alumni in Newark rates three Newark girls well good family well recommended I don't know them nor anyone who knows them. Bea trying to get information on Brooklyn and Lawrence girls. She will wire you if she gets any. Looking up NY girls virtually impossible."[85]

In the Midwest: Hillel Rabbis Confront
New York Communist Jewish Students, 1937

Hillel rabbis also feared socially careless and disruptive New York Jews, along with what they perceived as their tendency to fill the ranks of the political radicals and rebels. As in the case of the leaders of the Menorah societies of the 1920s, the nature of the rhetoric of these religious and communal leaders—particularly those who themselves did not originate from anywhere near the New York area—was not always dissimilar from that of their secular Greek contemporaries.

At their annual meeting held in Martinsville, Indiana, in 1937, an address entitled "The Migratory Student and His Adjustment" given by Rabbi Max Kadushin, Hillel Director at the University of Wisconsin, opened a spirited discussion on the subject between rabbis from across the country.[86] The discussion incidentally does much to reveal the depth of antisemitism which Jewish students as a whole suffered on American college campuses during those years. This included restrictions on acceptance into medical school and the special difficulties and suspicions experienced by single Jewish female students trying to rent rooms in college town boarding houses. It also suggests how fear and resentment of New Yorkers coalesced into an attitude of fear and resentment of all those Jews who would not conform to accepted standards of behavior and thus might bring great danger down upon the entire people.

By the 1930s the term "migratory student" had become synonymous with New Yorkers, who for the communal leaders responsible for them had become synonymous with "trouble." As Rabbi Kadushin explained to his fellow Hillel directors:

> The term "New Yorkers" has, unfortunately, become a term of opprobrium on our campus. It designates the Jewish students who come from the east generally, of whom there are about three hundred. . . . The Eastern Jewish student, sophisticated by reason of his life in the large city, has a tendency to look down on the mid-westerner, whom he regards as a very simple sort. The Eastern student is often doctrinaire as a result of his radical political and economic sympathies. . . . In the classroom, too, the Eastern Jewish student is regarded with some disfavor. His fellow-students declare that, because of his loquaciousness in discussion, he takes up too much class time; and his professors complain that he is more apt than his fellow to wrangle about grades. It is enough that these things be true of only a proportion of the Jewish students from the East. . . . for the entire Jewish student-body to be stigmatized. Latent anti-Semitism finds in these qualities an excuse to come out in the open.

According to Kadushin, the Eastern Jewish student contingent not otherwise indistinguishable from his or her midwestern counterpart consisted of a shrinking number with "Hebraic backgrounds" who wished to continue with their Jewish interests, along with Ethical Culture school graduates who tended to maintain social bonds among themselves. However, the largest group "by far" he noted, were "members of the Young Communist League and their sympathizers," and it was this group of "New Yorkers" who represented their most serious problem on the campus. His Wisconsin campus alone, he noted, contained sixty members of the YCL and another 75 to 100 sympathizers, and most of these were "Eastern" Jews. (In the course of the discussion that fol-

lowed, Abram Sachar of Illinois contributed that he had a "problem" of
at least forty Communist Jewish students on his campus.) Even though
the Communist students scorned Judaism or indeed any religion as an
opiate of the people, Kadushin observed, it was a major effort for the
Hillel Rabbi to prevent the activities of the Communists—admittedly,
many of them of fine minds and great intellect—from bringing disfavor
upon the entire Jewish student body.[87]

Kadushin also revealed a characteristically fearful American
Jewish attitude in the 1930s toward public activism when he criticized
the Communist students for undertaking campaigns on behalf of Jews.
These included attempts to publish clear proof that the medical school
discriminated against them, or speaking out against the exclusion of
young Jewish women from private roominghouses. To have publicly attacked the medical school, in the rabbi's opinion, would only result in
out-of-state Jewish students being excluded altogether.

As for the rooming house problem, Kadushin declared:

> This evil is, of course, not confined to our campus. I have been occupied
> with mitigating it in various ways, and much can be done with the coop-
> eration of the university authorities. . . . The great error which the Com-
> munists make is this: They believe that by calling a case of anti-Semitism
> to the attention of the public the public conscience will be aroused. I am
> convinced that in this case the effect will be the opposite. Very many Gen-
> tile girl-students simply refuse to live in the same house with Jewish girls,
> and these will only take courage when they find how wide-spread their
> prejudice is.[88]

On the other hand, Rabbi Kadushin advised against pleading
with the communist students to keep silent out of consideration for the
Jewish people. This, he conceded, would violate the precious values of
free speech and conscience and would only further convince such students that organized Judaism was a reactionary force. Instead, he advised, it was better to pay attention to these students' pressing economic
needs, to give them a place on the Jewish student governing councils,
and to attempt to draw them in to Hillel classes. Precisely that thought-
fulness and social conscience characteristic of those drawn to Communism made these students, in his opinion, potentially the greatest leaders
in the Jewish community.[89]

In the discussion that followed, Kadushin's fellow rabbis did not
even refer to the case of Wisconsin's medical school or the current residential discrimination against single young Jewish women, which was

worse than that against Jewish men. These incidents were apparently
far too common in 1937 to be worthy of special attention. As early as
1925 the Dean of Women at the University of Michigan had informed
a visiting Alpha Epsilon Phi representative that "the problem of housing Jewish girls becomes harder every year."[90] By September 1936, at
the University of Illinois, Abram Sachar reportedly had found himself
at the start of the school year confronting an outbreak of antisemitism
in town so severe that fifty young Jewish women were forced to leave
school because they could not find a place to live.[91] Nor did Rabbi
Kadushin and his fellows discuss methods of dealing with student communism or concrete ways of fulfilling the students' needs. Instead, the
topic of conversation shifted quickly toward general criticism of "Eastern" or New York Jewish student behavior, as indicated by the verbatim

> *Rabbi Max J. Merritt (California):* In our Foundation we do not find the
> New York Jew repellant and obnoxious. However, because of the greater
> distance, we have but few New York Jews in California and I imagine we
> get a better type of New York Jew . . .
>
> *Rabbi Maurice Pekarsky (Cornell):* The New York students are obnoxious
> only in mass and therefore we cannot generalize on the basis of California.
>
> *Rabbi Martin Perley (Illinois):* I may say in defense of these obnoxious
> New York Jews that they come to Illinois primarily because the tuition is
> cheap. They come from poorer families, under-privileged families. They
> come to school in September and do not leave until the middle of June.
>
> *Rabbi Bernard Zeiger (North Carolina):* At North Carolina the feeling is
> so intense that when a signpost of New York is flashed on the screen in
> a moving picture theatre, there is a hiss . . . This is the indictment: The
> New York Jew is loud, vulgar, a chiseler for marks. . . . The Hillel cabinet
> visited the Northern boys and pointed out to them what was expected
> on a Southern campus. I sanctioned a letter going out to prospective stu-
> dents telling them the don'ts, such as being loud, shaving, and dressing
> properly . . .
>
> *Rabbi Bernard Heller (Michigan):* Doesn't [this] antagonism . . . reveal a
> psychological weakness on the part of students—something in our nature
> that we hate, give vent to it by hating New York students? Isn't that feeling
> the result of stereotyped judgment? . . . .
>
> *Rabbi Zeiger:* On the whole I think that the metropolitan Jew is obnox-
> ious and repellent and believe that the indictment is justified. At North
> Carolina it is a practical problem and the question is how to deal with it.[92]

The Greater Threat

Life and death issues lay behind the sharpness of fraternity and sorority rhetoric, and the fear and revulsion of the Hillel rabbis. For all, the economic difficulties of the Great Depression could be overcome or at least endured. Not all were equally affected, and if many were forced to drop out of colleges or chapters for lack of funds, others came to take their places. As for campus prejudice, quotas, and other limitations, these were already a familiar story. If Jews were shut out from some schools, they could still go to others. If Jewish students could not find rooms in one or the other boarding house, they could find a place to live somewhere else, or rely on their own fraternity system.

The worst problems of the 1930s, however, stemmed from those factors over which Jewish college students and those responsible for them exercised no direct control. These were the lengthening shadow of Hitlerism and Fascism in Europe and the terror that it would engulf them in the United States. The new generations and their mentors could not help but fear that hopes for safety and success in America were in jeopardy as they scrambled to respond to this new threat from across the seas.

Chapter 9

In the Shadow of Hitler

Social Life, Snobbery, and Jewish Identity

When Jewish college students and fraternity members encountered evidence of anti-Jewish feeling and discrimination during their years at school, their pain and resentment was usually tempered by awareness that conditions had been far worse for their immediate ancestors. In the 1930s their pain and resentment was also tempered by awareness that conditions were infinitely worse at that very moment for extended family trapped overseas. A newly married Elizabeth Eldridge and her husband found themselves pouring every penny of their wedding gifts toward rescuing two relatives from Nazi Germany and bringing them to America;[1] such stories and desperate attempts, not always successful, could be heard among American Jews of German heritage across the country. Prayers of thanksgiving for the ancestors who decided to leave for the United States in time soon became part of the private liturgy of thousands of citizens. Meanwhile fraternity travelers in the late 1930s were already well able to communicate their gratitude to friends at home.

"Europe, with the exception of perhaps France and England, is a hell of a place for the Jew to live," wrote Leo R. Markey, M.D., on January 29, 1937. A Phi Epsilon Pi and recent medical school graduate from Ohio State University, he was spending the winter and spring of that year traveling and working in Hungary, Austria, and France.

> Really and truthfully, I thank GOD I was born in the United States and that I am a citizen of that country. The land of the FREE and the HOME of the brave is no idle boast. It is more and more appreciated after seeing

and living in countries that limit the freedom, money, and pursuit of happiness of its citizens. I feel more and more each day that I will be the most happiest man in the world when I can set foot again on American soil and inhale a pure breath of American air . . . the LORD was good and kind when he made me an American.[2]

Fighting Nazism at Home: Protests and Condemnations

At that time, the faith of American Jews that they would be safe in their land was strong, but not strong enough to take for granted. Fraternities were concerned with fighting Nazism on their own campuses. In one instance, in December 1933, a Sigma Alpha Mu delegate from the University of Washington chapter traveled to a national committee meeting to complain that one of the Gentile fraternity houses had flown a Nazi flag for the period of one week without any interference from the university. In the ensuing discussion, officers agreed that similar occurrences could not be tolerated and that the National Interfraternity Conference must be enlisted to help prevent them in the future.[3]

During the same period Phi Epsilon Pi found itself confronting directly not only an American Nazi, but someone who was no less than *their* American Nazi. Back in the founding days of the fraternity at City College, German-born poet, playwright, publisher, and journalist George Sylvester Viereck '06 had been a dedicated member of the allegedly nonsectarian Phi Epsilon Pi. There he shared his love of German culture with his Jewish fraternity brothers, who in those days also came from a predominantly German cultural background. Their paths began to diverge, however, when during World War I Viereck became a leading pro-German propagandist, editing a newspaper known as *The Fatherland.* By 1920, he resigned in disgust when he comprehended that Phi Epsilon Pi had become an entirely Jewish organization. Periodically he let the press know his feelings regarding the religious-ethnic affiliations of his former fraternity brothers. By 1939 Viereck was, in the words of Maurice Jacobs, "one of the biggest Jew-baiters in America," and a Secretary of the German American Bund, the representatives of the Nazi Party in the United States. Who would have thought that their early experiments in nonsectarianism would have gone so awry? Still, in this case, as the Phi Epsilon Pi officers pointed out to indignant inquiries, Viereck had long since been struck from their membership rolls and there was nothing else they could do but ignore him.[4]

In the home front war against Nazism, the Jewish fraternities chose to take a firmer stand in some areas than in others. For Phi Ep-

silon Pi, the true plunge into political arena took place in January 1934
when the fraternity as a group threw its support behind Senate Resolution 154, which condemned the German Reich's treatment of its Jewish
subjects.[5] On the other hand, a Phi Epsilon alumnus heading the Chicago Committee for the Defense of Human Rights Against Nazism was
unable to obtain his fraternity's mailing list for use in the boycott against
German-made goods. As Maurice Jacobs replied to his inquiry, an informal meeting of Jewish fraternity officials in late 1933 concluded that
the fraternities as a group could not become involved in so controversial
and divisive a cause. In addition, none of them looked with favor upon
their mailing lists being used for anything but fraternity purposes.[6] The
attempt to organize an American Jewish boycott of German goods, as
it happened, was not successful in any quarter. Among other factors, no
one could be sure that a boycott of German goods might not harm German Jews as much as it helped them. Furthermore, a boycott might play
right into the hands of the Nazis, who charged that Jews were pulling
the economic strings of the United States.

Community Relations: Dickinson College

"Community relations," or the formation of educational and interfaith
programs to promote better relations between Jews and Christians, was
a particular area in which the Jewish fraternities could excel in fighting
back against Nazism and antisemitism. Their corporate nature made
them particularly well suited for it. In addition, it had always been
an important goal of the Jewish Greek subsystem to prove that Jewish students were the same as everybody else. In performing such work
students became expert in skills that would stand them in good stead
in later years working and volunteering for such organizations as the
Anti-Defamation League (ADL), the American Jewish Committee,
and other Jewish defense and human rights organizations.

In March 1936, for example, Norman Ranz, a young Phi Epsilon Pi attending the coeducational Dickinson College and head of the
Jewish Committee on Religious Affairs there, asked Maurice Jacobs for
"programming" and "public relations" tips for an upcoming campus religious program. It was the Jewish students' turn to present the regular
religious program that Sunday evening at a nearby church, and Ranz was
planning the content with special care. A Sigma Tau Phi student would
speak on "various Talmudic tales and how much of the old Hebrew law
has been basically incorporated into our American law system," Ranz

reported. Another Jewish fraternity student planned to give a speech refuting the alleged economic dominance of the Jew in the U.S. and Germany, while "one of the co-eds" would "perform and verbally explain certain musical numbers of Jewish tradition such as 'Eli, Eli,' and 'Kol Nidre.'"

All that remained to write was Ranz's own speech. He wished to end the evening with as "effective and forceful" an address as possible, without "boring the audience." As the undergraduate put it to Jacobs, "I would like to talk on some topic which is 'alive' and of utmost interest to a mixed group of students. That is, I'd rather avoid such topics as might border too much on the question of Anti-semitism, or the oppression of the Jews in Germany and America. In other words, I don't particularly care for a topic that might be considered 'stock.'" Ranz was afraid that his Dickinson College audience had reached the saturation point on bad news from overseas, and would not be willing to listen to more. Jacobs, himself an accomplished public speaker, understood exactly what the young man wanted and, appreciating his desire not to make a "stock" talk, gave him a detailed outline of alternative speech topics.[7]

Also at Dickinson College in 1937, the Jewish students' committee, which included the heads of the various fraternities, decided to confront the idea that "Jewish students have no love for Alma Mater"—a familiar charge since the days of the Harvard affair in 1922–1923—by organizing an annual project to do something "good and appropriate for the university as a whole." The previous year, as the Dickinson delegate informed his national convention, they had donated a set of books on American history to the library, in memory of a departed professor. That year, they had decided to donate a set of books "on the customs and holidays of the Jewish race, in order to get students acquainted with the race as a whole." In an arrangement that hearkened back to traditional European communities, the collection was being financed by a mandatory tax of two dollars from every Jewish student at Dickinson, which, the delegate reported, they were trying to collect "in as painless a fashion as possible."[8]

The Push to End Separate Jewish and Gentile Councils at Penn

At the same December 1937 convention, the Phi Epsilon Pi delegate from the University of Pennsylvania, which had thirteen Jewish men's national fraternities and two sororities, spoke in a similar fashion at roundtable discussions of the Louis Marshall Society of their school.

The Society's immediate goal was to unite all Jewish fraternity and non-fraternity men in order to "continually combat the Jewish prejudice on campus." "Do you try to combat the Jewish feeling, or just let it ride?" asked the delegate from the University of Michigan, using the general term—"Jewish feeling"—which the undergraduates meant to refer to anti-Jewish prejudice on their campuses. "We try to combat it, as far as we ourselves are concerned," replied the head of Phi Epsilon Pi's Penn chapter. "You have to admit that some of the Jewish students are objectionable." According to his report, the "Big Five" of the Jewish fraternities (that is, the five largest and most powerful men's fraternities in residence there) had recently gotten together and were doing their best to "break that feeling." As proof of their progress, the Penn delegate discussed the ongoing movement to merge the Group A (Gentile) and Group B (Jewish) Interfraternity Councils at Penn, and noted that several Jews were serving on the Gentile interfraternity ball committee for the first time.[9] Penn in this case was well behind New York University, where Mitchell Fisher had led the struggle to break the Gentile fraternities' exclusive control over the New York University Prom in 1923–25.

To some extent the Jewish fraternities had accepted and even desired the long-standing separation of Jewish and Gentile fraternities at Penn. To be members of the Gentile IFC's and panhellenics also meant being under the jurisdiction of strict Gentile rushing regulations designed to limit cutthroat competition. As on many campuses, at Penn, Gentile IFC regulations forbade rushing students until they actually set foot on the campus. Also, they could not join the fraternity immediately; initiation had to wait until later in their freshman year. By contrast Jewish fraternities, with a wider geographical area to cover and a smaller pool of potential applicants, enjoyed their freedom of rushing members while they were still in high school and then pledging them as soon as possible. Besides, no one expected the day would come when significant numbers of Jews would be rushed by Gentile fraternities or otherwise invited to socialize with them. Therefore, while restriction to Group B meant second-class citizenship, the motivation to end it was not strong.[10]

Nevertheless, the separation irked. As events developed overseas, the perception grew among communal leaders that a major principle was at stake in the Group A/Group B dichotomy among Penn's fraternities. To permit that separation to stand would represent a danger to Jewish rights and the preservation of American democracy. In

February 1938 the national head of Zeta Beta Tau called for a conference of representatives from all the Jewish national fraternities, almost all represented at Penn, for the express purpose of consolidating the two groups. The outbreak of World War II just at the start of the 1939–1940 academic year led further impetus to the effort. "This represents a 'ghetto' situation," asserted Richard L. Lowenstein of Penn's Phi Epsilon Pi chapter in 1940, "and particularly in these critical times, it is important to break up any such manifestation of discrimination on a campus as prominent in collegiate circles as Pennsylvania." His chapter joined forces with the independent students and successfully lobbied all the Group B fraternities to change their rushing regulations in conformity to those of Group A. They next enlisted the support of prominent university officials, including President Thomas Gates, Provost William McClellend, and the Dean of Student Affairs.[11]

These efforts were ultimately successful. It would be many more years before Jews and Christians attending the University of Pennsylvania routinely crossed fraternity lines. However, by the time World War II ended, the two groups at least found themselves in the same local interfraternity council.

The ADL's Fireside Discussion Groups Project: Success at Nebraska

For self-education in the cause of intercommunity relations, an effective agent available to fraternities and similar groups included the pamphlets of the Fireside Discussion Groups Project. This program was conceived in 1937 by personnel of the Anti-Defamation League and modeled after President Roosevelt's popular radio speeches. "No greater injury can befall any people than to stand mute to a fictitious charge," urged the ADL's Sydney B. Lavine, director of the program. "Avail yourself of all facts, information, and history of your own people so that no slander or libel be permitted to remain unchallenged."[12] Over 50,000 subscribers received a series of twenty or more pamphlets to be read and discussed in groups in homes, lodges, fraternities, sororities, clubs, and temples. The pamphlets provided specific suggestions on how to answer anti-Jewish charges that readers were assumed to encounter each day along with information calculated to bolster their level of self-knowledge and self-respect.

Fraternity house residents and their parents were especially well-suited to the dissemination of the pamphlets and the accompanying discussions. In the case of Sigma Alpha Mu, the national head of the fraternity noted with pleasure in September 1938 that the project had "touched off like a spark a tremendous pool of latent Jewish interest and leadership" among the young men, and that more than twenty-five chapters across the country were making it a regular weekly part of their activities. Leading them all was the Sigma Alpha Mu chapter at the University of Nebraska at Lincoln, which had already completed the third subject in the series and was planning to complete the entire project by the end of the school term. In addition, the meetings at Nebraska were open to members of other fraternities and nonfraternity students, as well as members' families. Some of the parents at these meetings reportedly participated in the discussions "with as much enthusiasm as the boys."[13]

A list of the topics for these Fireside Discussion Group pamphlets reveals well the challenges and accusations that American Jews were facing every day and their need for well-researched material to combat them. "What can I do to alleviate the situation?" was the title of the first pamphlet. The second pamphlet, entitled "The Myth of Jewish Economic Dominance," attempted to refute the idea that Jews controlled the entire business and professional worlds of both the U.S. and Germany. Then came "The Truth About the Protocols of the Wise Men of Zion," the antisemitic forgery that was enjoying renewed vigor and circulation under Nazi support; "The Ritual Murder Accusation"; "Communism" ("authentic data showing conclusively that Jews form a very small percentage of the Communist Party"); "The Aryan Race and the Nordic Myth," in which leading non-Jewish anthropologists condemned "the fallacious reference of the so-called 'Semitic nose' and the 'pure race'"; and "Three Questions Jews Must Answer," an analysis of possible answers to the eternal inquiry whether Jews were a race, a nation, or a religion. Other pamphlets included "Jews as Nobel Prize Winners"; Zionism and the progress of the Jews in Palestine; the debt that Christianity owed to the Hebrew Bible and to Jewish law and ideals; the participation of American Jews in their country's history from the first days of the Pilgrim Fathers up to the days of the Great War; The Jews in Medicine and Science, American Jews in Philanthropy, Jews in Music, Jews in American Literature, the Jew and His Faith, "Reform Judaism: Pro and Con," and finally "The Tragedy of Poland" ("three million corpses and their plight. Facts that will startle even the most casual observer").[14]

The German Jewish Student Refugee Program

For the actual rescue of European Jews, fraternity houses held within their grasp a response to Hitlerism far more concrete than mere discussion groups. They were ideally suited to supply room, board, and school materials for selected refugee students. Initiated by Phi Sigma Delta and joined by the others, between 1934 and 1941 the German Jewish Student Refugee program brought dozens of brilliant but penniless students who had been forced out of their universities by Nazism to the safety of the United States, where they continued their education from the haven of Jewish fraternity and sorority houses.[15] The project meant extensive and often tense negotiations with university administrators and U.S. immigration officials. In one instance in 1940, two of the German Jewish student refugees, bound for the University of Michigan and Tufts College, were instead detained in New York at Ellis Island. Only the strenuous petitions of the fraternities' refugee committee before the Department of State protected them from deportation back to Europe.[16]

Not all German Jewish student refugees found their stay in American colleges to be a happy one. Some suffered from feelings of displacement and culture shock at the remoteness of the towns in which they found themselves. Still, many did well enough to go on to academic careers; a few were able to bring their parents and siblings over as well; several served in the Armed Forces during World War II and at least two served in the OSS.[17] Most importantly, many became close friends with their American hosts, wearing their clothes, learning their slang, helping their fellow students with their German, widening their cultural horizons, and in some cases inspiring other students to raise special funds for the refugees so that they could be initiated as brothers and sisters into the fraternities.

Quite unexpectedly, the German Jewish Student Rescue Fund also helped to justify the existence of the fraternities and to bring in the support of adults who might otherwise have dismissed the Greek system. Having a refugee became a valuable rushing point each fall as chapters competed for potential members. Administrations, faculty, and fellow students looked upon a Jewish fraternity house with greater respect, knowing that it sheltered such a person. Alumni who had broken contact for years renewed their tie with the fraternity in order to participate in so worthy a project. Parents rushed to pay house bills on time knowing that their child's chapter was supporting an exile from the land of Hitler.

"Overcrowded" Professions and Vocational Guidance

Fraternities also responded to antisemitism and to the threat of Hitlerism on American soil by intensifying their efforts in the Jewish vocational guidance movement, already an area of concern because of the Depression. The phrase "vocational guidance," when used in reference to young American Jews, had multiple meanings and nuances. In its simplest sense, "vocational guidance," or helping members to find positions after graduation, was an accepted function of any good college fraternity. Indeed, both Jewish and Gentile young men specifically sought out the Greek system in the hopes that the contacts and networks established through them would help in the working world after college.

For Jewish young people, however, the goals of making a living or pursuing professional training presented special challenges. For them, vocational guidance meant help finding jobs when they were barred from many positions and companies, and quotas and restrictions kept all but the most brilliant from achieving their dreams of professional school. "Vocational guidance" also became a euphemism in the battle to convince Jewish families that not all was lost if their sons could not become doctors or lawyers and that other lines of work had to be considered. Among Jewish fraternity alumni and others, the desire also existed to disprove a staple of Nazi propaganda that Jews controlled the world and American economy, and to steer them away from what were perceived as overcrowded professions.

American Jews, as had their predecessors in modern Western Europe before them, did indeed gravitate disproportionately to the free professions. According to an elaborate study on American Jews in higher education conducted by Lee Levinger of B'nai B'rith Hillel's Research Bureau in 1937, although they were 3.5 percent of the U.S. population Jews made up more than a quarter (26%) of all the nation's professional students in dentistry, one quarter (25%) percent in law, 22 percent in pharmacy, 16 percent in commerce, and 16 percent in medicine. In the last field, they were still represented in vastly disproportionate numbers although their entrance was restricted and most schools imposed a specific Jewish quota.[18]

With the gradual implementation of Nazi anti-Jewish racial laws in Germany and the disenfranchisement and disbarment of German professionals there, the rush of young American Jews toward the professions and the traditional fraternity role in such placements became cause for serious communal criticism. In one of the earliest examples, a Phi Epsilon Pi alumnus in the Philadelphia municipal administration,

who for many years had helped to steer medical students in his fraternity to good Philadelphia hospitals, vowed in November 1933 that he
would to do nothing more to aid any Jewish youth in either law or medicine. Moreover, he claimed that no other Jew should sponsor any other
Jew for that purpose, "because of the overcrowding of the field" and
fear that American Jewish overconcentration in the professions would
lead to the same situation as had happened in Germany. "So there you
are, Joe," wrote Maurice Jacobs regretfully to a young Phi Epsilon Pi
who was seeking an internship and residency at Philadelphia General
Hospital and who could no longer count on aid from his fraternity's
accustomed source. "We are not wanted as Jews. The German bugaboo
has frightened everyone so that people can't think sanely or clearly and
everything is interpreted a la Hitler. . . . Every day we hear more of this
coming trouble, which I personally believe is more or less imaginary, but
who knows."[19]

As the years went by, the fear of Hitlerism increased, and Jewish
youth and their families stubbornly insisted on pursuing the free professions in the face of all criticism, more fraternity alumni grew alarmed.
"I attended a men's club round table meeting the other day in which the
question of saturation of Jews in the professions came up," wrote one
alumnus, an insurance broker in Cleveland, in February 1936.

> It was agreed that one of the pressing problems of Jewry today was voca-
> tional guidance for the young Jews to correct this maladjustment that is
> harming our cause so much and it occurred to me the college fraternity
> is in an enviable position to do a good deal along these lines. . . . The fu-
> ture will be filled with this problem of too many Jewish lawyers, doctors,
> judges, politicians, and whatnot. Isn't that one of the difficulties that led
> to the Nazi antisemitism? Perhaps Phi Ep as a fraternity can point the
> way of proper vocations to its members and to Jewish youth as a whole.[20]

Jacobs' consistent reply to these numerous, and to him annoying, inquiries was that the question was important, but he did not think the
fraternity was necessarily the agent to act upon such a "delicate" subject.
"We get the boy after his parents have already decided that he is going
into professional work and the damage has already been done," he wrote
back to Cleveland.[21]

Some young fraternity graduates had no expectation or hope
of attending professional school, and would have been happy to obtain any job at all. For these Sigma Alpha Mu in 1938 set up a placement service to cooperate with the local vocational guidance bureaus

of the B'nai B'rith, which specialized in finding jobs for young Jewish men and women in other Jewish or Jewish-run firms and organizations or companies that were known not to have discriminatory policies. A "Jobs wanted" column appeared regularly in the fraternity's periodical, and graduating seniors were directed to alumni who needed workers.[22] When possible, applicants were also given the names and addresses of alumni engaged in the same field in which the student was interested.[23] The Alpha Epsilon Phi sorority, although it did not organize a formal job placement program, regularly ran articles in its magazine with information on various careers, the advisability of different professional training courses, and the achievements of alumnae in such fields as dentistry, law, and chemistry.

In Phi Epsilon Pi, the need for jobs was less immediate, for a questionnaire distributed by Vocational Guidance Committee chairman Albert A. Hutler in 1939 revealed that fifty percent of the respondents intended to go into their family's business. For those without that option, the committee mailed out bulletins on different occupations and trades, published vocational articles in the fraternity's quarterly, set up alumni advisory committees, and sent out notices of civil service examinations—particularly in the area of the federal employment. The latter field employed thousands of college-educated young Jews and non-Jews during the years of the Great Depression and President Roosevelt's New Deal, and their presence helped to change the face of Washington, D.C.[24]

The effectiveness of this vocational guidance movement among the Jewish fraternities in the 1930s was best illustrated by the attendance of all at a special conference for them sponsored by the B'nai B'rith Hillel. At the Park Central Hotel in New York City on October 15, 1939, six weeks after the Nazi invasion of Poland and the beginning of World War II in Europe, delegates from every surviving national Jewish fraternity and sorority gathered. Even Pi Lambda Phi, which normally shunned such gatherings as a way of emphasizing its official nonsectarian status, sent representatives to the event.[25] At this unprecedented conference of Jewish fraternal unity, the delegates voted to form a permanent body, with a standing delegate from each group, solely for disseminating vocational guidance and employment information.

These efforts turned out not to be necessary. With the movement of the United States toward wartime production in late 1940 and 1941, the entrance of the U.S. into the war itself, and the drafting of millions into the armed forces, the employment fears of the Great Depression evaporated amidst an acute labor shortage. Still, this did not detract from the surprise of participants and observers that for once, fraternities that normally stood in fierce competition with one another had been able to cooperate in time of crisis in a cause that concerned them all.

Washing Dirty Linen: Conflict Management at Wisconsin and Ohio State, 1939

The agreement that characterized the Jewish fraternities' approach to problems of employment was unusual. Unity among groups that during the Depression were competing fiercely for the same pool of potential applicants was the exception rather than the rule under the shadow of Hitler. The president of the University of Wisconsin Phi Epsilon Pi chapter in December 1939 lamented at his annual convention that the hatred and competition between the five Jewish men's fraternities on his campus actually presented a far graver problem than antisemitism expressed by Gentiles against Jews. In the previous three years, he reported, Jewish fraternities against other Jewish fraternities had brought up two serious complaints before the Gentile Dean of Men.[26]

Traditionally, betraying a fellow Jew, informing on him to Gentile authorities, or bringing him before a hostile Gentile court, was one of the worst offenses one Jew could commit against another. If at all possible, disputes were to be settled by internal Jewish courts of law. Dr. Abram Sachar of the University of Illinois no doubt had this tradition in mind when in 1939 he made a special trip up to Madison to persuade Jewish fraternities to cease and desist from these tactics. At Illinois, Sachar made sure that his students maintained a special forum to settle fraternity disputes among themselves, and he urged the students at Wisconsin to do the same.[27]

Not all the Wisconsin students, however, could agree with Sachar's proposed solution. The right to join the mainstream interfraternity councils had been hard-won, after all. Suppose Gentiles heard about these modern internal Jewish courts and then made the equally disturbing charge that Jews were sticking too much to themselves and thus deserved to be treated differently? "If you are going to wash the dirty linen out in public, that is bad; Jews cannot get along among themselves, and that does not look good," the Wisconsin Phi Epsilon Pi chapter president noted at a his annual convention's roundtable meeting on the matter. Yet the Illinois method was not ideal either: "If you do that, you are clannish. If there is no barrier, you are making it a double one."[28]

A lively discussion ensued among the delegates. Near the end, the Ohio State representative commented that for his chapter the question of clannishness was entirely moot. Joint sessions or cooperation with Gentile fraternities on his campus at Columbus were an "utterly ridiculous" idea. No Jewish fraternity boy at Ohio State had ever been invited to a Gentile fraternity party, nor did Gentile students associate with Jewish students in any way. With no cooperation between Jews and Gentiles, he advised, one might as well have cooperation between the Jewish houses. Phi Epsilon Pi Executive Secretary Maurice G. Gurin, who was moderating the discussion, summed up by agreeing that conditions differed from campus to campus, and that if Jewish students enjoyed "the pleasure of not having any distinction," then they should not try to create one. On the other hand, he concluded, "If there is any dirty linen, you should get together in a very informal body and wash it."[29]

Greater or Lesser Jewish Identity? The Burning Controversy

When faced with an unknown threat, disunity from within could be as sharp as disunity from without. By far one of the most sensitive and controversial sources of disunity in certain Jewish fraternities, or those officially nonsectarian fraternities that were de facto Jewish, could be their Jewish identity itself. The question of just how Jewish these fraternities should or should not be had been asked at their founding and was asked anew with each generation. In many ways, the varying answers to that question throughout the twentieth century served as a barometer of the changing eras.

In the 1930s, the issue assumed greater urgency. Fraternities were already under attack for their alleged frivolity and anti-intellectualism. In addition, events in Europe were causing Jewish fraternity undergraduates to become more aware of their identity and the responsibilities it could impose whether they wished to or not. This led certain alumni leaders to try adding more Jewish material to their fraternity's programming where it did not already exist. By so doing, they hoped both to help members deal with new pressures and responsibilities and also prove to outside critics that fraternities were capable of serious undertakings.

Such plans were bound to meet resistance from those undergraduates and alumni who wished to stress the social aspect of their fraternities, not the Jewish ones. According to the alternate attitude, if a student wished to pray or to do Jewish organizational work there a were myriad of other groups available—such as Hillel, B'nai B'rith, or the National Federation of Temple Brotherhoods—which were more appropriate outlets. Besides, a period of intensifying antisemitism and encroaching Hitlerism hardly seemed the most propitious time to make one's Jewish background any more conspicuous than it already was. Under the circumstances, did it not behoove them to keep as low a profile as possible?

Keeping a low Jewish profile did not happen to be part of the worldview of the American-born Maurice Jacobs, University of Maine '17, long-time secretary and executive leader of Phi Epsilon Pi. In the 1930s, this tendency drove him in an unsuccessful and highly divisive struggle to inject more Jewish programming into his officially nonsectarian fraternity. A self-described rebel from an Orthodox Jewish childhood and a dedicated layman in the U.S. Reform Jewish movement, the Philadelphian was as capable as anyone in the upper echelons of judging the manners and cultural backgrounds of his fellow Jews with special ire, as we have seen, reserved for those originating in New York and Brooklyn.

Nevertheless, in all these pronouncements against individuals it was never the overall value of Judaism or Jewish peoplehood that he judged. Jacobs was a prominent communal leader, active in many causes beyond his fraternity, and a scholar as well. As an indicator of his interests, background, abilities, and working skills in both Hebrew and Yiddish, by 1932, when he was appointed Phi Epsilon Pi's Executive Director for a small annual salary, Jacobs simultaneously served as director and editor for the Jewish Publication Society of America.[30] Both headquarters were located down the hall from each other in the same Philadelphia office building, and at times he ran both offices at once by working eleven-hour days and keeping five stenographers busy. Jacobs was determined that his Phi Epsilon Pi would serve as a vehicle to encourage active Jewish identification and broad communal leadership among its younger members.

As early as the December 1923 convention, it will be recalled, traveling secretary Jacobs had led the fight for the Grand Council to remove the cross and crescent from the fraternity's crest. He had also lent his voice to the group insisting that they cease from hobbling expansion through recruitment of then-unattainable Gentile members in the name of an alleged nonsectarianism. When Jacobs assumed the position of Executive Director in 1932, in line with his previous fraternity policies, he at first arranged for generous portions of reading material—including religious tracts, pamphlets, and copies of a Reform Jewish youth movement magazine—to be sent to the various chapters. Later, he urged greater cooperation between chapters and local Hillel Foundations and rabbis.[31] Soon after, Jacobs also established a close friendship with Dr. Abram Leon Sachar, who was already an honorary member of the Phi Epsilon Pi chapter at the University of Illinois. A professor of history, Sachar at the time was also the National B'nai B'rith Hillel director. (After an early retirement from Hillel, Abram Sachar became in 1948 the first president of Brandeis University, a Jewish-sponsored institution). Jacobs, slightly in awe of Sachar, easily persuaded the academician to serve on the fraternity's Grand Council as its semiofficial consultant on Jewish affairs.

In July 1934, at Jacobs' behest, Sachar composed and presented to the fraternity a "National Service Plan" program, which the other national officers quickly dubbed with his name. The "Sachar Plan" called for an increase in the Jewish content of fraternity life in six ways. These included the reading of Jewish books as part of the pledge period, regular distribution of Jewish magazines and periodicals to the chapter houses, more articles of Jewish interest in the fraternity's quarterly magazine, more cooperation with local Hillel foundations and Jewish congregations, and more direct encouragement of alumni participation and leadership in Jewish institutional life.[32] With Sachar present, delegates at the Phi Epsilon Pi 1934 convention unanimously voted to adopt the plan.

Revolt Against the Sachar Plan

Subsequently, however, none but Jacobs and a handful of supporters seemed eager to implement the plan's measures.[33] Instead, a full-scale alumni revolt against the Sachar Plan broke out, centered in the Reform Jewish strongholds of Chicago and Cincinnati as well as, ironically, the Phi Epsilon Pi chapters at Ohio State University and Sachar's own University of Illinois. At those campuses, undergraduate members possibly resented the overpowering influence of this history professor, Hillel director, and eminent Jewish communal leader. The rebels were appalled at what they saw as an attempt to inject unwanted Jewish religious influences into their purely social/cultural/ethnic organization and demanded that the efforts cease immediately. Sachar suffered the ultimate insult when two undergraduate members of his very own Illinois

Phi Epsilon Pi chapter sent out a national letter condemning both him and his plan and dared to reproduce it on chapter house stationery.

One leader of the revolt, Jean Wertheimer, an alumnus and banker living in Cincinnati, warned against the "rabbinical tendencies" taking over his fraternity. He claimed to be hearing comments among the membership such as, "When our initiation becomes a Bar Mitzvah and our quarterly a *B'nai B'rith Monthly*, I and many of my fraters are going to take a walk." In an impassioned letter warning that the implementation of the Sachar Plan would tear the fraternity apart, Wertheimer wrote to the Grand Superior of the fraternity Louis M. Fushan on March 28, 1936:[34]

> The Grand Council and the Fraternity are both riding for a fall, if this thing continues, and if you continue in your effort to try to make kids swallow a lot of baloney that they do not sincerely accept, and forget as soon a they are out of college and into the world, it is going to kill the Alumni who don't go into the "pow-wows" of Jewish patriotism, worked into a fever heat by Rabbis at a pep meeting and crammed down their throats at conventions in the form of a sweet pill from silver-tongued speakers. . . . You certainly don't see the lawyers preaching and practicing law in the Fraternity, and demanding of the boys that they cooperate with the lawyer's aid society, or read the court index, or worry about what Hitler is doing to the bar and bench in Germany, and all that crap. . . . To be very frank, I don't know if it means anything to you or the other boys or the Fraternity, but I am losing my interest in it, and only because of the "Jewishness" or "Jewish consciousness" in the Fraternity, that I don't like and won't have. . . . An outstanding Jewish social worker or Rabbi tells a Fraternity that it must *be* Jewish, *write* Jewish, *read* Jewish, etc. and a weak-kneed Grand Council groping for a policy, or some plan to use, forgets the college boy, and Alumni, and forgets the principles and purposes of the college fraternity, and grabs a religious strain and tries to go to town with it. I tell you it won't work!

Jacobs' first response to Wertheimer's letter was not to take it seriously. When called upon for an explanation, Jacobs informed the Grand Superior that Wertheimer's fraternal loyalties were suspect because he had in fact once tried to desert Phi Epsilon Pi for Pi Lambda Phi (possibly because of its greater commitment to the ideology of nonsectarianism), and that the Cincinnati circle he headed had never done anything worthwhile for the fraternity anyway. Futhermore, they had allowed the University of Cincinnati chapter to die because they did not want to be associated with Hebrew Union College students (Hebrew Union College rabbinical students were permitted to pursue their BA degrees simultaneously at the University of Cincinnati and thus were a common source of material for Jewish fraternities there). The comparison between lawyers and rabbis was ridiculous, Jacobs charged, and the Sachar Plan was the only thing that would save the fraternity from oblivion. Finally, he wrote angrily, "if we're riding for a fall then I say let's take the fall and go out of business."[35] Jacobs also insisted that a great fuss was being made over nothing, since little of the proposed Jewish programming had in fact been implemented.

Sachar concurred. In an icy reply to a protest from the president of the Chicago Alumni Association about the "over-emphasis" of Jewish affairs in their fraternity, Sachar wrote back that he "had not been aware of the tremendous Jewishness of the Phi Ep chapters throughout the country."[36] He furthermore assured the alumni that only one chapter, Cornell, had even bothered to send in a report in hopes of obtaining a new award for the chapter with the best record in Jewish activities. "I do not believe that you have to worry about over-Judaizing the boys who come into Phi Ep. No chapter has been really infected," Sachar concluded. "I appreciate your writing to me, and I only hope that sometime such a problem will actually arise."[37]

Seeing this reaction to his efforts, Sachar broke contact with Phi Epsilon Pi and retained a lifelong animosity toward Jewish fraternities. None were officially allowed to set foot on the campus of Brandeis University so long as he was President or Chancellor there. To the end of his life, he was hardly able even to discuss the subject of Jewish fraternities without becoming visibly choked with rage.

Jewish Rituals?

In addition to supporting the Sachar Plan, Jacobs in the mid-1930s further tried to bring into the fraternity's national leadership approximately a half dozen young Reform rabbis. These men had joined Phi Epsilon Pi as undergraduates and had later received ordination at the Reform movement's Hebrew Union College seminary. Since these rabbis knew what the life of a typical American college student was like and were so thoroughly Americanized themselves, their religious input would presumably be more acceptable than that of older rabbis or authorities from more traditional denominations. The group included Rabbi L. Elliot Grafman, who was appointed the fraternity's National Pledgemaster; Washington and Lee graduate Rabbi David H. Wice; and Rabbi Albert G. Minda, who became the fraternity's Scholarship Commissioner.

Without consulting other officers of the fraternity, Jacobs commissioned Wice to rewrite the fraternity's secret rituals in order to inject more Jewish content into them.

For almost two years Wice worked on the quasi-liturgical project, drawing upon Jewish texts, motifs and prayers for his inspiration. He and Jacobs discussed eliminating the traditional skull and bones from the initiation ceremony in favor of a Menorah and other traditional Jewish symbols. The Hebrew *Kaddish* mourner's prayer was to be read at the fraternity's memorial service for departed members. Verses from the Twenty-third Psalm and the Book of Isaiah ("How good and how pleasant it is for brethren to dwell together in unity") would be recited. The Superior of the chapter, in explaining the mysteries and symbols of the fraternity, would invoke the memory of the Biblical friendship of David and Jonathan, along with the ideals of freedom celebrated in the Jewish holiday of Passover.[38]

The final version of the new Judaized ritual came up for a vote at the annual convention in 1936. It did not even come close to passing. Jacobs, who about that time was deciding on whether to give up on Phi Epsilon Pi and instead go to work for the Jewish Publication Society full-time, thereafter faced the unpleasant task of writing to Wice (then serving as a pulpit rabbi in Omaha, Nebraska) to apologize. "Some of the boys are still afraid of the word Jewish," he wrote, "and do not want to accept anything smacking of a typical prayer service"—although Jacobs hastened to assure the rabbi that his efforts had merited him an appointment as the fraternity's Grand Chaplain.[39] "Thanks loads for your letter of the twenty-first," wrote Wice back, obviously miffed. "I was a little surprised to see Phi Ep go Nordic. Perhaps they think I wear a beard and can't speak campus English."[40] At the 1939 convention, four months after the outbreak of World War II in Europe, Phi Epsilon Pi in convention assembled further confirmed a new ritual which deliberately had not a single Jewish reference in it.[41]

When the Wice ritual was rejected, Jacobs received comfort from one of his few supporters, attorney and Chicago Alumni Association member Samuel J. Sherman. Like him, Sherman was a dedicated Reform Jewish layman and a product of a traditional Jewish childhood. As Jacobs had once tried to explain the mysteries of New York Jews to Sherman, Sherman now tried to explain to his Philadelphian colleague why Midwesterners might desire assimilation and feared being too conspicuous as Jews in any way. "There is a situation here which an Easterner like you will find hard to appreciate at all," he wrote, and that is that the second and third generation here are entirely disinterested in things Jewish. . . . I imagine some of our boys feel our so-called "nonsectarianism" was a virtue, and the project of making the ritual "more Jewish" and giving the fraternity a Jewish direction is undesirable. . . . Fundamentally they believe in a philosophy which is based on worry, fear, or downright shame because they are Jews. For the fear they can't be entirely blamed these days . . . It's hard for you to picture it because you—like me—have taken the necessity for interest in things Jewish for granted. People here in the mass don't. In fact, they prefer to be not even reminded about it.[42]

Jacobs replied with resignation, saying that the problems they faced were not to be found only in the American Midwest: "It is the same problem we have everywhere in the country today with our so-called educated young Jewish men. Where it is going to lead to, I don't know, but evidently we have not learned from the tragedy in Germany and will have to wait until the same thing is given to us here."[43]

Jacobs' attitude was shared in part by Arthur D. Schwarz of Zeta Beta Tau, himself a child of the old German Jewish elite. Schwarz by this time had become well-known within his fraternity for penning hilarious parodies and satires of that culture along with other humorous aspects of Greek life in the pages of the *Zeta Beta Tau Quarterly*. (In 1922 he had entertained his readers with an essay entitled "Rushing as It Wunst Wuz.") In 1936 however, when reviewing a book by scholar and author Marvin Lowenthal that described the situation of the Jews in Hitler's Germany, Schwartz abandoned his customary lightheartedness. Specifically, he lashed out at the tendency of members and their families to disregard the principle of Jewish unity and to scorn the traditions of the East European Jews:

The greatest tragedy to this reviewer of the German situation was that time just before Hitler's election when our smug, self-satisfied German-American families—yours and mine—smiled knowingly and said, "Ach, Hitler isn't worrying about our German Jews—it's those verdammte Polacks we, as well as they, want kicked out of Der Vaterland." Have you ever listened in at a bridge or Mah Jong klatsch and heard Tante Debby say, "I certainly hate that Yiddish jargon—I despise it—where did that language ever start? Where did those kikes learn it?" The answer is they learned it in Germany from the South Germans. Do you have any recollection of remarks like this, "The Jew will never be hurt in Germany; that's the one country where the Jew is respected because he is, like the German himself, a super-mensch, far ahead of Jews anywhere else in the world." Do you remember your rabbi or your father saying, "What the devil do we Germans need Palestine and Zionism. It's all right for those Jews of Russia, but we Germans are better off in America or in Germany. They should have their Palestine, those *Ostjuden*."[44]

The "Phi Ep Gentleman's Code"

After the failure of the Sachar Plan and the Wice plan to Judaize the Phi Epsilon Pi rituals, Jacobs learned from his mistakes and turned to young alumnus Rabbi L. Elliot Grafman to transform a different segment of his fraternity's membership literature. From 1937 through 1941, Grafman developed a new program of pledge training that stressed Jewish identity. This time, however, it eschewed particularistic details of Jewish ritual and stressed wider values upon which all segments of the community could agree.

Grafman was close enough to his college days to understand campus traditions and the teenaged boy's longing for acceptance within mainstream, Gentile American society. In a series of ten lessons sent to all chapters, Grafman therefore supplied college freshmen with concrete and cautionary explanations of antisemitism along with specific ways to combat it.[45] Most, in an extension of the old Best Behavior Syndrome and Mission of Manners greatly intensified by fear of encroaching Hitlerism, stressed a combination of maintaining unimpeachable standards of behavior and good citizenship. By the 1930s, this had crystallized into a new code of behavior. In a stance not dissimilar to the "pro-Semitism" philosophy of ZBT's Harold Riegelman in the 1920s, the standards were meant not only to elevate individual lives. If followed properly, it was believed, they could help the entire Jewish community to deflect and prevent lethal manifestations of anti-Jewish prejudice.

These new pledge lessons included what Grafman chose to call the "Phi Ep Gentleman's Code," later incorporated into the fraternity's initiation ritual. It was not an original idea, a "Gentleman's Code" being part of the lore of some Gentile fraternities. "A Phi Ep is always a Gentleman! A Phi Ep *commands* respect and *gives respect* at all times and under all circumstances" read his version.[46] In another lesson, the men were taught that all the Jews on the campus would be judged by their every act and attitude. "It's truer than most men realize—especially when they are Jews—that they reflect in themselves the demands and achievements of their social group. . . . The man who remembers this is clothed with the necessary armor; the man who forgets or shirks bares the ugly nudity of dishonor of his fellows and thus betrays."[47] Another lesson was on the "General Manly Requirements" of fraternity etiquette, including the need to accept correction cheerfully from others.[48] "It is more important than ever," he warned his undergraduates from 1937, "that the Jewish student's loyalty be above reproach! He must in fact be MORE loyal, MORE interested, MORE active, and always, without being promiscuous. For it is an undeniable fact that on many a campus, the *Jewish* student has to do much better in demonstration of loyalty than his non-Jewish fellow students, in order to be equally acceptable."[49]

Phi Epsilon Pi's alumni could not all agree on the desirability of requiring synagogue attendance or Jewish magazines and books in the chapter houses. All, however, could apparently agree with that final statement. Rabbi Grafman was gratified to see his pledge program enthusiastically endorsed at every Phi Epsilon Pi national convention between 1937 and 1941. After that, the U.S. entry into World War II put a halt to the annual meetings for the duration.

Response: Fear of Success

The written Rabbi Grafman pledge lessons of 1937 were symptomatic of the deepest, most widespread, and in many ways the simplest of the reactions and responses of middle-class American Jewry to antisemitism in the shadow of Hitler. The basic rules of the game and the paradigms of the reactions had not changed much since the days of the Harvard affair and Henry Ford in the 1920s. However, now the stakes had become higher and the hoped-for victory smaller. No longer upward mobility but sheer survival and staving off disaster were the main goals. The rules were: watch your manners, behave like ladies and gentlemen, avoid impropriety, keep your head low, be good and loyal citizens, and contribute to the welfare of your community. At the same time, avoid calling attention to yourself and never flaunt or permit other Jews to flaunt their money or abilities in the face of Gentiles for fear of arousing criticism or jealousy.[50]

Observing the latter section of this code put Jews in a difficult position of daily walking the finest of lines. They naturally desired to do well for themselves and for their families, to increase their own security, to enjoy their hard-earned affluence, to gain credit for the good name of their people, and to win the approval of Gentiles. This goal called for just enough participation in public affairs to prove that they were not clannish or inassimilable, as the antisemites would have the world believe. On the other hand, they did not want to be so conspicuous in their leadership or so dominant in public or artistic affairs or so financially successful as to lend any credence to the claim of the dreaded *Protocols* that Jews were actually taking over the nation or the world.

Lee Dover of Zeta Beta Tau, as head of a fraternity that ordinarily took pride in the wealth of its members, took the latter aspect of the Code with special seriousness. In 1937 and again in 1941 on the eve of the war he enacted for his chapters something near to the sumptuary laws that had governed the lives of Jews in Europe and the Middle East for hundreds of years. No chapter, he wrote, should collect fees beyond those which were necessary to carry out the programs of the chapter "in a successful manner;" and no chapter, he continued, "regardless of the financial ability of the families of its members should allow its operations to be de luxe or pretentious. ZBT chapters should operate along modest but adequate lines and should provide no reason for their campus associates to consider them ostentatious."[51]

Beyond simple wealth, conspicuous intellectual or political achievement could also arouse anxiety. Most American ethnic or religious groups, for example, might have been proud to contribute a member to the U.S. Supreme Court. Yet when Felix Frankfurter was appointed to the Court in 1938, a Washington reporter stated that ninety percent of the protests against Frankfurter came on the grounds that he was a Jew, and eighty percent of those complaints came from other Jews.[52] Harold Riegelman, who had led Zeta Beta Tau through the 1920s and never lost the cachet of having been the first Jewish president of the National Interfraternity Conference, angrily denounced what he called the "posture of apology" Jews were adopting regarding the Frankfurter appointment. The premises of antisemitism, he warned, were being unconsciously embraced "by the very people whom it would destroy." "Is it bad business in these unsettled times for a Jew to make himself conspicuous by serving his government?" he demanded of his audience. "Is it not worse business in these or any times for a Jew to refuse a service which any government has the right to expect of every citizen?"[53]

Do Unto Others First

From late antiquity and medieval times bribery and promises of potential tax contributions as ways to placate hostile political authorities had been a technique central to Jewish communal survival. In the United States, for one of the few periods in their long history Jews had for some time enjoyed the luxury of voluntarily choosing to enrich individuals or communities other than their own. They had invoked that privilege for any number of reasons. In the shadow of Hitler, the hopeful purchase of security and clout through the conspicuous contribution of money toward non-Jewish causes in the name of good citizenship became one more line of defense.

For example, when Jewish fraternity officials confronted the quotas and restrictions rampant at colleges and universities in the 1930s, it was common for them to receive and to accept the explanation that insufficient monetary contributions by their group were to blame. When Sigma Alpha Mu Executive Secretary Jimmy Hammerstein reported to the Supreme Council in March 1935 that Jewish fraternities at McGill University in Montreal faced a fight for their existence because the administration had decided to reduce Jewish enrollment to twenty-five men a year, the only explanation he could give for the reduction was that "contributions by Jews to the Endowment Funds have been proportionately so small."[54] Similarly, in 1936 the Sigma Alpha Mu alumni of Syracuse University announced their intention of setting up a scholarship to be used by a deserving student of any faith. Their motive was "to prove to the trustees that Jews ARE interested in alma mater. This is important, as there is some talk of cutting down students from the metropolitan district which means, in effect, curtailing the number of Jewish students."[55]

The second World War and the catastrophe of European Jewry was already in progress across the seas, yet Jewish causes did not rank high on the list when in April 1941 the National Council of Alpha Epsilon Phi debated the topic of what their "National Project," or chief charitable endeavor, should be. The women eventually decided on scholarships to any deserving college student, regardless of whether he or she was a Jewish refugee. General scholarships were not just an appropriate cause for a sorority; they were a way, as supporters of the motion put it specifically, "to help combat antisemitism." In the past, they agreed, Jewish groups as a rule had not sufficiently supported educational activities and thus were criticized as being interested only in charities for their own people. Scholarships granted in the name of Alpha Epsilon Phi, a Jewish sorority, might help to erase that impression, and ultimately do their people greater service.[56]

Fear of Political Activity

In condemning the activities of Jewish Communist students at American colleges, Rabbi Max Kadushin, speaking at the annual Hillel director's conference in Indiana in 1937, at least praised their intelligence, spoke with concern for their needs, and advocated drawing them in to communal activities rather than shunning them.

The alumni officers of Alpha Epsilon Phi sorority, however, along with the Jewish fraternity world's more conservative elements, were not so forgiving of possible Communist activity within their ranks, especially after the events of 1939 and the signing of the Nazi-Soviet non-agression pact. They lived in mortal fear that the political activities of their undergraduates could bring great harm to the good name of their group and to the Jewish people as a whole. Involvement in anything even resembling Communist activity led credence to charges that Jews were inherently a disruptive force that sought to rule the world, and violated parts of the Code calling for Jews to be good citizens and to be as quiet and inconspicuous as possible. They were apprehensive to learn that four members at New York University were active in the American Student Union, an organization that was feared to be a front for the Young Communist League.[57]

Apprehension turned to horror when the following mimeographed petition, festooned with the Alpha Epsilon Phi logo and signed by the four offending students, was found to be circulating on the NYU campus in December of 1939:

SNOBBERY IS OUTMODED / WE SORORITY WOMEN SINCERELY BELIEVE that discrimination, be it on the basis of race, creed, or color, is highly unbecoming to ladies. America was not built on the principle that one individual is better than another. Americans must work together for a common cause. / WE HAVE SEEN HOW THIS POLICY OF DISCRIMINATION AGAINST RACIAL GROUPS AND PEOPLES HAS BROUGHT ABOUT THE DOWNFALL OF EUROPE. *IT IS HAPPENING HERE! YOU MUST BELIEVE IT!* THESE PEOPLE WHO SIT AT HOME in their arm chairs and say "It can't happen here," are fooling themselves to a degree that is unmentionable. IT IS A SERIOUS PROBLEM./ WE WOMEN ARE ALERT to the causal factors and results, and will do our utmost to see that *IT WILL NOT HAPPEN HERE!* (signed) / Members of the ALPHA EPSILON PHI Sorority / Jenny Braekman / Naomi Bloom / Joyce Grossman / Judith Silverman.

Disapproval of this statement against the selective basis of their sorority paled in comparison, however, to their shock when they heard in early March 1941 that Naomi Bloom (NYU '42) and six other NYU students calling themselves the Committee for Racial Equality had been suspended from school for circulating a forbidden petition in the NYU cafeteria, alleging that NYU was discriminating against its Negro athletes by agreeing not to send them to an upcoming track meet with the Catholic University of America in Washington, DC.[58] The incident created national headlines. Hundreds of NYU students protested, sporting buttons reading "Reinstate the 7 Fighters Against Jim Crow."[59] On April 3, 1939, Eleanor Roosevelt addressed an audience of seven hundred in a nearby church in order to lend support to the student protesters, though she added a "verbal spanking" that the students had been perhaps too violent and hasty in their methods.[60] For weeks, the NYU student government and prominent public figures appealed to the university's chancellor and dean to reverse their decision, to no avail.

For the members of Alpha Epsilon Phi's National Council, however, their main concern was not the future of race relations in the United States nor the questionable legality of the college's suspension process, but the unfavorable publicity which their sorority had received and the question of what they should do about the errant Naomi Bloom. For six weeks they investigated and debated: should she be reprimanded, put on probation, suspended, or expelled from the sorority altogether? In the end, the Council acted on the side of leniency by voting only to put her on probation during the term of her suspension from the college. The decision came in part because evidence emerged that she was the least responsible of the seven students and had never meant to drag the sorority's name into the controversy. In fact, by all reports she was a dedicated, active, and well-liked member of her chapter.[61] The reasons that those advocating stronger action gave, however, reflected their fear that association with radical student activity of any kind could ultimately destroy them.

"I have always been so terribly opposed to those of our faith taking part in such activity, that I cannot feel that we should be lenient in this case," wrote Field Secretary Florence S. Orringer from Pittsburgh, Pennsylvania, in expressing her original opinion that they should request Bloom's resignation. "Her actions and her suspension from school have done Zeta [NYU chapter] immeasurable harm, and cannot help but reflect badly on the name of Alpha Epsilon Phi."[62] "I do feel strongly in this case that at the present time we as a Jewish organization cannot afford to be tied up in any way with communistic organizations," wrote Irma Loeb Cohen from Shaker Heights, Ohio, in recommending that all Alpha Epsilon Phi members be asked to resign from campus political organizations or else be expelled from the sorority. "We *must* see that not *one* of our members has any doubtful political connections. And I do think refusals should result in immediate disaffiliation. I know we were afraid of just such a possibility when we discussed ASU affiliation at NYU before. And now we have it! So we'd better act *now* before worse happens."[63]

Exaggerated Etiquette

Social polish had always been important as a way for fraternity members to distinguish themselves from lower classes of Jews, to build self-respect, and to gain valuable allies among Gentiles. The art of overcoming antisemitic stereotypes by good manners had been part of Zeta Beta Tau's rationale for existence for many generations. Never before the rise of Adolf Hitler, however, had the subject been such a crucial part of the fraternity's curriculum. The last pre-war *Zeta Beta Tau Manual for Chapter Administration*, authored by Lee Dover in 1937 and revised and republished only one week before Pearl Harbor, was permeated with the concept. The esoteric manual predictably dealt with such routine fraternity matters as finances, collection procedures, rituals, meal plans, and descriptions of officers' duties. However, specific instructions on the maintenance of manners and good behavior, with special emphasis on the desirability of remaining as inconspicuous as possible, filled many pages.

"There are certain conventions in ZBT which are taught to and observed by all undergraduates from the time they are freshmen," Dover wrote, in describing his fraternity's ideal. "They eschew extreme styles in clothing, and loud colors. They are quiet in voice and manner. Their table manners are unobtrusive and correct. In short, ZBT's are gentlemen." No ZBT undergraduate, for example, was permitted to wear a mustache.[64] Exhibiting intoxication at a university dance or "similar ungentlemanly behavior" in public would result in a withdrawal of weekend social privileges.[65] Coats and ties had to be worn at all meals and on most campuses any time a young member stepped out the front door of his fraternity house. The chapter president could allow more casual dress on special occasions, but never when guests were present.[66] There was to be no discussion between tables or the passing of food or condiments from one table to another. In short, "Decorum and proper modulation of voices" was the guiding rule, whether or not guests were present. The degree of the real culture of the membership of a fraternity chapter, Dover stipulated, could be gauged in the dining room by a sound meter, reading it in reverse.[67]

Many of these rules were common among fraternities, and had been in force long before the eve of World War II. Yet the tenacity with which some Zeta Beta Tau members clung to their training during these years of anxiety was enough to arouse comment, as in this item by a Kansas City Star columnist appearing on August 3, 1936:

> Members and Alumni of the Missouri chapter of Zeta Beta Tau were holding a rush party in the Ambassador Hotel dining room on a recent night. The place was air-cooled, but, nevertheless, in the weather it looked odd to see sixty or more men sitting dignifiedly around a table with their coats on. The only other guests in the room comprised a boy and a girl twosome, some distance away. Both halves of the date were more than surprised when two of the ZBT's walked up, addressed the girl and said, "We beg your pardon, but would you mind a lot if we took off our coats at our table?" Just a fraternity with manners![68]

At Alpha Epsilon Phi, an entire office within the sorority's national roster, known as the "Courtesy Chairman," was created in the late 1930s. In January of 1938 Joan Loewy Cohn, who had received the appointment, inaugurated a column entitled "Greek P's and Q's" in order to school members in the arts of proper dress, good grooming, and entertaining with grace and style.[69] Her articles on giving a formal tea covered in detail such items as setting the table, securing corsages for the guests of honor and the housemother, how to dispense the honor of "pouring," when it was proper to receive in long dresses, and how to use a pastry tube and vegetable dye to create imaginative refreshments in green and white, the sorority colors.[70]

Charm and attractiveness at all times became a pursuit of the entire sorority. At the University of Illinois chapter, "straggling coiffures, hanging slips and excess pounds have all been banned," she wrote. Notes were hung on the mirrors of the house to ask offending sorors, "How's your make-up?" "Are your seams straight?" "How's your color combination?" and "Where's that girdle?" Those with weight to lose were seated at a special diet table in the dining hall. At the University of Minnesota, similar criticisms were handled more subtly and impersonally through the use of a "charm box." Each Monday night the head of the "charm committee" passed out sealed envelopes, and the pointers inside were read by the members in private.[71] Loewy herself cautioned members in her writings: don't chew gum on campus, don't dance with any other part of the body but your feet, don't forget porch etiquette (for neighbors could see and hear), don't smoke cigarettes while walking down the street, replace nail polish the moment it starts to crack or peel, keep wool dresses dry-cleaned, have anklets that match your dresses and do not sag down into the backs of your shoes, and above all keep cottons and linens "immaculately laundered and pressed."[72]

Looking "Too Jewish"

Distance from immigrant origins along with money and family background had always been prized in the membership selection process of the upper tier fraternities, but with the rise of Hitler, the stakes became higher. Like chameleons who sought to blend into their environment by the use of protective coloring, members equated propriety, respectability, security, and safety with looking and acting as much like Gentiles as possible—or, at the very least, the way they imagined Gentiles should look and act. The result, as we have seen, is that expressions of intra-Jewish snobbery and the shunning of candidates who were too stereotypically "Jewish" in manner or appearance reached its height during the 1930s.

Saying of someone that he or she "did not look Jewish" had become, over the years, one of the highest compliments any person could pay to a Jew. By the eve of World War II, young college students were apparently taking the attitude to extremes. Lee Dover of Zeta Beta Tau, in the "Membership Standards" section of his manual on chapter administration, found it necessary in 1941 to chide the undergraduates against this tendency:

> Some chapters have not pledged men for the sole reason that certain, unintelligent members have offered the opinion that they were "too Jewish." By this they have meant, although they do not express their real opinion, that the man in question, if known on the campus as a member of their chapter would set it and its membership apart from the rest of the student body. This is a stupid attitude. No Jewish student or organization can masquerade successfully as a Gentile. The matter of honesty and conscience alone should prohibit such an attempt. All Jewish students are known to be Jews by their non-Jewish contemporaries. If the undergraduates in the chapter will take the attitude that being a Jew is a personal thing like being a member of any other faith or racial group, they will not be disturbed in their own minds on this point and their attitude will tend to be accepted by their contemporaries on the campus.[73]

The admonitions of "Mr. ZBT" notwithstanding, some fraternity members continued the long-time quest of looking as non-Jewish as possible, routinely changing their names, resorting to specialized hairdressing, and occasionally submitting to plastic surgery—especially rhinoplasty, colloquially known as "nose-fixing." This option had first become available in the early 1920s and dozens of Jewish entertainers and movie stars, beginning with Fanny Brice, had already availed themselves of it.[74]

Avoiding Jewish Women

The desire to escape one's Jewishness had its effects on relationships between young Jewish men and women. If a young Jewish man could not make himself look like a Gentile, then he could still aspire to the goal of being accepted by a Gentile woman, helped along perhaps by vast expenditures of money upon his date and liberal application of his most gentlemanly behavior. The Zeta Beta Tau men of Alabama had been so eager to have compatible Jewish women attend their school that they had supplied Alpha Epsilon Phi sorority with a ready-made rushing list; this eagerness, however, was not always matched by ZBTs at other campuses.

In the case of Zeta Beta Tau's chapter at the University of Missouri, consistent reports from the Anti-Defamation League, community rabbis and ZBT alumni were continually surfacing throughout the 1930s that older members were either discouraging or outright forbidding the younger ones to date Jewish girls. When confronted, the chapter officers had always denied it, and the national alumni officers had always backed them up in responding to the fraternity's accusers, but as time passed, the mounting accusations could no longer be ignored.

The matter came to a head in October 1941, when Rabbi David Jacobson of Temple Beth-El in San Antonio, Texas, reported that a Jewish senior at Stephens College—a women's school also located in the city of Columbia, Missouri—claimed to have discovered that the chapter levied a fine against any member who brought a "Jewess" to the spring dance. The amount of the fine, depending on the importance of the social occasion, allegedly varied between five and ten dollars.[75] If they were indeed using this technique, then the young men of Missouri's ZBT did not conceive of it themselves, but had learned it from the Gentile world. Certain restricted country clubs that did not outright forbid Jews from joining were known to levy fines against members who brought Jews onto the premises as guests.[76]

Lee Dover responded to the charge by writing to the undergraduate officers to demand an explanation. He also alerted the ZBT alumni directors of the chapter in Kansas City that they had better go in to see the students and to set the matter straight. "I do not feel that any of our chapters should tell their members who they shall or shall not date," he wrote, and warned of the undesirable repercussions that such stories could cause among the community:

> The matter which he brings up is not a new one as you will remember. Although Omega [University of Missouri chapter] has denied in the past that it has a rule which prevents its members from dating Jewish girls, at least on certain occasions, I am not convinced that it does not have some sort of a rule which the fraternity cannot countenance . . . I am probably one of the few members of the Fraternity who has understood Omega's attitude relative to mixing freely with the Gentile students. I do not desire to eliminate this as a chapter policy, but I do feel that we must definitely get rid of the chapter's policy which causes the constant comment throughout the country that Omega is antisemitic towards Jewish coeds and that it forces its freshmen to comply with its ruling in this connection.[77]

The president of the Missouri ZBT chapter insisted that the allegations were "utterly ridiculous" and the product of jealous troublemakers. "In the past we have ignored such foolish accusations and intend to do so in the future," he wrote.[78] Dover passed the denial on to Rabbi Jacobson with the mollifying comment, "From time to time a few young ladies, who go to the University of Missouri and who do not have an enjoyable social time there have, through the past years, taken to their home cities similar trouble-making reports. . . . There is no way that either you or I can control the preferences of the young Jewish men in college as to feminine company."[79]

To the undergraduates at Missouri, however, Dover did not take nearly so indulgent a tone, nor did he accept the young men's protestations of innocence. "It is my knowledge that your chapter has, in the past, had certain rules, call them traditional customs, if you will, which have caused freshmen pledges to feel that they have to date Gentile coeds," he wrote.

> If this policy still exists, I believe it is unwise. It is one thing to tell freshmen that they should not confine their associations to Jewish students on the campus (no one has advocated more than the writer the breaking down of ghetto lines on the American campus) but it is quite another thing to lead such pledgees to suppose that they are encouraged to avoid association with their co-religionists at the University be they male or female.[80]

He promised personally "in the very near future" to visit the chapter to discuss the allegations. In the meantime, in order for the chapter to do what was "best for it and for American Jewry," the young men would have to do a "public relations job with the Jewish coeds" at Missouri. "Your chapter must handle itself so well on this particular point in the future," he threatened, "that there will be no opportunity for trouble-makers to misinterpret its policy, or if you like it better, lack of policy relative to dating Jewish and Gentile girls." They must go out of their way, at least once a year, to "entertain and make friends with the Jewish co-eds, not only those who are 'Hedy Lamarrs' but also those who are not so fortunately endowed." Finally Dover refused, in answer to the Missouri president's demands, to divulge the name of the Stephens College senior who had betrayed them, since doing so would "serve no purpose—and if you do discover this later, I advise you against reprisals."[81]

Fear of "Out-of-State" Students: Vice Charges at Iowa State, 1935

The old fear of bringing shame upon campus Jews by ill-bred behavior in public could also turn to terror if a Jewish fraternity was caught in violation of campus rules, which in the heyday of the *in loco parentis* philosophy completely governed student movements and contacts with the opposite sex. In such cases Jewish fraternity men might discover that the rest of the world did not look with favor upon their forays into relationships with non-Jewish young women. Regulations were stricter and far more difficult to circumvent in those days. Simply violating the traditional midnight curfew or having female guests in the house without a chaperone present was grounds for trouble. No more did being caught besmirch only the integrity of Jewish college students or the Greek system in general; now, the entire good name of Judaism appeared at stake. When the Phi Beta Delta chapter at Iowa State University made national headlines in April 1935 for allegedly "maintaining a disorderly house" by "housing two juvenile girls within their quarters for immoral purposes,"[82] (the members insisted that they were innocent) Anti-Defamation League director and Phi Epsilon Pi alumnus Richard E. Gutstadt immediately demanded that all Jewish fraternity chapters in the country meet to discuss the situation.

The entire Jewish student migrant movement that had served as such an important outlet for American Jewry appeared to be endangered by the charges. Gutstadt was clearly upset that the Iowa newspa-

pers had published the obviously Jewish names of all the chapter members. The paper had also not failed to point out that Phi Beta Delta's
headquarters were in "New York," and had published on the front pages
a photograph—full-faced and untouched—of the fraternity chapter's
president. Furthermore, the mayor and local authorities were grasping
at the exposé as an opportunity to declare a war against vice in the town
of Ames. "The unhappy publicity which attended this breach of morals
and of university regulations will indubitably produce very undesirable
repercussions," Gutstadt, whose own son was a Phi Epsilon Pi at Illinois, wrote in a warning letter to the heads of all Jewish fraternities on
April 10, 1935:

> The Anti-Defamation League has for many years concerned itself with
> the good name of American Jewry. For the last several years, with the
> increase of antisemitic sentiment throughout the country, it has striven
> mightily to counteract all false propaganda and to secure the position of
> the American Jew. . . . All of the aspects of this specific problem [i.e. vice
> charges against fraternity houses] should be placed before your groups and
> they be urged to exercise every possible precaution. It should be made
> clear to them that their individual and collective conduct should be above
> reproach and that the utmost care should be exercised to maintain such
> aspects of Jewish dignity and Jewish rectitude of conduct as to afford no
> basis for criticism.[83]

At issue, apparently, was also the ADL's fear that charges of
"immorality" against Jewish fraternity houses located in small midwestern towns might arouse antisemitic stereotypes of Jews as white slavers,
pimps, and prostitutes, and thus result in the state universities closing
their doors to Jews—or at least to out-of-state students, since the two
groups were often one and the same. It was beside the point, Gutstadt
wrote, "in view of the tenor of publicity which accompanied the expose,"
to insist that members of Jewish fraternities were most certainly not
alone in violations of campus rules prohibiting unchaperoned women in
male student quarters. Revelations in one Jewish area could easily lead
to investigations of Jews in others, he wrote. Unless Jewish fraternity
men scrupulously guarded their contact with women and avoided even
the appearance of violating regulations, further investigations could turn
up ample material "which could be used to heighten anti-Jewish sentiment." "How this may be exploited for the purpose of evoking prohi-
bitions against extrastate admissions to State Universities can easily be
discerned," Gutstadt warned.[84]

No one in the Jewish fraternity world seemed to think that Gutstadt might be exaggerating the gravity of the situation. In fact, so im-
pressed was Maurice Jacobs of Phi Epsilon Pi with Gutstadt's handling
of the Iowa vice charges, that he offered the ADL director free Life
Membership in the fraternity as a tribute. Throughout the rest of 1935,
the Anti-Defamation League, Jacobs, and community rabbis worked
"tactfully and quietly" in tandem to educate their young charges in the
realities of just how much trouble their foibles might cause. Jacobs himself ordered the closing of all of Phi Epsilon Pi's fraternity houses during the summer so that no unauthorized and unsupervised personnel
might wander in and harm the fraternity's name, a policy which Gutstadt agreed should be mandatory for every national Jewish fraternity.[85]

    Their worst fears were realized in the first week of July, when an-
other Jewish fraternity was "raided"—this time Sigma Tau Phi, a small
national with a chapter at Temple University, although the administration claimed that none of the names of the people taken to the local
police station were of registered students. "Some organizations are not
taking their responsibilities seriously and we must do something about
it," wrote Jacobs to Gutstadt, upon reading about the incident in his
newspaper. He urged more stringent education among the undergraduates about the responsibility their groups held for "the protection of the
Jewish name."[86]

"What if It Happens Here?"

When Nazism began making inroads into Austria in 1934, delegates
from all the Jewish men's fraternities met to appoint a committee to
draw up a plan of action in case the movement spread to the United
States. The committee reportedly met, drew up a plan, and distributed
copies to all the groups, although fortunately there was never a need to
refer to it.[87]

    Whatever plans were made or discussed, the first line of defense
in the shadow of Hitler was that most close at hand: personal behavior. In the middle of a routine presentation by the Grand Superior on
fraternity finances at the December 1937 Phi Epsilon Pi convention, a
member interrupted by handing the speaker a newspaper with headlines
proclaiming Rumania's revocation of the citizenship of its Jews. "I see in
the papers that another country has announced a campaign to liquidate
the Jews," the speaker announced to the assembly. Then, without long
pause and without expressing shock or outrage, the fraternity's Grand

Superior immediately connected the events in Rumania with possible similar events in the U.S., and cautioned that good manners would go far toward averting such evil decrees in their own land. "There are sufficient bigots in this country to take any excuse at all to carry on such a campaign," he warned. "The Jewish student body on the campus is the most important element of the Jewish people as a whole in combating the sort of thing that is attempting to ruin us. Let's go back to our various chapters and see that we keep our own houses in order. . . . See that all the men in your chapter always conduct themselves as gentlemen at all times."[88]

Over a period of six weeks, from December 1938 to January 1939, in her investigatory travels to six colleges—Illinois, Northwestern, Wisconsin, Minnesota, Syracuse, and Cornell—Reba B. Cohen, by then the national president of Alpha Epsilon Phi sorority, noted with gratitude the genuine interest and concern of some Gentile college officials as they asked her questions about religion, Germany, Palestine, and Jewish refugees. At the same time she expressed her apprehension for the future and concern that poor public behavior was harming the position of Jews on campus. She called for unity among all the Jewish women's groups and for a special sorority conference to address these concerns:

> The more I talked with deans, community leaders, and college leaders both Jewish and non-Jewish—the more convinced I became that steps should be taken for better understanding between all Jewish fraternity women. . . . Present world-wide conditions should make us realize that it is not sufficient to give a secret handclasp and talk about high ideals. . . . So many gigantic world problems face us at present that the pettiness of wholesome competition plus the incompatibility of Jewish groups fills the average person with disgust. Much criticism and censure has been heaped upon us in connection with rushing, cliquing, and arousing unnecessary attention in public places. Unethical rushing is certainly a problem for all sensible fraternity women to consider; but at present we must also concentrate on proper conduct and proper dress. We can shout from the house tops that it can't happen here, but personally, I think we should do less shouting and more acting so that it WILL be less apt to happen here.[89]

"We can, as college women," she concluded, "best serve our people by creating better understanding between Jews and non-Jews, by paying special attention to our dress, manners, and speech, and by cooperating among ourselves."

In time, American Jews would learn that proper dress, good manners, quiet speech, and gentle behavior alone would not be sufficient to protect the Jewish people from great tragedy. It says worlds about them, however, to see from the records on the eve of World War II, just how many of them believed that it would.

Epilogue

World War II and the Beginning of the End
for the Jewish Fraternity System

The entrance of the United States into World War II paradoxically came almost as a relief to leaders of the American Jewish community. For years, and particularly since the outbreak of the War in 1939, they had agonized over the triumph of Nazism while fearing to speak out lest they bring harm to themselves and fulfill the antisemitic charge that the Jews were fomenting war. Large segments of the population and the Congress had been staunchly isolationist. Now, American Jews could join their fellow citizens of all faiths in fully and patriotically opposing the Axis foe.

Half a dozen members of Zeta Beta Tau and Phi Epsilon Pi, along with other young Jewish men, had been unable to wait and traveled to Canada in order to enlist in His Majesty's forces. Their comrades soon followed, voluntarily or involuntarily. With the draft age lowered from 21 to 18, a majority of college-aged men doing military service, and most of their chapter houses taken over by the Armed Forces for the duration of the war, fraternity life as it had been known on the American campus virtually ceased to function. Sororities were less depleted by the war than the men's groups, although their journals are filled with stories of members serving in some capacity, including as WACs, WAVEs, and nurses at the front. For the most part, however, they discontinued most of their usual activities, turning their energies to supporting the general war effort as well as their individual boyfriends and husbands in any way they could.

A rash of hasty marriages, resulting in a wife who had to follow her serviceman husband to bases around the country, brought an end to many a college and sorority career. On the other hand, the wartime shortage of men served as a window of opportunity, bringing unprece-

dented professional and technical advancement for college-trained women and opening the portals of certain previously all-male colleges and
educational programs to the other gender. It also led to repeated suspensions of peacetime rules of propriety and etiquette. The ubiquitous
U.S.O. dances with sorority women serving as hostesses and dance partners to men on leave were one example. In another case at the University
of Arizona in 1943, the members of Alpha Epsilon Phi sorority and Zeta
Beta Tau fraternity—by then almost empty with most of its members
in the army—decided to stretch their ration coupons and help maintain the ZBT chapter house by sharing meals together. Accompanied
by their chaperone (as the national office insisted) the women joined
their remaining comrades at the ZBT house twice each day, as well as
entertaining at their own house any ZBT servicemen who happened to
be near.[1]

For the men, even though the system as such almost ceased to
function and scores of fraternity houses were taken over by the armed
forces to quarter men in campus military training programs, fraternal
bonds and friendships reached perhaps the apogee of their strength. As
long as the journals could continue publishing, articles by early enlistees
instructed and warned their apprehensive fraternity brothers at home
what to expect, how to succeed in army life, and the importance of
their cause. The national fraternity office was one of the few institutions that could keep track of literally thousands of men scattered all
over the globe and bring them in touch with each other—and also to
spread word that one of their number was missing, had been taken pris-
oner, was wounded, or had been confirmed as killed in action. This
news prompted letters of condolence to family and friends and also
letters to one another expressing grief, anger, and an inability to believe that the friends of school days such a short time ago were gone
forever.

Hundreds of letters from overseas, some written directly from
soldiers and some forwarded by their families, poured into fraternity
offices, describing their activities. Sometimes for security reasons the
letters had no return addresses save Somewhere in North Africa, Somewhere in the Pacific, Somewhere in England, Somewhere in Australia,
or Somewhere in the Aleutian Islands. The letters were in turn excerpted, printed, and sent out again in national and chapter newsletters
reaching membership and their loved ones. Through these newsletters,
fraternity brothers based in the same vicinity or stationed on the same
Pacific island who would never have known of each other's existence so

close by were able to renew old friendships at a time when they were badly needed.[2]

Fraternity bonds extended to include nonmembers as well. As the only chapter of any Jewish fraternity at the University of Arizona in 1942, the ZBT house there reportedly became the social gathering center for all Jewish servicemen at David-Montham Field at the Tucson Air Base.[3] As part of their wide-ranging "Service Men's Service" (SMS) program, Zeta Beta Tau sent thousands of care packages filled with tea, coffee, cookies, delicacies, toiletries, and copies of the *New York Times* to its members. The U.S. Armed Forces, knowing how important such packages were for the fighting men's morale, allocated valuable shipping space for them, although as the war went on the allowable size and weight of the packages decreased.[4]

Religious traditions and symbols, even when they were considered of slight importance during college years, also provided a sense of comfort and stability to young Jewish men overseas. Capt. Arnold D. Swartz, Miami '37 (U.S.M.C., Unit 650), wrote on January 23, 1943, from Guadalcanal that while walking through the cemetery there, he noticed the name of a fraternity brother from Columbia College. Immediately, he arranged for a Star of David to be placed on the crosspiece at the head of the grave.[5] (His brother, like many others, had likely declined to have an "H" engraved on his dog tag.) Jewish fraternity men not observant in their civilian life reported attending whatever Jewish services were available, sometimes leading services themselves when able and being pressed into duty as unofficial chaplains to their fellow Jews.[6] One Western Reserve graduate, raised with relatively little Jewish education, described his attendance at traditional High Holy Day services in a small room in a tiny town "somewhere in England" in September 1942: "The sincerity and vitality that these old-timers put into their service made it as sacred as if it were the most ornate synagogue," he wrote:

> For the first time in my life, I observed the orthodox service. I say "observed" because that's about what it was. I didn't know what they were doing or saying most of the time. And you know how this orthodox service is—every man for himself. Not like our reformed service, where we just sit, and let the Rabbi do all the work. It was, however, a strange and good feeling to be there in that group of civilians, officers, British soldiers and American soldiers, all brought together from all over the world on those days by our common, though somewhat indefinable bond. An English chap in front of me remarked how strange it was "you get a bunch of Jews together from all over the world, and they all read out of the same book."

I smiled. Especially because I, among many others, could not read out of the same book. But he had something there anyway.[7]

As the war drew to a close the fraternities' soldiers wrote longingly of being together at home again and their hope of attending the huge "Victory Conventions" to be held after it was finally over. Several members of Zeta Beta Tau humorously suggested holding the convention, rather than in the usual American cities, in Tokyo, Rome, or Berlin instead. All agreed that location was not as important as the fact that it take place as soon as possible.[8]

When World War II finally ended and ten million American soldiers demobilized, among them approximately half a million Jews, it appeared at first that the picture for fraternities was bright.[9] When the U.S. Congress passed the Servicemen's Readjustment Act of 1944—popularly known as "the G.I. Bill of Rights," which among other measures guaranteed full tuition and stipends to most veterans and their families at the college of their choice—it was as a dream come true for millions of Americans of modest circumstances who could never have gone to college otherwise. Once on the verge of closing during the war, the universities of the nation literally overflowed with new and returning students. The resulting desperate housing shortage made residence in fraternity and sorority houses especially desirable.

However, the post-war period brought its own challenges to Jewish Greek-letter societies. Sharp inflation had vastly raised the cost of food and services. Traditions and leadership techniques that had been forgotten now had to be relearned. Veterans, some of whom had been wounded in action, did not wish to tolerate the foolishness, the paddling, or the hazing which, despite constant attempts at regulation or elimination, had always been a part of fraternity life. It was extremely difficult for them, after having faced death in combat, to embrace what seemed to them to be the more juvenile aspects of these organizations.[10] In the years after the war they coexisted in chapter houses with teenagers much younger and more inexperienced than they were, and although the younger ones benefited from exposure to more mature models, some tensions inevitably resulted.[11]

However, by far the greatest post-war challenge for Jewish fraternities and sororities was what came to be known euphemistically as the "S" question—or the "sectarian" question. After generations of taken-for-granted strict segregation by religion, race and class, sometimes *de facto* and sometimes *de jure*, a complex variety of factors and historical forces caused a post-war movement to far greater democratization of American social and educational institutions—at least in theory, if not always in fact. The lowering of traditional social barriers during the war, the anger of minorities at not being granted full rights in the country they had laid down their lives to defend, the need to forestall Communist criticism of American racism, the growing need for academically and technically trained personnel no matter what their background, and an awareness of just how appallingly far racism and religious prejudice had so recently been taken, all played a role. As tax-exempt institutions and, increasingly, recipients of public funds, American universities were especially vulnerable to these trends. The results changed the face of American society. The struggles of the Civil Rights movement and the 1954 Supreme Court decision in *Brown v. Board of Education of Topeka* that the doctrine of "separate but equal" was inherently unequal and unconstitutional, were major turning points.

For members and leaders of Jewish fraternities and sororities all of these changes had enormous ramifications and caused them to be caught on the horns of an acutely painful dilemma.[12] On the one hand, great pressure was placed on them, from both within and without the Jewish community, to go along with what appeared to be the longed-for dawning of a new day in America and to remove from their charters the clauses restricting membership to Jews, or in cases where no such clause existed, to follow a fully nondiscriminatory pledging policy. Pressure was especially strong from the American Jewish Committee and the B'nai B'rith Anti-Defamation League, whose ranks included several prominent Jewish fraternity members and who met with representatives of the Jewish Greek system continuously through the late 1940s and early 1950s to discuss this issue.[13] How, these critics asked, could Jews in good conscience push for an end to restricted schools, corporations, summer camps, law firms and country clubs while themselves discriminating against others on the basis of religion, especially after the example of Hitlerism?[14]

On the other hand, at the same time the Gentile Greek-letter groups in the National Interfraternity Conference and the National Panhellenic Congress were asking for Jewish fraternal groups to make a common cause of fighting back the veritable rain of federal, state, and local legislation demanding that social Greek-letter groups demonstrate lack of discrimination within set deadlines or else get off campus. Highlights of this movement were the 1948 decision at Amherst College to ban any fraternities with membership restrictions based on race, color, or creed, and the 1953 decision by the authorities of the State University of New York system to abolish national fraternities altogether.[15] Campus after campus was requesting all fraternities and sororities to open their constitutions and rituals to public view, reveal whether or not they had discriminatory clauses, and risk expulsion if any were found.[16] Jewish fraternity and sorority leaders had always striven to be loyal members of the general Greek system, whether or not they were fully permitted into its institutions, and they all supported the right to maintain free association and selective membership—after all, these were the very basis of fraternity life. Indeed, to some extent the older and more conservative Jewish and Gentile Greek system alumni could easily make a common cause of the issue of not being forced to accept Black students, which quickly became a *cause célèbre* for both groups. But overall, to offer public support on this issue to the Gentile groups, some of whom had for years and still were discriminating against Jews, was like "being asked to hunt with the hounds and run with the hares," in the words of Alpha Epsilon Phi president Joan Loewy Cohn in 1957.[17]

Pressure was also strong from both the Christian and Jewish undergraduates, who tended to be far more liberal in their views on membership policy than the alumni. This fact led to numerous inter-generational conflicts especially when undergraduate members of Jewish fraternities took the lead in doing the formerly unthinkable and pledging Blacks to their fraternity. In one of the earliest examples, a major uproar ensued in May 1950 when the Phi Epsilon Pi chapter at the University of Connecticut at Storrs attempted to initiate Alfred Rogers, a Black student who was an excellent scholar, president of the Freshman class, and a varsity football player. When the national organization threatened to expel the chapter, the undergraduates mobilized fourteen other sympathetic undergraduate chapters across the country and threatened to secede en masse over the issue. In the meantime, dozens of alumni wrote in to resign their membership. The incident attracted national attention, not just among the American Jewish community but also among prominent non-Jewish social activists as well. These included Eleanor Roosevelt, who in her role as member of the U.S. delegation to the United Nations and proponent of its Human Rights Covenant, heard about the incident and wrote to the leaders of Phi Epsilon Pi fraternity to demand an explanation for their behavior. Finally, at a Special Grand Convention convened December 28, 1950, to consider this issue only, a resolution was adopted that membership in Phi Epsilon Pi would not be denied to anyone because of race, color, or creed. Alfred Rogers was duly initiated, and the fraternity survived.[18]

Throughout the 1950s it became more acceptable for the historically Jewish fraternities to accept Blacks and other non-White or non-Christian students. By 1954 all with the exception of Alpha Epsilon Phi, Zeta Beta Tau, and Sigma Alpha Mu had at least one Black member if not more, while eight of the Gentile fraternities—Beta Theta Pi, Alpha Kappa Lambda, Theta Delta Chi, Delta Kappa Epsilon, Alpha Delta Phi, Tau Kappa Epsilon, Sigma Tau Gamma, and Zeta Psi— had initiated Black students.[19] Before his graduation Michael "Mickey" Schwerner (Cornell '61), who later lost his life in Mississippi along with fellow civil rights workers Andrew Goodman and Seth Chaney, successfully led the fight to pledge the first Black student to his Alpha Epsilon Pi chapter.[20] In 1955 Leonard Jeffries '59, one of four Black freshmen at Lafayette University, was approached by the officers of Pi Lambda Phi and asked to join them. He accepted and in his senior year became "Rex" or president of the chapter. In later years Jeffries earned his Ph.D. and became director of African American Studies at the City College of New York.[21] At Columbia, the Phi Sigma Delta chapter in 1958 included Jews, Catholics, Protestants, Armenians, Japanese Americans, and Blacks, to the degree that some other fraternity houses, rather than referring to it by the customary abbreviation "Phi Sig," began to call the house derogatorily "Phi Nig."[22] In a number of cases, if alumni objected, members resigned from their fraternities over the issue, went back to being "locals," or took the initiative and declared that they would pledge whomever they pleased, something which the power structure of a national fraternity did not allow them to do.[23]

Among American Jews there could not help but be a certain amount of pleasure and pride that for the first time, it was actually possible for Jewish students to be accepted into formerly exclusively Christian fraternities, a phenomenon that occurred with increasing frequency through the late 1940s and 1950s. However, the awareness of the recent devastation of European Jewry and the inability or unwillingness of Gentiles to stop it, though rarely mentioned, colored all decisions on the maintenance of community solidarity. There was a sense of resentment that Jews should have to make sacrifices in order to eliminate a situation which had been originated by Gentiles, and a strong sense of doubt that, once their doors were opened to non-Jews, the non-Jewish groups would fully reciprocate the favor. The relaxation of unguarded speech might disappear; and it was feared that the especially close ties of brotherhood, sisterhood, and intrafraternal marriage and friendship that was so characteristic of Jewish fraternities and sororities would be irreparably damaged if Gentiles were admitted as well.

Obviously the separate religious identity of the Jewish fraternities and sororities also seemed at stake. While the degree of specifically Jewish content in their activities varied widely from group to group and from campus to campus and was usually never enough to satisfy rabbis and communal leaders, nevertheless any review of fraternity and sorority periodicals and minutes, as well as alumni interviews, reveals that it was a significant factor through the 1950s as well as a source of comfort to parents. Philanthropy and participation in Jewish communal affairs after graduation was taken for granted, and national meetings of such organizations as the National Council of Jewish Women, the National Federation of Temple Brotherhoods, and B'nai B'rith are frequently mentioned as serving as quasi-reunions for Jewish fraternity and sorority members.

Jewish identification was not limited to times of crises but was woven into the fabric of daily fraternity life in myriad ways. In the "pledge period" which preceded initiation into a fraternity, the reading of at least one book on Jewish history had been a typical requirement. Trading phrases in broken Yiddish learned from parents or grandparents and indulging in typical in-group "Jewish humor" was a feature of life in some fraternity houses. The placing of a *Mezuzah* on chapter house doorposts and avoidance of pork and shellfish at chapter house meals was also not unusual. Some Alpha Epsilon Phi chapters, while not preventing their members from attending parties elsewhere, would avoid scheduling their own parties for Friday nights, the eve of the Jewish Sabbath. Before meals, a Jewish-style Grace over bread, or the chanting of a brief prayer over wine and lighted Sabbath candles on Friday night was customary at certain chapter houses and national conventions. At times a Jewish sorority member would join the men in order to light the candles and a man would go over to the sorority house to say the traditional blessing over the wine. Hillel rabbis in their correspondence would often criticize these practices as insufficient and superficial, but on young college students they made a deep impression.

The cycle of Jewish holidays was also acknowledged in fraternity chapters. In September and October, a practical reason for acquiescing to separate "Jewish" and "Gentile" rush weeks was the ability to schedule recruitment events that would not conflict with the Jewish High Holidays. In December, chapter house abstention from putting up a Christmas tree or joining the singers of Christmas carols could also be an identifying mark. In the spring, chapter houses would hold some form of a communal Passover seder meal, however truncated, for students not going home for the holiday. At least one monthly Friday night attendance for the house as a whole at synagogue or Temple was urged by the national officers of several fraternities, though the undergraduates might make light of it. With even one Gentile member in the house all of these observances and in-group forms of identification were of course made highly problematic. Moreover, the concern of Jewish students that their Gentile friends be made comfortable and the resulting elimination of any vestige of Jewish ritual was reportedly rarely matched by the willingness of Christian fraternities to give up their traditional religious practices for the sake of their new Jewish members.

In debates on the "S" question an important consideration also included the ever-present dynamics of prestige and social desirability, which were as much based on subjective perception as they were on any objective, historically measurable reality. In the beginning, the Jews now being taken by the formerly all-Christian fraternities were the "best" students, the ones who would bring luster to any group—the best-looking, the brightest, the richest, the best athletes. Jewish fraternity officials in the 1950s, as well as alumni parents, were perturbed to find that their best pledging prospects were now the objects of interest of the leading Gentile fraternities, eager to demonstrate their magnanimity and compliance with new nondiscriminatory policies.[24] But after all, they asked one another, what kind of Gentile would want to join a Jewish fraternity, with all the others to choose from? Jews, they feared, could not hope to compete in a truly integrated Greek system. Particularly for the more elite groups, much hard work had gone into cultivating and building their prestige and selecting and training only the "best" members. If Jewish fraternities were forced to cease being Jewish and open their doors to non-Jews, it was greatly feared, too many Christian students who might not be accepted by elite groups elsewhere might join, and the size and character of their beloved fraternities would quickly deteriorate. "It has taken us sixty years to build what we have," wrote Maurice Jacobs in 1961, making this and other arguments. "Let's not destroy it so quickly, merely because of a theory of the sociologists, who have been wrong before and will be wrong again."[25]

Finally and most importantly, Jewish parents, some of whom for generations had urged their college-aged children to join Jewish Greek-letter groups and had supported the chapters through Parents', Fathers', and Mothers' Clubs, feared for the loss of their children and the inevitable rise in intermarriage which was sure to ensue once the national Jewish Greek matchmaking system broke down. "Many marriages are made in heaven," commented one Jewish mother of a college-age son in 1960, in an article expressing her views that Jews should maintain their own separate fraternity system despite legal pressures to the contrary. "Many more are made on college campuses."[26] Christian parents too, who otherwise supported the movement toward equality of Jews, Blacks and other minorities in American society, shared these fears, as noted by a prominent spokesman of the Gentile fraternity world who described the problem from a non-Jewish perspective:

> It was on this basis that some of them [parents], while joining efforts to equalize opportunities in classrooms, employment, voting, housing, and other spheres, felt justified in opposing the integration of chapters; for these were perceived as very much involved with exchange parties and dances, with getting dates and double dating and going steady, with pinnings and serenades and sweetheart songs, with the passing of cigars at fraternity houses and the pouring of ice water at sorority dinners, with bachelor's dinners and the showering of gifts to brides, with the lining up of "brothers" to serve as ushers and of "sisters" as bridesmaids, and all the other elaborate rituals of middle class Americans that help bring compatible young people of marriageable age together. . . . [These] were near the core for explaining much of the reluctance to experiment with unsegregated and possibly awkward social arrangements.[27]

The sectarian and racial controversy rocked the entire fraternity and sorority world for years, beginning in 1946 and continuing through the early 1960s. The lines were sharply drawn and many friendships of long standing were broken. In the end, the new mood of the country and the relentless legal pressure against official bigotry of any kind proved to be too strong. Officials in the fraternity world realized that they were dependent upon the universities and were there only by their sufferance. On many campuses, Greek-letter societies with discriminatory clauses in their constitutions were simply not allowed.

Approximately half of the eleven historically Jewish fraternities and sororities still in operation in the early 1950s, including Alpha Epsilon Pi, were less of a target on this issue. Ironically, their constitutions had never had clauses limiting membership to Jews in the first place. Either they had always maintained official nonsectarianism or, despite or perhaps because of an overwhelmingly Jewish membership, had never conceived that anyone else would want to join them and so had not specified Jewish background as a condition for entrance. For Zeta Beta Tau and Sigma Alpha Mu, however, the "S" Question could not be sidestepped. Both had specific Jewish sectarian clauses written into their constitutions and their secret rituals, and both required a fraternity-wide vote at the annual convention in order to remove them. After several attempts, years of debate, and continued pressure, Sigma Alpha Mu removed the last of such clauses in 1953 and Zeta Beta Tau did the same in the summer of 1954. In the case of ZBT, an impassioned discussion on the resolution went on for more than three hours, and the final resolution to remove the clause passed by a mere three votes.[28] In the eyes of the law, they thus ceased to be officially Jewish. That they continued to be identified as such and to a great extent still are, is only evidence that one cannot so easily change social characteristics simply by removing a clause from a charter.

The zeal for fraternity reform lessened for a time from the mid-1950s through the early 1960s, partly because World War II and the Korean War were receding from the memories of students and the general public. Observers of U.S. campuses during the Eisenhower years spoke of a return to more conservative "collegiate values," and the practice of fraternity hazing, which had never been entirely eliminated, enjoyed a revival. Colleges and universities appeared relatively peaceful, their students docile. No one surveying the campus scene in 1959, wrote one historian of American college student life, could have predicted the campus upheavals that would follow a few short years later.[29] Discriminatory clauses were gone from most fraternity constitutions, but the crossing of traditional lines, especially in the midwestern and southern parts of the country, did not become a routine. On many campuses, Jewish, Gentile, and Black fraternities continued to go their separate ways.

Nevertheless, under the surface, rebellion was brewing, and the power and influence of the Greek system was undergoing a gradual decline. A second stage of forced change during the era of the Vietnam War and student protest from the mid-1960s through the early 1970s dealt the final blow to the traditional Jewish fraternity and sorority system. The passage by Congress in 1964 of the Civil Rights Act and other related legislation in following years that formally outlawed segregation and discrimination on the basis of race or religion provided the legal nails for its coffin. By then, motivation to fight for the Greek system against its detractors was waning, as the entire social structure and complex of aspirations that had buttressed it came tumbling down.

The Jewish Greek subsystem had been distinguished from its Gentile counterpart by the intensity of its commitment to social training along the lines of mainstream, Anglo-Saxon Protestant culture. Its leaders in the 1920s and 1930s displayed a sense almost of religious and communal mission as they taught their members everything from the importance of school loyalty to playing golf to making proper introductions to how to use a pastry tube. The learning of these skills would insure the happiness and success of the individual, enhance the status of the group, and disprove the collective stereotype of the dirty, money-grubbing, disloyal, uncouth, and uncultured Jew. Without outright religious conversion, the embracing of such values within the Greek system appeared to be the ticket of admission to respectable, bourgeois American society.

From the late 1940s until the early 1960s, the focus of public debate had shifted toward making fraternities and sororities more democratic and responsible for fulfilling social needs. Enough Jewish students and their parents, many of whom had been members themselves as undergraduates and had met each other that way, still considered membership in a good fraternity or sorority to be a desirable goal. Enough students were still willing to submit to the discipline of Greek life, which required such things as pledge education, group service, regulated study hours, constantly signing in and out of the house, not having unchaperoned guests, refraining from indulging in liquor (much less illegal drugs), constant submission to group guidance and criticism, or the chanting of ritual and the wearing of jackets and ties or dresses and stockings to required Monday night chapter meetings.

However, the "baby boomers" that flooded the campuses now questioned the need for Greek-letter societies to exist at all. It appeared that one could have a perfectly satisfactory college career without one. In 1968, approximately 300,000 Jewish youth were attending colleges and universities in the U.S. and Canada on a full-time basis, and 90 percent of affiliated Jewish youth planned to attend, as opposed to 50 percent in the general population.[30] Among American college students membership in these groups was increasingly considered outdated or "irrelevant," a favorite term of derision in the 1960s and early 1970s. College women in particular, whose parents had supported sororities for their Jewish daughters even more than fraternities for their Jewish sons because of the supposed protection, polish, chaperonage, and marriage opportunities it offered them, now went against parental wishes and gladly jeopardized their morals and their virtue by abandoning the sorority house for independent living in apartments.[31]

Fraternities and sororities fell among the first victims of far-reaching changes in American university culture and governance. Formerly, universities had exercised strict *in loco parentis* control over their students, regulating every aspect of living, dining, socializing, traveling, and sexual activity (or lack of it). Until the mid-1960s, at most U.S. women's colleges, for a female student to leave campus and openly sleep over at her boyfriend's apartment had been, amazingly enough, grounds for expulsion. Whether American college officials truly had changed their minds that such regulation was desirable or simply lost the energy to battle with their students, the barriers came tumbling down. With them went homecoming queens, campus beauty contests, proms, elaborate dating rituals, corsages and formals; a contemporary observer noted with shock that a female college student might now pack off to college with only three pairs of Levis and four workshirts in one bag.[32] One group of four Alpha Epsilon Phi women who remained close friends after graduation remembered entering the University of Pennsylvania in 1966, when men and women were housed separately, men were only allowed to visit women in their rooms every other Sunday if they kept both feet on the floor and the door open at least a book's width, and skirts were required wear to dinner and to classes. By the time they graduated in 1970, one woman recalled, "we had co-ed dorms."[33]

For those who did join, the social hierarchy of fraternities and the age-old requirements of "good family," breeding, and wealth no longer seemed so important, in part because the American Jewish community had become more homogenous since the 1920s and 1930s and such former distinctions as those between "Germans" and "Russians" had lost any meaning. "We just have to understand that things have changed," wrote Alpha Epsilon Phi president Blanche Greenberger in July 1965, in insisting that "any decent girl from a decent family against whom there is nothing that can be said morally" should receive a reference for membership. "One has only to pick up the newspaper any day of the week to realize that we are living in a completely different world than that in which we grew up."[34]

All segments of the Greek system in the United States suffered in the late 1960s, but the Jewish groups suffered more, both because they were relatively younger and smaller to begin with, and because their members exhibited a disproportionate tendency to participate in or at least sympathize with liberal causes and the protest movement. A director in the B'nai B'rith Hillel Foundations in 1967 estimated that, while Jewish students were approximately ten percent of all college and university students, they made up no fewer than one-third of the campus protesters.[35] The sociologist Nathan Glazer, in an influential article in *Fortune* magazine entitled "The Jewish Role in Student Activism," estimated that Jews made up anywhere from one-third to one-half of the small number of college militants who actively courted arrest.[36]

What was even more remarkable about this phenomenon, Glazer noted, was that these militant young Jews "make nothing of it. Indeed, they are scarcely conscious of it, and are not aware of it at all in connection with their political activities." Unlike their parents and grandparents, these children of a new age could not even conceive that anyone might think that their actions might bring a pogrom upon their communities. Richard Gutstadt, head of the Anti-Defamation League in the 1930s, along with many other college-educated Jewish men and women who graduated before World War II ended, would have been shocked. For such blithe heedlessness and feelings of security to exist, either the world had been transformed, the civil rights and American Jewish defense agencies had done an excellent job since the end of World War II, or both; perhaps the latter had helped to bring about the former. The author himself took this into account in his squib for the article. "This is not a period in American history in which there is much danger that Jews will suffer from unequal treatment, prejudice, or discrimination," he wrote, reassuring his readers and perhaps salving his own guilty conscience. "If it were, I for one would hesitate to discuss in a non-Jewish periodical the interesting and peculiar phenomenon that Jews, who are very likely the most prosperous religious group in the country, are strikingly prominent among young radicals both on and off campus today."[37]

Strikingly prominent they were, and the Jewish fraternities felt the consequences. In a symbol of an era, the Phi Epsilon Pi house at Columbia University was abandoned and closed during that school's spring 1968 campus riots as members joined the demonstrations. Shortly afterward, it was taken over as campus headquarters for the SDS (Students for a Democratic Society).[38] The Jewish sororities showed more stability; but virtually overnight, Jewish fraternities closed, merged, or lost half their chapters, and one executive director was forced to temporarily give up the office and to run the entire operation from his basement.[39]

The American college Greek system as a whole did not die out during these years of upheaval, nor did the historically Jewish segment of it ever disappear entirely. After a few lean years, college fraternities rebounded in the late 1970s and 1980s. Today no college fraternity is officially permitted to set religious tests for membership. Jewish students can and do join fraternities and sororities that were once restricted against them. This can be a source of feelings of joy and triumph on the one hand and feelings of dismay on the other in older Americans who know or remember how the system used to work. As for the historically Jewish organizations, of the nine remaining groups at the turn of the twenty-first century perhaps three choose to emphasize their historical Jewish identity consistently and go out of their way to recruit Jewish students. Another three tend to acknowledge their heritage with pride while trying to retain official neutrality. The national leaders of the other three are adamant in their preference that the world forget they ever had any Jewish connections at all, and their membership today is indeed predominantly non-Jewish. No national organization is as capable as it would wish to be of wielding strong central control, however, and there are wide variations in chapters from campus to campus. Within the same national fraternity, chapters in one part of the country can be predominantly Jewish while chapters in another part of the country can consist entirely of non-Jews.[40]

In the minds of the public, however—as well as in the minds of occasional campus vandals—the impression persists that all these fraternities are still Jewish. Among active alumni and national officers the question of how they should or should not relate to their fraternal heritage is cause for continued impassioned debate and internal factionalism.

Regardless of the outcome of these debates, it is unlikely that the Jewish Greek subsystem will ever again function with the same insularity, cohesiveness, and communal support that it enjoyed in the first two thirds of the twentieth century. Legal considerations alone and strict interpretations of the church/state separation principle make a revival of the old system untenable. Too much time has passed, and no one can turn back the clock. Furthermore, as can be seen here, the complex of factors that gave birth to it and helped it to flourish no longer exists, due to a series of developments that from a communal point of view are largely positive.

The Greek system as a whole, once riddled with discriminatory clauses, no longer enjoys the centrality and prestige it once had. Social, residential, occupational and resort discrimination against Jews that helped to make their own fraternity houses necessary either disappeared or slipped underground. Hostile administrations are no longer a common problem. By the 1980s American Jews were well represented not only among the students but also among the faculty, deans, and presidents of the nation's most elite universities. As Hillel rabbis and other observers began to note with pleasure from the late 1950s onward, American Jewish college students appeared far less self-conscious about their Jewish identity than their predecessors in the 1920s and 1930s and less eager to escape it. Keeping quiet and blending in were no longer supreme values. Public celebration of one's ethnicity became a common occurrence. Young Jewish men who in previous generations might never have dreamed of wearing a *kippah* in public in the post-1967 years now strode to classes wearing their distinctive crocheted skullcaps with aplomb. On the most elite Ivy League campuses college administrations supported the creation of kosher living and dining options.[41] Mass Jewish student migrancy became a phenomenon of the past; attending school thousands of miles from home became a matter of personal choice, not necessity. After graduation, with wider economic opportunities available to Jews, a tight Jewish communal network was no longer so essential; the friends and acquaintances that provided referrals and job contacts were as likely to be Gentiles as Jews. Most of all, in the post-1960s era American Jews no longer needed to put their faith in the armor of Americanization, loyalty to school and country, and faultless manners in order to feel safe. Nor was it any longer necessary for them to attach acute danger to the allegedly uncouth and un-American behavior of their coreligionists.

As for the traditional social and matchmaking functions of the Jewish subsystem, the end of official sectarianism also brought an end to the support and cooperation of parents and the extended American Jewish community. Among the non-Orthodox majority emphasis on the communal arrangement of endogamous marriages in the face of all odds has declined, as has the idea that getting married is somehow mandatory. Jewish men and women, once limited in their choices, are freer to choose their mates, and to be chosen, from a much wider pool. Meanwhile, Gentile families are as likely to welcome a Jewish spouse into the family as to reject him or her. After all the years and energy expended by American Jewish defense organizations to win social approval, no one could wish for a level of greater acceptance.

The new freedom from oppression and official bigotry that was such an important gift of the post-World War II era helped to eliminate American antisemitism as a significant force. The battle against it had been at the very core of much of American Jewish communal and organizational life for most of the century. Ironically, however, antisemitism and segregation at the nation's colleges and universities had also been a crucial ingredient in the birth and flourishing of separate fraternity systems in the first place. When that was eliminated, so too was much of the justification for the Jewish Greek subsystem.

Contemporary Jewish parents, rabbis, communal leaders, Hillel directors and other observers might be tempted to look back today with some nostalgia at the positive functions the Jewish Greek subsystem once served in fostering identity, training students for communal lay leadership and, most of all, fostering endogamous marriage. As we have seen, college fraternities were an important technique used and encouraged by non-Orthodox American Jews of the middle class to keep their young people's intermarriage rates negligible. This was and is a daunting challenge on residential college campuses where students are so far removed from the influence of family and community. Precious few historical alternatives remain. Surviving institutions and organizations that stress the more affirmative aspects of American Jewish education, identity, fellowship and marriage remained seriously underfunded and underdeveloped during years of channeling the bulk of philanthropic time and energy into sheer survival. For generations the U.S. communal ethos appears to have been dominated by the idea that being Jewish was a thing to rescue people from, certainly not something to be loved or embraced.

Who could wish to return for even a moment to precisely those college days of fear, antisemitism, internal divisions, snobbery and self-hatred that served as such a solid backdrop to the Jewish Greek subsystem's most successful era? As it is, adults who spent their most formative years under the old system—or the children raised by them—too often seem to be caught in a temporal vise. By force of training and habit they scramble to meet external standards or to disprove accusations that either no longer exist or are no longer as pressing as they once were. In a new era of freedom and choice, new, creative and fully voluntary forms of campus organizations would be necessary to maintain that same positive level of campus social, ethnic, and religious solidarity that apparently reigned in those recent days of so long ago.

The surviving fraternities and sororities in the subsystem, even after decades of pursuing the goal of nonsectarianism, could conceivably retool themselves, by reaching back through the generations and trying to take up a similar positive role once more. But first, they themselves would have to choose to assert their historical role as Jewish organizations—a step most painful to their many loyal non-Jewish members and officers and seemingly almost impossible under the prevailing legal system. Second, they would require as they once had the strong support or at least the responsible supervision and concern of alumni and the adult organized Jewish community, including that of the Hillel Foundations.

As these questions continue to be debated, scholars will still look back at the history of Jewish immigrants and their descendants in America in the twentieth century and marvel at their success in higher education, at the speed of their flight up to the heights of American intellectual, business, professional, and artistic achievement. But education comes in many forms. The records of Jewish college fraternities show us, in detail that the participants would probably prefer to forget, some of the obstacles these great achievers had to overcome as they made that flight, and some of the personal and collective sacrifices they had to make along their way.

Appendix A

Chapter Rolls of the National Jewish
College Fraternities and Sororities to 1968

Chapter lists and membership figures are derived from the *American Jewish Year Book* and from the 18th and 20th editions of *Baird's Manual of American College Fraternities*, which appeared in 1968 and 1991. Fraternities are listed in the order of the organization's founding. Dates in parentheses indicate the known year or years when a chapter became inactive. Economic challenges of the 1930s and 1940s and, to an even greater extent, the impact of the Vietnam War, student protest, and general campus upheaval in the late 1960s helped to bring about the expiration or consolidation of several of these groups. An asterisk * indicates those fraternities that no longer exist as independent organizations. Several that do survive were nonsectarian in spirit and ritual from their origins or else can no longer be considered specifically Jewish fraternities. For the most up-to-date information available, readers should consult the national headquarters of the surviving groups.

JEWISH FRATERNITIES

Pi Lambda Phi

Founded at Yale University in 1895 by Henry Mark Fisher, Louis Samter Levy, and Frederick Manfred Werner. Periodical: *The Tripod of Pi Lambda Phi*. Mergers: absorbed Phi Beta Delta in 1940 and Beta Sigma Rho in 1972. Membership: 1945, 7,000; 1968, 21,500.

1895   Iota, Yale University (1932)
1896   Alpha, Columbia University (1964)

1896   NY Beta, College of the City of New York (1902; 1935–1959; 1971)
1896   NY Delta, Cornell University (1976)
1896   NY Gamma, New York University (1973)
1896   Nu, Harvard University (1900)
1896   PA Epsilon Zeta, University of Pennsylvania (1901–1912)
1897   MA Theta, Massachusetts Institute of Technology (1901)
1897   Xi, Union College [Schenectady, NY] (1900)
1914   PA Gamma Sigma, University of Pittsburgh
1915   PA Lambda, Lehigh University [Bethlehem, PA]
1916   NJ Theta, Stevens Institute of Technology
1918   Beta, Fordham University (1934)
1919   IL Omicron, University of Chicago (1949)
1919   NY Delta Delta, Brooklyn Polytechnic Institute (1934)
1920   CA Kappa, University of Southern California (1969)
1921   Canada Eta, McGill University (1942–1988)
1922   CA Upsilon, University of California, Los Angeles (1969)
1922   Canada Kappa, University of Toronto (1966–1980)
1922   MA Rho, Worcester Polytechnic Institute (1932)
1922   OK Iota, University of Oklahoma (1963)
1922   PA Beta Zeta, Carnegie-Mellon University [Pittsburgh, PA]
1922   WV Mu, University of West Virginia (1959)
1924   MA Xi, Tufts University (1931)
1924   NH Pi, Dartmouth College (1971)
1925   FL Delta, University of Florida
1925   IA Psi, Drake University [Des Moines] (1930)
1925   MD Rho, Johns Hopkins University (1940–1980)
1926   CO Alpha Beta, University of Denver (1967)
1926   WI Omega, University of Wisconsin (1968–1983)
1927   AL Alpha Eta, University of Alabama (1940)
1927   IA Phi, University of Iowa (1937)
1927   OH Alpha Epsilon, Ohio State University (1977)
1927   PA Alpha Delta, Temple University [PA]
1927   Upsilon, Amherst College (1931)

1928   IN Alpha Theta, Indiana University (1959)

1928   NE Chi, Creighton University [Omaha] (1952)

1928   SC Alpha Zeta, University of South Carolina (1950)

1929   CO Alpha Iota, University of Colorado (1934; 1963)

1929   RI Phi, Brown University (1963)

1929   VA Psi, College of William and Mary

1932   VA Omega Alpha, University of Virginia (1945–1966)

1934   IL Tau Delta, University of Illinois

1935   NJ Beta Theta, Rutgers University [Newark] (1983)

1939   NC Omega Beta, University of North Carolina (1984)

1940   PA Sigma, Lafayette College [Easton, PA] (1983)

1942   PA Omega Gamma, Pennsylvania State University

1943   NY Omega Epsilon, University of Buffalo (1968–1988)

1945   Canada Kappa Iota, University of Western Ontario (1968–1983)

1946   FL Omega Eta, University of Miami (1963)

1947   PA Tau Omega, Franklin and Marshall College [Lancaster, PA]

1948   OH Beta Sigma, Ohio Wesleyan University [Delaware, OH] (1968)

1948   OH Beta Tau, Baldwin-Wallace College [Berea, OH]

1948   PA Omega Kappa, Washington and Jefferson College [PA] (1981)

1949   Beta Sigma Kappa, University of Kentucky (1953)

1949   MA Alpha Epsilon, University of Lowell [MA] (1986)

1949   NY Beta Lambda, Syracuse University

1951   NY Omega Mu, New York University (1966)

1954   NY Kappa Tau, Rensselaer Polytechnic Institute [Troy, NY]

1958   IN Alpha Delta, Indiana State University [Terre Haute, IN]

1958   NY Sigma Tau, Brooklyn College (1973)

1959   ME Beta Chi, Colby College [Waterville, ME] (1984)

1959   VA Lambda Kappa, Roanoke College [Salem, VA]

1961   NY Alpha Lambda, Rutgers University (1969)

1963   NY Phi Lambda, Adelphi University [NY]

1965   PA Delta Iota, Drexel University [PA]

1966   CT Alpha Chi, University of Hartford (1969)
1967   MA Kappa Nu, University of Massachusetts (1981)
1967   NY Alpha Mu, Hunter College (1970)
1967   NY Delta Epsilon, Long Island University (1970)
1967   NY Lambda Delta, Queens College [NY] (1971)
1968   CT Delta Kappa, University of Bridgeport [CT] (1971)
1968   CT Tau Kappa, Quinnipiac College (1975)
1968   NM Sigma Chi, New Mexico Highlands University (1972)
1968   NY Beta Omicron, St. John's University [NY]
1968   NY Eta Chi, Hobart College [Geneva, NY] (1975)
1968   PA Gamma Chi, West Chester University of Pennsylvania
        (1977)
1968   PA Phi Delta, Alliance College [Cambridge Springs, PA]
        (1988)
1968   TX Alpha Sigma, University of Texas (1973)

Zeta Beta Tau

Founded 1898 at Jewish Theological Seminary by a group of young men
attending several universities in New York City: Herman Abramowitz,
Bernhard Bloch, Isidore Delson, Aaron Drucker, Bernard C. Ehrenre-
ich, Menachem M. Eichler, Aaron Eiseman, David Levine, Aaron W.
Levy, David Liknaitz, Louis S. Posner, Bernard D. Saxe, Herman B.
Sheffield, and Maurice L. Zellermayer. Publication: *The Zeta Beta Tau
Quarterly.* Mergers: ZBT today preserves elements and records of five
historically Jewish fraternities, having absorbed Phi Sigma Delta/Phi
Alpha in 1969 and Phi Epsilon Pi/Kappa Nu in 1970. Membership:
1945, 7,800; 1968 [pre-mergers] 35,000.

1898   Home Fraternity (1903)
1902   Alpha, College of the City of New York (1971)
1903   Beta, Long Island Medical College (1914)
1904   Gamma, New York University [Heights Campus] (1972–
        1989)
1905   Delta, Columbia University (1972–1974)
1907   [Unnamed] Jefferson Medical College (1908)
1907   Theta, University of Pennsylvania

1907   Kappa, Cornell University (1982–1988)
1908   Mu, Boston University (1939–1949; 1957)
1909   Lambda, Western Reserve University
1909   Zeta, Case Institute of Technology (1928)
1909   Sigma, Tulane University
1909   Eta, Union College (1938)
1910   Iota, Brooklyn Polytechnic Institute (1920)
1911   Nu, Ohio State University (1989)
1911   Xi, Massachusetts Institute of Technology (1927)
1911   Omicron, Syracuse University (1986–1987)
1911   Pi, Louisiana State University (1989)
1911   Rho, University of Illinois
1912   Tau, Harvard University (1933)
1912   Phi, University of Michigan
1913   Upsilon, McGill University (1969)
1915   Chi, University of Virginia (1985)
1916   Psi, University of Alabama
1917   Omega, University of Missouri
1918   Alpha Beta, University of Chicago (1975)
1918   Alpha Gamma, Vanderbilt University [Nashville, TN]
1918   Alpha Delta, University of Southern California (1972)
1920   Alpha Epsilon, Washington and Lee University [Lexington, VA] (1988)
1920   Alpha Eta, University of California, Berkeley
1921   Alpha Lambda, Yale University (1933)
1921   Alpha Zeta, University of Florida (1933–1948; 1956)
1922   Alpha Theta, University of Nebraska (1962)
1922   Alpha Kappa, University of Wisconsin (1983–1987)
1923   Alpha Xi, Washington University [St. Louis, MO]
1924   Alpha Mu, University of Washington (1973–1974)
1926   Alpha Omicron, University of Arizona (1969–1983)
1927   Alpha Pi, University of North Carolina (1985)
1927   Alpha Rho, University of California, Los Angeles
1931   Alpha Sigma, University of Texas (1934)

1931   Alpha Tau, Franklin and Marshall College (1988)
1935   Alpha Epsilon, Duke University (1971)
1936   Alpha Phi, Miami University [Oxford, OH] (1974–1989)
1942   Alpha Nu, University of Tennessee (1969)
1942   Alpha Chi, University of British Columbia (1970–1979)
1942   Alpha Iota, University of Kentucky (1973)
1946   Alpha Psi, Pennsylvania State University (1971–1988)
1946   Alpha Omega, University of Miami
1947   Beta Alpha, University of Colorado
1947   Beta Gamma, Indiana University
1947   Beta Delta, Rutgers University
1947   Beta Epsilon, Michigan State University (1971)
1948   Beta Zeta, University of Maryland
1948   Beta Eta, Bowling Green State University [OH]
1948   Beta Theta, University of Manitoba (1972)
1949   Beta Iota, University of Minnesota (1953)
1950   Beta Kappa, University of Arkansas (1955)
1951   Beta Lambda, San Diego State College (1968–1988)
1956   Beta Tau, Johns Hopkins University (1990)
1957   Beta Mu, Rider College [NJ]
1960   Beta Xi, Brooklyn College (1973–1990)
1960   Beta Pi, California State University, Long Beach (1975)
1961   Beta Rho, New York University [Washington Square Campus] (1972)
1962   Kappa Nu Kappa, Rensselaer Polytechnic Institute
1962   Beta Upsilon, Youngstown State University [OH] (1979)
1962   Beta Phi, University of Pittsburgh
1963   Beta Iota, Long Island University (1968)
1963   Beta Psi, American University [Washington, DC] (1971–1984)
1963   Gamma Alpha, Washington and Jefferson College
1964   Gamma Beta, California State University, Northridge
1964   Gamma Delta, C. W. Post College (1990)
1965   Gamma Epsilon, Marshall University [Huntington, WV] (1978)

1965   Gamma Zeta, University of Louisville [KY] (1972)

1966   Alpha Phi, Parsons School of Design [NY] (1972)

1966   Beta Xi, Baruch College [NY] (1968)

1966   Gamma Eta, Bradley University [Peoria, IL] (1973)

1966   Gamma Theta, Queens College (1973)

1967   Gamma Iota, Western Michigan University (1971)

1967   Gamma Kappa, Adelphi University (1972)

1967   Gamma Lambda, University of Hartford (1967–1985)

1967   Gamma Mu, Memphis State University (1972)

1967   Lambda, DePauw University (1972)

1968   Beta Phi, West Chester University of Pennsylvania (1973)

1968   Beta Tau, Widener College (1988)

1968   Gamma Nu, California State University, Los Angeles

1968   Gamma Omicron, University of Wisconsin, Milwaukee
        (1972)

1968   Gamma Xi, California State University, Santa Barbara
        (1970–1985)

1968   Zeta Tau, Seton Hall University [NJ] (1989)

*Phi Epsilon Pi

Founded in 1904 at College of the City of New York by Max Shlivek, Alvin P. Bloch, Arthur Hamburger, Siegfried F. Hartman, Arthur Hirschberg, William A. Hannig, and Abraham E. Horn. Publication: *The Phi Epsilon Pi Quarterly*. Mergers: absorbed chapters of Sigma Lambda Phi in 1932 and Kappa Nu in 1961. Membership: 1945, 6,000; 1968, 26,000.

1904   Alpha, College of the City of New York

1905   Beta, Columbia University (1928–1958)

1911   Kappa Alpha, University of Rochester

1911   Epsilon, Cornell University

1913   Zeta, University of Pittsburgh

1914   Eta, University of Pennsylvania

1914   Theta, Pennsylvania State University

1914   Iota, Dickinson College

1914   Kappa, New York University [Washington Square Campus]
        (1922–1949)
1915   Kappa Beta New York University [Heights Campus]
1915   Lambda, Rutgers University
1915   Mu, University of Georgia
1915   Nu, University of Virginia
1915   Kappa Delta, Union College (1925)
1916   Xi, Georgia Institute of Technology
1916   Omicron, Tufts University
1916   Pi, University of Maine (1925)
1916   Rho, Rhode Island State University (1922)
1916   Sigma, Brown University (1918)
1916   Tau, Auburn University [GA] (1920)
1916   Upsilon, University of Connecticut (1964)
1916   Phi, Carnegie Institute of Technology [Pittsburgh] (1922)
1917   Kappa Zeta, University of Buffalo
1917   Kappa Iota, Union College
1917   Chi, Syracuse University
1920   Gamma, Northwestern University [IL]
1920   Delta, Washington and Lee University
1920   Psi, University of Illinois
1920   Omega, University of Cincinnati (1935)
1920   Alpha Alpha, Dartmouth College (1922)
1920   Alpha Beta, University of Iowa
1920   Alpha Epsilon, Johns Hopkins University
1921   Alpha Gamma, University of Michigan (1942–1957)
1921   Kappa Omicron, University of Chicago (1934)
1921   Kappa Pi, University of Alabama
1921   Kappa Nu, University of California, Berkeley
1922   Kappa Sigma, Tulane University (1956)
1923   Alpha Delta, University of Minnesota
1925   Alpha Eta, University of Wisconsin (1937–1966)
1926   Alpha Zeta, Harvard University (1935)
1928   Alpha Theta, University of South Carolina
1929   Alpha Iota, University of Miami

1930   Alpha Mu, George Washington University (1952)
1932   Kappa Upsilon, University of Arkansas (1941)
1932   Alpha Nu, Muhlenberg College
1932   Alpha Omicron, Ohio State University (1964)
1932   Alpha Xi, Boston University
1933   Alpha Kappa, Western Reserve University (1955–1966)
1933   Kappa Phi, Alfred University
1933   Alpha Pi, Louisiana State University (1958)
1933   Alpha Rho, Ohio University [Athens, OH]
1935   Alpha Sigma, University of Mississippi
1948   Alpha Tau, Queens College
1949   Alpha Upsilon, Memphis State University (1959)
1949   Alpha Phi, North Carolina State University (1962)
1950   Alpha Chi, University of Omaha (1955)
1951   Alpha Psi, McGill University
1952   Kappa Alpha Delta, University of California, Los Angeles
1952   Kappa Alpha Gamma, Wayne State University (1963)
1956   Beta Alpha, University of Houston
1957   Beta Beta, American University
1958   Beta Gamma, Brooklyn College
1959   Beta Delta, Rensselaer Polytechnic Institute
1960   Beta Epsilon, University of Florida
1961   Beta Zeta, Philadelphia College of Textiles and Science
1961   Beta Eta, Indiana University
1962   Beta Theta, University of Maryland
1963   Beta Iota, Long Island University
1965   Beta Lambda, Northern Illinois University
1966   Beta Mu, C. W. Post College
1966   Beta Xi, Baruch College
1967   Beta Omicron, De Paul University
1967   Beta Sigma, Southampton College [NY]

Sigma Alpha Mu

Founded 1909 by eight students attending College of the City of New York: Ira N. Lind, Jacob Kaplan, Lester Cohen [Cole], Samuel Ginsburg [Gaines], Hyman I. Jacobson, David D. Levinson, Abraham N.

Kerner, and Adolph Fabis. Publication: *The Octagonian*. Membership: 1945, 7,500; 1968, 25,500.

1909	Alpha, College of the City of New York (1983)
1911	Beta, Cornell University (1982)
1911	Delta, Long Island Medical College (1934)
1911	Gamma, Columbia University
1912	Epsilon, Columbia College of Physicians and Surgeons (1922)
1912	Zeta, Cornell Medical College (1915)
1913	Eta, Syracuse University
1914	Theta, University of Pennsylvania
1915	Iota, University of Kentucky (1924)
1915	Kappa, University of Minnesota
1916	Lambda, Harvard University (1936–1989)
1916	Nu, University of Buffalo
1917	Omicron, University of Cincinnati
1917	Pi, Yale University (1934)
1917	Xi, Massachusetts Institute of Technology (1973)
1918	Rho, University of Illinois
1919	Chi, McGill University (1986)
1919	Phi, Washington University
1919	Psi, University of Pittsburgh
1919	Sigma, Dickinson College (1920)
1919	Tau, University of Alabama (1961)
1919	Upsilon, University of Utah (1951)
1920	Omega, University of Toronto (1972)
1920	Sigma Alpha, University of Oklahoma (1982)
1920	Sigma Beta, Ohio State University
1920	Sigma Gamma, Tulane University (1971–1976; 1980–1987)
1921	Sigma Delta, Rutgers University
1922	Sigma Epsilon, Illinois Institute of Technology (1952)
1922	Sigma Eta, Purdue University [IN] (1989)
1922	Sigma Theta, University of Texas
1922	Sigma Zeta, Indiana University

1923 Sigma Iota, University of Michigan

1923 Sigma Kappa, Lehigh University

1923 Sigma Lambda, University of Kansas (1936)

1926 Sigma Nu, University of Washington (1983–1988)

1926 Sigma Omicron, University of Nebraska

1926 Sigma Pi, University of California, Los Angeles

1926 Sigma Xi, University of Manitoba

1928 Sigma Rho, University of Missouri

1929 Sigma Sigma, University of California, Berkeley

1930 Sigma Tau, University of Oregon (1962)

1930 Sigma Upsilon, Dartmouth College (1935)

1932 Sigma Phi, Bucknell University [Lewisburg, PA]

1933 Sigma Chi, University of Maryland

1937 Sigma Psi, Mississippi State University (1950)

1938 Sigma Omega, North Carolina State University

1939 Mu Alpha, Southern Methodist University [Dallas, TX] (1976)

1941 Mu Beta, University of Alberta (1972)

1945 Mu Gamma, Case Western Reserve University

1946 Mu Epsilon, University of Miami (1970–1987)

1947 Mu Eta, Drexel University

1947 Mu Zeta, Washington State University (1950)

1948 Mu Iota, Butler University [Indianapolis, IN] (1957)

1948 Mu Kappa, Wayne State University (1971)

1948 Mu Theta, University of Southern California

1949 Mu Lambda, Pennsylvania State University (1970–1983)

1949 Mu Omicron, New York University (1966–1989)

1949 Mu Xi, University of British Columbia (1959)

1953 Mu Pi, University of Colorado (1960)

1955 Mu Sigma, Queens College (1973)

1957 Mu Rho, University of Rochester

1957 Mu Upsilon, Brooklyn College (1971–1988)

1958 Mu Phi, Long Island University (1987)

1959 Mu Chi, Michigan State University (1983–1986)

1959   Mu Psi, Miami Unversity [Oxford, OH]

1961   Mu Omega, University of Toledo

1962   Beta Alpha, University of Texas, El Paso (1972)

1962   Beta Beta, Ferris State College [MI] (1979)

1962   Beta Gamma, University of Arizona (1964–1988)

1963   Beta Delta, San Jose State University [CA]

1965   Beta Zeta, St. Mary's University of San Antonio [TX] (1967)

1966   Beta Eta, California State University, Northridge (1971–
          1984)

1966   Beta Iota, University of Wisconsin (1972–1983)

1966   Beta Kappa, Hunter College (1971)

1966   Beta Lambda, Lehman College [NY] (1970)

1966   Beta Theta, University of New Orleans (1972)

1967   Beta Nu, Portland State University (1971)

1967   Beta Omicron, George Washington University (1971–1987)

1967   Beta Pi, Northwestern University (1973)

1967   Beta Rho, University of Houston (1972–1989)

1967   Beta Sigma, North Texas State University (1987)

1968   Beta Chi, Eastern Michigan University (1971)

1968   Beta Phi, Youngstown State University (1975)

1968   Beta Psi, University of Virginia

1968   Beta Tau, Northeastern University (1978–1988)

1968   Beta Upsilon, Boston University (1971–1986)

*Phi Sigma Delta

Founded in 1909 at Columbia University by William L. Berk, Herbert L. Eisenberg, Maxwell Hyman, Alfred Jason, Joseph Levy, Herbert K. Minsky, Joseph Shalleck, and Robert Shapiro. Publication: *The Deltan.* Mergers: absorbed Phi Alpha in 1959. Membership: 1945, 3,800; 1968, 19,500.

1909   Alpha, Columbia University (1933–1955)

1912   Beta, Cornell University

1913   Gamma, Rensselaer Polytechnic Institute

1913   Delta, New York University [Heights Campus]

1914   Epsilon, Union College

1916   Zeta, University of Pennsylvania
1916   Eta, University of Michigan
1919   Theta, University of Colorado
1920   Iota, University of Denver
1920   Kappa, Western Reserve University
1920   Lambda, University of Texas
1921   Mu, University of Chicago
1921   Nu, Massachusetts Institute Of Technology (1927)
1921   Xi, Boston University (1933)
1921   Omicron, Ohio State University
1922   Pi, University of Wisconsin
1923   Rho, Johns Hopkins University
1925   Tau, Lehigh University (1933)
1927   Sigma, Pennsylvania State University
1927   Upsilon, University of West Virginia
1928   University of Vermont
1929   Chi, Duke University (1936)
1929   Psi, University of Alabama (1939)
1931   Omega, University of Missouri (1964)
1943   Alpha Alpha, University of Connecticut
1947   Alpha Beta, University of California, Los Angeles
1947   Alpha Gamma, University of Illinois
1948   Alpha Delta, Ohio University
1949   Alpha Epsilon, Syracuse University
1949   Alpha Zeta, University of Miami (1966)
1952   Alpha Eta, Colorado State University
1952   Alpha Theta, Rutgers University
1952   Alpha Iota, New York University [Washington Square Campus](1966)
1955   Alpha Kappa, University of Utah (1961)
1957   Phi Alpha Kappa, Hunter College
1957   Alpha Lambda, University of Detroit
1957   Alpha Mu, University of Massachusetts
1957   Alpha Nu, University of Wisconsin, Milwaukee

1958   Alpha Xi, C. W. Post College
1959   Alpha Omicron, Pratt Institute [Brooklyn, NY]
1959   Phi Alpha Mu, College of the City of New York
1961   Kappa Nu, Brooklyn College
1963   Alpha Pi, University of Rhode Island
1963   Alpha Rho, Washington University
1963   Alpha Sigma, Michigan State University
1964   Alpha Tau, Long Island University
1965   Alpha Upsilon, Adelphi University
1965   Alpha Phi, Parsons School of Design

Tau Epsilon Phi

Founded in 1910 at the Columbia School of Pharmacy by ten men: Robert L. Blume, Julius M. Breitenbach, Charles M. Driesen, Ephraim Freedman, Leo H. Fried, Harold Goldsmith, Samuel Greenbaum, Julius Klauber, Israel Schwartz, and Julius Slofkin. The group switched its emphasis from professional to collegiate/social with the addition of the NYU chapter in 1912. Publication: *The Plume of Tau Epsilon Phi.* Membership: 1945, 5,300; 1968, 23,400.

1910   Alpha, Columbia School of Pharmacy
1912   Beta, New York College of Dentistry (1927)
1912   Gamma, New York University
1913   Delta, Cornell University
1919   Mu, Emory University [Atlanta] (1991)
1919   Nu, University of Georgia
1919   Xi, Massachusetts Institute of Technology
1921   Rho, University of Pennsylvania (1981)
1922   Sigma, Syracuse University
1924   Omega, University of North Carolina
1924   Psi, University of Illinois
1925   Tau Alpha, University of Florida
1925   Tau Beta, University of Maryland
1926   Tau Gamma, University of Southern California (1990)
1927   Tau Delta, Ohio State University (1989)
1929   Tau Zeta, University of Maine

1932   Tau Mu, University of Connecticut (1988)
1932   Tau Theta, George Washington University (1986)
1936   Tau Nu, University of Virginia (1988)
1947   Rho Delta Rho, Illinois Institute of Technology
1947   Tau Epsilon, University of California, Los Angeles (1989)
1947   Tau Psi, New Jersey Institute of Technology
1955   Epsilon Eta, Drexel University
1956   Epsilon Theta, Queens College (1988)
1957   Epsilon Iota, Rensselaer Polytechnic Institute (1989)
1958   Epsilon Lambda, Brooklyn College
1959   Epsilon Kappa, Tulane University
1959   Epsilon Nu, Rochester Institute of Technology
1959   Phi Eta, Johns Hopkins University
1960   Alpha Beta, American University (1990)
1960   Epsilon Pi, Marietta College [OH]
1961   Epsilon Xi, Clark University (1989)
1961   Kappa Zeta Phi, Northeastern University (1988)
1962   Epsilon Tau, Bradley University
1963   Alpha Kappa, Adelphi University (1989)
1963   Epsilon Phi, Pennsylvania State University
1965   Alpha Phi, Rutgers University (1987)
1966   Sigma Epsilon, Rutgers University, Camden
1967   Phi Beta, University of South Florida [Tampa, FL]
1967   Phi Mu, University of Hartford (1989)
1967   Sigma Lambda, Bryant College [RI]
1967   Tau Alpha Kappa, Lehigh University
1968   Lambda Phi Epsilon, Clarkson University

Tau Delta Phi

Founded 1910 at College of the City of New York by Maxwell S. Goldman, Alexander B. Siegel, Maximilian A. Coyne, Milton Goodfriend, Max Klaye, Samuel Klaye, Benjamin Gray, Gustave Scheib, and Benjamin Epstein. Annual Publication: *The Pyramid.* Mergers: Absorbed Omicron Alpha Tau in 1934. Membership: 1945, 4,500. 1968: 13,000.

1914   Alpha, College of the City of New York

1914 Gamma, New York University [Washington Square Campus]

1916 Delta, Columbia University (1949)

1917 Epsilon, Boston University (1951)

1918 Zeta, Harvard University (1929)

1919 Eta, Massachusetts Institute of Technology (1929)

1920 Theta, Armour Institute of Technology [IL] (1923)

1920 Iota, University of Pennsylvania (1970)

1921 Lambda, University of Chicago (1935)

1921 Mu, Vanderbilt University (1923)

1922 Nu, University of Michigan (1968)

1923 Xi, Northwestern University (1968)

1924 Omicron, Ohio State University (1931)

1924 Pi, University of Illinois (1975)

1926 Rho, University of Texas (1975)

1927 Sigma, University of Southern California (1968)

1927 Tau, Lehigh University(1973)

1928 Chi, University of California, Los Angeles (1969)

1928 Phi, University of Minnesota (1952)

1929 Upsilon, University of North Dakota (1941)

1929 Psi, Carnegie Institute of Technology (1973)

1932 Omega, University of Manitoba (1957)

1933 Tau Alpha, Colby College (1972)

1934 Tau Gamma, Rutgers University (1976)

1943 Gamma Upsilon, New York University [Heights Campus] (1969)

1947 Tau Delta, University of Arizona (1968)

1949 Tau Zeta, Syracuse University

1950 Tau Theta, Norwich University [VT] (1960)

1951 Tau Iota, Rutgers University, Newark

1952 Tau Kappa, Queens College

1952 Tau Lambda, Alfred University (1970)

1952 Tau Mu, University of Miami (1971)

1952 Tau Nu, Hunter College (1968)

1956 Tau Omicron, Temple University (1971)

1957   Tau Pi, Roosevelt University [Chicago, IL] (1968)
1959   Tau Rho, Brooklyn College
1962   Tau Sigma, Pratt Institute
1965   Tau Tau, Pennsylvania State University (1973)
1966   Tau Upsilon, Michigan State University (1968)
1967   Tau Phi, Seton Hall University
1968   Tau Chi, University of Chicago (1970)
1968   Tau Psi, C. W. Post College (1971)
1968   Tau Omega, Corpus Christi State University (1972)

Beta Sigma Rho

Originally named Beta Samach, "the Greek Beta and the Hebrew Samach suggesting the application of the Greek society idea to the social and cultural life of the Jewish undergraduate," this society was founded at Cornell in 1910 by M. H. Milman, M. M. Milman, Nathaniel E. Koenig, and Lester G. Krohn. It was renamed Beta Sigma Rho with the addition of the Columbia chapter in 1919. Mergers: absorbed by Pi Lambda Phi in 1972. Membership: 1945, 1,500; 1968, 5,000.

1910   Alpha, Cornell University
1913   Beta, Pennsylvania State University
1919   Gamma, Columbia University
1920   Delta, University of Buffalo
1922   Epsilon, University of Pennsylvania
1922   Zeta, Carnegie Institute of Technology
1930   Eta, University of Toronto
1935   Theta, Rutgers University, Newark
1945   Iota, University of Western Ontario
1949   Kappa, University of Kentucky (1952)
1950   Lambda, Syracuse University
1958   Mu, University of Miami
1962   Nu, New York University (1965)
1964   Xi, College of the City of New York
1969   Omicron, St. John's University

Kappa Nu

Founded in 1911 at the University of Rochester by Joshua Bernhardt, Louis Gottlieb, Joseph A. Lazarus, Morris Lazerson, Harold Leve, and Abraham Levey. Mergers: absorbed by Phi Epsilon Pi in 1961. Membership: 1945, 3,000; 1961, 5,500.

1911   Alpha, University of Rochester
1915   Beta, New York University [Heights Campus]
1915   Gamma, Columbia University (1926)
1915   Delta, Union College [Albany, NY] (1925)
1916   Theta, New York State Teachers College, Albany (1919)
1917   Epsilon, Boston University (1934)
1917   Zeta, University of Buffalo
1917   Iota, Union College
1918   Eta, Harvard University (1934)
1918   Kappa, Rensselaer Polytechnic Institute
1919   Lambda, Western Reserve University (1932)
1919   Mu, University of Michigan (1953)
1919   Nu, University of Pennsylvania
1921   Xi, University of Pittsburgh
1921   Omicron, University of Chicago (1934)
1921   Pi, University of Alabama
1921   Rho, University of Cincinnati (1923)
1922   Sigma, Tulane University
1922   Tau, University of California, Berkeley
1932   Upsilon, University of Arkansas (1941)
1933   Phi, Alfred University [NY]
1939   Chi, Louisiana State University (1942)
1951   Omega, New York University [Washington Square Campus]
1951   Alpha Beta, Cornell University
1952   Alpha Omega, Wayne State University
1952   Alpha Delta, University of California, Los Angeles

*Phi Beta Delta

Founded at Columbia University in 1912. Publications: *The Phi Beta Delta News Letter* and *The Tripod of Phi Beta Delta.* Mergers: absorbed by Pi Lambda Phi in 1940. Membership: 3,000.

1912   Alpha, Columbia University (1929)
1912   Gamma, College of the City of New York
1912   Lambda, New York College of Dentistry (1926)
1912   Sigma, Cornell University (1918–1934)
1915   Zeta, New York University
1918   Beta, Fordham University
1918   Mu, Brooklyn Polytechnic Institute
1919   Eta, University of Pennsylvania
1919   Epsilon, University of Chicago
1920   Theta, Massachusetts Institute Of Technology
1920   Mu, University of Cincinnati
1920   Kappa, University of Southern California
1921   Omicron, University of Michigan
1921   Rho, Worcester Polytechnic Institute (1925)
1921   Xi, Tufts University (1930)
1921   Pi, Washington University
1922   Tau, University of California, Berkeley
1922   Upsilon, University of California, Los Angeles
1922   Iota, University of Oklahoma
1923   Phi, University of Iowa
1924   Chi, University of Wisconsin (1934)
1924   Psi, Drake University (1930)
1925   Delta, University of Florida
1925   Omega, University of Pittsburgh (1931)
1925   Alpha Alpha, University of Minnesota (1933)
1925   Alpha Beta, University of Denver, 1934
1927   Alpha Gamma, Lehigh University (1933)
1927   Alpha Delta, Temple University
1927   Alpha Epsilon, Ohio State University
1928   Alpha Zeta, University of South Carolina

1928   Alpha Eta, University of Alabama
1928   Alpha Theta, Indiana University
1931   Alpha Iota, University of Colorado
1934   Alpha Kappa, University of Illinois

Omicron Alpha Tau

Founded at Cornell in 1912 by Joseph Seidlin, James Castelle, Jack Grossman, Benjamin Brickman, Nat Shiren, Jules Jokel, and Abraham Haibloom. Publication: *The Oath*. Through the 1920s the fraternity grew to 15 chapters, but it could not last through the Great Depression and disintegrated in 1934. Most of its chapters were absorbed by Tau Delta Phi.

1912   Alpha, Cornell University
1915   Beta, College of Dental and Oral Surgery [later combined with Gamma Chapter]
1916   Gamma, Columbia University
1919   Epsilon, New York University
1919   Zeta, Syracuse University
1928   Eta, Rutgers University
1922   Lambda, University of Pennsylvania
1924   Nu, Valparaiso University [IN]
1925   Xi, University of Buffalo
1927   Omicron, University of Alabama
1927   Pi, University of Illinois
1927   Rho, McGill University
1927   Sigma, University of Chicago
1928   Tau, George Washington University
1928   Upsilon, Marquette University [Milwaukee, WI]

Phi Alpha

Founded in 1914 in Washington, DC, by David Davis, Maurice H. Herzmark, Edward Lewis, Reuben Schmidt, and Hyman Shapiro. Publication: *The Phi Alpha Quarterly*. Mergers: absorbed by Phi Sigma Delta in 1959. Membership: 1945, 3,900; 1959, 6,400.

1914   Alpha, George Washington University

1915   Beta, University of Maryland [Baltimore]

1916   Gamma, Georgetown University

1919   Delta, Northwestern University (1924)

1919   Epsilon, University of Maryland

1920   Zeta, Yale University (1925)

1920   Eta, Johns Hopkins University (1938)

1920   Theta, New York University

1920   Iota, Columbia University (1923)

1921   Kappa, University of Pennsylvania (1939–1952)

1921   Lambda, De Paul University (1927)

1922   Mu, University of Virginia

1924   Nu, Clark University

1924   Omicron, University of New Hampshire

1924   Pi, Boston University

1925   Rho, University of Richmond [VA]

1925   Sigma, Brooklyn Polytechnic Institute

1927   Tau, College of William and Mary

1927   Upsilon, University of Chicago

1927   Phi, Duquesne University [Pittsburgh, PA]

1927   Chi, Trinity College (1929)

1928   Psi, University of Tennessee (1930)

1928   Omega, University of North Carolina

1928   Alpha Alpha, University of West Virginia (1935)

1929   Alpha Beta, Temple University

1930   Alpha Gamma, Wayne State University

1930   Alpha Delta, University of Detroit

1937   Alpha Epsilon, St. John's College [MD]

1938   Alpha Zeta, St. John's University

1940   Alpha Eta, College of the City of New York

1941   Alpha Theta, Washington University (1942)

1953   Alpha Iota, Cornell University

Alpha Epsilon Pi

Founded in 1913 at the Washington Square campus of NYU by
Charles C. Moskowitz, Isador M. Glazer, Herman L. Kraus, Arthur E.

Leopold, Arthur M. Lipkint, Emil J. Lustgarten, Benjamin N. Meyer, Charles J. Pintel, Maurice Plager, David K. Schafer, and Hyman Schulman. Publication: *The Scroll*; since 1948, *The Lion of Alpha Epsilon Pi*. Mergers: absorbed Sigma Omega Psi in 1940 and Sigma Tau Phi in 1947. Membership: 1945, 4,000; 1968, 30,500.

1913   Alpha, New York University
1917   Beta, Cornell University
1919   Gamma, University of Pennsylvania
1920   Delta, University of Illinois
1920   Epsilon, Emory University [Atlanta]
1920   Omicron Deuteron, University of Cincinnati
1920   Zeta, Georgia Institute of Technology (1923–1946)
1921   Eta, Ohio State University
1921   Pi Deuteron, Pennsylvania State University (1974–1982)
1921   Theta, Auburn University (1923–1965; 1984)
1923   Iota, Columbia University (1932–1951)
1924   Kappa, Ohio Northern University (1981)
1925   Lambda, University of Chicago (1932) [charter transferred to
          Illinois Tech in 1948]
1925   Mu, University of Virginia
1925   Nu, Marquette University (1974)
1925   Rho Deuteron, University of Delaware
1926   Omicron, University of Georgia
1927   Pi, University of Wisconsin (1973–1982)
1928   Rho, Rhode Island State University
1928   Sigma, Washington University (1972–1977)
1929   Tau, Vanderbilt University
1930   Xi, Wayne State University (1934–1947; 1973–1977)
1931   Upsilon, University of Southern California
1933   Phi, University of Massachusetts (1973–1981)
1934   Chi, Michigan State University (1972–1979)
1936   Psi, Johns Hopkins University (1971)
1937   Omega, University of North Carolina (1951–1987)
1937   Alpha Deuteron, Drake University

1938   Beta Deuteron, Louisiana State University (1952–1965; 1972)
1939   Gamma Deuteron, University of Texas
1940   Delta Deuteron, University of Maryland
1940   Epsilon Deuteron, Worcester Institute of Technology (1973)
1940   Eta Deuteron, Tufts University
1940   Zeta Deuteron, Boston University (1972–1984)
1941   Theta Deuteron, University of Akron (1973)
1942   Iota Deuteron, University of Alabama (1982)
1947   Chi Deuteron. Washington University (1961)
1947   Kappa Deuteron, George Washington University
1947   Lambda Deuteron, University of Miami
1947   Mu Deuteron, University of Missouri
1947   Nu Deuteron, University of Missouri, Rolla
1947   Sigma Deuteron, Syracuse University (1973–1977)
1947   Tau Deuteron, Western Reserve University (1974)
1947   Upsilon Deuteron, University of New Mexico (1965)
1948   Alpha Upsilon, New York University [Heights Campus]
          (1972)
1949   Beta Upsilon, Bradley University
1949   Chi Alpha, University of California, Berkeley (1964–1985)
1949   Kappa Chi, Queens College (1972–1987)
1949   Kappa Sigma, Kansas State University (1963)
1949   Kappa Upsilon, University of Kansas (1977–1982)
1949   Mu Upsilon, University of Minnesota (1973)
1949   Omega Deuteron, University of Michigan
1949   Phi Deuteron, Kent State University [OH] (1972–1977)
1949   Psi, Deuteron, University of Tennessee (1953–1962)
1950   Upsilon Tau, University of Toledo (1973)
1951   Alpha Sigma, Arizona State University
1951   Iota Upsilon, University of Iowa
1951   Mu Tau, Massachusetts Institute Of Technology
1951   Phi Gamma, University of Florida
1951   Rho Pi, Rensselaer Polytechnic Institute
1951   Tau Upsilon, Tulane University (1974–1977)

1952　Gamma Alpha, Georgia State University

1953　Beta Pi, New York Polytechnic Institute (1973)

1954　Pi Upsilon, Purdue University (1970–1975)

1954　Upsilon Rho, University of Richmond (1972)

1954　Zeta Pi, University of Vermont (1972–1987)

1956　Alpha Pi, Temple University (1972–1977)

1956　Kappa Mu, University of Missouri, Kansas City (1972)

1956　Phi Theta, Brooklyn College (1973–1988)

1956　Rho Upsilon, Rutgers University

1956　Upsilon Kappa, University of Connecticut

1957　Mu Epsilon, University of Wisconsin, Milwaukee (1974)

1958　Beta Iota, Indiana University

1958　Sigma Chi, Brooklyn College (1973)

1958　Upsilon Beta, University of Buffalo (1972–1984)

1959　Eta Chi, Lehman College (1973)

1959　Omega Upsilon, University of Oklahoma (1973–1983)

1960　Beta Sigma, Baruch College (1973)

1962　Alpha Epsilon, C. W. Post College (1973–1984)

1962　Lambda Upsilon, Long Island University (1973)

1962　Rho Beta, Rutgers University, Newark (1973)

1962　Sigma Kappa Psi, Northeastern University

1962　Upsilon Chi, University of Tennessee, Chattanooga (1972)

1963　Pi Zeta, Old Dominion University [Norfolk, VA] (1972)

1964　Alpha Tau, Miami Unversity [Oxford, OH]

1964　Rho Nu, University of Rochester (1973)

1964　Upsilon Alpha, University of Arizona

1965　Epsilon Kappa, East Carolina University [Greenville, NC]
　　　　(1972)

1965　Pi Chi, Parsons School of Design (1972)

1966　Rho Iota, Rochester Institute of Technology

1966　Rho Mu, Randolph-Macon College [Ashland, VA] (1985)

1967　Delta Pi, Utica College (1972)

1967　Delta Tau, Detroit Institute of Technology (1972)

1967　Phi Chi, Cleveland State University (1974)

1967   Upsilon Omicron, University of Nebraska, Omaha (1972)

1968   Kappa Gamma, Clarkson University [NY]

1968   Nu Alpha, Northern Arizona University [Flagstaff] (1975)

1968   Nu Eta, Quinnipiac College (1975)

1968   Nu Sigma, University of Nevada, Las Vegas (1971–1977)

1968   Phi Tau, Florida State University [Tallahassee]

1968   Rho Eta, Hunter College (1970)

1968   Upsilon Eta, University of Houston (1974–1988)

Alpha Mu Sigma

Founded at Cooper Union in 1914 by Irwin S. Chanin, Henry Charles Dinney, Irving H. Fisher, Edward D. Fox, Henry I. Gilbert, Theodore F. Haynes, Julius Liebing, Benjamin Rothstein, Saul Shaw, Samuel H. Solodar, Jonas I. Speciner, and Joseph Spies. Publication: *The Shield.* Mergers: the fraternity gradually expired by 1963, with chapters becoming inactive or being absorbed by other groups. Membership: in 1945, 1,500.

1914   Alpha, Cooper Union Institute of Technology (1971)

1917   Beta, College of the City of New York (1963)

1917   Gamma, Brooklyn Polytechnic Institute (1919)

1919   Delta, Massachusetts Institute Of Technology (1920)

1920   Epsilon, Columbia University (1920)

1921   Zeta, New York University

1922   Eta, Harvard University (1922)

1922   Theta, Bellevue Hospital Medical College (1922)

1922   Iota, Yale University (1922)

1923   Lambda, University of Pennsylvania (1923)

1925   Mu, University of Maryland (1925)

1925   Nu, University of Virginia

1926   Omicron, University of Southern California (1926)

1927   Xi, Union College (1927)

1928   Rho, University of Alabama (1927)

1928   Pi, Long Island University (1928)

1929   Kappa, Boston University (1929)

1930   Sigma, Lewis Institute of Chicago (1930)

1932   Tau, George Washington University (1937)
1937   Upsilon, Brooklyn College (1960)
1939   Phi [1] St. John's University (1963)
1958   Phi [2] Pratt Institute [joined Tau Epsilon Phi] (1962)

Sigma Omega Psi

Founded 1914 at College of the City of New York. At various times it had chapters at New York University, Columbia University, Harvard University, Lowell Institute of Technology, Bellevue Medical College, Syracuse University, New York College of Dental and Oral Surgery, Worcester Polytechnic Institute, Tufts University, Northeastern University, and the Massachusetts Institute of Technology. With the Great Depression only five chapters remained active, and it merged with Alpha Epsilon Pi in 1940.

Sigma Lambda Pi

Founded at NYU in 1915 by Herbert J. Roeder, Matthew W. Sherman, Abraham Weinberg, and Milton R. Weinberger. Mergers: in 1932 the national society disintegrated, with chapters either closing, becoming "locals," or being absorbed by other fraternities. Membership: 600.

1915   Alpha, New York University
1920   Delta, New York College of Dental and Oral Surgery
1920   Phi, Fordham University
1920   Kappa, Columbia University
1921   Theta, University of West Virginia (1925)
1922   Beta, University of Pennsylvania
1923   Rho, Western Reserve University
1923   Mu, University of Michigan (1925)
1924   Zeta, Boston University
1926   Gamma, Muhlenberg College
1927   Omicron, Ohio State University

Sigma Tau Phi

Founded originally as a professional engineering fraternity by undergraduate students studying both engineering and architecture at the University of Pennsylvania in 1918. Publication: *Sigma Tau Phi Recorder.*

Mergers: absorbed by Alpha Epsilon Pi in 1947. Membership: 1945, 1,100.

1918   Alpha, University of Pennsylvania
1920   Beta, University of Cincinnati
1921   Gamma, Pennsylvania State University
1925   Delta, University of Delaware
1926   Epsilon, Dickinson College

JEWISH SORORITIES

Iota Alpha Pi

Founded in 1903 by Hannah Finkelstein Swick, Olga Edelstein Ecker, Sadie April Glotzer, Rose Posner Bernstein, Rose Delson Hirschman, May Finkelstein Spiegel, and Frances Zellermayer Delson. Publications: *The J.A.P. Bulletin*. Membership: 1945, 1,000; 1968, 6,300. The national organization disbanded in 1971.

1903   Alpha, Normal College [later Hunter College] (1913)
1913   Beta, Hunter College [chapter renamed] (1965)
1913   Gamma, Brooklyn Law School (1941)
1922   Delta, New York University [Washington Square Campus]
1922   Epsilon, New Jersey Law School (1942)
1926   Zeta, Adelphi University
1927   Eta, University of Denver (1942)
1929   Kappa, University of Toronto (1956)
1930   Iota, Long Island University
1931   Lambda, Brooklyn College
1932   Mu, University of Manitoba (1965)
1935   Nu, Wayne State University
1938   Omicron, Queens College
1942   Pi, Syracuse University
1946   Rho, Miami University [Oxford, OH] (1956)
1946   Sigma, Temple University
1947   Upsilon, Rider College (1955)
1954   Phi, University of Illinois

1960   Psi, New York University [Heights Campus] (1965)
1962   Beta Alpha, Pennsylvania State University
1965   Beta Beta, College of the City of New York
1966   Beta Delta, Cornell University
1966   Beta Epsilon, C. W. Post College

Alpha Epsilon Phi

Founded at Barnard College in 1909 by Ida Beck, Lee Ries, Helen Phillips, Rose Salmowitz, Stella Straus, Rose Gerstein, and Augustina Hess. Publication: *The Columns of Alpha Epsilon Phi.* Membership: 1945, 6,400; 1968, 25,000.

1909   Alpha, Barnard College (1914)
1909   Beta, Hunter College (1970)
1915   Gamma, Teachers College [Columbia University] (1917)
1916   Delta, Adelphi University
1916   Epsilon, Sophie Newcomb College [Tulane University]
1917   Eta, New York State Teachers College [State University of New York at Albany] (1955–1985)
1917   Theta, University of Pennsylvania (1931–1959; 1970)
1917   Zeta, New York University (1970–1986)
1919   Iota, Syracuse University
1920   Kappa, Cornell University
1920   Lambda, University of Denver (1924)
1920   Mu, University of Illinois
1920   Nu, University of Pittsburgh
1921   Omicron, Northwestern University (1988)
1921   Pi, University of Michigan
1921   Rho, Ohio State University
1921   Sigma, University of Wisconsin (1972–1983)
1921   Xi, University of Southern California (1985–1990)
1923   Tau, University of California, Berkeley
1924   Phi, University of California, Los Angeles
1924   Upsilon, University of Akron (1931)
1925   Chi, Vanderbilt University (1965)

1925   Omega, University of Texas

1925   Psi, Washington University (1934–1960)

1927   Alpha Alpha, University of Toronto (1955)

1929   Alpha Beta, University of Missouri

1930   Alpha Gamma, George Washington University (1937–1959; 1970–1985)

1932   Alpha Delta, University of Washington (1987)

1934   Alpha Epsilon, Duke University (1965–1975)

1937   Alpha Zeta, Pennsylvania State University (1978)

1938   Alpha Eta, University of Miami

1938   Alpha Iota, University of Minnesota (1978)

1938   Alpha Theta, Louisiana State University (1984)

1940   Alpha Kappa, Miami University [Oxford, OH] (1980–1986)

1940   Alpha Lambda, University of Arizona

1943   Alpha Mu, University of Maryland

1944   Alpha Nu, Carnegie-Mellon University (1971)

1944   Alpha Xi, University of Connecticut (1970)

1945   Alpha Omicron, University of Vermont (1970)

1945   Alpha Pi, University of South Carolina (1949–1967; 1978)

1945   Alpha Rho, University of Alabama (1967)

1948   Alpha Sigma, University of Tennessee (1977)

1948   Alpha Tau, University of Florida

1948   Alpha Epsilon, Purdue University (1951–1968; 1976)

1951   Alpha Chi, Boston University (1974–1985)

1951   Alpha Phi, Ohio University (1971–1981; 1984)

1952   Alpha Omega, Drake University (1973)

1952   Alpha Psi, University of Colorado (1971–1990)

1952   Epsilon Alpha, Michigan State (1973)

1954   Epsilon Beta, Brooklyn College (1976)

1956   Epsilon Delta, Queens College (1971)

1956   Epsilon Gamma, University of Oklahoma (1979)

1958   Epsilon Epsilon, Indiana University

1958   Epsilon Zeta, Arizona State (1972)

1959   Epsilon Eta, Emory University

1959　Epsilon Theta, American University (1970–1987)
1962　Epsilon Iota, New York University [Heights Campus]
1962　Epsilon Kappa, Rhode Island (1965–1980; 1986)
1962　Epsilon Lambda, University of Texas, El Paso (1969)
1962　Epsilon Mu, C. W. Post College (1972)
1964　Epsilon Nu, San Diego State University (1971)
1965　Epsilon Xi, Kent State University (1970–1980; 1984)
1966　Epsilon Omicron, Brooklyn College (1971)
1966　Epsilon Pi, California State University, Long Beach (1971)
1966　Epsilon Rho, San Jose State University (1968)
1968　Epsilon Chi, Bradley University (1983)
1968　Epsilon Phi, University of Iowa (1974)
1968　Epsilon Sigma, California State University, Northridge (1971)
1968　Epsilon Tau, University of California, Santa Barbara (1971)

Phi Sigma Sigma

Founded at Hunter College in 1913 by Rose Sher Seidman, Josephine Ellison Breakstone, Estelle Melnick Cole, Fay Chertkoff, Gwen Zaliels, Ethel Gordon Kraus, Jeanette Lipka Furst, Lillian Gordon Alpern, Shirley Cohen Laufer, and Claire Wonder McArdle. Publication: *The Sphinx*. Membership: 1945, 3,500; 1968, 13,000.

1913　Alpha, Hunter College (1976)
1918　Gamma, New York University (1963)
1920　Delta, University of Buffalo (1984)
1920　Epsilon, Adelphi University
1921　Zeta, University of California, Los Angeles
1922　Eta, University of Michigan
1923　Theta, University of Illinois
1924　Iota, University of Pittsburgh
1924　Kappa, George Washington University (1971–1986)
1926　Lambda, University of Cincinnati (1971)
1926　Mu, University of California, Berkeley (1966)
1926　Nu, University of Pennsylvania
1926　Xi, Temple University
1927　Omicron, Louisiana State University (1933)

1927   Pi, Syracuse University
1928   Rho, Ohio State University (1958)
1929   Sigma, Long Island University
1929   Tau, University of Texas (1933)
1930   Phi, University of Wisconsin (1969)
1930   Upsilon, University of Manitoba (1955)
1932   Chi, University of Utah (1943)
1934   Psi, Sophie Newcomb College (1946)
1935   Omega, University of Missouri (1955)
1936   Beta Alpha, University of Maryland
1940   Beta Beta, University of Washington
1941   Beta Delta, Ohio University (1951–1997)
1941   Beta Gamma, Boston University (1966)
1943   Beta Epsilon, University of Connecticut
1945   Beta Zeta, University of Southern California (1953)
1946   Beta Eta, Pennsylvania State University (1970)
1947   Beta Iota, Southern Methodist University (1953)
1947   Beta Kappa, Florida Southern University (1953)
1947   Beta Theta, University of Miami (1985)
1950   Beta Lambda, Wayne State University (1970)
1952   Beta Mu, University of Kentucky (1957)
1954   Beta Nu, Brooklyn College (1969)
1954   Beta Xi, Cornell University (1969)
1956   Beta Pi, Queens College (1967)
1961   Beta Rho, Drexel University
1962   Beta Upsilon, American University (1983)
1965   Beta Phi, Georgia State University [Atlanta, GA]
1965   Beta Tau, California State University, Northridge
1966   Beta Chi, University of Wisconsin, Milwaukee
1967   Beta Psi, University of Florida
1968   Alpha Alpha, Lehman College

Sigma Delta Tau

Founded at Cornell in 1917 by Inez Dane Ross, Amy Apfel Tishman, Regene Freund Cohane, Marian Gerber Greenberg, Dora Bloom

Turteltaub, Lenore Blanche Rubinow, and Grace Srenco Grossman. Publication: *The Torch*. Membership: 1945, 3,000; 1968, 16,000.

1917   Alpha, Cornell University
1920   Beta, University of Pennsylvania
1921   University of Buffalo (1976–1983)
1923   Epsilon, University of Cincinnati
1924   Eta, University of Georgia
1924   Zeta, Louisiana State University (1969)
1925   Theta, University of Nebraska (1970)
1926   Iota, McGill University (1971)
1926   Kappa, University of Illinois
1927   Lambda, University of California, Los Angeles (1987)
1927   Mu, University of Southern California (1935)
1929   Nu, University of Minnesota
1929   Xi, University of Oklahoma
1933   Pi, University of Iowa (1971–1982; 1988)
1934   Omicron, University of West Virginia (1969)
1935   Rho, University of Alabama
1938   Sigma, Northwestern University (1983)
1939   Tau, University of Texas
1940   Upsilon, Indiana University
1943   Phi, Pennsylvania State University (1971–1978)
1944   Chi, University of Michigan
1945   Psi, University of Massachusetts
1946   Alpha Beta, University of Rhode Island
1946   Omega, Syracuse University (1977–1984)
1947   Alpha Delta, University of Colorado (1971)
1948   Alpha Epsilon, Purdue University (1953)
1950   Alpha Zeta, University of Pittsburgh
1951   Alpha Eta, Washington University (1973)
1952   Alpha Theta, University of Maryland
1955   Alpha Iota, Sophie Newcomb College
1957   Alpha Kappa, University of South Carolina (1962)
1957   Alpha Mu, University of Miami

1958   Alpha Nu, University of Wisconsin (1971–1982)
1959   Alpha Omicron, Brooklyn College
1959   Alpha Pi, University of Arizona (1974–1988)
1959   Alpha Xi, Boston University (1962–1986)
1960   Alpha Rho, New York University (1970)
1960   Alpha Sigma, Hunter College (1973)
1961   Alpha Tau, George Washington University (1971–1985)
1962   Alpha Phi, Memphis State University (1976)
1963   Alpha Chi, Miami University [Oxford, OH] (1987)
1963   Alpha Psi, University of Akron (1970)
1964   Alpha Omega, University of Toledo (1976)
1964   Beta Beta, Michigan State University (1972–1984)
1965   Beta Alpha, University of Denver (1984)
1965   Beta Gamma, University of Houston (1971)
1966   Beta Epsilon, Colorado State University (1968)
1967   Beta Delta, Parsons School of Design (1969)
1967   Beta Eta, Northern Illinois University (1975)
1967   Beta Iota, University of Missouri, Kansas City (1971)
1967   Beta Theta, C. W. Post College (1972)
1967   Beta Zeta, Queens College (1971–1986)
1968   Beta Sigma, Lehman College (1973)

Delta Phi Epsilon

Founded by five students attending the New York University Law School in 1917: Minna Goldsmith Mahler, Eva Effron Robin, Ida Bienstock Landau, and Sylvia Stierman Cohen. Publication: *The Triangle, The Triad.* Membership: in 1945, 2,000; in 1968, 11,000.

1917   Alpha, New York University (1966–1983)
1920   Beta, Barnard College (1922)
1921   Gamma, Syracuse University (1923–1949)
1922   Delta, Hunter College (1969–1971; 1983)
1922   Epsilon, McGill University
1924   Zeta, University of Toronto (1958)
1925   Eta, University of Pittsburgh (1944–1966)

1925   Iota, Florida State University (1950–1968; 1971)
1926   Kappa, University of Manitoba (1964)
1926   Lambda, Adelphi University (1937–1958; 1971)
1926   Mu, University of Cincinnati (1951)
1926   Nu, University of Pennsylvania (1970)
1926   Theta, University of Denver (1957)
1926   Xi, Brenau College [Gainesville, GA] (1930)
1927   Omicron, University of Louisville (1951)
1927   Pi, University of Alabama (1932–1953; 1973)
1927   Rho, University of Illinois (1933–1945)
1928   Sigma, Ohio State University (1948; 1987–1990)
1929   Tau, University of Minnesota (1932)
1930   Upsilon, Long Island University (1934–1962; 1970)
1931   Phi, Brooklyn College (1970–1972; 1984)
1934   Chi, University of Texas (1990)
1935   Psi, University of Georgia
1939   Delta Alpha, University of Vermont (1954)
1939   Omega, University of Miami (1980–1987)
1940   Delta Beta, University of Colorado (1966)
1946   Delta Delta, Indiana University (1952)
1946   Delta Gamma, University of British Columbia (1972–1981)
1947   Delta Epsilon, Drexel University (1951)
1948   Delta Zeta, University of California, Berkeley (1968)
1954   Delta Eta, University of Michigan (1974–1985)
1955   Delta Iota, Queens College (1980–1990)
1955   Delta Kappa, University of Florida
1955   Delta Theta, Wayne State University (1971)
1956   Delta Lambda, University of California, Los Angeles (1971)
1958   Delta Mu, Georgia State University (1960)
1959   Delta Nu, Temple University
1960   Delta Omicron, New York University [Heights Campus] (1968)
1960   Delta Pi, Pennsylvania State University (1966)
1960   Delta Rho, Cornell University (1988)
1960   Delta Xi, University of Maryland

1962   Delta Sigma, Rider College
1963   Delta Tau, Washington University (1971)
1965   Delta Upsilon, University of Tampa (1976)
1966   Delta Chi, George Washington University (1971–1987)
1966   Delta Phi, University of Oklahoma (1969)
1967   Delta Omega, Monmouth College [NJ]
1967   Phi Alpha, College of the City of New York (1972)
1967   Phi Beta, Baruch College (1970)
1968   Delta Psi, University of Hartford (1977)
1968   Phi Delta, Eastern Michigan University (1970)
1968   Phi Epsilon, Lehman College (1972)
1968   Phi Eta, Northeastern University
1968   Phi Gamma, Indiana University (1974–1989)
1968   Phi Theta, Oglethorpe University [Atlanta, GA] (1973)
1969   Phi Zeta, North Texas University (1973)

Pi Alpha Tau

Founded at Hunter College in 1919. This sorority remained small and as a national organization was inactive by the 1950s. In 1927 its fourth, or Delta, chapter was listed as being at St. Lawrence University in Canada. The following is its chapter roll as it appeared in the 1940 edition of *Baird's Manual*:

1919   Alpha, Hunter College
1920   Beta, New York University
1921   Gamma, Adelphi College (1938)
1923   Delta, Brooklyn Law School
1925   Epsilon, New York State Teachers' College
1927   Eta, University of Cincinnati
1929   Kappa, St. John's University
1930   Lambda, Brooklyn College

Some Historically Jewish Professional Fraternities

Medical: Phi Delta Epsilon was founded in 1904 at Cornell and had 20,000 members and 42 active graduate clubs in 1968. Phi Lambda

Kappa, founded in 1907 at the University of Pennsylvania, had 3,250 members in 1945 and 4,800 in 1968. In 1921 it absorbed the Chicago-based Jewish medical fraternity Aleph Yod He, also founded in 1907.

Dental: Sigma Epsilon Delta was established at the New York College of Dentistry in 1901. It had 900 members in 1945 and 2,400 in 1968. Alpha Omega was founded in Maryland in 1909 with the union of the Ramach Fraternity at the Pennsylvania College of Dental Surgery and the Alpha Omega Dental Fraternity at the University of Maryland. Alpha Omega also absorbed the Jewish dental fraternities Alpha Zeta Gamma in 1932 and the Mt. Sinai Dental Society of Toronto in 1942. Its membership was 5,300 in 1945 and 18,000 in 1968. Alpha Omega's philanthropic activities included, in 1953, the funding of a modern dental school at the Hebrew University in Jerusalem.

Law: Iota Theta Law Fraternity, founded in 1918, had 850 members in 1945. Nu Beta Epsilon, founded in 1919 at the University of Maryland and Northwestern University, had 850 members in 1945 and 1,750 in 1968. Tau Epsilon Rho, founded in 1920 at Western Reserve and Ohio State University Law Schools, had 1,700 members in 1945 and 6,000 members in 1968. Lambda Gamma Phi, founded in 1921, had 600 members in 1945.

Pharmacy: Alpha Zeta Omega was founded at the Philadelphia College of Pharmacy in 1919. It had 950 members in 1945 and 6,700 in 1968. Rho Pi Phi was founded also in 1919 at the Massachusetts College of Pharmacy in Boston. It had 2,500 members in 1945 and 12,000 in 1968.

Other: for Osteopaths, Lambda Omicron Gamma, founded 1924 (membership 650 in 1968); for Optometrists, Mu Sigma Pi, founded 1932 (membership 354 in 1945); for veterinarians, Sigma Iota Zeta, founded 1933 (250 members in 1945).

Appendix B

Directory of Jewish Fraternity and Sorority Chapters at Selected Colleges and Universities

This list is derived from various editions of *Baird's Manual of American College Fraternities* and shows fraternity and sorority chapters according to geographical region. Dates in parentheses indicate the known year or years that the chapter became inactive.

NEW YORK CITY

Columbia University (New York, NY)

1896	Pi Lambda Phi (1964)
1905	Phi Epsilon Pi (1928–1958)
1905	Zeta Beta Tau (1972–1974)
1909	Phi Sigma Delta (1933–1955)
1910	Tau Epsilon Phi
1911	Sigma Alpha Mu
1912	Phi Beta Delta (1929)
1915	Kappa Nu (1926)
1916	Omicron Alpha Tau
1916	Tau Delta Phi (1949)
1919	Beta Sigma Rho
1920	Alpha Mu Sigma (1920)
1920	Phi Alpha (1923)
1920	Sigma Lambda Pi
?	Sigma Omega Psi

NEW YORK STATE

Cornell University (Ithaca, NY)

1896   Pi Lambda Phi (1976)
1907   Zeta Beta Tau (1982–1988)
1910   Beta Sigma Rho
1911   Phi Epsilon Pi
1911   Sigma Alpha Mu (1982)
1912   Omicron Alpha Tau
1912   Phi Beta Delta (1918–1934)
1912   Phi Sigma Delta
1913   Tau Epsilon Phi
1917   Alpha Epsilon Pi
1917   Sigma Delta Tau
1920   Alpha Epsilon Phi
1951   Kappa Nu
1953   Phi Alpha
1954   Phi Sigma Sigma (1969)
1960   Delta Phi Epsilon (1988)
1966   Iota Alpha Pi

Rensselaer Polytechnic Institute (Troy, NY)

1913   Phi Sigma Delta
1918   Kappa Nu
1951   Alpha Epsilon Pi
1954   Pi Lambda Phi
1957   Tau Epsilon Phi (1989)
1959   Phi Epsilon Pi
1962   Zeta Beta Tau

University of Rochester (Rochester, NY)

1911   Phi Epsilon Pi
1911   Kappa Nu

1957   Sigma Alpha Mu
1964   Alpha Epsilon Pi (1973)

Syracuse University (Syracuse, NY)

1911   Zeta Beta Tau (1986–1987)
1913   Sigma Alpha Mu
1917   Phi Epsilon Pi
1919   Alpha Epsilon Phi
1919   Omicron Alpha Tau
?   Sigma Omega Psi
1921   Delta Phi Epsilon (1923–1949)
1922   Tau Epsilon Phi
1927   Phi Sigma Sigma
1942   Iota Alpha Pi
1946   Sigma Delta Tau (1977–1984)
1947   Alpha Epsilon Pi (1973–1977)
1949   Phi Sigma Delta
1949   Pi Lambda Phi
1949   Tau Delta Phi
1950   Beta Sigma Rho

Union College (Schenectady, NY)

1897   Pi Lambda Phi (1900)
1909   Zeta Beta Tau (1938)
1914   Phi Sigma Delta
1915   Phi Epsilon Pi (1925)
1917   Kappa Nu
1927   Alpha Mu Sigma (1927)

New England

Boston University (Boston, MA)

1908   Zeta Beta Tau (1939–1949) (1957)
1917   Kappa Nu (1934)

1917　Tau Delta Phi (1951)
1921　Phi Sigma Delta (1933)
1924　Phi Alpha
1924　Sigma Lambda Pi
1929　Alpha Mu Sigma (1929)
1932　Phi Epsilon Pi
1940　Alpha Epsilon Pi(1972–1984)
1941　Phi Sigma Sigma (1966)
1951　Alpha Epsilon Phi (1974–1985)
1959　Sigma Delta Tau (1962–1986)
1968　Sigma Alpha Mu (1971–1986)

University of Connecticut (Storrs, CT)

1916　Phi Epsilon Pi (1964)
1932　Tau Epsilon Phi (1988)
1943　Phi Sigma Sigma
1943　Phi Sigma Delta
1944　Alpha Epsilon Phi (1970)
1956　Alpha Epsilon Pi

Dartmouth University (Hanover, NH)

1920　Phi Epsilon Pi (1922)
1924　Pi Lambda Phi (1971)
1930　Sigma Alpha Mu (1935)

Harvard University (Cambridge, MA)

1896　Pi Lambda Phi (1900)
1912　Zeta Beta Tau (1933)
1916　Sigma Alpha Mu (1936–1989)
1918　Kappa Nu (1934)
1918　Tau Delta Phi (1929)
1922　Alpha Mu Sigma (1922)
1926　Phi Epsilon Pi (1935)

University of Maine (Orono, ME)

1916   Phi Epsilon Pi (1925)
1929   Tau Epsilon Phi

Massachusetts Institute of Technology (Cambridge, MA)

1897   Pi Lambda Phi (1901)
1911   Zeta Beta Tau (1927)
1917   Sigma Alpha Mu (1973)
1919   Alpha Mu Sigma (1920)
1919   Tau Delta Phi (1929)
1919   Tau Epsilon Phi
1920   Phi Beta Delta
1921   Phi Sigma Delta (1927)
1951   Alpha Epsilon Pi
?   Sigma Omega Psi

Tufts University (Medford, MA)

1916   Phi Epsilon Pi
1921   Phi Beta Delta (1930)
1924   Pi Lambda Phi (1931)
1940   Alpha Epsilon Pi
?   Sigma Omega Psi

University of Vermont (Burlington, VT)

1928   Phi Sigma Delta
1939   Delta Phi Epsilon (1954)
1945   Alpha Epsilon Phi (1970)
1954   Alpha Epsilon Pi (1972–1987)

Worcester Polytechnic Institute (Worcester, MA)

1921   Phi Beta Delta (1925)
1922   Pi Lambda Phi (1932)

?   Sigma Omega Psi
1940   Alpha Epsilon Pi (1973)

Yale University (New Haven, CT)

1895   Pi Lambda Phi (1932)
1917   Sigma Alpha Mu (1934)
1920   Phi Alpha (1922)
1921   Zeta Beta Tau (1933)
1922   Alpha Mu Sigma (1923)

MIDDLE ATLANTIC

George Washington University (Washington, DC)

1914   Phi Alpha
1924   Phi Sigma Sigma (1971–1986)
1928   Omicron Alpha Tau
1930   Alpha Epsilon Phi (1937–1959; 1970–1985)
1930   Phi Epsilon Pi (1952)
1932   Alpha Mu Sigma (1937)
1932   Tau Epsilon Phi (1986)
1947   Alpha Epsilon Pi
1961   Sigma Delta Tau (1971–1985)
1966   Delta Phi Epsilon (1971–1987)

Johns Hopkins University (Baltimore, MD)

1920   Phi Alpha (1938)
1920   Phi Epsilon Pi
1923   Phi Sigma Delta
1925   Pi Lambda Phi (1940–1980)
1936   Alpha Epsilon Pi (1971)
1956   Zeta Beta Tau (1990)
1959   Tau Epsilon Phi

University of Maryland (College Park, MD)

1919   Phi Alpha
1925   Alpha Mu Sigma (1925)
1925   Tau Epsilon Phi
1933   Sigma Alpha Mu
1936   Phi Sigma Sigma
1940   Alpha Epsilon Pi
1943   Alpha Epsilon Phi
1948   Zeta Beta Tau
1952   Sigma Delta Tau
1960   Delta Phi Epsilon
1962   Phi Epsilon Pi

University of Pennsylvania (Philadelphia, PA)

1896   Pi Lambda Phi
1907   Zeta Beta Tau
1914   Phi Epsilon Pi
1914   Sigma Alpha Mu
1916   Phi Sigma Delta
1917   Alpha Epsilon Phi (1931–1959) (1970)
1918   Sigma Tau Phi
1919   Alpha Epsilon Pi
1919   Kappa Nu
1919   Phi Beta Delta
1920   Sigma Delta Tau
1920   Tau Delta Phi (1970)
1921   Phi Alpha (1939–1952)
1921   Tau Epsilon Phi (1981)
1922   Beta Sigma Rho
1922   Omicron Alpha Tau
1922   Sigma Lambda Pi
1923   Alpha Mu Sigma (1923)
1926   Delta Phi Epsilon (1970)
1926   Phi Sigma Sigma

Rutgers University (New Brunswick, NJ)

1915 Phi Epsilon Pi
1921 Sigma Alpha Mu
1928 Omicron Alpha Tau
1934 Tau Delta Phi (1976)
1947 Zeta Beta Tau
1952 Phi Sigma Delta
1956 Alpha Epsilon Pi
1961 Pi Lambda Phi (1969)
1965 Tau Epsilon Phi (1987)

SOUTH

University of Alabama (Tuscaloosa, AL)

1916 Zeta Beta Tau
1919 Sigma Alpha Mu (1961)
1921 Kappa Nu
1921 Phi Epsilon Pi
1927 Delta Phi Epsilon (1932–1953; 1973)
1927 Omicron Alpha Tau
1927 Pi Lambda Phi (1940)
1928 Alpha Mu Sigma (1928)
1928 Phi Beta Delta
1929 Phi Sigma Delta (1939)
1935 Sigma Delta Tau
1942 Alpha Epsilon Pi (1982)
1945 Alpha Epsilon Phi (1967)

University of Arkansas (Fayetteville, AR)

1932 Phi Epsilon Pi (1941)
1932 Kappa Nu (1941)
1950 Zeta Beta Tau (1955)

Duke University (Durham, NC)

1929   Phi Sigma Delta (1936)
1934   Alpha Epsilon Phi (1965–1975)
1935   Zeta Beta Tau (1971)

University of Florida (Gainesville, FL)

1921   Zeta Beta Tau (1933–1948; 1956)
1925   Phi Beta Delta
1925   Pi Lambda Phi
1925   Tau Epsilon Phi
1948   Alpha Epsilon Phi
1951   Alpha Epsilon Pi
1955   Delta Phi Epsilon
1960   Phi Epsilon Pi
1967   Phi Sigma Sigma

University of Georgia (Athens, GA)

1915   Phi Epsilon Pi
1919   Tau Epsilon Phi
1924   Sigma Delta Tau
1935   Delta Phi Epsilon

University of Kentucky (Lexington, KY)

1915   Sigma Alpha Mu (1924)
1942   Zeta Beta Tau (1973)
1949   Pi Lambda Phi (1953)
1949   Beta Sigma Rho (1952)
1952   Phi Sigma Sigma (1957)

Louisiana State University (Baton Rouge, LA)

1911   Zeta Beta Tau (1989)
1924   Sigma Delta Tau (1969)

1927   Phi Sigma Sigma (1933)
1933   Phi Epsilon Pi (1958)
1938   Alpha Epsilon Phi (1984)
1938   Alpha Epsilon Pi (1952–1965; 1972)
1939   Kappa Nu (1942)

University of Miami (Coral Gables, FL)

1929   Phi Epsilon Pi
1938   Alpha Epsilon Phi
1939   Delta Phi Epsilon (1980–1987)
1946   Pi Lambda Phi (1963)
1946   Sigma Alpha Mu (1970–1987)
1946   Zeta Beta Tau
1947   Alpha Epsilon Pi
1947   Phi Sigma Sigma (1985)
1949   Phi Sigma Delta (1966)
1952   Tau Delta Phi (1971)
1957   Sigma Delta Tau
1958   Beta Sigma Rho

University of Mississippi (Oxford, MS)

1935   Phi Epsilon Pi

University of Missouri (Columbia, MO)

1917   Zeta Beta Tau
1928   Sigma Alpha Mu
1929   Alpha Epsilon Phi
1931   Phi Sigma Delta (1964)
1935   Phi Sigma Sigma (1955)
1947   Alpha Epsilon Pi

University of North Carolina (Chapel Hill, NC)

1924   Tau Epsilon Phi
1927   Zeta Beta Tau (1985)
1928   Phi Alpha
1937   Alpha Epsilon Pi (1951–1987)
1939   Pi Lambda Phi (1984)

University of South Carolina (Columbia, SC)

1928   Pi Lambda Phi (1950)
1928   Phi Epsilon Pi
1928   Phi Beta Delta
1957   Sigma Delta Tau (1962)
1945   Alpha Epsilon Phi (1949–1967; 1978)

University of Tennessee (Knoxville, TN)

1928   Zeta Beta Tau (1942–1969)
1928   Phi Alpha (1930)
1949   Alpha Epsilon Pi (1953–1962)
1948   Alpha Epsilon Phi (1977)

University of Texas (Austin, TX)

1920   Phi Sigma Delta
1922   Sigma Alpha Mu
1925   Alpha Epsilon Phi
1926   Tau Delta Phi (1975)
1929   Phi Sigma Sigma (1933)
1931   Zeta Beta Tau (1934)
1934   Delta Phi Epsilon (1990)
1939   Alpha Epsilon Pi
1939   Sigma Delta Tau
1968   Pi Lambda Phi (1973)

Tulane University/Sophie Newcomb College (New Orleans, LA)

1909   Zeta Beta Tau
1916   Alpha Epsilon Phi
1920   Sigma Alpha Mu (1971–1976; 1980–1987)
1922   Kappa Nu
1922   Phi Epsilon Pi (1956)
1934   Phi Sigma Sigma (1946)
1951   Alpha Epsilon Pi (1974–1977)
1955   Sigma Delta Tau
1959   Tau Epsilon Phi

Vanderbilt University (Nashville, TN)

1918   Zeta Beta Tau
1921   Tau Delta Phi (1923)
1925   Alpha Epsilon Phi (1965)
1929   Alpha Epsilon Pi

University of Virginia (Charlottesville, VA)

1915   Phi Epsilon Pi
1915   Zeta Beta Tau (1985)
1922   Phi Alpha
1925   Alpha Epsilon Pi
1925   Alpha Mu Sigma
1932   Pi Lambda Phi (1945–1966)
1936   Tau Epsilon Phi (1988)
1968   Sigma Alpha Mu

Washington and Lee University (Lexington, VA)

1920   Zeta Beta Tau (1988)
1920   Phi Epsilon Pi

University of West Virginia (Morgantown, WV)

1921   Sigma Lambda Pi (1925)
1922   Pi Lambda Phi (1959)
1927   Phi Sigma Delta
1928   Phi Alpha (1935)
1934   Sigma Delta Tau (1969)

College of William and Mary (Williamsburg, VA)

1927   Phi Alpha
1929   Pi Lambda Phi

MIDDLE WEST

Carnegie Institute of Technology (Pittsburgh, PA)

1916   Phi Epsilon Pi (1922)
1922   Beta Sigma Rho
1922   Pi Lambda Phi
1929   Tau Delta Phi (1973)
1944   Alpha Epsilon Phi (1971)

Case Institute of Technology (Cleveland, OH)

1909   Zeta Beta Tau (1928)
1945   Sigma Alpha Mu

University of Chicago (Chicago, IL)

1918   Zeta Beta Tau (1975)
1919   Phi Beta Delta
1919   Pi Lambda Phi (1949)
1921   Kappa Nu (1934)
1921   Phi Epsilon Pi (1934)
1921   Phi Sigma Delta
1921   Tau Delta Phi (1935)

1927   Omicron Alpha Tau
1927   Phi Alpha
1968   Tau Delta Phi (1970)

University of Cincinnati (Cincinnati, OH)

1917   Sigma Alpha Mu
1920   Alpha Epsilon Pi
1920   Phi Beta Delta
1920   Phi Epsilon Pi (1935)
1920   Sigma Tau Phi
1921   Kappa Nu (1923)
1923   Sigma Delta Tau
1926   Delta Phi Epsilon (1951)
1926   Phi Sigma Sigma (1971)

Dickinson College (Carlisle, PA)

1914   Phi Epsilon Pi
1919   Sigma Alpha Mu (1920)
1926   Sigma Tau Phi

Drake University (Des Moines, IA)

1924   Phi Beta Delta (1930)
1925   Pi Lambda Phi (1930)
1952   Alpha Epsilon Phi (1973)

Franklin and Marshall College (Lancaster, PA)

1931   Zeta Beta Tau (1988)
1947   Pi Lambda Phi

University of Illinois (Champaign-Urbana, IL)

1911   Zeta Beta Tau
1918   Sigma Alpha Mu
1920   Alpha Epsilon Phi

1920   Alpha Epsilon Pi
1920   Phi Epsilon Pi
1923   Phi Sigma Sigma
1924   Tau Delta Phi (1975)
1924   Tau Epsilon Phi
1926   Sigma Delta Tau
1927   Delta Phi Epsilon (1933–1945)
1927   Omicron Alpha Tau
1934   Phi Beta Delta
1934   Pi Lambda Phi
1947   Phi Sigma Delta
1954   Iota Alpha Pi

Illinois Institute of Technology (Chicago, IL)

1922   Sigma Alpha Mu (1952)
1925   Alpha Epsilon Pi (1932–1948)
1947   Tau Epsilon Phi

Indiana University (Bloomington, IN)

1922   Sigma Alpha Mu
1928   Phi Beta Delta
1928   Pi Lambda Phi (1959)
1940   Sigma Delta Tau
1946   Delta Phi Epsilon (1952–1968; 1974–1989)
1947   Zeta Beta Tau
1958   Alpha Epsilon Phi
1958   Alpha Epsilon Pi
1961   Phi Epsilon Pi

University of Iowa (Iowa City, IA)

1920   Phi Epsilon Pi
1923   Phi Beta Delta
1927   Pi Lambda Phi (1937)
1933   Sigma Delta Tau (1971–1982; 1988)

1951   Alpha Epsilon Pi
1968   Alpha Epsilon Phi (1974)

University of Kansas (Lawrence, KS)

1923   Sigma Alpha Mu (1936)
1949   Alpha Epsilon Pi (1977–1982)

Lehigh University (Bethlehem, PA)

1915   Pi Lambda Phi
1923   Sigma Alpha Mu
1925   Phi Sigma Delta (1933)
1927   Phi Beta Delta (1933)
1927   Tau Delta Phi (1973)
1967   Tau Epsilon Phi

Miami University (Oxford, OH)

1936   Zeta Beta Tau (1974–1989)
1940   Alpha Epsilon Phi (1980–1986)
1946   Iota Alpha Pi (1956)
1959   Sigma Alpha Mu
1963   Sigma Delta Tau (1987)
1964   Alpha Epsilon Pi

University of Michigan (Ann Arbor, MI)

1912   Zeta Beta Tau
1916   Phi Sigma Delta
1919   Kappa Nu (1953)
1921   Alpha Epsilon Phi
1921   Phi Beta Delta
1921   Phi Epsilon Pi (1942–1957)
1922   Phi Sigma Sigma
1922   Tau Delta Phi (1968)
1923   Sigma Alpha Mu

1923   Sigma Lambda Pi(1925)
1944   Sigma Delta Tau
1949   Alpha Epsilon Pi
1954   Delta Phi Epsilon (1974–1985)

Michigan State University (East Lansing, MI)

1927   Sigma Alpha Mu (1950)
1934   Alpha Epsilon Pi (1972–1979)
1947   Zeta Beta Tau (1971)
1952   Alpha Epsilon Phi (1973)
1959   Sigma Alpha Mu (1983–1986)
1963   Phi Sigma Delta
1964   Sigma Delta Tau (1972–1984)
1966   Tau Delta Phi (1968)

University of Minnesota (Minneapolis, MN)

1915   Sigma Alpha Mu
1923   Phi Epsilon Pi
1925   Phi Beta Delta (1933)
1928   Tau Delta Phi (1952)
1929   Delta Phi Epsilon (1932)
1929   Sigma Delta Tau
1938   Alpha Epsilon Phi (1978)
1949   Alpha Epsilon Pi (1973)
1949   Zeta Beta Tau (1953)

University of Nebraska (Lincoln, NE)

1922   Zeta Beta Tau (1962)
1925   Sigma Delta Tau (1970)
1926   Sigma Alpha Mu

University of North Dakota (Grand Forks, ND)

1929　　Tau Delta Phi (1941)

Northwestern University (Evanston, IL)

1919　　Phi Alpha (1924)
1920　　Phi Epsilon Pi
1921　　Alpha Epsilon Phi (1988)
1923　　Tau Delta Phi (1968)
1938　　Sigma Delta Tau (1983)
1967　　Sigma Alpha Mu (1973)

Ohio State University (Columbus, OH)

1911　　Zeta Beta Tau (1989)
1920　　Sigma Alpha Mu
1921　　Alpha Epsilon Phi
1921　　Alpha Epsilon Pi
1921　　Phi Sigma Delta
1924　　Tau Delta Phi (1931)
1927　　Phi Beta Delta
1927　　Pi Lambda Phi (1977)
1927　　Sigma Lambda Pi
1927　　Tau Epsilon Phi (1989)
1928　　Delta Phi Epsilon (1948; 1987–1990)
1928　　Phi Sigma Sigma (1958)
1932　　Phi Epsilon Pi (1964)

Ohio University (Athens, OH)

1933　　Phi Epsilon Pi
1941　　Phi Sigma Sigma (1951–1991)
1948　　Phi Sigma Delta
1951　　Alpha Epsilon Phi (1971–1981; 1984)

Pennsylvania State University (University Park, PA)

1913   Beta Sigma Rho
1914   Phi Epsilon Pi
1921   Alpha Epsilon Pi (1974–1982)
1921   Sigma Tau Phi
1927   Phi Sigma Delta
1937   Alpha Epsilon Phi (1978)
1942   Pi Lambda Phi
1943   Sigma Delta Tau (1971–1978)
1946   Phi Sigma Sigma (1970)
1946   Zeta Beta Tau (1971–1988)
1949   Sigma Alpha Mu (1970–1983)
1960   Delta Phi Epsilon (1966)
1962   Iota Alpha Pi
1963   Tau Epsilon Phi
1965   Tau Delta Phi (1973)

University of Pittsburgh (Pittsburgh, PA)

1913   Phi Epsilon Pi
1914   Pi Lambda Phi
1919   Sigma Alpha Mu
1920   Alpha Epsilon Phi
1921   Kappa Nu
1924   Phi Sigma Sigma
1925   Delta Phi Epsilon (1944–1966)
1925   Phi Beta Delta (1931)
1950   Sigma Delta Tau
1962   Zeta Beta Tau

Purdue University (West Lafayette, IN)

1922   Sigma Alpha Mu (1989)
1948   Sigma Delta Tau (1953)
1948   Alpha Epsilon Phi (1951–1968; 1976)
1954   Alpha Epsilon Pi (1970–1975)

Washington University (St. Louis, Missouri)

1919   Sigma Alpha Mu
1921   Phi Beta Delta
1923   Zeta Beta Tau
1925   Alpha Epsilon Phi (1934–1960)
1928   Alpha Epsilon Pi (1972–1977)
1941   Phi Alpha (1942)
1951   Sigma Delta Tau (1973)
1963   Delta Phi Epsilon (1971)

Western Reserve University (Cleveland, OH)

1909   Zeta Beta Tau
1919   Kappa Nu (1932)
1920   Phi Sigma Delta
1923   Sigma Lambda Pi
1933   Phi Epsilon Pi (1955–1966)
1947   Alpha Epsilon Pi (1974)

University of Wisconsin (Madison, WI)

1921   Alpha Epsilon Phi (1972–1983)
1922   Phi Sigma Delta
1922   Zeta Beta Tau (1983–1987)
1924   Phi Beta Delta (1934)
1925   Phi Epsilon Pi (1937–1966)
1926   Pi Lambda Phi (1968–1983)
1927   Alpha Epsilon Pi (1973–1982)
1930   Phi Sigma Sigma (1969)
1958   Sigma Delta Tau (1971–1982)
1966   Sigma Alpha Mu (1972–1983)

WEST AND SOUTHWEST

University of Arizona (Tucson, AZ)

1926   Zeta Beta Tau (1969–1983)
1940   Alpha Epsilon Phi
1947   Tau Delta Phi (1968)
1959   Sigma Delta Tau (1974–1988)
1962   Sigma Alpha Mu (1964–1988)
1964   Alpha Epsilon Pi

University of California, Berkeley

1920   Zeta Beta Tau
1921   Kappa Nu
1922   Pi Lambda Phi
1922   Phi Beta Delta
1923   Alpha Epsilon Phi
1926   Phi Sigma Sigma (1966)
1929   Sigma Alpha Mu
1948   Delta Phi Epsilon (1968)
1949   Alpha Epsilon Pi (1964–1985)

University of California, Los Angeles

1921   Phi Sigma Sigma
1922   Phi Beta Delta
1922   Pi Lambda Phi (1969)
1924   Alpha Epsilon Phi
1926   Sigma Alpha Mu
1927   Sigma Delta Tau (1987)
1927   Zeta Beta Tau
1928   Tau Delta Phi (1969)
1947   Phi Sigma Delta
1947   Tau Epsilon Phi (1989)
1952   Kappa Nu
1952   Phi Epsilon Pi
1956   Delta Phi Epsilon (1971)

University of Southern California (Los Angeles, CA)

1918 Zeta Beta Tau (1972)
1920 Phi Beta Delta
1920 Pi Lambda Phi (1969)
1921 Alpha Epsilon Phi (1985–1990)
1926 Alpha Mu Sigma (1926)
1926 Tau Epsilon Phi (1990)
1927 Sigma Delta Tau (1935)
1927 Tau Delta Phi (1968)
1931 Alpha Epsilon Pi
1945 Phi Sigma Sigma (1953)
1948 Sigma Alpha Mu

University of Colorado (Boulder, CO)

1919 Phi Sigma Delta
1929 Pi Lambda Phi (1934)
1931 Phi Beta Delta
1940 Delta Phi Epsilon (1966)
1947 Sigma Delta Tau (1971)
1947 Zeta Beta Tau
1952 Alpha Epsilon Phi (1971–1990)
1953 Sigma Alpha Mu (1960)

University of Denver (Denver, CO)

1920 Alpha Epsilon Phi (1924)
1920 Phi Sigma Delta
1925 Phi Beta Delta (1934)
1926 Delta Phi Epsilon (1957)
1926 Pi Lambda Phi
1927 Iota Alpha Pi (1942)
1965 Sigma Delta Tau (1984)

University of Oklahoma (Norman, OK)

1920   Sigma Alpha Mu (1982)
1922   Phi Beta Delta
1922   Pi Lambda Phi (1963)
1929   Sigma Delta Tau
1956   Alpha Epsilon Phi (1979)
1959   Alpha Epsilon Pi (1973–1983)
1966   Delta Phi Epsilon (1969)

University of Oregon (Eugene, OR)

1930   Sigma Alpha Mu (1962)

University of Utah (Salt Lake City, UT)

1919   Sigma Alpha Mu (1951)
1932   Phi Sigma Sigma (1943)
1955   Phi Sigma Delta (1961)

University of Washington (Seattle, WA)

1922   Zeta Beta Tau (1973–1974)
1926   Sigma Alpha Mu (1983–1988)
1932   Alpha Epsilon Phi (1987)
1940   Phi Sigma Sigma
1947   Alpha Epsilon Pi (1961)

CANADA

University of Alberta (Edmonton, AB)

1941   Sigma Alpha Mu (1972)

University of British Columbia (Vancouver, BC)

1942   Zeta Beta Tau (1970–1979)
1946   Delta Phi Epsilon (1972–1981)
1949   Sigma Alpha Mu (1959)

University of Manitoba (Winnipeg, MB)

1926   Sigma Alpha Mu
1926   Delta Phi Epsilon (1964)
1930   Phi Sigma Sigma (1955)
1932   Tau Delta Phi (1957)
1932   Iota Alpha Pi (1965)
1948   Zeta Beta Tau (1972)

McGill University (Montreal, QC)

1913   Zeta Beta Tau (1969)
1919   Sigma Alpha Mu (1986)
1921   Pi Lambda Phi (1942–1988)
1922   Delta Phi Epsilon
1926   Sigma Delta Tau (1971)
1927   Omicron Alpha Tau
1951   Phi Epsilon Pi

University of Toronto (Toronto, ON)

1920   Sigma Alpha Mu (1972)
1922   Pi Lambda Phi (1966–1980)
1924   Delta Phi Epsilon (1958)
1927   Alpha Epsilon Phi (1955)
1929   Iota Alpha Pi (1956)
1930   Beta Sigma Rho

University of Western Ontario (London, ON)

1945   Pi Lambda Phi (1968–1983)
1945   Beta Sigma Rho

Appendix C

Some Distinguished Alumni

Major League Baseball: Sandy Koufax, Pi Lambda Phi; Mike Epstein, Zeta Beta Tau; Barry Latman, Zeta Beta Tau; Al Rosen, Pi Lambda Phi; Steve Stone, Alpha Epsilon Pi.

Pro Basketball: "Red" Auerbach (Basketball Hall of Fame) Tau Epsilon Phi; Artis Gilmore, Pi Lambda Phi; Harry Glickman, Sigma Alpha Mu; Art Heyman, Zeta Beta Tau; Danny Schayes, Sigma Alpha Mu; Zollie Volchok, Sigma Alpha Mu.

Football: Ernie Davis, Sigma Alpha Mu; Mike Garrett, Tau Epsilon Phi; Sid Gillman (Pro Football Hall of Fame), Zeta Beta Tau; Sid Gordon, Floyd Little, Tau Delta Phi; Alpha Epsilon Pi; Sid Luckman (Pro Football Hall of Fame), Zeta Beta Tau; Jim Nance, Zeta Beta Tau; Merv Pregulman, Sigma Alpha Mu; Aaron Rosenberg, Zeta Beta Tau.

Football Executives and Coaches: Carroll Rosenbloom (owner of the Baltimore Colts), Zeta Beta Tau; Herman Sarkowsky, Zeta Beta Tau; "Sonny" Werblin, Zeta Beta Tau.

Sports Broadcasting: Mel Allen, Zeta Beta Tau; Howard Cosell, Zeta Beta Tau; Dick Schaap, Zeta Beta Tau.

Olympians: Louis Clarke, 1924 Gold Medalist, Track and Field, Phi Epsilon Pi; Lillian Copeland, 1928 Silver Medalist and Gold Medalist, both for Track and Field and discus 1932, Alpha Epsilon Phi (USC); Marty Glickman, Track and Field, Sigma Alpha Mu.

The Arts: Mildred Berry, entertainer, Sigma Delta Tau

Music: Martin Broones, composer and producer, Phi Epsilon Pi; Art Garfunkel, vocalist, Alpha Epsilon Pi; Jay Gorney, composer (author of "Brother, Can You Spare a Dime?"), Kappa Nu; Marvin Greenberg, composer, Alpha Epsilon Pi; Lorenz Hart, composer, Phi Sigma Delta; Richard Rodgers, composer, Phi Sigma Delta; Dorothy Sarnoff, vocalist, Alpha Epsilon Phi; Allan Sherman, vocalist, Sigma Alpha Mu; Paul Simon, vocalist, Alpha Epsilon Pi; Peter Yarrow (of Peter, Paul and Mary), Phi Alpha.

Film and Stage: Charles Coburn, motion picture actor, Zeta Beta Tau; Melvin Douglas, motion picture actor, Zeta Beta Tau; Samuel Goldwyn, Jr., motion picture producer and director, Zeta Beta Tau; Arnold M. Grand, president of Columbia Pictures, Zeta Beta Tau; Cy Howard, motion picture writer, director, and producer, Phi Epsilon Pi; Joseph Mankewicz, motion picture producer, Phi Sigma Delta; Walter Mirisch, motion picture producer, Zeta Beta Tau; Michael Ovitz, Disney, Zeta Beta Tau; Tony Roberts, Broadway and movie actor, Tau Delta Phi; Gene Saks, motion picture and Broadway director and actor, Zeta Beta Tau; Irving Shulman, novelist and playwright, Phi Epsilon Pi; Preston Tisch, motion picture executive, Sigma Alpha Mu; Jack Warner, motion picture and TV producer, Zeta Beta Tau; Gene Wilder, motion picture actor, Alpha Epsilon Pi.

TV and Radio: Martin Agronsky, radio and TV commentator, Sigma Alpha Mu; Jack Barry, TV host, Phi Sigma Delta; Wolf Blitzer, TV commentator, Alpha Epsilon Pi; Leonard Goldenson, president of CBS, Sigma Alpha Mu; Robert Klein, TV comedian and actor, Zeta Beta Tau; Irv Kupcinet, TV host and newspaper columnist, Tau Delta Phi; Sheldon Leonard, TV actor and producer, Zeta Beta Tau; Richard Lewis, TV actor and comedian, Alpha Epsilon Pi; William Paley, Chairman of the Board of CBS, Zeta Beta Tau (*Nasi* of the University of Pennsylvania chapter); Charlotte Rae, TV actress, Alpha Epsilon Phi; Alan Rafkin, TV director and producer, Sigma Alpha Mu; David Sarnoff, broadcasting executive, Tau Delta Phi; Dinah (née Fanny Rose) Shore, Alpha Epsilon Phi (Dean of the Vanderbilt University chapter); Lawrence Spivak, TV producer, Sigma Alpha Mu; Mike Wallace, TV commentator, Zeta Beta Tau;

Walter Winchell, radio commentator and newspaper columnist, Alpha
Epsilon Pi.

Writing and Publishing: William F. Adler, magazine publisher, Phi
Epsilon Pi; Walter H. Annenberg, publisher, Phi Sigma Delta; David
Dietz, journalist (winner of the 1937 Pulitzer Prize), Zeta Beta
Tau; Joseph Epstein, writer, Phi Epsilon Pi; Benjamin Fine, editor,
Alpha Epsilon Pi; Edwin O. Guthman, journalist (winner of the
1950 Pulitzer Prize), Zeta Beta Tau; Eugene Meyer, publisher of the
Washington Post c. 1950s–1960s, Zeta Beta Tau; Philip Roth, novelist,
Sigma Alpha Mu; Sara Snelling, journalist, Sigma Delta Tau; Irving
Stone, author, Kappa Nu; Sylvia Porter, Sigma Delta Tau; Robert
Gessner, author, Phi Sigma Delta.

Politicians: Rudolph Boschwitz, U.S. senator from Minnesota, Zeta
Beta Tau; Thomas J. Downey, U.S. representative from New York,
Sigma Alpha Mu; Jacob Hecht, U.S. senator from Nevada, Sigma
Alpha Mu; Henry Horner, governor of Illinois, Zeta Beta Tau;
Henry M. Morgenthau, Jr., Secretary of the Treasury, Zeta Beta
Tau; Richard L. Neuberger, U.S. senator from Oregon, Zeta Beta
Tau; Abraham Ribicoff, U.S. senator from Connecticut and former
Secretary of Health, Education, and Welfare, Zeta Beta Tau; Edward
Zorinsky, U.S. senator from Nebraska, Sigma Alpha Mu.

Law: Abraham M. Bloch, Judge, Phi Sigma Delta; Edward N. Cahn,
attorney, author, and educator, Zeta Beta Tau; Henry J. Friendly,
judge, Sigma Alpha Mu; Ruth Bader Ginsburg, U.S. Supreme Court
justice, Alpha Epsilon Phi; Arthur J. Goldberg, U.S. Supreme Court
associate justice and Secretary of Labor, Phi Epsilon Pi; Samuel I.
Rosenman, judge, speechwriter, White House Legal Counselor for
Franklin Delano Roosevelt Administration, Phi Epsilon Pi (president
of the Columbia University chapter).

Other: Max Abramovitz, architect, Tau Epsilon Phi; George Alpert,
railroad president, Zeta Beta Tau; Dr. Joyce Brothers, psychologist
and TV personality, Sigma Delta Tau; Bernard F. Gimbel, Board
chairman of Gimbel Brothers department store chain, Zeta Beta Tau;
Donald A. Glaser, physicist (winner of the 1960 Nobel Prize), Sigma
Alpha Mu; Lewis Webster Jones, President of Rutgers University, c.
1950s, Zeta Beta Tau; Judith Resnick, astronaut (Challenger mission),

Alpha Epsilon Phi; Judith Rodin, president of the University of Pennsylvania, Delta Phi Epsilon; Harold Shapiro, president Princeton University, Zeta Beta Tau (Secretary of the McGill chapter); James D. Zelterbach, diplomat and industrialist, Zeta Beta Tau.

Religious Leaders: Joseph G. Fink, past president of the Central Conference of American Rabbis, Beta Sigma Rho; Frank Goldman, international president of B'nai B'rith, Zeta Beta Tau; Rabbi Roland B. Gittelsohn '31, Phi Sigma Delta (President of chapter),U.S. Navy chaplain 1943–1946, President CCAR 1968.

Appendix D

Songs of the Jewish Fraternities and Sororities
c. 1920s–1950s (published versions)

SIGMA ALPHA MU

Don't Take My Pin (By Allan Sherman, University of Illinois '44. Sung to the tune of "Don't Fence Me In")

If I should drink and you think that I'm thinking of romance
Don't take my pin
Although you're swell, what the hell, give the other girls a chance
Don't take my pin
I know I'm the guy and there is no other, I know you'd like to take
me home to mother
But can't you get a pin from my fraternity brother? Don't take my
pin.
Oh take my heart and my flowers, you can while away the hours
at a picture show with me.
Oh take the change from my pocket or a sterling silver locket, or
a branch from my family tree
Oh, take my gray Chevrolet with the windshield wipers, take
Tommy Dorsey and the four Pied Pipers
But if you take my pin I'm gonna lose my diapers—Don't take my
pin!

Sammies Are a Girl's Best Friend (Sung to the tune of "Diamonds Are a Girl's Best Friend")

A Deke may look sleek in his new Continental
But Sammies are a girl's best friend.

A Sig thinks he's big but he's inconsequential,
So don't go wrong, just grab a Sammy big and strong
The elite meet on   Street
And we've yet to turn a coed down
Down de-down down down,
But Sammy's your buddy, he never gets smutty,
Sammies are a girl's best friend.

Now a D.U. is swell and to some girls he's ample
But Sammies are a girl's best friend;
But a D.U. won't jell with a girl who's had a sample
Of that precious gem: a gorgeous hunk of S.A.M.
Some guys got dough, but dough don't glow
Like the fire that burns in every S.A.M.
Da de-ah da da,
When love life's belated, just come get cremated
Sammies are a girl's best friend.

Fast and Firm (fraternity anthem)

Fast and firm is our union, Strong its ties that bind
Held by links of friendship together,
Now and for all time.
Ever lasting, every faithful, ever staunch and true
Stands the brotherhood we formed
In Sigma Alpha Mu.

My Girl of Sigma Alpha Mu (National Sweetheart Song)

The wind croons me a melody;
The stars shine down more heavenly
I realize my dreams come true.
The rapture of your fond embrace
Has made this world a dreamed-of place,
My girl of Sigma Alpha Mu.
Now I had always hoped to find
Your love for me was true.
And now your heart beats close to mine
I know my longing's through.

The fantasy that's haunted me
Has now become reality,
My girl of Sigma Alpha Mu.

Build Me a Castle

I'm gonna build me a castle painted purple and white,
I'm gonna hold a bull-fest ev'ry night,
I'm gonna lay the damn pledges all over the floor,
Sigma Alpha Mu crest over the door
I'm gonna marry a gal from old   U.
Gonna change her blood from red to blue.
Entertain royalty ev'ry night,
In my little castle painted purple and white,
Castle painted purple, castle painted white,
MMMMMMM . . . Some
castle!

The Grand Old Gang (Sung to the tune of "It's a Grand Old Flag")

When the grand old gang gets together we'll hang
till the waters of hell freeze o'er
From the Lone Star State to the Golden Gate,
From New Orleans to Baltimore (and back again)
Oh many moons have shone on the Purple and White,
With never a scar or a stain;
When good corn whiskey can be got, Just remember this old
    refrain:
Wah-wah-wah Who owns this town? Wah-wah-wah Who owns
    this town?
Wah-wah-wah Who owns this town?—the people cry.
WE own this town, WE own this town,
S A M M Y !

Fairest of the Angels

Down at   where the devil rules
You'll find the S.A.M.'s
with the rest of the fools
You'll find them high in the skies above

With their wings locked together, wings locked together
With their wings locked together in brotherly love.
S.A.M. fairest of the angels, S.A.M. shining and bright, S.A.M.
  mother's little cherubs
We only go to hell on Saturday night.

Here's to the Pledges

Here's to the pledges, drink 'er down, drink 'er down
Here's to the pledges, drink 'er down.
For they are best, they're better than the rest
Oh, here's to the pledges, drink 'er down, down down,
Here's to the pledges, they are men.
Here's to the pledges, they're damn fine men.
Eins, Zwei, Drei, Vier, Who's going to buy the beer?
Here's to the pledges, drink 'er down.

I Want to Be a College Boy

I want to be a college boy—boom—and a little bit more
I want to wear a fraternity pin—boom boom—and a little bit
  more
I want to have a fleur-de-lis, hanging on my door
I want all that's coming to me—Boom boom—and a little bit
Boom—and a little bit
Boom—and a little bit more.
Now I am a college boy—boom—and a little bit more
Now I wear a Sammy pin—boom boom—and a little bit more
Now I have a fleur-de-lis, hanging on my door,
I've got all that's coming to me—Boom—and a little bit—
Boom—and a little bit—
Boom—and a little bit more—boom boom!

ALPHA EPSILON PHI

Sing, Sisters, Sing

Sing, sisters, sing! Sing, sisters, sing!
And let AEPhi ring, sisters, sing, sing, sing.

And when we go to dances, with boychums nice and neat, We
    always try our darndest, to step right on their feet.
I—tell—you—(Chorus "Sing, sisters," etc.)
And when we all are married, with babies who will cry,
We'll teach them that the Alphabet begins with AEPhi,
Then—they—will (Chorus)
And when we go to Hades, we know very well,
That AEPhi is known all over . . . (Chorus)

A Little Bit More

I'd like to be a friend of yours
Mmmmmm—and a little bit more
I'd like to be a pal of yours
Mmmmm—and a little bit more
I'd like to be the little flower
That grows beside your door—
I'd like to give you all I own
Mmmm—and a little bit,
Mmmm—and a little bit,
Mmmm—and a little bit more!

I'd like to be a college girl
Mmmm—and a little bit more
I'd like to be a sorority girl
Mmmm—and a little bit more,
But if I could be an AEPhi,
I'd never want to be any more,
'Cause then I'd be all I wanted to be
Mmmmm—and a little bit
Mmmmm—and a little bit
Mmmmm—and a little bit more!

When I left my home settee
My Daddy said to me
"Be careful darling child—
They say that college is wild.
Why, the tricks that they play

Would make my hair turn gray
And I'm par-tic-a-lic
Lic-lic-lic-a-lic-
I'm par-tic-u-lar."
Said I to Daddy dear
"For me you need not fear—
I swear to do or die
To be an AEPhi.
They've got the rep and the pep
And they make you keep in step,
And they're par-tic-a-lic
Lic-lic-lic-a-lic
They're par-tic-u-lar."

Sing Me a Song

Sing me a song of sororities
Tell me what to go;
The Pi Phis for their pretty girls,
The Thetas for their beaus;
D.G.'s for their scholars,
The Kappas for their keys,
But for faith and loyalty—the A.E.Phis for me!

SIGMA DELTA TAU

"Take Good Care of Yourself"

Always wear that flashing pin
Walk the streets with glee,
Take good care of yourself
You're an SDT.

Don't go out with SAMs
When you're on a spree
Take good care of yourself
You're an SDT.

Be careful dating TEPs, Ooo Ooo,
Or Phi Eps, Ooo Ooo Or you may lose your reputation,
Why not try a ZBT,
Break monotony.
Take good care of yourself
You're an SDT.

(Later variant)
Don't go out with SAM's
Good as they may be
Take good care of yourself,
You're an SDT.

Don't go out with Pi Lam Phi's
When they're on a spree
Take good care of yourself
You're an SDT

Don't take Phi Sig's pin—Umm, Umm,
Laugh and grin—Umm, Umm,
Don't give in—Umm, Umm!
If you want to rate the formals.
Don't go out with Z.B.T.'s
Take a tip from me,
Take good care of yourself
You're an SDT

Some Fine Girls

Some fine girls go Pi Beta Phi
Sophisticates go Kappa,
Gamma Phi's the home of the social butterflies,
The D.G.'s will take you if you're very, very wise.
Some fine girls go no club at all,
But that's not the way for me;
It takes a prim, a pure, an old-fashioned girl
To be an SDT

He Wore His College Frat Pin

He wore his college frat pin, right above his heart
And with his college frat pin, he swore he'd never part
Through the long years of college
The pin stood firm and pat,
And he wore his college frat pin
In honor of the frat.
Now along came a pair of big brown eyes
A smiling SDT.
She took that college frat pin
from where it used to be.
And now they live in a bungalow
With welcome on the mat,
And they pin the baby's diapers
In honor of the frat.

PHI EPSILON PI

He's a Phi Ep As Sure as You're Born (Sung to the tune of "Sure as You're Born")

When you see a fellow with a smile
Who's got all others beat a mile—
Why he's a Phi Ep sure as you're born.
When you see a fellow who charms the girls
Who sports a pin with sixteen pearls—
Why he's a Phi Ep sure as you're born.
If he treats you fine, shows you a great time
And he wins you completely;
If he steals your heart,
And you're hoping you'll never part;
If you find that no one else will do
And he's the man for you—
Why he's a Phi Ep sure as you're born.

Drinking Song

In Phi Ep Pi
In Phi Ep Pi
Where every man's a king-ng-ng
In Phi Ep Pi In Phi Ep Pi
We'll laugh, we'll shout, we'll sing-ng-ng
With a big stein on the ta-a-ble,
We'll drink while we are a-a-ble
And we don't give a damn for any old man
In Phi Ep Pi.

Don't Send My Boy

Don't send my boy to S A M
The dying mother said,
Don't send my boy to Z B T
I'd rather see him dead.
But send my boy to old Phi Ep,
I know they'll treat him well,
Rather than see him go Phi Sig,
I'd see him first in (h   ),

Adam

Adam was the first man to wear the Phi Ep pin,
Socrates, the wise, was the next one in,
Napoleon, the third, although he had the itch
If Caesar were alive today
We'd pledge the son of a gun.
Oh, we are, we are, we are, we are, the boys of Phi Ep Pi,
We are, we are, we are, we are, the boys of Ph Ep Pi,
For we're all jolly good fellows, And here's the reason why,
We are, we are, we are, we are, the boys of Phi Ep Pi.

Now if I had a daughter, I'd dress her in scarlet and gray
And send her on the campus to cheer the boys all day
But if I had a son, boys, here's how he would die
A rootin,' tootin,' shootin' crap with the boys of Phi Ep Pi.

Take Down the Silver Goblet

Take down the old silver goblet
With the Phi Ep crest upon it;
And we'll all have another keg of beer
For it's not for knowledge
That we come to college
But to raise hell while we're here.
So take a Zebe for his money
Or a Sammy 'cause he's funny
Or a Tep, or an Alpha Epsilon Pi,
But if you want to go out drinking
And you want to come home stinking
Take a man from Phi Ep Pi.

Phi Epsilon Pi for Aye

Let us gather and do homage to this brotherhood of ours
The harbor of good feeling where we spend the happy hours
May her standard ever guide us as we march on thru life's fray
For the spirit of Phi Ep Pi will live on for aye.

Let us honor our brave fraters who their country's call obey
And stand ready to uphold it in the good old Phi Ep way
May their deeds be ever glorious as they march on thru war's fray
For the spirit of Phi Ep must live on for aye.

Should passing years estrange us, and our bonds of love relax
Should fraters be taken from us and our numbers thinner wax
Then remember Phi Ep Fraters, as you march on thru life's fray
That the spirit of Phi Ep Pi will live on for aye.

ZETA BETA TAU

Here's to Our Fraternity (Sung to the tune of "Gaudeamus Igitur")

Here's to our Fraternity, may it live forever,
May we always faithful be, and its bonds ne'er sever.
Though the troubles may be nigh, boys,

With our standard raised on high, boys,
We'll be loyal to our ZBT
Ever loyal to our Zeta Beta Tau.

Let us raise our glasses boys, and pledge our friendship ever,
Though life may have its cares and joys, that friendship we'll ne'er
   sever.
In life's sorrow and in its sadness,
In its joys and in its gladness,
We'll be brethren of the ZBT
Always brethren of Zeta Beta Tau.

Lord of Heaven and of Earth, keep watch o'er us ever,
Fill our hearts with love and mirth; let our bonds ne'er sever.
By the heavens that smile above us,
By the faith of those that love us,
God protect our ZBT
God protect our Zeta Beta Tau.

My Brother, Here's My Hand (Written at the University of Nebraska by Lawrence Gavenman '42, Norman Rips '44, and Norman Smeerin '44, shortly before their departure into the armed forces)

The friends I love, I'll leave behind
No truer friends I'll ever find
We've won and lost and yet we stand
My brother, here's my hand.

And if this year should be our last,
We'll ne'er forget the glorious past
We've launched the ship, the course is planned,
My brother, here's my hand.

Oh ZBT, you shall remain
More honors yet you shall attain,
Your future's bright, with courage stand
My brother, here's my hand
Take my hand, take my hand, take my hand.

Notes

ABBREVIATIONS AND ACRONYMS USED IN NOTES

AEPhi	Alpha Epsilon Phi sorority archives, Stamford, CT
AEPi Scroll	*The Scroll of Alpha Epsilon Pi*
AEPi	Alpha Epsilon Pi fraternity archives, Indianapolis, IN
AJA-HUC	American Jewish Archives, Hebrew Union College, Cincinnati, OH
AJC	American Jewish Committee archives, Jacob Blaustein Library, New York, NY
AJHS-PHIEP	Phi Epsilon Pi Papers, American Jewish Historical Society, Center for Jewish History, New York, NY
Baird	*Baird's Manual of American College Fraternities*
Columns	*The Columns of Alpha Epsilon Phi*
Egotist	*The Eta Egotist*, published by Eta [University of Pennsylvania] Chapter of Phi Epsilon Pi
Fane Papers	Irvin Fane Papers, Manuscript Collection No. 177, American Jewish Archives-Hebrew Union College, Cincinnati, OH
HUC	Klau Library, Hebrew Union College, Cincinnati, OH
Octagonian	*The Octagonian of Sigma Alpha Mu*
PhiEpQ	*Phi Epsilon Pi Quarterly*
SAM Bulletin	*SAM: The Confidential Monthly Bulletin of Sigma Alpha Mu*
SAM	Sigma Alpha Mu fraternity archives, Carmel, IN
SDT	Sigma Delta Tau sorority archives, Indianapolis, IN
ZBTQ	*Zeta Beta Tau Quarterly*

CHAPTER 1

1. For descriptions of the ritual, song, poetry, and general student life of medieval times, see Charles Homer Haskins, *The Rise of the Universities* (Ithaca:

Cornell University Press, 1957), 59–93, and Henry D. Sheldon, *Student Life and Customs* (New York: D. Appleton & Co., 1901), 1–9.

2. Sheldon, 10–36.
3. See Marsha L. Rozenblit, *The Jews of Vienna, 1867–1914: Assimilation and Identity* (Albany: State University of New York Press, 1983), 161–162 and 239, note 59.
4. Alex Bein, *Theodore Herzl: A Biography*, trans. Maurice Samuel, (Philadelphia: Jewish Publication Society, 1948), 30–31, 40–42.
5. *Kadimah* appears prominently in the historical literature of the Jews of Vienna. For one excellent account of their founding and development, see Rozenblit, 161–166, 171.
6. See Richard Nelson Current, *Phi Beta Kappa in American Life: The First Two Hundred Years* (New York: Oxford University Press, 1990).
7. Union College was then among the most prominent and influential of U.S. colleges, having the third largest enrollment and the largest endowment of any college in the U.S. before the Civil War. See Frederick Rudolph, *The American College and University: A History* (New York: Knopf, 1962), 114. For details on the founding and expansion of the American college fraternity system, I am indebted to Jack L. Anson, Jr., and Robert F. Marchesani, Jr., eds., *Baird's Manual of American College Fraternities* [hereafter cited as Baird], 20th ed. (Indianapolis, IN: Baird's Manual Foundation, Inc., 1991).
8. See Sheldon, 97–106 and Baird, 20th ed., I-3.
9. Rudolph, 145: "Few American colleges were untouched by this movement which so ably characterized the enterprise and initiative of the 19th century undergraduate. Before they quite knew what had happened, most college presidents found that their undergraduates had ushered into the American college community a social system that they had neither invited nor encouraged."
10. Helen Lefkowitz Horowitz, *Campus Life: Undergraduate Cultures from the End of the 18th Century to the Present* (New York: Knopf, 1987), 5; Laurence R. Veysey, *The Emergence of the American University* (Chicago: University of Chicago Press, 1970), 2
11. Mark C. Carnes, *Secret Ritual and Manhood in Victorian America* (New Haven: Yale University Press, 1989), 1.
12. William Raimond Baird (1858–1917), a lawyer and mineralogist by profession and a devotee of fraternities by avocation (he was himself a member of Beta Theta Pi), authored eight editions of *A Manual of American College Fraternities* between 1879 and 1915. After his death, others edited the publication, but the manual was always given his name.
13. *Fraternity Month* magazine began publishing in 1934 and ceased in 1971; *Banta's Greek Exchange* was published from 1912 to 1973.
14. Baird, 20th ed., I-12.
15. For post-Civil War developments in American higher education, see Rudolph, 241–263, and Baird, 20th ed., 1–2.
16. For a classic defense of the usefulness of college fraternities written from the perspective of the Dean of Men at the University of Illinois, see Thomas Arkle Clark, *The Fraternity and the College* (Menasha, WI: George Banta Publishing Co., 1931).

17. On the relationship between fraternities and college alumni, see Clark, 18–19. That fraternity alumni tended to be disproportionately able and willing to fund their schools generously was an anecdotal observation of long standing among college presidents and administrators. Statistical support for this view, along with abstracts of comparative studies of alumni support from different universities, are available in the text and annotated bibliography of W. Thomas Nelson, Jr., *The Undergraduate Experiences of Alumni Who Support Their Alma Mater* (Bloomington, IN: Center for the Study of the College Fraternity, 1988). The reference to New York University appears on page 46.

18. Baird, 20th ed., 1–2. For discussion of fraternity rushing, see also Sheldon, Rudolph, and Horowitz.

19. Horowitz advances an interesting theoretical structure to explain different segments of the student population. She argues that it is a myth to contend that all "student culture" was monolithic, or that it always conformed to the values of what she calls "college life," of which fraternities were an important part. In fact, university student populations can be divided into three "contending cultures . . . [which] arose from particular historical contexts and were linked to socioeconomic position and personal style" (11): the "college men and women," who indulge in football, drinking, fraternity life, extracurricular activities, etc., and who give little thought to studying; the "serious" or "good students," who have neither the time nor the money to indulge in such things and who attend diligently to their studies and to their professors; and the "college rebels," those who question the conformity expected of them and challenge the university administration. In any one era, she asserts, "one of these appears to be dominant and catches the public eye: in the 1920s it was college life; in the 1930s, rebellion; between 1948 and 1955, the world of the outsider; from 1955 to 1965, college life again; from 1965 to 1970, rebellion once more; since 1970, the ethos of the New Outsider. Other student worlds did not vanish, however. They were simply less visible or less interesting to reporters." She argues that in the 1960s, the power of traditional college life was broken (290).

20. Baird, 13th ed. (1935), quoted in Stanley I. Fishel, "The Greeks Have Words," *Zeta Beta Tau Quarterly* [hereafter cited as ZBTQ] 17, 3, (December 1935): 52.

21. A profile on Ronald Reagan during his days as an actor entitled "Famous Star Lauds Fraternities" appeared in the magazine *Fraternity Month* (April 1957): 26.

22. For descriptions of the origins of discriminatory clauses as well as specific texts and membership practices, see Alfred McClung Lee, *Fraternities Without Brotherhood: A Study of Prejudice on the American Campus* (Boston: The Beacon Press, 1955), *passim*, especially 24, 28–31, 48–52, 63–82, 85–87, 92–95, 124. See also an extensive journalistic investigation by Howard Whitman, "The College Fraternity Crisis," parts 1 and 2, *Collier's* 123, no. 2 (January 8 1949): 9; no. 3 (January 15, 1949): 34, which noted the following restrictive clauses in the constitutions of national fraternities: "Members must be of the Aryan race and not of the black, Malayan, or Semitic race . . . must not be of Mongolian, Malaysian, Negro or Jewish blood. . . . Must be white persons of full Aryan blood." See also Louis Krapin, "The Decline of Fraternity Bias,"

Barriers: Patterns of Discrimination Against Jews, ed. N. C. Belth (Washington, D.C.: Anti-Defamation League of B'nai B'rith, 1958), 78–88.

23. Lawrence G. Blochman, "The Rishus Circle," ZBTQ 12, 2 (December 1927): 3.

24. Lee, 24–25

25. For a discussion of East European Jewish immigrants's attitudes toward and use of American higher education, see Leonard Dinnerstein's fine and insightful essay, "Education and the Advancement of American Jews," *American Education and the European Immigrant, 1840–1940,* ed. Bernard J. Weiss (Champaign and Urbana: University of Illinois Press, 1982), 44–60.

26. Arthur Goren, *The American Jews: Dimension of Ethnicity* (Cambridge: Harvard University Press, 1982), 30. See also Nathan Glazer, *American Judaism,* 2nd ed., revised (Chicago: The University of Chicago Press, 1972), 23, and chapter 3, 22–42, *passim*; Naomi W. Cohen, *Encounter With Emancipation: The German Jews in the U.S., 1830–1914* (Philadelphia: Jewish Publication Society, 1984).

27. Harold S. Wechsler, *The Qualified Student: A History of Selective College Admission in America* (New York: John Wiley & Sons, 1977), 5, 7.

28. For background on the years of mass Jewish migration from Eastern Europe to the U.S., see Goren, 43–44, and Howard M. Sachar, *A History of the Jews in America* (New York: Knopf, 1992), 116–142.

29. The theme of conflict and cooperation between "German" and "Russian" Jews permeates much of American Jewish history between 1880 and World War II. For background and discussion of this conflict, see Moses Rischin, "Germans vs. Russians," *The American Jewish Experience,* ed. Jonathan D. Sarna (New York: Holmes & Meier, 1986), 118–132, and Cohen, 303–305, 312–314, 317–344.

30. Bureau of Jewish Social Research. "Professional Tendencies among Jewish Students in Colleges, Universities, and Professional Schools." In the *American Jewish Year Book, 1920–1921,* 22 (Philadelphia: Jewish Publication Society, 1921), 383.

31. John Higham, *Send These to Me: Jews and Other Immigrants in Urban America* (New York: Atheneum: 1975), 154–155.

32. Bernard Baruch, *My Own Story* (New York: Holt, 1957), 58.

33. Wechsler, *The Qualified Student,* 164.

34. Stephen Steinberg, "How Jewish Quotas Began," *Commentary* 52 (September, 1971): 69. On the growth of quotas, see Marcia Graham Synnott, "Anti-Semitism and American Universities: Did Quotas Follow the Jews?" *Anti-Semitism in American History,* ed. David A. Gerber (Urbana and Chicago: University of Illinois, 1986), 233–271.

35. See Winton U. Solberg, "The Early Years of the Jewish Presence at the University of Illinois," *Religions and American Culture* 2, 2 (summer 1992): 22. My thanks to Jonathan Sarna for bringing this article to my attention.

36. Dan Oren, *Joining the Club: A History of Jews and Yale* (New Haven: Yale University Press, 1985), 98.

37. Heywood Broun and George Britt, *Christians Only: A Study in Prejudice* (New York: Vanguard Press, 1931), 52–53.

38. Joseph Gollomb, "City College vs. Columbia," *The Unquiet* (New York: Dodd, Mead: 1935), excerpted in *The Golden Land*, ed. Azriel Eisenberg (New York: T. Yosseloff, 1964), 179.
39. Gollomb, 180–181.
40. Broun and Britt, 79; also Whitman.
41. Broun and Britt, 121; also, Jay Stanley Ruder, "Greeks, Barbarians, and Jews: The Early Years of American Jewish College Fraternities," (B.A. Honors Thesis, Harvard College, 1976): 4.
42. Lee, 21.
43. Clyde Sanfred Johnson, *Fraternities in Our Colleges* (New York: National Interfraternity Conference, 1972), 39.
44. Baird, 20th ed., s.v. "Theta Phi Alpha."
45. The number of African American students attending colleges and universityies doubled between 1970 and 1977. For information on the Black fraternities and sororities, see Baird, 20th ed., I-41 and publications of the National Pan-Hellenic Council, International headquarters, Bloomington, IN.

CHAPTER 2

1. In his prologue to *Identity: Youth in Crisis* (New York: W. W. Norton & Co., 1968), 15–22, Erik H. Erikson discusses the twenty-year development and evolution of the term "identity crisis" and quotes material written in 1926 by Sigmund Freud as he reflected upon the difficulties and conflicts posed by his own Jewish identity.
2. Clarence K. Weil, *ZBT 1898–1923: The First Twenty-Five Years* (New York: Zeta Beta Tau, 1923); Marianne Sanua, *Here's to Our Fraternity: One Hundred Years of Zeta Beta Tau 1898–1998* (Hanover, NH: University Press of New England, 1998).
3. See Baird, 20th ed., s.v. "Pi Lambda Phi,"; Lee, 35; and, most importantly, Oren's description of the founding of Pi Lambda Phi, 25–26, 36.
4. Oren, 26.
5. Oren, 26; Baird, 11th ed. (1927), s.v. "Pi Lambda Phi"; and Ruder, 31–33. See also Baird, 20th ed., s.v. "Pi Lambda Phi." The early records of the fraternity have been lost. However, it is clear that between 1895 and 1897, Pi Lambda Phi added nine chapters, most of which became defunct. A new one did not appear on the roll until 1912–1913, with the addition of Penn State. According to Maurice Jacobs of Phi Epsilon Pi, the reborn Columbia chapter of Pi Lambda Phi was responsible for the general revival of the fraternity.
6. See Maurice Jacobs, *Universal Jewish Encyclopedia*, vol. 4 (1941), s.v. "Fraternities, Jewish," which identifies Pi Lambda Phi's founders as Jewish, as well as Oren, 26, and Marianne Sanua, "Non-Recognition of Jewish Fraternities: The Cases of Columbia and Brown Universities," in *American Jewish Archives* 45, 2 (fall/winter 1993): 125–145. Entries in Baird as well as all of Pi Lambda Phi's accounts of itself insisted that the fraternity was founded by "undergraduates of different faiths" or that the three founders had consisted of a Protestant, a Catholic, and a Jew. However, examination of the class records, yearbooks, and obituaries available at the Manuscripts and Archives

section of the Yale University Library confirms the Jewish identity of two founders and strongly suggests the Jewish origins of the third. Henry Mark Fisher (Yale '97) is openly listed as Jewish in Yale's records and was ordained a rabbi at Hebrew Union College in Cincinnati in 1903, whereupon he served in several pulpits and followed a distinguished public career. Frederick Manfred Werner (Yale '98), another founder who prepared for college at the well-known Dr. Sach's Collegiate Institute, whose pupils were primarily German Jews, died in New York City on March 8, 1909, of acute nephritis. His obituary in the *Decennial Record: Class of Eighteen Hundred and Ninety-Eight, Yale College* (New Haven: Yale College, 1910) specifically notes when describing his untimely passing, "he was of the Jewish faith." The third founder, Louis Samter Levy (Yale '98) born in Forklands, AL, to Maurice Levy and Jennie Samter, reveals no specific religious background at all in his published Yale records, which is itself unusual; however, his entry appears in the 1938–1939 edition of *Who's Who in American Jewry*, vol. 3, ed. John Simons (New York: National News Association Inc.), 643.

7. "The Fraternity Issue at Brown University; Corporation to Decide; Pi Lambda Phi Chapter Disbands," *Jewish Daily Bulletin*, Friday, May 3, 1929, 6. A clipping of this article appears in the American Jewish Archives, Hebrew Union College, Cincinnati, OH [hereafter cited as AJA-HUC], Mss. Coll. 1, Intercollegiate Menorah Society, Folder: "Fraternities." For related material, see Box 70, Folder 14, "Brown University, clippings."

8. Oscar Hammerstein II, one of America's most prolific and best-loved lyricists, was the grandchild of German Jewish immigrants and the son of William Hammerstein, who did not practice his religion and who remained distant from Judaism for most of his life. His mother Alice was brought up as an Episcopalian and had both of their sons baptized in that faith. Oscar himself reportedly never joined a formal religious group nor attended weekly services. However, he was often assumed to be Jewish and suffered because of it. It is perhaps for this reason that the theme of unjust racial discrimination appears so often in his work, most notably in the musicals *Show Boat, Carmen Jones, South Pacific,* and *The Flower Drum Song.* He entered Columbia in 1912 and soon afterward joined Pi Lambda Phi. See Hugh Fordin, *Getting to Know Him: A Biography of Oscar Hammerstein II* (New York: Random House, 1977).

9. In much historical literature on Jews and selective college admissions, as well as in memoirs of students and faculty who taught at Columbia, Nicholas Murry Butler has tended to emerge as an almost villainously antisemitic figure, and his personal friendships with wealthy Jews are ascribed to the mercenary motive of not wishing to cut off a sizable potential source of funds for his university. See the work of Wechsler, especially *The Qualified Student*, where the reference to "Tsar Nicholas" appears; Marcia Graham Synnott, *The Half-Opened Door: Discrimination and Admissions at Harvard, Yale, and Princeton, 1900–1970* (Westport, CT: Greenwood Press, 1979); and Susanne Klingenstein, *Jews in the American Academy 1900–1940: The Dynamics of Intellectual Assimilation* (New Haven: Yale University Press, 1991), 145–146, who quotes Estelle Gilson, Letter to the Editor, "Butler at Columbia," *Commentary* (April 1986): 9–10. In Gottheil's surviving correspondence (he or-

dered most of his Columbia papers destroyed before his death), the absence of any complaint or allusion to personal antisemitism he may have suffered at Columbia is notable. However, on at least one occasion he hinted at his difficulties in a letter to Horace Kallen dated September 5, 1914: "Columbia, entre nous, is not a good berth for a Jew, through both Woodbridge and Dewey are quite far from any bias." (Correspondence with Horace Kallen, AJA-HUC, Mss. Coll. No. 1, Intercollegiate Menorah Association Collection, Box 12, Folder 1: "Gottheil, Richard 1914–1918."

10. Paul Ritterband and Harold S. Wechsler, *Jewish Learning in American Universities: The First Century* (Bloomington: University of Indiana Press, 1994), 55.

11. See Weil, and memoirs of former Columbia students in tribute to Gottheil after his death in a memorial issue of ZBTQ 18, 2, (September 1936). A file on Emma Leon Gottheil, a young Beirut-born Jewish widow with two sons at the time of her marriage to Richard (the Gottheils had no children together), can be found among the Small Collections at AJA-HUC, and obituaries of her can be found there in Mss. Coll. No. 127, Richard Gottheil Papers, Box 1 Folder 11.

12. For Gottheil's own account of his growing interest in Zionism, see his biography of his father, *The Life of Gustav Gottheil: Memoir of a Priest in Israel* (Philadelphia: Jewish Publication Society, 1936), as well as his history of the early Zionist movement in America, *Zionism* (Philadelphia: Jewish Publication Society, 1914).

13. Progress Reports and Descriptions of Richard Gottheil's early Zionist activity and travel in the United States and Europe can be found in AJA-HUC, Mss. Coll. No. 127, Gottheil Papers, Box 1, Folder 1: "Actions Committee Vienna 1898–1903."

14. See Weil, 14. Gottheil's desire to bring Jewish college men directly into the Zionist fold through their organization into a Zionist student society is evident in his correspondence with the Actions Committee in Vienna (see AJA-HUC, Mss. Coll. No. 127, Gottheil Papers, Box 1, Folder 1: "Actions Committee, Vienna 1898–1903," See also Ritterband and Wechsler, which contains discussion of Gottheil's career at Columbia and in particular his relationship to Zeta Beta Tau on 88–89.

15. "Religious Work in the Universities," *Central Council of American Rabbis Yearbook* [hereafter cited as *CCAR Yearbook*] 6, (1896): 85, quoted in Jenna Weissman Joselit, "Without Ghettoism: A History of the Intercollegiate Menorah Association, 1906–1930," *American Jewish Archives* 30, 2 (November 1978): 133–154.

16. The idea that ZBT was formed from a reorganization of the Young American Zionists, of which Ehrenreich was a leader (he served as the first Recording Secretary of the Federation of American Zionists) is suggested in Byron L. Sherwin's monograph, "Portrait of a Romantic Rebel: Bernard C. Ehrenreich, 1876–1955," *Turn to the South: Essays on Southern Jewry*, ed. Nathan M. Kaganoff and Melvin I. Urofsky (Charlottesville: American Jewish Historical Society and the University Press of Virginia, 1979), 3.

17. Joseph E. Glaser, "1898–1935—ZBT's Founders Today" in ZBTQ 17, 3

(December 1935): 16; Sherwin, 3; Harold S. Wechsler, "Rabbi Bernard C. Ehrenreich: A Northern Progressive Goes South," *Jews of the South: Selected Essays from the Southern Jewish Historical Society,* ed. Samuel Proctor and Louis Schmier (Macon, GA: Mercer University Press, 1984), 45–63. Ehrenreich's papers are preserved at the American Jewish Historical Society in New York.

18. *The American Hebrew* 64, 19 (March 10, 1899): 653, and 66, 9, (January 5, 1900): 300. Quoted in Ruder, 35.

19. A.A. Brill apparently did not remain in close contact with ZBT after his graduation from New York University and Columbia. However, he remained on the membership rolls and the fraternity did not lose sight of one of its most distinguished early graduates. At the annual Zeta Beta Tau Old Timer's Day Ball held in New York City in the winter of 1939, Brill was presented with their Alumni Achievement award. See ZBTQ 21, 1, (June 1939): 3.

20. See Weil, 15, and Irving Leonard Slade, "An Introductory Survey of Jewish Student Organizations in American Higher Education" (Ed.D. Thesis, Teachers College, New York, 1966): 26–27. Founder Louis S. Posner recalled the early days in detail in an address at the fraternity's fortieth annual convention. His speech was reprinted in full in ZBTQ 20, 4 (March 1939): 16–19.

21. *The American Hebrew* 66, 1 (November 10, 1899): 14, quoted in Ruder, 36–37.

22. Slade, 26, and Baird, 10th ed. (1923), 11th ed. (1927), 13th ed. (1935), and 14th ed. (1940), s.v. "Zeta Beta Tau."

23. Weil, 17. For a fascinating account of student life at the Jewish Theological Seminary during this period, see Mel Scult, *Judaism Faces the Twentieth Century: A Biography of Mordecai Kaplan* (Detroit: Wayne State University Press, 1993), 38–51.

24. For a description of the City College merger and ZBT's transformation, see Slade, 27–28. According to Weil (17), the local fraternity Omicron Epsilon Phi was established at City College in 1902. On February 2, 1903, Bernard Robinson, the "Arxon" or president of the group, authored the resolution merging the two fraternities.

25. Baird, 7th ed. (1912), 235.

26. Weil, 25.

27. Zeta Beta Tau Fraternity, *Esoteric Rituals,* pamphlet (n.p., March 2, 1920), 14. My thanks to the national officers of the fraternity for permitting me to see this document.

28. See "Minutes of the Supreme Beth Din, known as the Supreme Council, of the Zeta Beta Tau Fraternity, October 21, 1906," manuscript, in the archives of the Zeta Beta Tau National Office, Indianapolis, IN.

29. Weil, 33–34.

30. On the origin and development of the Menorah, see Joselit's fine study, 133–154. Also helpful is a brief discussion of the founding of Menorah and the Hillel Foundations in Sachar, 417–418.

31. Richard Gottheil, "Our Proper Position," ZBTQ 2, 3 (April 1916): 197, quoted in Ruder, 41. See also Richard Gottheil, "The True Basis of Zeta Beta Tau," ZBTQ 3, 1 (March 1917): 14–15, quoted in Ruder, 40. Gottheil's attitude toward the Menorah Society, however, was not entirely without reser-

vations. In a letter to Horace Kallen on July 22, 1915, after a visit to the ZBT chapter at Tulane University in New Orleans, Gottheil wrote, "I must say there is an earnestness and a quota of leadership among our boys that I find lacking in the hot air of the Menorah. I wish we could somehow capitalize that leadership more effectively" (correspondence with Horace Kallen AJA-HUC, Ms. Coll. No. 1, Intercollegiate Menorah Association Collection, Box 12, Folder 1: "Gottheil, Richard 1914–1918").

32. Henry Hurwitz, "ZBT and Menorah," ZBTQ 4, 3 (March, 1920): 9–10, quoted in Ruder, 40. Ruder's 1976 B.A. Honors Thesis at Harvard College appears to be one of the only sources for the earliest issues of the *Zeta Beta Tau Quarterly*, which contain extensive coverage of the Gottheil/Menorah/fraternity undergraduate struggle along with reports of Gottheil's resignation in 1920. At the fraternity's national office, all issues of ZBTQ published before September 1922, as well as those appearing between 1924 and 1927, are missing.

33. Joselit, 148; Slade, 26.

34. Richard Gottheil, "A Crisis," ZBTQ 2, 1 (April 1915): 8–9, 10, quoted in Ruder, 41.

35. Richard Gottheil to Horace Kallen, January 3, 1914, Menorah Association Collection, Box 12, Folder 1: "Gottheil, Richard 1914–1918."

36. Gottheil, "Our Proper Position," 197–198, quoted in Ruder, 42.

37. Letter to the Editor, ZBTQ 4, 2 (December 1919): 13, quoted in Ruder, 43.

38. Weil, 54. More details of Gottheil's resignation presumably appeared in that year's quarterlies.

39. Letter to the editor, ZBTQ 4, 3 (March 1920): 28–30, quoted in Ruder, 44.

40. "Fundamentals," editorial in ZBTQ 4, 4, (May 1920): 28–30, quoted in Ruder, 45.

41. See Gottheil's letter of a year and half before his death to Stephen S. Wise, January 28, 1935, AJA-HUC Mss. Coll. No. 49. Stephen Wise Papers, Box 3, Folder 8: "Gottheil, Richard 1933–1936."

42. According to Baird, 20th ed., s.v. Phi Epsilon Pi was officially established on November 23, 1904. The fraternity's own records (AJHS-PHIEP) sometimes state that they had been in existence, perhaps on an informal basis, since 1902.

43. This declaration appears in the first issue of the *Phi Epsilon Pi Quarterly* [hereafter cited as PhiEpQ] 1, 1 (December 1915): 41.

44. The crest of Phi Epsilon Pi went through great evolution in the space of a few years, all traceable within the pages of the fraternity's quarterlies, which appeared from 1915 to 1923. The first step, as insisted upon by secretary and leader Maurice Jacobs, was to change the star to the correct shape; thereafter, he called for changing the crest altogether, and eliminating the cross and the religious symbols. After brief experimentation with substituting a Jewish Scroll of the Law, it was decided that the final crest would contain the more neutral figures of a sailing ship and a rising sun.

45. Baird, 20th ed.(1991), s.v. "Phi Epsilon Pi."

46. See Jacobs, "Fraternities, Jewish," 453; Edward Calisch, "The Jewish Student in American Colleges," PhiEpQ 6, 2 (June 1923): 9.

47. Jesse Acker to Louis Zimmerman, January 12, 1916, AJHS-PHIEP, Box

16, Folder: "Early Fraternity Correspondence, 1916." Philip Weisberg was Phi Epsilon Pi's contact at the University of Michigan. A member of the fraternity, he had recently graduated from the University of Pennsylvania (Phi Epsilon Pi's Eta chapter), was then attending law school at the University of Michigan, and through the efforts of the local "Eta Club," was helping to form another chapter of the fraternity at his new campus.

48. Jesse Acker to Herman Kline, January 19, 1916, AJHS-PHIEP, Box 16, Folder: "Early Fraternity Correspondence, 1916."

49. Philip Weisberg to Jesse Acker, May 14, 1916, AJHS-PHIEP, Box 16, Folder: "Early Fraternity Correspondence, 1916."

50. Jesse Acker to A. N. Krieger, November 29, 1916, AJHS-PHIEP, Box 16, Folder: "Early Fraternity Correspondence, 1916."

51. Ruder, 47.

52. Ralph Dubin (Secretary of Alpha) March 20, 1917, AJHS-PHIEP, Box 21, Folder: "Alpha" [City College].

53. Dean Bernard Loeb to Alfred Reineman, April 5, 1916, AJHS-PHIEP, Box 16, Folder: "Early Fraternity Correspondence, 1916."

54. Jesse Acker to Al Reineman (in Louisiana, Missouri) May 9, 1916, AJHS-PHIEP, Box 16, Folder: "Early Fraternity Correspondence, 1916."

55. Norton J. Lustig, Secretary, Extension Division, University of Missouri, Columbia, to Alfred Reineman, Louisiana, Missouri, May 26, 1916, AJHS-PHIEP, Box 16, Folder: "Early Fraternity Correspondence, 1916."

56. Evidence of Maurice Jacobs's strenuous efforts to "Judaize" Phi Epsilon Pi in the 1920s and 1930s appears throughout the fraternity's records of that period. In the months before the convention, he authored several strong editorials, which appeared in issues of PhiEpQ, supporting the changing of the crest and the revocation of the nonsectarian ideal. See his personal Phi Epsilon Pi correspondence dating from 1921–1938 in AJHS-PHIEP, Box 17, Folder: "Maurice Jacobs," especially a letter to Simon Goldsmith of the Baltimore Alumni Association, November 23, 1932. For the life and activities of Jacobs at the Jewish Publication Society, see Jonathan Sarna, "The Maurice Jacobs Years," in *JPS: The Americanization of Jewish Culture, 1888–1988* (Philadelphia: Jewish Publication Society, 1989), 175–218.

57. Ralph E. Cohn (University of Michigan) "The Cross, the Crescent, and the Star," PhiEpQ 6, 3 (September 1923): 30.

58. Samuel Melvin Kootz, "Air Castles and Dissimulation," PhiEpQ 6, 2 (June 1923): 10–11.

59. Samuel M. Kootz, editorial, PhiEpQ, 6, 4 (December 1923): 23.

60. Joseph C. Hyman, "After Twenty-Five Years," *Frater of Pi Lambda Phi* 16 (August 1933): 6, quoted in Slade, 26.

CHAPTER 3

1. "And It Came to Pass in Those Days (Handed down by "Chief" Cohen, CCNY '12, to "Will I" Levy, M.I.T.)," *Octagonian of Sigma Alpha Mu* [hereafter cited as *Octagonian*] 12, 1 (March 1923): 31.

2. Howard S. Levie and Benjamin Goldman, "Here's How It All Began . . . ," *Octagonian* 47, 4 (November 1959): 6.
3. Morris Urich (Cincinnati). "Sigma Alpha Mu: Is it a Reflection of Bourgeois Society?" *Octagonian* 12, 1 (March 1923): 31.
4. "And It Came to Pass in Those Days," 11.
5. "And It Came To Pass In Those Days," 12. The following passage describes precisely the different techniques by which the bounds of the fraternity were spread: "Beta (Cornell) was started by five Brooklyn men who were initiated in the summer of 1911 before returning to Cornell for the fall term. Gamma (Columbia) was sponsored by the famous Charlie Nadler who was also responsible for Delta (Long Island), Epsilon (Columbia Medical), and Theta (Penn). Beta started Eta (Syracuse), Theta was responsible for Kappa (Minnesota) and Iota (Kentucky), and Iota started Omicron (Cincinnati). Omicron and Kappa started Rho (Illinois), Lambda and Pi (Harvard and Yale) were started by missionaries, Murry Horwood of Alpha started Xi (M.I.T.), Eta and Beta men started Nu (Buffalo), and so we grew."
6. Hyman I. Jacobson. "Votes for Women," *Octagonian* 2, 4 (April 1913), 2.
7. Hyman I. Jacobson. "Executive Notices," *Octagonian* 6, 4 (April 1916): 1.
8. Hyman I. Jacobson, "Executive Notices," *Octagonian* 6, 4 (April 1916), 3.
9. Hyman I. Jacobson. "Who's Your Friend?" *Octagonian* 6, 2 (February 1916), 2.
10. Evyatar Friesel. "The Age of Optimism in American Judaism, 1900–1920," in *A Biecentennial Festschrift for Jacob Rader Marcus,* ed. by Bertram Wallace Korn (New York: Ktav Publishing House, 1976), 131–155.
11. Herman "Heinie" Klein to Jesse Acker, January 16, 1916, AJHS-PHIEP, Box 16, Folder: "Early Fraternity Correspondence, 1916."
12. Jesse Acker to Lou Zimmerman (in Philadelphia) February 12, 1916, AJHS-PHIEP, Box 16, Folder: "Early Fraternity Correspondence, 1916."
13. "Chapter Roll," *Pledge Manual for 1945* (February 1, 1945), 47, AJHS-PHIEP, Box 46A, Publications, Folder: "Pledge and Rush Manuals." This list includes both the founding dates and the names of the local societies from which the chapters of Phi Epsilon Pi were formed. They were: Pittsburgh (Alpha Kappa Pi, 1913), Dickinson (Phi Kappa Delta, 1914), Rutgers (Theta Phi, 1915), Georgia (Eay Daleth Sigma, 1895), Tufts (Delta Phi Delta, 1916) Maine (Lambda Sigma Pi, 1916) Rhode Island State (Sigma Rho, 1916) Connecticut (Kappa Beta Iota, 1916), Carnegie Tech (Sigma Delta Chi, 1916), Syracuse (Delta Psi Epsilon, 1917), Northwestern (Lambda Club, 1920), Illinois (Theta Club, 1920), Dartmouth (Alpha Omega, 1920), Michigan (Cacique Club, 1921), Minnesota (Phi Club, 1923), Wisconsin (Tri Phi Club, 1925), Harvard (Phi Club, 1926), South Carolina (Troubadour Club, 1928), University of Miami (Pi Kappa Mu, 1929), Ohio State, Muhlenberg, and Boston University (formed from defunct chapters of the former Jewish national Sigma Lambda Pi, 1932), Western Reserve (Phi Delta Gamma, 1933), Louisiana State (Sigma Kappa Phi, 1933), Ohio University (Phi Upsilon, 1933), and University of Mississippi (Alpha Mu, 1935).
14. *Phi Epsilon Pi Pledge Manual for 1945,* 47, AJHS-PHIEP, Box 46A, Folder: "Pledge and Rush Manuals." The name "Eay Daleth Sigma" is problematic,

since "Eay" does not correspond to either a Greek or a Hebrew letter. It is quite possible that, as frequently happened with Jewish fraternities who attempted to included Hebrew in their symbolism and rituals, through lack of familiarity with the language the words and letters were misspelled, mispronounced, or improperly transliterated.

15. Hyman I. Jacobson. "Alumni Notes," *Octagonian* 2, 5 (May 1913), 4.

16. "Alumni Notes," *Octagonian* 6, 4 (April 1916): 3.

17. I have been unable to trace the existence of any institution named Dwight Memorial Hospital. It is possible that "Dwight" was an in-group reference to a particularly antisemitic hospital official who was known to deny positions to Jews.

18. Hyman I. Jacobs. "Alumni Notes" *Octagonian* 3, 4 (April 1914), 3.

19. For one general discussion of the historically important German-Russian Jewish "uptown-downtown" tensions that resulted in the Mt. Sinai/Beth Israel Hospital dichotomy in New York City, see Gerald Sorin, *A Time for Building: The Third Migration, 1880–1920*, vol. 3, *The Jewish People in America* (Baltimore: Johns Hopkins University Press, 1992), 98.

20. "Legal Notices," *Octagonian* 2, 4 (April, 1913), 3.

21. "News from Delta chapter [Long Island Medical College]," *Octagonian* 6, 4 (April 1916), 4; Moses Rischin, *The Promised City: New York's Jews, 1870–1914* (Cambridge: Harvard University Press, 1977), 92–93.

22. According to Baird, 6th ed. (1905), 125, Delta Phi Sigma was founded at Columbia "upon a non-sectarian basis, that is, providing for the admission of Christians and Jews," In Baird, 11th ed. (1927), the defining statement confined invitations to candidates "whose ideals and beliefs are those of a modern Christian civilization" (85). This information is noted in Johnson, 43–44.

23. Baird, 20th ed. (1991), s.v. "Fraternities That Are No More."

24. Kappa Nu Ritual, n.p., n.d. [c. 1930s] (mimeographed), Zeta Beta Tau archives. Shown to me with the kind permission of Zeta Beta Tau Fraternity.

25. Edward F. Perlson (of Alpha Epsilon Pi), "The Jewish Collegian in Greek Letter Fraternities," *Banta's Greek Exchange* 21, 1 (January 1933): 24. This article contains a list and valuable thumbnail sketch of sixteen of the national men's Jewish fraternities.

26. Rischin, *The Promised City*, 258.

27. Sidney Dunn, Executive Director Alpha Epsilon Pi, interview with the author, Indianapolis, IN, Fraternity national headquarters, May 24, 1992.

28. AEPI Fraternity history appearing in pledge manual, *A Guide to Alpha Epsilon Pi*, (Indianapolis, IN: AEPi Archives, 1964).

29. From Baird, 20th ed., especially s.v. "Fraternities That Are No More," and Sidney S. Suntag, "The Heritage of the Predominantly Jewish Fraternity Movement," *The History of Tau Epsilon Phi: 75 Years of Friendship 1910–1985* (Atlanta: The TEP Foundation, Inc., 1986), 3–4. See also George S. Toll, "Colleges, Fraternities, and Assimilation," *Journal of Reform Judaism* 32, 4 (summer 1985), 93–103 as well as Toll's "The Jewish Fraternities, Their Rise and Fall," *Alpha Epsilon Pi: The First Sixty-five Years, 1913–1978* (The Alpha Epsilon Pi Foundation, Inc., 1980), 1–47.

30. See Baird, 20th ed., s.v. "Fraternities That Are No More," article on Iota Alpha Pi, 32.

31. Gloria Ansell Krulik, interview with the author, January 10, 1999, Boca Raton, FL. "They never called themselves 'Japs,' and the term wasn't popular. We were not affluent. We were supposed to be just a plain sorority . . . not snobs, nothing special about us." On the disbanding of Iota Alpha Pi, see Baird, 20th ed., s.v. "Fraternities That Are No More."

32. Between 1922 and 1926 Delta Phi Epsilon added three Canadian chapters: McGill, University of Toronto, and University of Manitoba, in Winniepeg. The chapter at the University of British Columbia was added in 1946. See Baird, 20th ed. (1991), s.v. "Delta Phi Epsilon."

33. Memoirs of a former student's days in the SATC and the tendency to refer to it as a "tea club" or "safe at the college" are found in an article by Dr. Maurice Smith, "The Development of the Bay Window," *ZBTQ* 15, 3 (June 1931): 17; its effects on college life at the time are recalled in an editorial by Lee Dover upon the outbreak of World War II, *ZBTQ* 21, 2 (October 1939): 3.

34. Percy Pachtman, Secretary, Phi Epsilon Pi 1919 Convention Committee, to Fraters, November 22 and December 9, 1919 (convention newsletters), AJHS-PHIEP, Box 6, Folder: "1919."

35. Percy Pachtman to Fraters, November 17, 1919, AJHS-PHIEP, Box 6, Folder: "1919."

36. Minutes of Phi Epsilon Pi Grand Council Meeting, Philadelphia, PA, January 21, 1920, 4–6, AJHS-PHIEP, Box 6, Folder: "1919."

37. Isaac Y. Olch to Jesse Acker, February 23, 1916, AJHS-PHIEP, Box 31, Folder "Sigma" (Brown University). See also Sanua, "Non- Recognition of Jewish College Fraternities," 125–145. Students of those days recalled secret meetings that broke up in confusion when they heard sounds at the door and feared that they had been discovered.

38. Until after World War II Gentile and Jewish fraternities at the University of Pennsylvania were listed as being either in the "Class A" or "Class B" group, while the 1915 edition of Baird's included the national Jewish fraternities only under the heading "Second Division" (Baird, 8th ed. [1915], 356).

39. Richard Gottheil to Felix Warburg, November 1, 1912, AJA, Felix Warburg Papers, Box 163 Folder 19, (copy of resolution attached to letter). See also Sanua, "The Non-Recognition of Jewish College Fraternities."

40. Richard Gottheil to Felix Warburg, November 18, 1912, Felix Warbug Papers, Box 163 Folder 19. Sanua, "The Non-Recognition of Jewish College Fraternities," 136

41. Richard Gottheil to Felix Warburg, November 21, 1912, AJA, Felix Warburg Papers, Box 163, Folder 19.

42. Louis Zimmerman to Jesse Ackerman, January 11, 1916, AJHS-PHIEP, Box 16, Folder: "Early Fraternity Correspondence, 1916."

43. Philip Weisberg to Jesse Acker May 14, 1916, AJHS-PHIEP, Box 16, Folder: "Early Fraternity Correspondence, 1916."

44. Cited in a letter from David Paull, executive secretary, to Lt. Charles A. Tepper, March 21, 1945, AJHS-PHIEP, Box 15, Folder: "WWII Correspondence, 1945."

45. Naomi W. Cohen offers some interesting insights into this phenomenon in chapter 3, "The Proper American Jew," esp. the section entitled "Manners and Virtues," 110–114. She writes:

    > A lasting effect of emancipation was to make the now legally free Jewish citizen more self-conscious than ever before. As long as the premodern Jew had accepted a way of life divorced from the dominant society . . . he worried little about the image he projected. His religious literature taught him how a proper Jew behaved toward his God, fellow Jews, and even faceless political authorities. He knew the dangers to himself and his community were he to cause a scandal in his dealings with Christians, but he never really believed that consistently virtuous deportment on his part would endear Jews to their host country or significantly alter the course of Jewish-Christian relations. Only when the modern Jew strove for social integration did the thought "Mah yomru ha-goyyim?" ("What will the gentiles say?") become well-nigh an obsession, coloring his behavior both within the Jewish community as well as within the larger society. The figure he cut by his manners and morals loomed all-important. (109)

46. Jesse Acker to Al Reineman, May 19, 1916, AJHS-PHIEP, Box 16, Folder: "Early Fraternity Correspondence, 1916."

47. Art W. Ager [name unclear] to Jesse Acker, February 20, 1916, Western Union Telegram, AJHS-PHIEP, Box 16, Folder: "Early Fraternity Correspondence, 1916": "Just wired Kline to cut off relations with local at Connecticut Agricultural College do not consider the college of high enough rank to warrant our establishing there at the present time."

48. Herman "Heinie" Kline to Jesse Acker, January 16, 1916, AJHS-PHIEP, Box 16, Folder: "Early Fraternity Correspondence, 1916."

49. Editorial, PhiEpQ 9, 1 (September 1923): 85.

50. Slade, 26.

51. *Central Conference of American Rabbis Yearbook* 23 (Cincinnati: May and Kriedler Publishers, 1913): 121ff, quoted in Slade, 31–33. For other discussions of fraternities in the *CCAR Yearbook*, see volume 6 (1896): 85; volume 15 (1905): 6; volume 16 (1906): 78, 188 ff.; and volume 19 (1909): 150–154.

52. Harold Riegelman. "The Promise of Z.B.T," ZBTQ 3, 1 (March 1917).

53. Louis E. Levinthal, "Jewish Brotherhood," editorial, *Octagonian* 4, 4 (April 1915), 1.

54. Jacob Turchinksy, "The Case Against Jewish Fraternities," *Octagonian* 2, 5 (May 1913), 1.

55. Turchinksy.

56. Hyman I. Jacobson, Editorial, *Octagonian* 2, 5 (May 1913), 1–3.

57. *Octagonian* 6, 4 (April 1916).

CHAPTER 4

1. Paula S. Fass, *The Damned and the Beautiful: American Youth in the 1920's* (New York: Oxford University Press, 1977), 124, 130, 407. For further background and statistics on the growth of student populations in the 1920s, see Horowitz, 8; Rudolph; and Veysey.

2. From article reprinted in Baird, 12th ed. (1930), 15–22.

3. Fass, 144. On the importance of college fraternities and their resilience through economic collapse and a second world war, Horowitz has written:

   > One element remained constant: from the 1920s through the 1950s the fraternity dominated American colleges. With their prestige confirmed by official under-graduate organizations, recognized by the administration, and broadcast in the student newspaper, fraternity men had powerful instruments for ruling the campus. It was they who had defined and continued to control the major social events of the college year: the proms, student plays and musicals, elections, freshman hazing. Their activities had strong appeal, especially the football games. As the expanding universities built larger stadiums, the Saturday afternoon game became the symbolic event that bound together all students, past and present (131).

4. Richard Flesch, "Disraelis I Have Known," ZBTQ 13, 2 (December 1928): 13.

5. Henry L. Feingold, "Investing in Themselves: The Harvard Case and the Origins of the Third American-Jewish Commercial Elite," *American Jewish History* 77, 4 (June 1988): 538.

6. The popularity of fraternity membership, as opposed to membership in Jewish religious, cultural, literary, or Zionist groups which were also active on campuses at the time, is confirmed by the other organizations's constant complaints that the Jewish fraternities were taking members away from them. This appears most markedly in the records of the Intercollegiate Menorah Association, whose leaders tended to blame the fraternities for their own demise. See Joselit, especially pages 136, 140, 145–149, for a discussion of the antagonistic relationship between Menorah and the Jewish fraternities.

7. H.S. Linfield, "The Communal Organization of the Jews in the United States, 1927," *American Jewish Yearbook* 31 (1929–1930): 141–143; also quoted in Harold S. Wechsler, "The Rationale for Restriction: Ethnicity and College Admission in America, 1910–1980," *American Quarterly* 36, 5 (winter 1984): 658.

8. According to Fass, the vast majority of youths on college campuses in the 1920s had adequate support from home to meet most of their expenses. Although at least one half of the men and one quarter of the women students worked to earn some outside money during their college years, much of this income fell under the category of "pocket money." Only 15 percent of all college students were completely self-supporting (134–35). Her figures are taken from Walter J. Greenleaf, "Self-Help for College Students," *U.S. Bureau of Education Bulletin* 2 (1929): 59–60.

9. Lawrence G. Blochman, "Professors of Platitude," ZBTQ 13, 1 (October 1928): 3.

10. Alfred B. Engelhard, "Ulysses Universitatis; or, Four and Twenty Hours from the Life of a College Youth," ZBTQ 12, 2 (December 1927): 17. The body of water in question was Madison's Lake Mendota.

11. For background on Prohibition and its effect on American life in the 1920s, see Thomas M. Coffey, *The Long Thirst: Prohibition in America: 1920–1933* (New York: Norton, 1975) and Frederick Lewis Allen, *Only Yesterday* (New York: Harper, 1931).

12. John B. Quigley, "Beer Busts," ZBTQ 14, 3 (March 1930): 13.

13. Quigley, 15.
14. Lawrence G. Blockman, "To a Lost Art: Drink 'er Down!" ZBTQ 14, 1 (October 1929): 13–15.
15. A description of the event and a partial text of Robert E. Segal's toast appeared in *ZBTQ* 19, 3 (March 1936): 44 See also Sanua, *Here's to Our Fraternity*, 44. For a penetrating look into the manners and mores of one city's German Jewish aristocracy, see Stephen Birmingham, *Our Crowd: The Great Jewish Families of New York* (New York: Harper and Row, 1967).
16. Arthur Donald "Aidee" Schwarz, "Why I Hate Jewesses," ZBTQ 7, 3 (March 1923): 25.
17. Arthur Donald Schwarz, "Rushing as it Wunst Wuz," ZBTQ 7, 1 (September 1922): 16.
18. "Report of the Committee on Standards of Membership," Minutes of the Supreme Council, Zeta Beta Tau, New York City, September 9, 1924 (ZBT archives in Indianapolis, IN). Richard Loeb (1905–1936) a member of the University of Michigan chapter, was indicted and convicted for the murder along with Nathan Freudenthal Leopold (1904–1971), a University of Chicago graduate. Both were the sons of wealthy Chicago Jewish families. Leopold and Loeb, who were defended by Clarence Darrow in what became one of the most sensational murder trials in the United States up until that time, were both sentenced to life imprisonment plus ninety-nine years. While in jail, the two men developed a correspondence school for the inmates of nineteen penitentiaries. In 1936 Loeb was murdered by a fellow inmate.
19. Minutes of the Supreme Council, Zeta Beta Tau, September 9, 1924.
20. Interview with James E. Greer, Executive Director, Zeta Beta Tau, New York City, April 6, 1996.
21. "Psi, University of Alabama," ZBTQ 12, 3 (March 1928): 39.
22. Minutes of Zeta Beta Tau Supreme Council, September 9, 1924; I am indebted to my colleague Ava F. Kahn for pointing out the latter implication of Cunard's offer to me.
23. Harry J. Galland, "Yes, I've Been To France," ZBTQ 13, 4 (May 1929): 15.
24. Lee Dover, editorial, "C., F., & S." ZBTQ 13, 4 (May 1929): 3.
25. Bernard S. Greensfeder, "In the Land of Pretzels and Beer," ZBTQ 13, 4 (May 1929): 7.
26. Greensfeder, 6.
27. Galland, ZBTQ 13, 4 (May 1929): 15.
28. Eustace Meyers, letter to the editor, August 12, 1929, ZBTQ 14, 1 (October 1929): 4. Eustace Meyers, of Kingston, Jamaica, was the son of Horace V. Meyers, also a ZBT member.
29. Lee Dover, editorial, "The Vacation Number," ZBTQ 14, 4, (May 1930): 3.
30. See Feingold, "Investing in Themselves."
31. Herbert Lippman, "Take It or Leave It," ZBTQ 14, 1 (October 1929): 7.
32. Clarence K. Weil, "Toward a Medical Career," ZBTQ 12, 2 (December 1927): 23–27.
33. Minutes of the Supreme Council of Zeta Beta Tau, November 13, 1924, ZBT Archives, Indianapolis, IN.
34. "Eta Man Works in German Plant: Son of American Millionaire Receives

Fifty Cents a Day," *The Eta Egotist* (Philadelphia: University of Pennsylvania [Eta] Chapter of Phi Epsilon Pi) [hereafter cited as *Egotist*] 3, 2 (May 1923): 1. The Bamberger family was only one of the prominent American Jewish families engaged in the manufacturing and department store business. For an interesting and humorous view of these families and the impact they had on their communities, see Leon Harris's popular history, *Merchant Princes: An Intimate History of Jewish Families Who Built Great Department Stores* (New York: Harper and Row, 1979).

35. *Egotist* 3, 2 (May 1923): 1
36. *Egotist* 3, 2 (May 1923): 4.
37. *Egotist* 3, 2 (May 1923): 2.
38. "Eta's Penn," *Egotist*, 3, 2 (May 1923): 2.
39. "Here's the Dope on Phi Ep's Biggest and Best," convention flyer, September 1927, AJHS-PHIEP, Box 6, Folder: "1927."
40. "Phi Ep's Biggest," convention flyer.
41. Lawrence G. Blochman, "Blind Man's Bluff," ZBTQ 13, 2 (December 1928): 8.
42. M. J. Rosenfeld, Jr., "The Hindu Secrets of Love," ZBTQ 7, 3 (March 1923): 16.
43. *SAM: The Confidential Monthly Bulletin of Sigma Alpha Mu* [hereafter cited as *SAM Bulletin*] 12, 7 (November 15, 1928): 1. The issue mentioned special celebrations in honor of the fraternity's eighteenth anniversary that year. The letters for the word "life" in Hebrew also represent the number eighteen.
44. *SAM Bulletin* 13, 8 [Convention Number] (December 15, 1929).
45. Marie Luhrs. "A Party with Boys: A Penetrating Up-to-the-Minute Sketch of College Life," *American Hebrew* (December 21, 1928): 258.
46. Luhrs.
47. Report of Sigmund H. Steinberg, Supreme Master, Minutes of the 13th Annual Supreme Council of the Alpha Epsilon Pi Fraternity, Hotel McAlpin, NYC, December 26, 1929, Alpha Epsilon Pi archives, Indianapolis, IN [hereafter cited as AEPi].
48. *The Scroll of Alpha Epsilon Pi Fraternity* [hereafter cited as *AEPi Scroll*] 2, 2 (April 15, 1921). The archives of the Alpha Epsilon Pi national office contain a touching montage of summer photographs taken at the Edgemere house during this period; these have since been enlarged and have been placed on the walls of the fraternity's present national offices in Indianapolis, IN.
49. *AEPi Scroll* 1, 4 (April 1920), 1.
50. Address by Nathan Wolf, Supreme Master of Alpha Epsilon Pi, minutes of the December 1920 convention, 50, Minute Book, AEPi Archives, Indianapolis, IN.
51. "Beta Entertains," *AEPi Scroll* 1, 4 (April 1920), 1–2. The article includes the full names and addresses of all the visitors to Ithaca; almost all resided in Brooklyn, NY.
52. For example, Western Union would not hire Jewish boys, nor could Jews hope to become bank tellers or salesclerks in non-Jewish stores. The New York Telephone Company claimed that it could not employ Jewish women as operators because their arms were supposedly "too short to handle the switch-

boards," Want ads in certain papers, in particular the *New York Herald Tri-bune*, routinely specified "Christian Only" or other euphemisms to make it clear that Jews were not wanted. See Henry Feingold, *A Time for Searching: Entering the Mainstream, 1920–1945*, vol. 4 in *The Jewish People In America* (Baltimore: Johns Hopkins University Press, 1992), 2.

CHAPTER 5

1. The term "counterrevolution" is used by Rudolph in reference to changes in U.S. higher education that took place between 1890 and 1910 (443). For another discussion of liberal culture and the "New Humanist" movement of the 1920s, see also Veysey, 180–251.
2. H.L. Mencken, "In the Halls of Learning," *Chicago Tribune*, 1927. Reprinted in ZBTQ 12, 2 (December 1927): 12–14.
3. Alfred B. Engelhard, "In Defense of Hell," ZBTQ 13, 2 (December 1928): 8.
4. Discussion of this phenomenon appears widely in the historical literature. For some examples, see Dinnerstein, "Education and the Advancement of American Jews" and Feingold, "Investing in Themselves," 530. The sociologist Glazer has noted that between 1920 and 1940 American Jewry underwent "a phenomenal advance in their social position," transforming themselves from a largely proletarian group to a middle-class one, a movement which was achieved by intense education and a shift in occupational patterns (81). See also Glazer and Daniel Patrick Moynihan, *Beyond the Melting Pot: The Negroes, Puerto Ricans, Jews, Italians and Irish of New York City* (Cambridge: MIT Press, 1970), who note that Jews rose to the middle class far earlier than other groups of the 'new immigration.' For a similar conclusion, see Thomas Kessner, *The Golden Door: Italian and Jewish Immigrant Mobility in New York City 1880–1915* (New York: Oxford University Press, 1977), esp. xi–xvii.
5. Wechsler, *The Qualified Student*, 133–136, 144–175.
6. Feingold, "Investing in Themselves," 540. The epithet "College of the Circumcised Citizens of New York" appears in many other articles and books dealing with Jewish college students as well.
7. In his memoirs *In Memory Yet Green: The Autobiography of Isaac Asimov, 1920–1954* (New York: Doubleday, 1979) the scientist and author recalls applying to Columbia College as a teenager and being shunted instead to Seth Low Junior College in downtown Brooklyn, which only offered a three-year program. The highest degree Seth Low granted was the Bachelor of Science degree; the college did not grant Bachelor of Arts degrees. When Brooklyn College, a branch of the City University of New York, opened in 1936, Seth Low Junior College allowed its students to finish their courses, then closed its doors in 1938. For discussion of Columbia president Nicholas Murray Butler's opposition to a Brooklyn University and the establishment of Seth Low, see Wechsler, *The Qualified Student*, 191–194. See also "Columbiana," Columbia University Archives, New York, Subject Folder: "Seth Low Junior College."

8. Stephen Steinberg, *The Academic Melting Pot: Catholics and Jews in American Higher Education* (New York: 1974), 19–20, and Synnott, *The Half-Opened Door*, 11 ff. Jews were less than 3.4 percent of the American population in 1934, but they supplied 10 percent of the national student population and even more in Jewish population centers. By 1957, 28.5 percent of Jews had graduated from college as opposed to 10 percent of the general population. In 1935 Jews supplied three times as many students as their proportion in the population. In the professional schools, and particularly in medicine, they were especially conspicuous. In 1923 the Jewish enrollment at Columbia's College of Physicians and surgeons was as high as 50 percent. By 1939, it had been cut to less than 7 percent. Rejected Jewish candidates turned to dentistry, podiatry, optometry, osteopathy, pharmacy, chiropractic, and veterinary schools, or else went abroad for their medical education.

9. Dr. A. A. Roback (Department of Psychology, Harvard University), "Must Your Son Go to College?" *Jewish Tribune*, June 5, 1925, 8.

10. See Higham, 159. There are numerous references and descriptions of specific techniques throughout American Jewish memoirs and historical literature. For examples of methods used to weed out Jewish students, see the work of Wechsler, in particular *The Well-Qualified Student*; Synnott, *The Half-Opened Door*; and Broun and Britt in their discussion on Jews in college, 102. Oren notes that Jewish boys from the Boston area in 1922 were offended that Harvard required an applicant to state his color, religious preference, father's birthplace, and whether or not he or his father had ever changed their name (47).

11. Arthur D. Schwarz, "Three Points for Beauty," ZBTQ 12, 1 (September 1927): 7.

12. Schwarz, "Three Points for Beauty," 8.

13. A. Lawrence Lowell became president of Harvard in 1909 against the wishes of Charles W. Eliot, who had served as president for forty years and who had been responsible for many of the liberalizing reforms that had turned the college into a major university. Lowell's conflicts with Eliot, his efforts to remake Harvard, and his successful attempt to limit the number of Jews admitted are discussed in Steinberg, *The Academic Melting Pot*, 19–31; Wechsler, *The Well-Qualified Student*, 161–162; and Synnott, *The Half-Opened Door*, 25–124. The scandal was complicated at first by charges that Jewish students themselves had "leaked" the story to the press and thus were in part guilty of spreading lies and slander about their alma mater. See Harry Starr, "The Affair at Harvard: What the Students Did," *The Menorah Journal* 8, no. 5 (October 1922): 263–76.

14. William C. Kranowitz, "What Does the Harvard Jewish Exposé Mean to Sigma Alpha Mu?" *Octagonian* 11, 3 (December 1922): 8.

15. William T. Ham [most likely a pseudonym], "Harvard Student Opinion on the Jewish Question," *The Nation* 115, no. 2983 (Sept. 6, 1922): 225–27. Reprinted in *ZBTQ* 7, 1. The article was based on a final examination essay question given by Dr. Richard C. Cabot of Harvard's Department of Social Ethics at the end of the school year in 1922. Of 83 men examined, 41 expressed the belief that "race limitation" on admissions was justified; 34 held

that it was not, including 7 Jews, and 8 expressed no clear opinion either way.
16. Ham, 6.
17. Cyrus McGinn Mulqueen, A Christian Collegian [pseud.], "Why I Hate Jews," ZBTQ 7, 2 (December 1922): 3.
18. Mulqueen, 6.
19. Harold Riegelman, Speech in New York City, reported in the *New York Times,* January 22, 1923, sec 5, 1. For a full chronology, explanation, and analysis of President A. Lawrence Lowell's actions during the Harvard affair of 1922–1923, see the works of Steinberg; Wechsler; and Synnott, *The Half-Opened Door,* 27. See also Oren, 45–48; Sachar, 328–331; and Feingold, *A Time for Searching, 1920–1945,* v. 4, 1 and 13–24. An interesting account of the Harvard affair and subsequent ill-feeling between Lowell and American Jewish leaders appears in *From the Diaries of Felix Frankfurter,* ed. Joseph Lash (New York: Norton, 1975). A close friend of Frankfurter, who was a professor at Harvard Law School at the time, told the author that the quota controversy had brought about a "vitriolic correspondence" between the Boston Brahmin Lowell and the Jewish Frankfurter—"Nobody but me has seen that exchange and it really was vitriolic" (37). The animosity developed even further in 1927 when Frankfurter became one of the leading advocates of the anarchists Sacco and Vanzetti, while Lowell headed the government commission whose report justified the execution of the two men. At that point, Frankfurter was asked whether he would resign from the Law School. "Why should I resign?" he reportedly answered. "Let Lowell resign" (124).
20. Feingold, "Investing in Themselves," 551.
21. Oren, 48.
22. See Toll, "Colleges, Fraternities, and Assimilation," 97. The one possible exception to this was Amherst, since there apparently existed a chapter of the nonsectarian Pi Lambda Phi there from 1927 to 1931. See Baird, 20th ed., s.v. "Campuses and Their Fraternities."
23. Letters of refusal of recognition from university officials, as well as extensive discussions and speculations on the reasons for such refusal and possible strategies for overcoming it, are found in the early records of all Jewish fraternities and sororities. See especially AJHS-PHIEP Collection, passim; also Louis Marshall correspondence in the American Jewish Committee Archives, Blaustein Library, New York City [hereafter cited as AJC] Folder: "Fraternities."
24. Excerpt of minutes of National Interfraternity Conference of December 1927 in a letter from Frederic R. Mann, National President of Tau Epsilon Phi, to Louis Marshall, February 14, 1928, AJC, Blaustein Library, Folder: "Fraternities." The excerpt had been obtained by Mann and was attached to his letter to Marshall as an example of the attitudes that Jewish fraternities were facing in the Greek-letter world. It was this letter that prompted Marshall to write to President Faunce of Brown University.
25. Herman "Heinie" Kline to Jesse Acker, January 16, 1916, AJHS-PHIEP, Box 16, Folder: "Early Fraternity Correspondence, 1916."
26. See Sachar, 521. For a description of Viereck's resignation and the desire of Phi Epsilon Pi to strike him from the roll, see Maurice Jacobs to Louis M.

Fushan, July 7, 1934, AJHS-PHIEP, Box 17, Folder: "Maurice Jacobs, 1931–37." See also correspondence between Pascal Greenberg and Kurt Gruenwald, February 21 and March 1,1939, AJHS-PHIEP, Box 12, Folder: "Alpha" (City College). A picture, biography, congratulatory letter, and poem of friendship written by George Sylvester Viereck to his Phi Epsilon Pi fraternity brothers appear in the first issue of PhiEpQ (1, 1 [December 1915], 1). Viereck was born in Munich on December 31, 1884 and came to the U.S. at the age of 11. For background on Viereck's life and pro-German activities, see Susan Canedy, *America's Nazis, A Democratic Dilemma: A History of the German American Bund* (Menlo Park, CA: Mark Graff, 1990), 5; Nathan C. Belth, *A Promise to Keep: A Narrative of the American Encounter with Anti-Semitism* (New York: Times Books, 1979), 120–123; and two full-scale biographies: Nil M. Johnson, *George Sylvester Viereck: German-American Propagandist* (Urbana: University of Illinois Press, 1972) and Elmer Gertz, *Odyssey of a Barbarian: The Biography of George Sylvester Viereck* (Buffalo: Prometheus Books, 1978).

27. Arthur J. Levy (Providence, RI) to Maurice Jacobs, March 8, 1921, AJHS-PHIEP, Box 31, Folder: "Sigma."

28. Benjamin Rowe (Tufts Chapter, Phi Epsilon Pi) to Emmanuel Wirkman, December 15, 1929, AJHS-PHIEP, Box 31, Folder: "Sigma." Rowe was writing to inquire why there was no Phi Epsilon Pi chapter at Brown. "There are over two hundred Jewish boys at Brown of which I can say fifty percent are of fraternity caliber. There are star football men, soccer players, swimmers, basketball stars, President and Manager of the orchestra, and many others who are participating in other activities such as the newspaper, etc."

29. William H. P. Faunce to Louis S. Lebenthal, January 20, 1928, AJC, Blaustein Library, Folder: "Fraternities."

30. Samuel M. Klivansky to Morris D. Waldman (Secretary, American Jewish Committee) December 27, 1928, AJC, Blaustein Library, Folder: "Fraternities."

31. Louis Pomiansky to Louis Marshall, November 12, 1928. AJC, Blaustein Library, Folder: "Fraternities."

32. Louis Marshall to Frederic R. Mann, February 16, 1928, AJC, Blaustein Library, Folder: "Fraternities."

33. Louis Marshall to William H. P. Faunce, February 21, 1928, AJC, Blaustein Library, Folder: "Fraternities," See also *American Jewish Yearbook* 31 (1929–1930): 354–358, s.v. "Jewish Secret Fraternities at Universities and Colleges."

34. William H. P. Faunce to Louis Marshall, March 1, 1928, AJC, Folder "Fraternities." See also *American Jewish Yearbook* 31, (1929–1930): 357.

35. See Eleanor F. Horvitz and Benton H. Rosen, "The Jewish Fraternity and Brown University," *Rhode Island Jewish Historical Notes* 8, 3 (November 1981), especially 305–333. For samples of the massive press coverage, including Yiddish newspapers, see Mss. Coll. No. 2, Henry Hurwitz collection, Folder 70 Box 4, "Brown University—Clippings" (c. April–May 1929), AJA. Note in particular "The Jewish Fraternity Issue at Brown University," 6.

36. Dr. Mitchell Salem Fisher. "For the Love of Alma Mater," in *The Brandeis*

Avukah Volume of 1936: A Collection of Essays on Contemporary Zionist Thought Dedicated to Justice Louis D. Brandeis, ed. Rabbi Joseph Shalom Shubow (Boston: Stratford Publishers, 1936), 604–614. I am indebted to Susan Aprill, then of the NYU archives, for her help in verifying the story.

37. Fisher, 605–606.
38. Fisher, 608.
39. Fisher, 609. The chancellor's real name was Elmer Ellsworth Brown.
40. Fisher's letter appeared in the March 15, 1923, issue of the *New York University Daily News*, 2. A copy of the letter, with accompanying note sent to Chancellor Elmer Ellsworth Brown of NYU and related correspondence, also appears in the NYU Archives, Elmer E. Brown Papers, Box 25, Folder 7, RG 3.0.4, "Fisher, Mitchell S., 1923," (Courtesy of Susan Aprill).
41. Fisher, "For the Love of Alma Mater," 611. The real name of NYU's Dean of Engineering in 1923 was Charles Snow.
42. A copy of the circular, printed in blue ink, headed with the Hebrew letters for "kosher" and with the words "New York University" in place of the pseudonymous "Da-Da," appears in the New York University Archives, Elmer E. Brown Papers, Box 9, Folder 12, RG.3.0.4, "Bouton, Archibald (Dean, College of Arts and Pure Science) 1922–1927." Accompanying it is a letter from Dean Bouton to Chancellor Brown, dated March 20, 1923: "I enclose a copy of a circular that was extensively posted on our campus this morning. The campus force was very busy very early in the morning cleaning up things and I think have succeeded. Nevertheless, the material is out. I spoke with a good deal of vigor about the matter in Chapel this morning. . . . I think you should know about the matter. Dean Snow thinks it is likely to bring us publicity. I do not know who is responsible for Mr. Fisher has been extremely active in bringing it to the attention of various people and seems to possess a large number of copies of the document," The folder also contains a clipping of a front-page *New York Herald Tribune* article on the matter (March 21, 1923); a copy of the Jewish student resolution authored by the NYU Menorah Society, signed by president Mitchell S. Fisher and vice-president David Cramer.
43. Fisher, "For the Love of Alma Mater," 612.
44. Fisher, "For the Love of Alma Mater," 613.
45. Fisher, "For the Love of Alma Mater," 614.

CHAPTER 6

1. Lionel A. Sperber, "Judaphobia," *Octagonian* 12, 3 (December 1923): 31.
2. A partial typescript copy of this study, done in 1926, can be found in AJHS-PHIEP, Box 17, Folder: "Council on American Jewish Student Affairs." 1500 questionnaires were sent to all the fraternities affiliated with the Council, asking the following questions: Does prejudice exist on your campus? If so is it slight, moderate, or intense? Does it exist in the student body, the faculty, or both? What are the causes, and are they controllable? What can be done to eliminate or minimize prejudice? The questionnaire also asked for a detailed statistical survey of the number of Jewish men and women students, the degree of their acceptance in specific institutions, and their level of participation

on varsity athletic teams, debate teams, and publications. The study found that of a total of 160,741 male college students, approximately 18,370 were Jewish; out of 75,653 female college students, 5,930 were Jewish, for a total of 24,217 Jewish students out of a college population of 237,507. Out of a total of 8628 students on varsity athletic teams, the study found 547 Jews, or roughly 7 percent of the total Jewish student population. Despite this respectable showing, in later years Riegelman criticized Jewish college students for being relatively underrepresented in the field of varsity athletics and overly represented in other areas, such as campus publications (20%) and debating (23%) See Harold Riegelman, "The Jewish Collegian: Missionary of Good Will," ZBTQ 14, 3 (March 1930): 7. Figures were derived as follows: out of a total of 758 on varsity debate teams, 69 were Jewish; out of a total of 4527 on student publications, 928 were Jewish. Out of 67 colleges and universities reporting, 52 did not admit Jews to Gentile fraternities and sororities at all, while on 15 they might be admitted occasionally.

3. The disproportion, however, did reveal itself later in the well-known tendency of Jewish fraternity graduates to become owners or managers of professional athletic teams.
4. Schwarz, "Why I Hate Jewesses," 25–26.
5. Ted Goldsmith, "In Defense of State Universities," ZBTQ 13, 3 (March 1929): 23.
6. Milton Adler, Supreme Master, Annual Report, December 29, 1921, 110, Alpha Epsilon Pi Minutes, AEPi.
7. Feingold, *A Time for Searching; 1920–1945*, 15–16.
8. Jerome M. Levy, "Squire Perkins' Remarks on Colleges in General," *Octagonian* 11, 3 (December 1922): 60.
9. Dorothy Linder, "Prejudice at a Women's College," ZBTQ 7, 4 (May 1923): 5.
10. Linder, 7.
11. Louis E. Wise, "The Jew's Position in College Today," PhiEpQ 6, 1 (March 1923): 16. This editorial mentions an article in the *New York Evening Post* of February 28, reporting that the student council appointed a committee of three to confer with the university authorities after members were said to have criticized Jewish students as lacking interest in athletics because of other activities. The council recommended that the number of Jews admitted to Syracuse be limited. The faculty of Syracuse reportedly quashed this move by the students.
12. Louis E. Wise, "American Universities and the Jewish Student," PhiEpQ 6, 2 (June 1923): 12.
13. Edward N. Calisch, "The Jewish Student in American Colleges," PhiEpQ 6, 2 (June 1923): 8.
14. In the Spring of 1921 the Supreme Board of Governors of Alpha Epsilon Pi moved its monthly meetings from Friday to Thursday in order to accommodate Supreme Sentinel M. Farber, who had been unable to attend meetings because of his Sabbath observance. AEPi Minutes, Jan–March 1922, 125, AEPi.
15. Nathan Wolf, Supreme Master of Alpha Epsilon Pi, Address, 1920 Convention Minutes, December 1920, 58, AEPi.

16. Philip D. Sang, "Fraternity Men and Their Jewish Obligations," *Octagonian* 11, 1 (March 1922): 10.
17. Dr. Charles I. Stoloff, "We Jews," *Octagonian* 11, 2 (June 1922): 44; and David I. Arbuse, "Intermarriage: A Point of View," *Octagonian* 12, 2 (June 1923): 3.
18. Emmanuel Abrahamson, "Zionism: The Solution of the Jewish Problem," *Octagonian* 11, 3 (December 1922): 11.
19. Harry S. Winer, "Internal Harmony," *Octagonian* 11, 3 (December 1922): 32.
20. Clipping from the *Indiana Jewish Chronicle*, n.d. [c. 1926], AJA-HUC, Mss. Coll No. 2, Henry Hurwitz Papers, Folder: "Fraternities."
21. Stoloff, 44.
22. William C. Kranowitz, "What Does the Harvard Jewish Expose Mean to Sigma Alpha Mu?" *Octagonian* 11, 3 (Dec. 1922): 8.
23. "A Plea for Snobbishness from an Outsider," ZBTQ 7, 1 (September 1922): 9.
24. "A Plea for Snobbishness," 10.
25. Harold Riegelman. "Pledging Dad: a One-Act Dialogue," ZBTQ 7, 1 (September 1922): 17. This dialogue was first composed by Riegelman in the late 1910s and was frequently reprinted.
26. Dr. Richard C. Cabot, head of the Department of Social Ethics at Harvard University, quoted by Arthur Gleason. The quote and Riegelman's reply to it appear in "The Reason for Jewish Fraternities," ZBTQ 7, 4 (May 1923): 21.
27. Riegelman, "The Reason for Jewish Fraternities," 23.
28. Paul Arthur Yawitz, "Well, ZBT Men *Are* Different," ZBTQ 7, 2 (December 1922): 7–8.
29. Initiation list for fall 1947, University of Washington, membership files (computer database), Alpha Epsilon Pi National Office, Indianapolis, IN. According to George S. Toll, executive director of Alpha Epsilon Pi, who claimed personally to have traveled to Seattle to start the chapter in 1947, the rapid upward mobility and acculturation of the Sephardic Jews of Seattle spelled the death knell of his efforts. Soon both ZBT and SAM were taking them as members, and the depleted Alpha Epsilon Pi chapter was forced to close in 1961. For the full account of the story of one Charles Alhadeff in 1926, see Oral History, University of Washington, Mss.v.f. 1263, No. 3290, transcript of an interview by Howard Droker, May 3, 1982, Seattle, Washington. Charles Alhadeff, whose father Nessim had emigrated from Rhodes, and his friend John Franco were rushed by ZBT in the fall of 1926, along with several other graduates of Temple DeHirsch's religious school. As a classical Reform Jewish institution, Temple DeHirsch was a natural recruiting ground for ZBT, and Charles had in fact been specifically sent there by his father rather than to the Sephardi synagogue school in order that his son might have contacts among the greater Seattle Jewish community. After six weeks, however, both Alhadeff and Franco were called in and depledged. "It was a matter of a tremendous amount of conversation and discussion in the community at the time," recalled Alhadeff fifty-six years later, "the feeling being that we, being 'Sephs,' were not welcome and were depledged. . . . It pretty well ruined my college life," In the late 1950s, Charles' son Jerry Alhadeff was rushed by ZBT. At first he refused to join because of what had been done to his father,

whereupon a delegation of ZBT reportedly visited Charles Alhadeff in his home to apologize for the fraternity's past actions, to say that in their time such a thing would not happen, and to ask Charles to please urge his son to join them. Charles Alhadeff did so. Both Jerry Alhadeff and later his brother Jack became full ZBT members, living in the chapter house. I am indebted to Julie Niebuhr Eulenberg of the University of Washington for her helpfulness and consideration in supplying me with this transcript.

30. Report from Beatrice Feingold, with handwritten comments by Bertha Feitel, n.d. [c. 1929] Alpha Epsilon Phi archives, Norwich, CT [hereafter cited as AEPhi], Box 3, Notebook 4: "Council Decisions 1929–1931." According to Baird, 20th ed., the Penn State chapter of Alpha Epsilon Phi was discontinued in 1931. It was revived in 1959, and then closed again in 1970.
31. Western Union Telegram from Bertha Feitel (New Orleans, LA) to Beatrice Feingold (33 Riverside Drive, New York City) n.d. [c. 1930], AEPhi, Box 3, Notebook 2: "Council Votes and Decisions December 1929–April 1932." Western Union telegrams were a typical method of performing quick investigations of candidates across the country during the sorority's rushing season.
32. Memo from Dorothea Slepyan, Field Secretary, to National Council, subject: Chapter Investigation (Eta: State Normal School, Albany), AEPhi, Box 3, Notebook 1: "Council Decisions 1921–1927," 9.
33. Report from Beatrice Feingold with Bertha Feitel's handwritten comments, AEPhi, Box 3, Notebook 4: "Council Decisions 1929–1931," 1.
34. Ruth I. Wien, National Scribe, to National Council, October 19, 1926, AEPhi, Box 3, Notebook 1: "Council Decisions 1921–1927."
35. Freda M. Rosenthal, National Dean, to Ruth I. Wien, October 23, 1926, AEPhi, Box 3, Notebook 1: "Council Decisions 1921–1927."
36. Stella Caplan Bloom, National Ritualist, to Ruth I. Wien, October 25, 1926, AEPhi, Box 3, Notebook 1: "Council Decisions 1921–1927"
37. Bertha W. Feitel, National Historian, to National Council, December 19, 1926, AEPhi, Box 3, Notebook 1: "Council Decisions 1921–1927."
38. *Alpha Epsilon Phi Rushing Manual* (c. 1920s), 17. Miscellaneous files.
39. Percy Pachtman, Province Master, Central Atlantic Province, Phi Epsilon Pi, to Maurice Jacobs, Grand Council, July 28, 1921, 6, AJHS-PHIEP, Box 18, Folder: "Mid Atlantic."
40. Maurice Jacobs to Percy Pachtman, July 29, 1921, AJHS-PHIEP, Box 18, Folder: "Mid Atlantic."
41. Harry L. Becker, corresponding secretary, to Maurice Jacobs, corresponding secretary, February 15, 1921, AJHS-PHIEP, Box 28, Folder: "Kappa."
42. "A Plea to the Conscience of the Fraternity," petition dated December 1921, signed by Robert I Rogin, Irving D. Lipkowitz, Saul W. Fleischer, Louis Mitchell, and Harry L. Wechsler, Chairman, AJHS-PHIEP, Box 28, Folder: "Kappa."
43. Hyman S. Mayerson, President, Brown University Menorah Society, to Julietta Kahn, Corresponding Secretary, Intercollegiate Menorah Association, April 17, 1922, AJA-HUC, Mss. Coll. No. 2, Henry Hurwitz Papers, Box 70, Folder 10: "Brown University 1921–1922."
44. Marcus H. Rabinowitz, President, University of Minnesota Menorah Society,

to Julietta Kahn, December 9, 1921, AJA-HUC, Mss. Coll. No. 2, Henry Hurwitz Papers, Box 73, Folder 7: "University of Minnesota 1921–1922." Dr. Moses Barron was on the faculty of the medical school.

45. Julietta Kahn, Semi-Annual Report, September 1923, AJA-HUC, Mss. Coll. No. 2, Henry Hurwitz Papers, Box 67, Folder 3: "Reports: Surveys and Membership Lists 1923–1930."

46. Arthur D. Schwartz. "An Intruder at the Supreme Council," ZBTQ 7, 2 (December 1922): 22.

47. George J. Hirsch, "Sans Rhyme or Reason," *Octagonian* 11, 1 (March 1922), 63–65.

48. David Paull, "Sartor Resartus," PhiEpQ 6, 3 (September 1923): 5–6.

49. Kalman R. Plessner, "Pioneers of Thought," ZBTQ 12, 2 (December 1927): 15.

50. ZBTQ (fall 1925), quoted in *Banta's Greek Exchange* (January 1925): 82.

51. Little Stone Pomeroy [pseud.], "Blackball," ZBTQ 14, 2 (January 1930): 10.

52. Bernard A. Bergman, "A Survey of Campus Prejudice," ZBTQ 7, 3 (March 1923): 20.

53. Benjamin D. Salinger, "On Being Too Jewish," ZBTQ 7, 4 (May 1923): 12.

54. Salinger, 15.

CHAPTER 7

1. Goodwin B. Auerbach, "The Four-Year Loaf and the Hungry Undergraduate," ZBTQ 15, 4 (October 1931): 22.

2. Kalman B. Druck, "They Came for the Ride," ZBTQ 17, 4 (March 1936): 13.

3. Jerome L. Schwartz, "We Grow Up, 1915–1938," ZBTQ 20, 3, (December 1938): 12–13.

4. Jerome L. Schwartz, 14.

5. See correspondence between Maurice Jacobs and Samuel J. Sherman (attorney and president of the Phi Epsilon Pi Chicago alumni association), November 22–24, 1933, AJHS-PHIEP, Box 21, Folder: "Gamma [Northwestern] to 1936." The folder contains a November 21, 1933, clipping from the *Chicago Daily News:* "Plan to Merge 2 Universities: No Change in Situation Since First Talk Last August."

6. Lee Dover, editorial, ZBTQ 15, 4 (October 1931): 3.

7. Supreme Council Minutes, September 18, 1939, 9, SAM Archives, Carmel, IN.

8. Elizabeth Eldridge, "On Our Way to the Corner," *Columns of Alpha Epsilon Phi* [hereafter cited as *Columns*] 17, 1 (January 1933): 22.

9. Supreme Council Minutes, December 6, 1933, 216, SAM.

10. Dr. Henry Suzzallo, "Fraternity System Problems," address delivered at the 23rd Annual Session of the National Interfraternity Conference in New York, November 27, 1931. Reprinted in ZBTQ 16, 1 (January 1932): 14–19.

11. Lee Dover, editorial, ZBTQ 17, 4 (March 1936): 7.

12. Correspondence between Samuel J. Sherman and Maurice Jacobs, November 22–24, 1933, AJHS-PHIEP, Box 21, Folder: "Gamma [Northwestern] to 1936." "You doubtless know that Chicago is definitely committed to an

anti-fraternity policy. It has no sororities and by means of new dormitories, offering luxurious quarters and excellent meals at greatly reduced rates, in the space of a year or two has crippled Chicago's fraternities and insured their early extinction."

13. Bruce H. McIntosh, compiler, "Statistics Regarding College Fraternities," May 1933, AJHS-PHIEP, Box 3, Folder: "History and Purpose of Phi Epsilon Pi." The list includes figures for all 72 NIC-member men's fraternities.

14. Eleventh meeting, Supreme Board of Governors, minutes, December 1, 1930. AEPi. A chart on the comparative mortality of Jewish fraternity chapters was prepared and presented by Edwarde [sic] Perlson.

15. Maurice Jacobs, Executive Secretary, memo to members of the Grand Council and the Extension Committee, June 21, 1934, 2, AJHS-PHIEP, Box 12, Folder: "Extension Committee."

16. Report on Sigma Zeta [Indiana] chapter, 193, Supreme Council minutes, April 2, 1935, SAM. The chapter had 23 actives and 4 pledges, all living in a former private dwelling at 421 Fess Ave. There were reportedly 110 Jews on campus, and the only other Jewish fraternity was Phi Beta Delta, which also had a full house.

17. Letter to the author from Hyman Meltz, Class of '41, N.Y. State College for Teachers at Albany (later the State University of New York at Albany), May 30, 1991. Meltz served as an English teacher and assistant principal in the New York City school system for 25 years. Members of the original group remained in close contact and celebrated the 50th anniversary of Kappa Beta's founding in 1986.

18. Supreme Council Minutes, May 23, 1939, 1, SAM.

19. "Round Table Discussion, December 30, 1937: Planning a Rush Program," minutes of discussions at the annual convention held at the Carter Hotel in Cleveland, 6–9, AJHS-PHIEP, Box 7, Folder: "1937."

20. Maurice Jacobs, *Phi Epsilon Pi Rush Manual*, ed. Maurice G. Gurin, Executive Secretary (1938 and 1941), 5, AJHS-PHIEP, Box, 46, Folder: "Rush Manuals."

21. Jacobs, *Rush Manual*, 29.

22. Jacobs, *Rush Manual*, 23.

23. Jacobs, *Rush Manual*, 28.

24. *Sigma Delta Tau Rush Manual*, ed. Louise Lehmann (summer 1937), 16, SDT.

25. Elizabeth Eldridge, National Dean, to National Council, April 2, 1935, 8, AEPhi, Box 3, Notebook 7, "Council Decisions and Votes 1934–1936."

26. Viola Lang Rusnak, National Field Secretary, to National Council, June 23, 1936, subject: "Expansion L.S.U," 1, AEPhi, Box: "Archives," Folder: "Petitioning Groups Not Accepted 1928–1936." According to the report, there were then 45 Jewish women on the L.S.U. campus. "The best" were all members of Sigma Delta Tau, while the 18 left unaffiliated were not considered AEPhi material—hence, the need to colonize.

27. Eleanor G. Reinach, 4th Province Director, to National Council, October 6, 1938, subject: "Minnesota," 3, AEPhi, Box: "Archives," Folder: "Petitioning Groups Not Accepted, 1928–1936."

28. Maurice Jacobs to Grand Council and Extension Committee, May 2, 1932,

subject: "Results of Survey," AJHS-PHIEP, Box 12, Folder: "Extension Committee."

29. See Maurice Jacobs's December 1932 speech before the Phi Epsilon Pi convention, AJHS-PHIEP, Box 10, Folder: "Secretary," for reference to the Dartmouth announcement (11). In addition, according to Jacobs, five or six other outstanding Jewish men at Dartmouth had been in effect lost to the Gentiles. For reference to the freshmen quota of 30 Jewish men a year and concern that this would mean the end of Jewish fraternities at Dartmouth, see the report of James C. Hammerstein, Executive Secretary, Supreme Council Minutes, March 17, 1935, 171, SAM.

30. James C. Hammerstein, Executive Secretary, visitation report on Dartmouth College, March 17, 1935, SAM.

31. Maurice Jacobs, speech before the Phi Epsilon Pi convention, December 1932, 11, AJHS-PHIEP, Box 10, Folder: "Secretary."

32. James C. Hammerstein, visitation report on Syracuse, March 17, 1935, 72, SAM. He reported that the chapter held a "fine" house at 712 Comstock Ave., which was owned by the alumni.

33. James C. Hammerstein, visitation report on McGill University, March 17, 1935, 171, SAM.

34. Maurice Jacobs, Executive Secretary, report to members of the Grand Council and the Extension Committee, June 21, 1934, 5, AJHS-PHIEP, Box 12, Folder: "Extension Committee." Reference to the restricted 3 percent Jewish enrollment at Duke appears in his December 1932 convention speech, 15, AJHS-PHIEP, Box 10, Folder: "Secretary." The one Jewish fraternity on campus that year was Phi Sigma Delta, which had pledged 18 out of 34 Jewish men on campus.

35. James C. Hammerstein, visitation report on Purdue University, May 21, 1935, Supreme Council Meeting, May 31, 1935, 194, SAM.

36. Ibid.

37. Maurice Jacobs, Executive Secretary, report, "To the Grand Superior and Fratres [sic] of the 1932 Convention," December 1932. 12–13, AJHS-PHIEP, Box 10, Folder: "Secretary."

38. Elizabeth Eldridge, National Dean, to National Council, March 31, 1933, subject: "Charter for William and Mary, No. 1," 6, AEPhi, Box: "Archives," Folder: "Petitioning Groups Not Accepted 1928–1936."

39. Elizabeth Eldridge, National Dean, to National Council, March 31, 1933, 6.

40. Elizabeth Eldridge to National Council, March 31, 1933, 6. Dr. Julian Alvin Carroll Chandler served as President of the College of William and Mary from 1919 to 1934.

41. Elizabeth Eldridge, National Dean, to National Council, May 25, 1933, subject: "Fate of Local at William and Mary No. 2, Letters," 2, AEPhi, Box: "Archives," Folder: "Petitioning Groups Not Accepted 1928–1936." The memo, along with an explanation of the circumstances of the denial, contains copies of the two letters, Eldridge's to Chandler on May 10 and Chandler's reply on May 17, 1933.

42. Elizabeth Eldridge to National Council, May 25, 1933.

43. Elizabeth Eldridge to National Council, May 21, 1933, subject: "Fate of Pe-

titioning Local at William and Mary," AEPhi, Box: "Archives," Folder: "Petitioning Groups Not Accepted 1928–1936." This memo contains the text of the letter from Lucille Fritz, who was president of the petitioning local and would have been Dean of the chapter under the national aegis of Alpha Epsilon Phi.

44. Maurice Jacobs, Executive Secretary, memo to members of the Grand Council, March 5, 1932, AJHS-PHIEP, Box 12, Folder: "Extension Committee."

45. Maurice Jacobs to Grand Council, March 5, 1932. See clipping, Austin M. Fisher, "Is Wesleyan Fair to the Jews?" *Wesleyan Argus*, February 18, 1932. The *Argus* appeared bi-weekly, on Monday and Thursdays.

46. Austin M. Fisher.

47. Maurice Jacobs to Grand Council, March 5, 1932. Alumni attending the meeting included attorney Louis Rosenfeld, Dave Levey, Eli Lifschuts, and Sam Susselman. The eighteen Wesleyan undergraduates were then placed under the supervision of Rabbi Feldman of Hartford, which was located only a half-hour drive from Middletown.

48. Clipping from the *Wesleyan Argus*, February 22, 1932, AJHS-PHIEP, Box 12, Folder: "Extension Committee": "McConaughy Defines University Position on Jewish Question; Situation Not Acute. 'Perhaps Over-emphasized,' by Mr. Fisher, But Latter's Article 'Thought-provoking.'"

49. M. M. Resnikoff, letter to the editor, *Wesleyan Argus*, Thursday, February 25, 1932. See clipping in AJHS-PHIEP, Box 12, Folder: "Extension Committee."

50. Resnikoff, letter to the editor.

51. Louis B. Rosenfeld (attorney and Phi Epsilon Pi alumnus in Hartford, CT) to Maurice Jacobs, March 15, 1932, AJHS-PHIEP, Box 12, Folder: "Extension Committee."

52. Herman E. Colitz to Maurice Jacobs, March 14, 1932, AJHS-PHIEP, Box 12, Folder: "Extension Committee."

53. Herman E. Colitz to Maurice Jacobs, March 14, 1932.

54. Herman E. Colitz to Maurice Jacobs, November 6, 1933, AJHS-PHIEP, Box 12, Folder: "Extension Committee."

55. Maurice Jacobs to Herman E. Colitz November 7, 1933, AJHS-PHIEP, Box 12, Folder: "Extension Committee."

56. Maurice Jacobs to Grand Council, March 5, 1932. In his description of the alumni meeting, Jacobs referred to the founding of Ivy Club and the belief of the alumni and undergraduates that the building could easily and inexpensively be obtained for a fraternity house.

57. Maurice Jacobs, "To the Grand Superior and Fratres [sic]," December 1932. See his report on the possibilities of extension at Amherst, Wesleyan, and Williams, 12.

58. AEPhi, Box 6, Notebook 2: "Council Minutes and Correspondence August 1937–September 1939." For discussion of what was termed "the prevailing Jewish problem " at the University of Maryland, see the reports of Marian Diamond to the National Dean, January 31, 1938, subject: "Visit to the University of Maryland Local: Alpha Sigma," 3–5, and Florence Orringer to the National Dean, February 27, 1939, subject: "Visits to University of Maryland

Local: Alpha Sigma No. 3," 2–3. Anti-Jewish feeling and the absolute refusal of the local IFC or Panhellenic to accept Jewish groups, along with the low number of and general lack of social life for Jewish students, convinced AEPhi officials not to establish a chapter there. Wrote Marian Diamond: "We would have this to fight against continually and I see no reason for going in when this has been made so obvious" (8).

59. Report of Executive Secretary James C. Hammerstein on visit to Sigma Chi [Maryland] chapter, March 27, 1935, Supreme Council Minutes, April 2, 1935, SAM. Hammerstein reported approximately 100 Jews on the campus with an average of 35 entering each year. Tau Epsilon Phi and Phi Alpha had already established chapters there.

60. See "Theta Chapter—University of Pennsylvania," Supreme Council Minutes, April 2, 1935, SAM, on Executive Secretary James C. Hammerstein's visit to the campus. All available Jewish fraternity records contain frequent references to the A and B division at Penn.

61. Elizabeth Eldridge, National Dean, to National Council, subject: "Panhellenic At California," December 13, 1934, AEPhi, Box 3, Notebook 7: "Council Decisions And Votes 1934–1936."

62. Elizabeth Eldridge to National Council, December 13, 1934, 3.

63. Elizabeth Eldridge to National Council, December 13, 1934, 5. Mortimer and later Herbert Fleishhacker were both Regents and prominent donors to the University of California at Berkeley. On November 27, 1934, a special meeting of the local Panhellenic was held to vote both Jewish sororities at the University of California into full membership, although a technicality in the resolution assured that their representatives would not be eligible for the presidency of that body for more than a quarter of a century.

64. See Baird, 20th.ed, s.v. "National Interfraternity Conference," and "National Panhellenic Conference."

65. For a description of NIC judicial activity and the role of Harold Riegelman of ZBT, see Baird, 12th ed., 19.

66. For examples of unsuccessful petitions of Jewish sororities to NPC in the 1920s, see memorandum from Alice B. Greene, National Dean, to the Field Secretary, subject: Pan-Hellenic Petition, October 25, 1921, AEPhi, Box 3, Notebook 1: "Council Decisions 1921–1927,": "Despite all our efforts, it is still very doubtful whether we will succeed this time"; Report on Pan-Hellenic petition, January 2, 1929, AEPhi, Box 3, Notebook 2: "Council Votes and Decisions December 1929–April 1932": "N.P.C. has refused our recent petition. Miss Leonard notified me very courteously and promptly. She says 'the negative vote was due to your restricted membership.' " See also minutes of the second biennial convention of Sigma Delta Tau, Buffalo, NY, December 22, 1924, and minutes of the annual meeting of the National Council of Sigma Delta Tau, Indianapolis, IN, September 1–3, 1925, SDT.

67. See reports of Alpha Epsilon Phi Panhellenic Chairman Elizabeth Eldridge, *passim*, AEPhi, Box 3, Notebook 7: "Council Decisions and Votes 1934–1936." Eldridge frequently used the example of the Phi Mu constitution in her efforts to prove that her own sorority was no less restrictive or limited in its membership than those who were already members of the NPC. It should

be noted, however, that the leaders of Phi Mu were among the earliest supporters coming out openly for admission of Alpha Epsilon Phi to the NPC.
The leaders of Chi Omega, however, consistently opposed it.
68. See AEPhi, Box 3, Notebook 7: "Council Decisions and Votes 1934–1936,"
which contains much of the abundant material relating to Alpha Epsilon Phi's
battle for NPC recognition. References to the Christian nature of NPC as a
basis for exclusion appear throughout the file. For the most specific instance,
see copy of a letter from L. Pearle Green, President, Kappa Alpha Theta, to
Mrs. Clyde L. Shepard, Chairman, NPC Committee on Eligibility of New
Groups, February 1935, describing the reasons formerly given for rejecting
AEPhi and her recommendation that they be admitted: "The dissenting fra-
ternities claim that they are strictly 'Christian' fraternities and would have
to withdraw from NPC if groups not 'Christian,' within their definition of
that word, were admitted," 2. See also memo from Elizabeth Eldridge to
National Council, April 21, 1936, subject: "Report of Convention of Urban
Panhellenics, April 17–18, 1936, Columbus," 2, AEPhi, Box 3 Notebook 8:
"Council Votes and Decisions 1934–1937," for a description of a speech by
Cora Rader, NPC delegate of Phi Mu, in which she refers to the "Christian"
nature of NPC sororities.
69. See memo from Elizabeth Eldridge, April 21, 1936.
70. Eldridge, April 21, 1936, 8.
71. Elizabeth Eldridge, National Panhellenic Chairman, to National Council,
October 22, 1938, subject: "National Panhellenic," 1, AEPhi, Box 3, Notebook 12: "Votes and Decisions of National Council 1938–1940."
72. Eldridge to National Council, October 22, 1938.
73. Executive Board Minutes, December 11–15, 1939, section: "Panhellenic,"
18–19, AEPhi, Box 6, Notebook 1: "Council Minutes 1934–1941."

CHAPTER 8

1. Lee Dover, editorial. ZBTQ 15, 4 (October 1931): 3; surveys quoted in Hy
Copins, "What's What Among the Chapters," ZBTQ 16, 3 (October 1932):
37; Elizabeth Eldridge. "On our Way to the Corner," *Columns* 17, 1 (January
1933): 22. By 1932 AEPhi's pledge class numbered 210 women across the
country and the numbers appeared to be increasing.
2. Noel Revod [pseud. of Leon Dover], "Who's Who Among the Alumni,"
ZBTQ 20, 2 (October 1938): 33. Paley appeared on the cover of *Time* 32, 12
(September 19, 1938).
3. Lee Dover. "ZBT's Second Rhodes Scholar," ZBTQ 18, 4 (March 1937): 6;
Leslie Epstein (Illinois '35) "Something About Oxford," ZBTQ 20, 3 (December 1938): 6.
4. Marty Glickman with Stan Isaacs. *The Fastest Kid on the Block: The Marty
Glickman Story.* (Syracuse: Syracuse University Press, 1996), 14–24, 41–42.
5. *Columns* 14, 2 (January 15, 1930). "A-Camping We Will Go" by Beta [Hun-
ter] chapter describes the chapters' summer weekends at a bungalow in Long
Branch on the Jersey shore (19). "The Rotenberg Family Embarks for Foreign
Lands," (*Columns* 16, 2 [March 1932]: 11) describes the cruise of a lead-

ing Toronto Jewish family to England for a "family reunion," The writer, Gertrude Rotenberg, describes meeting Sir Herbert Samuel, Gandhi, John Masefield, George Bernard Shaw, and other British luminaries. Her sister Hilda was staying on in Geneva with a Monsieur Dalcroze to study "both the art of dancing and French," In the same issue, "Meet Mrs. Peter Seitz!" (20) described the successes of Myra Patricia Tolins, who followed a brilliant scholastic career at Cornell 1924–1929 with a year at the University of Paris where she earned her M.A. in French. "Alpha Delta Goes to Sea" (18, 3 [May 1934]: 38) describes the spring house parties of the University of Washington chapter; twenty-two couples boarded a yacht on Lake Washington to watch the crew races between California and Washington. The races were followed by a cruise around the lake, supper served on board the yacht, and dancing.

6. Lee Dover, editorial. ZBTQ 15, 3 (June 1931): 3.
7. Alumni Notes, ZBTQ 17, 1 (June 1935): 33.
8. AJA-HUC, Mss. Coll. No. 177, Irvin Fane Papers [hereafter cited as Fane Papers], Box 31, Folder: "ZBT Correspondence 1939." The folder contains a complete list of the furnishings for the University of Missouri chapter house.
9. Alfred M. Coplon, "What's What Among the Chapters," ZBTQ 19, 2 (October 1937): 27.
10. Elizabeth Eldridge, National Dean, to National Council, April 2, 1935, subject: "Alabama," 3–7, AEPhi, Box 3, Notebook 7: "Council Decisions and Votes 1934–1936."
11. Minutes of Supreme Council meeting, May 17, 1931, 5, SAM. At that meeting, the officers rejected as "not desirable" petitioning chapters from Temple University, Long Island University, and New York University's downtown division.
12. AEPi, Minutes of 19th Convention in Atlanta, GA, December 28, 1932.
13. Description of the upcoming convention in Chicago, *The Periodical Newsletter* 1, 5 (November 23, 1934), AJHS-PHIEP, Box 7, Folder: "1934."
14. Richard A. Freiberger, Chairman of the Women's Committee, to Fratres [sic], October 30, 1937, AJHS-PHIEP, Box 7, Folder: "1937."
15. Irvin Fane to Mrs. S.F. Kiely of Kansas City, Missouri, April 9, 1938, Fane Papers, Box 30, Folder: "ZBT Correspondence 1930–1938." "Complying with your request, the following are young, unmarried members of the Alumni Club of Zeta Beta Tau."
16. Arthur Donald Schwartz. "A Day at the Central Office [New York City]; or, Imitating Seventeen Hawaiians," ZBTQ 17, 1 (June 1935): 22.
17. Dr. Lee J. Levinger, *The Jewish Student in America: A Study Made by the Research Bureau of the B'nai B'rith Hillel Foundations* (Cincinnati, 1937), 18, 42–44, 91–95. Heywood Broun and George Britt, in their report *Christians Only* (New York: Vanguard Press, 1931) wrote: "Hundreds of Jewish college students from the East every year go South and to the Middle West, fleeing discrimination. It would be possible to trace this motive, rather than to money and professionalism, the presence on obscure Southern church college teams of many star Jewish athletes from the North" (83).
18. For the most valuable and detailed numerical survey of Jewish students at different campuses in the 1930s, see Synnott, "Anti-Semitism and American Universities", 244–248 and Levinger, *The Jewish Student in America.*

19. See *The Hillel Digest* 1, 4 (May 1940), Student Periodical Collections, HUC, Cincinnati, 1.
20. Maurice Jacobs, "To the Grand Superior and Fratres [sic]" December 1932, 13.
21. Supreme Council Minutes, November 1, 1937, 133, SAM.
22. Maurice Jacobs, Traveling Secretary, report on Theta [Penn State] chapter, April 10, 1922, quoting 1915 report, AJHS-PHIEP, Box 12, Folder 20, "Secretary."
23. Louis Fushan, Grand Vice-Superior, report to members of the Grand Council, December 1927, AJHS-PHIEP, Box 12, Folder: "Vice-Superior."
24. Letter from Charles Schlow to Maurice Jacobs, January 14, 1934, AJHS-PHIEP, Box 27, Folder: "Theta [Penn State] 1934–1947." Charles Schlow, who lived near Penn State, was devoted to the Jewish students in attendance there and in particular became a combination of advisor, mentor, and father-figure to the members of Phi Epsilon Pi. He was known to several generations of Penn State Jewish students as "Uncle Charlie."
25. AEPhi, Box: Archives, Folder: "Petitioning Groups Not Accepted, 1928–1938." Marion Diamond to National Council, November 21, 1935. Subject: Investigation of L'Amite at Penn State College.
26. Pascal A. Greenberg, Executive Secretary, to members of the Grand Council, re: April 28–30, 1939, visitation to Penn State and Muhlenberg colleges, May 3, 1939, AJHS-PHIEP, Box 26, Folder: "Theta" [Penn State]. The report noted that 112 alumni and their wives attended the weekend events.
27. Maurice Jacobs to Rabbi Martin Weitz (Hillel Foundation, Northwestern University), October 26, 1935, AJHS-PHIEP, Box 21, Folder: "Gamma" [Northwestern] to 1936." For another description of the standing-room only High Holy Day services at Penn State, see Maurice Jacobs to Abram Sachar, October 6, 1935, AJHS-PHIEP, Box 17A, Folder: "Abram L. Sachar 1925–1955."
28. For a front-page photograph of Phi Epsilon Pi's first *sukkah* at Penn State along with full coverage of the event, see *The Hillel Digest* 2, 2 (December 1939): 1, available in the Jewish Student Periodicals Collection, HUC, Cincinnati.
29. Maurice Jacobs, "Results of Survey," memo to Grand Council and Extension Committee, May 2, 1932, AJHS-PHIEP, Box 12, Folder: "Extension Committee." The questionnaire was sent to 120 colleges and universities, and 75 responded. There were eight questions: 1. Number of male Jewish students registered this year. 2. Average number of Jewish male students registering past five years. 3. Are Jewish students admitted to general fraternities? 4. Are there Jewish fraternities on campus? 5. If so, which ones? 6. Are these fraternities recognized by the authorities? 7. Are they members of the local Interfraternity Council? 8. Would your administration permit Jewish fraternities to organize? Of the 70 colleges responding which had more than five Jewish students on campus, 51 categorically would not admit Jews to their general fraternities; eight would admit Jews seldom or occasionally, and nine answered "Yes." Other schools with notable Jewish populations and one or more Jewish fraternities described in the survey included Western Reserve (254, Phi Sigma Delta, Zeta Beta Tau); Rhode Island State (58, Alpha Ep-

silon Pi); University of Maine (52, Tau Epsilon Phi); University of Nebraska, (72, down from a 5–year average of 107, with Zeta Beta Tau and Sigma Alpha Mu on campus); Tulane (150, Zeta Beta Tau, Sigma Alpha Mu, Kappa Nu); University of West Virginia (136, Phi Sigma Delta, Pi Lambda Phi, Phi Alpha); University of Oklahoma (65, Sigma Alpha Mu and Phi Beta Delta); University of Texas (175, down from an average of 200, Phi Sigma Delta, Sigma Alpha Mu, Tau Delta Phi, Zeta Beta Tau); University of Colorado (54, Phi Beta Delta, Phi Sigma Delta); State University of New York at Buffalo (279, Beta Sigma Rho, Kappa Nu, Omicron Alpha Tau, Sigma Alpha Mu); University of Southern California (200, Alpha Epsilon Pi, Phi Beta Delta, Tau Delta Phi, Tau Epsilon Phi, and Zeta Beta Tau); University of North Dakota (25, Tau Delta Phi); University of Richmond (42, Phi Alpha); Union College (81, Zeta Beta Tau, Kappa Nu, Alpha Mu Sigma and Phi Sigma Delta); Franklin and Marshall (59, up from an average of 50, Zeta Beta Tau) and the University of Vermont (55, Phi Sigma Delta, Tau Epsilon Phi).

30. Maurice Jacobs, Executive Secretary, to Members of the Grand Council and the Extension Committee, April 24, 1935, 2, AJHS-PHIEP, Box 12, Folder: "Extension Committee."

31. Louise W. Wolf to Elizabeth Eldridge, November 9, 1933. Also see correspondence between Louise W. Wolf, Elizabeth Eldridge, and Ruth B. Rosenthaler, November 9–19, 1933, AEPhi, Box 3, Notebook 5: "Council Votes 1932–1934." An extensive discussion took place between national officials on the wisdom of establishing chapters at the state universities of Georgia, Alabama, and Maryland, where local groups were petitioning them for membership.

32. Maurice Jacobs, report to the Grand Convention in Pittsburgh, December 1935, 18, AJHS-PHIEP, Box 10, Folder: "Secretary."

33. James Hammerstein, Executive Secretary, report on visits to eleven chapters, February 10–March 27, 1938, Supreme Council Minutes, 181, SAM.

34. Maurice Jacobs, report before the 1932 Convention, December 1932, 28, AJHS-PHIEP, Box 10, Folder: "Secretary."

35. Fanny Dennery (alumna of Newcomb, resident of Birmingham, AL) to National Council, November 8, 1933, subject: "Report on Petitioning Group at University of Alabama," 1–3, AEPHi, Box 3, Notebook 5: "Council Votes 1932–34."

36. Elizabeth Eldridge, National Dean, to National Council, April 2, 1935, subject: "Alabama," 3, AEPhi, Box 3, Notebook 7: "Council Decisions and Votes 1934–36."

37. Maurice Jacobs, memo to the Grand Council and the Extension Committee, February 25, 1937, 3, AJHS-PHIEP, Box 12, Folder: "Extension Committee." The information in the Phi Epsilon Pi files on the University of Alabama is inexplicably in variance with the chapter roster published in the 20th ed. of Baird, which shows a chapter established at Alabama in 1921 (VIII-15).

38. Maurice Jacobs, report to the Grand Council and the Extension Committee, June 21, 1934, 3, AJHS-PHIEP, Box 12, Folder: "Extension Committee."

39. See Baird, 20th.ed, VIII-15.

40. Maurice Jacobs, memo to the Grand Council and the Extension Committee, June 21, 1934, 3, AJHS-PHIEP, Box 12, Folder: "Extension Committee." Fourteen men at St. John's belonged to a Jewish local called the Key Society, and Jacobs recommended keeping close watch on them as a potential chapter. However, Phi Epsilon Pi lost its opportunity when the group was pledged by Phi Alpha in 1936.

41. Maurice Jacobs, Executive Secretary, speech to the 1932 Grand Convention, AJHS-PHIEP, Box 10, Folder: "Secretary."

42. Maurice Jacobs, Executive Secretary, speech to the 1932 Grand Convention, December 1932, 16. Maurice Jacobs reported a well-established and well-recognized Jewish local at Ohio University there by the name of Phi Upsilon.

43. Mary Wiener to National Council, October 2, 1932, subject: "Report on Miami U at Oxford, Ohio," AEPhi, Box: "Archives," Folder: "Petitioning Groups Not Accepted, 1928–1938." An AEPhi chapter was eventually installed there in 1940.

44. See results of survey in Maurice Jacobs to Grand Council and Extension Committee, May 2, 1932, AJHS-PHIEP, Box 12, Folder: "Extension Committee."

45. Maurice Jacobs to Grand Council and Extension Committee, May 2, 1932. In 1932 there were 61 Jewish men attending Alfred University, up from an average of 44 in the previous five years.

46. Lillian Newmans, 4th Province Director, to National Council, March 29, 1932, subject: "Disc" Local at Butler University, 1–2, AEPhi, Box: "Archives," Folder: "Petitioning Groups Not Accepted, 1928–1938."

47. Ruth Newman, 5th Province Director, to National Council, March 31, 1932, subject: "Additional Remarks on Butler Investigation," 2, AEPhi, Box: "Archives," Folder: "Petitioning Groups Not Accepted, 1928–1938."

48. Newman to National Council, March 31, 1932, 2.

49. Roz J. Silver to National Council, October 7, 1932, subject: "Report on Butler," 1, AEPhi, Box: "Archives," Folder: "Petitioning Groups Not Accepted, 1928–1938."

50. May Elish Markewich to Executive Board, March 21, 1938, subject: "Investigation of Delta Eta Phi, University of Newark," AEPhi, Box 3, Notebook 10: "Council Votes April 1937–August 1938."

51. John H. Cohen, Chairman of the Extension Committee, "Report of the Extension Committee," December 1939, AJHS-PHIEP, Box 12, Folder: "Extension Committee."

52. The University of Akron (Theta Deuteron) chapter of Alpha Epsilon Pi became inactive in 1973.

53. Maurice Jacobs, Executive Secretary, memo to members of the Grand Council and the Extension Committee, June 21, 1934, 1, AJHS-PHIEP, Box 12, Folder: "Extension Committee."

54. National Field Secretary to National Council, November 21, 1930, subject: "Investigation of Sigma Tau Petitioning from University of Maine," 2, AEPhi, Box: "Archives," Folder: "Petitioning Groups Not Accepted, 1928–1986." The report noted that there were eight sororities on the campus, two of them local and the rest national.

55. Elizabeth Eldridge, National Dean, to National Council, April 1, 1933, subject: "Condition of Alpha Gamma" [University of Washington], 1, AEPhi, Box 3, Notebook 2: "Council Votes and Decisions December 1929–April 1932."
56. Elizabeth Eldridge, National Dean, and Viola Rusnak, National Editor, to National Council, March 7, 1933, subject: "Investigation of Iowa University Local Sorority Petition No. 2," 2, AEPhi, Box: "Archives," Folder: "Petitioning Groups Not Accepted, 1928–1938." The terms "milchig" and "fleishig" —Yiddish for dairy and meat products—were used by Jews who observed the dietary laws and kept the two separate.
57. Elizabeth Eldridge, National Dean, to National Council, March 9, 1933, subject: "Charter for Indiana No. 1," 1, AEPhi, Box 3, Notebook 6: "Votes and Decisions National Council 1933–1934."
58. Eldridge to National Council, March 9, 1933, 3–4.
59. Elizabeth Eldridge to National Council, March 14, 1933, AEPhi, Box 3, Notebook 6: "Votes and Decisions National Council 1933–1934."
60. Elizabeth Eldridge, National Dean, to National Council, March 31, 1933, subject: "Charter for William and Mary No. 1," 4, AEPhi, Box: "Archives," Folder: "Petitioning Groups Not Accepted 1928–1936."
61. Elizabeth Eldridge, National Dean, to National Council, May 1, 1933, subject: "Local at University of West Virginia," 1, AEPhi, Box: "Archives," Folder: "Petitioning Groups Not Accepted, 1928–1936."
62. Eldridge to National Council, May 1, 1933, 2.
63. Ruth Eldridge, National Editor, to National Council, May 15, 1936, subject: "Report on Investigaton of Alpha Phi Omega, University of Arizona," 1, AEPhi, Box: "Archives," Folder: "Petitioning Groups Not Accepted, 1928–1936."
64. Ruth Eldridge to National Council, May 15, 1936, 5.
65. Marion Diamond to National Council, December 5, 1935, subject: "Investigation of L'Amite at Penn State College—November 21, 1935," 2, AEPhi, Box: "Archives," Folder: "Petitioning Groups Not Accepted, 1928–1936."
66. Marion Diamond to National Council, December 5, 1935, 1.
67. Elizabeth Eldridge, National Dean, to National Council, January 13, 1932, subject: "Investigation, University of Oklahoma," 2, AEPhi, Box: "Archives," Folder: "Petitioning Groups Not Accepted, 1928–1936." In this case, a chapter of Sigma Delta Tau already existed on the campus. There were 30 Jewish women attending Oklahoma at the time, with approximately 16 more planning to attend from the state's public high schools.
68. National field Secretary to National Council, November 21, 1930, subject: "Investigation of Sigma Tau Petitioning from the University of Maine," 1, AEPhi, Box: "Archives," Folder: "Petitioning Groups Not Accepted, 1928–1938."
69. Virginia D. Frolichstein to Elizabeth Eldridge, April 5, 1932, subject: "Investigation of Randolph-Macon Report," 2, AEPhi, Box 3, Notebook 2: "Council Votes and Decisions, December 1929–April 1932."
70. National Ritualist Aline Lazard Roos to National Council, January 19, 1934, subject: "Investigation of Local Nu Beta Phi at Duke University, Durham, NC," 3, AEPhi.

71. See Marianne Sanua, "We Hate New York: Negative Images of the Promised City as a Source for Jewish Fraternity and Sorority Members, 1920–1940," *An Inventory of Promises: Essays on American Jewish History in Honor of Moses Rischin,* ed. Jeffrey S. Gurock and Marc Lee Raphael (Brooklyn: Carlson Publishing, 1995), 235–263.

72. "Problems of an Urban Chapter" was a subject of great concern to the Jewish fraternities. For an interesting discussion on this from the point of view of the students, see Grand Convention Minutes, Roundtable Discussion II, December 31, 1940, 73–75, AJHS-PHIEP, Box 7, Folder: "1940."

73. Lee Dover, "1932 Directory," ZBTQ 16, 1 (January 1932): 7–8.

74. Charles H. Fleishman, Grand Secretary, to Eugene G. Zacharias (in Atlanta), April 24, 1930, 3, AJHS-PHIEP, Box 12, Folder: "Extension Committee."

75. Maurice Jacobs to Herbert Fuhrman, Superior Alpha, September 23, 1936, AJHS-PHIEP, Box 21, Folder: "Alpha" [CCNY]. Jacobs used the expression in congratulating Fuhrman on his recent election as Superior of the chapter.

76. On the financial problems of their Alpha Chapter, also CCNY, see Supreme Council Minutes, February 6, 1934, SAM. The "Prior," or head of the SAM City College chapter, Morton Freedman, visited the Supreme Council meeting to plead his case. Consul James Hammerstein and William Ober, both of them Alpha alumni, offered to assist in the collection of funds from the chapter's alumni.

77. Pascal A. Greenberg, Assistant Executive Secretary, to the Members of the Grand Council, January 29, 1938, "Report on visitation to Alpha chapter at the College of the City of New York," 1, AJHS-PHIEP, Box 21, Folder: "Alpha" [CCNY].

78. Irvin Fane, Midwest Regional Director (in Kansas City) to Lee Dover, General Secretary, November 4, 1944, Fane Papers, Box 33, Folder: "Zeta Beta Tau Correspondence, 1944." The student's name was Eugene Kauffman; his home address was actually given as South Fallsburg, NY (located in the Catskill Mountains), although he had attended a year of high school at De-Witt Clinton High School in New York City.

79. Maurice Jacobs, Executive Secretary, to the Grand Council, January 23, 1932, subject: "Chapter Survey No. 2: Epsilon Chapter—Cornell University, Ithaca, NY," p. 2, AJHS-PHIEP, Box 23, Folder: "Epsilon" [Cornell].

80. Samuel J. Sherman, Grand Councilor, Chicago, to Maury Jacobs, April 10, 1937, AJHS-PHIEP, Box 17, Folder: "Maurice Jacobs."

81. Maurice Jacobs, Executive Secretary, to Samuel J. Sherman, April 20, 1937, AJHS-PHIEP, Box 17, Folder: "Maurice Jacobs."

82. Supreme Council Minutes, June 7, 1937, 124, SAM.

83. See AJHS-PHIEP, Box 29, Folder: "Mu" [University of Georgia], esp. Maurice Jacobs to Rabbi Abraham Shusterman, April 3, 1932; Jacobs' correspondence with Max Michael, Jr., an undergraduate member of the Georgia chapter, November 10 and 23, 1932; Jacobs to Ralph Fineberg, Superior, Mu Chapter, October 1, 1936; Maurice G. Gurin, Executive Secretary, Visitation Report, March 1, 1940.

84. Lee Dover, General Secretary, to Irvin Fane, Trustee Omega [Missouri] Chapter, in Kansas City, August 22, 1945, Fane Papers, Box 34, Folder: "Zeta

Beta Tau, 1951–52." Fane was also requesting references for potential pledges from small towns in Georgia, Maryland, and Missouri.

85. Elizabeth Eldridge, National Dean, to National Council, March 31, 1933, subject: "Charter for William and Mary No. 1," 6, AEPhi, Box: "Archives," Folder: "Petitioning Groups Not Accepted 1928–1936."

86. Rabbi Max Kadushin, "The Migratory Student and His Adjustment," paper presented at a meeting of B'nai B'rith Hillel Foundation Directors, June 2–3, 1937, Martinsville, Indiana, 3. The full transcript of this meeting can be found in the Klau Library, Hebrew Union College, Cincinnati.

87. Kadushin, 5.

88. Kadushin, 4.

89. Kadushin, 5.

90. AEPhi Box 3, Notebook 1: "Council Decisiions 1921–1927." Dorothea Slepyan, field secretary, to National Council, December 13, 1925, 14. Subject: "Field Investigation."

91. AEPhi Box 3, Notebook 8, "Council Votes and Decisions 1934–1937." Evylyn Silverstine, September 21–24, 1936, 2. "Went to see Dr. Sachar . . . to my surprise he hedged and said he was unable to help us. Discovered that he is in a difficult position due to sudden outburst of antisemitism in town. Fifty Jewish girls have left campus being unable to find a place to stay."

92. Kadushin, 6.

CHAPTER 9

1. Interview with Elizabeth Eldridge by author via telephone, November 13, 1994. By then a grandmother of 88, she spoke with wonder and pride of the accomplishments of her own daughters, one of them a college professor and head of her department. Of attitudes and judgments recorded sixty years earlier she confirmed with regret, "Yes, Russian Jews were 'Kikes.' Does that sound crude? It was a question of who got there first. But the fraternity didn't draw those distinctions. It was the community that drew those distinctions. And these were based on the evaluation of the Jewish community by Gentile outsiders."

2. Leo R. Markey, M.D. to Maurice Jacobs, January 29, 1937, AJHS-PHIEP, Box 13, Folder: "Holocaust."

3. Supreme Council Minutes, December 6, 1933, 248, SAM.

4. Discussion of Viereck's connections to Phi Epsilon Pi appear in Maurice Jacobs to Eugene G. Zacharias, Grand Councilor, June 12, 1934, AJHS-PHIEP, Box 13, Folder: "Holocaust," in which he mentions Viereck's description of his resignation in that day's *Jewish Daily Bulletin;* see also Kurt Gruenwald to Pascal A. Greenberg, Assistant Executive Secretary, February 21, 1939, Box 21, Folder: "Alpha" (CCNY) and Greenberg's reply of March 1. Further material on Viereck appears in Sander A. Diamond, *The Nazi Movement in the United States, 1924–1941* (Ithaca: Cornell University Press, 1974).

5. Maurice Jacobs, Executive Secretary, to the Foreign Relations Committee, U.S. Senate, Washington DC, January 30, 1934, AJHS-PHIEP, Box 13, Folder: "Holocaust,"; see attached resolution.
6. David L. Bazelon, Chicago Committee for the Defense of Human Rights Against Nazism, to Maurice Jacobs, July 3, 1934, AJHS-PHIEP, Box 13, Folder: "Holocaust"; see Jacobs' reply.
7. Norman Ranz, Dickinson College Phi Epsilon Pi House, to Executive Secretary Maurice Jacobs, March 9, 1936, 1–2, AJHS-PHIEP, Box 13, Folder: "Holocaust." Jacobs' reply is attached.
8. Convention minutes, Round Table Discussion, December 30, 1937: "Program of Jewish Activity," 1, AJHS-PHIEP, Box 7, Folder: "1937." The last name of the Dickinson student was Lazovick. At Dickinson, as was the custom at many colleges, attendance at chapel was compulsory for students three times each week. Jewish students in part fulfilled their own religious obligations by maintaining a close association with the Young Men's Hebrew Association (YMHA) located in Harrisburg, twenty miles away.
9. "Program of Jewish Activity," 4.
10. Supreme Council Minutes, February 7, 1938, 178, SAM.
11. Convention minutes, Round Table Discussion II, December 31, 1940: "A Jewish Activity Program," presentation by Richard L. Lowenstein of Eta [Penn] chapter, AJHS-PHIEP, Box 7, Folder: "1940."
12. Circular letter addressed "Dear Friend" from Sydney B. Lavine, Director of the Fireside Discussion Groups, September 30, 1937, AJHS-PHIEP, Box 16, Folder: "Anti-Defamation League."
13. Supreme Prior Schwartz, report on the Fireside Discussion Groups Project, Supreme Council Minutes, September 22, 1938, 194, SAM.
14. Letter from Louis M. Fushan, Grand Superior, to Maurice Jacobs, October 5, 1937, attaching September 30, 1937, letter from Richard E. Gudstadt of the Anti-Defamation League (himself a Phi Epsilon Pi alumnus) and Sydney B. Lavine, director of the Fireside Discussion Groups, AJHS-PHIEP, Box 16, Folder: "Anti-Defamation League." The list, "A Synopsis of Fireside Discussion Pamphlets," is dated September 1937.
15. The refugee student program was conceived by the late Arnold I. Shure '27 of Phi Sigma Delta at the University of Chicago and spread to other Jewish fraternities and then sororities; it operated from 1934 through 1941. Student journals of the period include photographs, descriptions, and interviews with the young refugees, along with stories of adjustment, reciprocal influence, and "Americanization" of dress, make-up, language and behavior which occurred among them and American-born members in fraternity and sorority houses. A detailed study of this refugee program, along with a follow-up on those who participated in it, would be most illuminating. For descriptions of Phi Epsilon Pi's German Jewish student refugee program, as well as the names of the specific students involved, see address by Grand Recorder Samuel J. Sherman, 6–7, AJHS-PHIEP, Box 7, Folder: "1935"; Samuel J. Sherman, "Report of the Committee on German Refugee Students," Convention, December 31, 1936, 17–20, Box 7, Folder: "1936,"; Maurice Jacobs to Irwin L. Freiberger, Grand Councilor, Cleveland, January 16, 1936, Box

13, Folder: "Holocaust,"; Sylvan L. May to Maurice Jacobs, March 18, 1936; Herbert Fuhrman, Past Superior of Alpha Chapter [CCNY], to Maurice Jacobs, February 8, 1938; "Report of the Refugee Students' Committee," Grand Convention, 50, Box 7, Folder: "1940"; Roundtable Discussion II, December 31, 1940: "The Refugee and the Chapter," address by Sylvan Cohen, undergraduate at Ohio University in Athens, OH, 71–73, and Lowenstein,"A Jewish Activity Program"; Pascal A. Greenberg, Executive Secretary, to the Members of the Grand Council, re: visitation to Penn State April 28–30, 1939, 2, Box 26, Folder: "Theta" [Penn State]. For Sigma Alpha Mu, see Supreme Council Minutes, February 10, 1936, 2; April 1936, 19, 36; and *passim*, SAM. For Alpha Epsilon Phi sorority, see Gudula Einstein,"My First Days at An American College [University of Illinois]," *Columns* 22, 1 (January 1938); Executive Board Minutes, March 15–22, 1938, 2, AEPhi, Box 6, Notebook 1: "Council Minutes 1934–1941"; National Dean Reba B. Cohen to National Council, January 4, 1939, subject: "Report of Eastern and Mid-Western Trips, Recommendations," 1, AEPhi, Box 3, Notebook 12: "Votes and Decisions of National Council 1938–1940"; list of refugee placements, Executive Board Minutes July 21–25, 1939, 12, AEPhi, Box 6, Notebook 1: "Council Minutes 1934–1941."

16. See "Report of the Refugee Students' Committee," AJHS-PHIEP, Box 7, Folder: "1940."

17. "Report of the Refugee Students' Committee."

18. *The Jewish Student in America: A Study Made by the Research Bureau of the B'nai B'rith Hillel Foundations, Dr. Lee F. Levinger, Director* (Cincinnati, Ohio, B'nai B'rith: 1937). Reviewed in ZBTQ 19, 2 (October 1937): 17. The study surveyed all of the institutions of higher learning in the U.S. and Canada and found that out of 1,150,000 students overall 105,000 or 9.13 percent were Jews, which was 2 1/2 times their percentage in the general population. They were not evenly distributed, but congregated in larger universities and professional schools. Levinger found that 113 colleges having 100 or more Jews as students had 90 percent of Jewish students as a whole; the other 729 colleges studied accounted for the other 10 percent, or 11,000.

19. Maurice Jacobs to Joseph W. Kohn (Ohio State Medical School '34), November 29, 1933, AJHS-PHIEP, Box 13, Folder: "Holocaust."

20. Irwin L. Freiberger to Maurice Jacobs, February 17, 1936, AJHS-PHIEP, Box 13, Folder: "Holocaust."

21. Maurice Jacobs to Irwin L. Freiberger, February 26, 1936, AJHS-PHIEP, Box 13, Folder: "Holocaust."

22. Supreme Council Minutes, November 3, 1938, 225, SAM.

23. Supreme Council Minutes, May 23, 1939, 1, SAM.

24. Albert A. Hutler, Report of the Vocational Guidance Committee, Grand Convention Minutes, December 31, 1939 Washington, DC, 59–62, AJHS-PHIEP, Box 7, Folder: "1939."

25. For the list of attendees at the October 15 conference see Executive Board Minutes, December 11–15, 1939, 21, AEPhi, Box 6, Notebook 1: "Council Minutes 1934–1941". These were: Alpha Epsilon Pi, Alpha Mu Sigma, Beta Sigma Rho, Delta Phi Epsilon, Iota Alpha Pi, Kappa Nu, Phi Alpha, Phi Beta Delta, Phi Epsilon Pi, Phi Sigma Delta, Phi Sigma Sigma, Pi Lambda

Phi, Sigma Alpha Mu, Sigma Delta Tau, Sigma Omega Psi, Sigma Tau Phi, Tau Alpha Omega, Tau Delta Phi, Tau Epsilon Phi, and Zeta Beta Tau, for a total of 20 groups. The only Jewish fraternities not accounted for were Omicron Alpha Tau, which had merged with Tau Delta Phi in 1934, and Sigma Lambda Pi, which disintegrated in 1932.

26. Victor Burstein, speaking at Roundtable Discussion II: "Interfraternity Relations," Minutes of Grand Convention, December 31, 1939, 83, AJHS-PHIEP, Box 7, Folder: "1939."
27. "Interfraternity Relations," 83.
28. "Interfraternity Relations," 83.
29. "Interfraternity Relations," 85.
30. For an account of Jacobs' career in publishing and his term as director of the Jewish Publication Society, see Jonathan D. Sarna's *JPS: The Americanization of Jewish Culture, 1888–1998* (Philadelphia: Jewish Publication Society, 1989) "The Maurice Jacobs Years": 175–218.
31. Series of letters and negotiations between Jacobs and UAHC on securing Jewish pamphlets and books for fraternity chapter libraries, May 1932, AJHS-PHIEP, Box 17A, Folder: "Union of American Hebrew Congregations."
32. Abram Leon Sachar to Members of the Grand Council, July 31, 1934, AJHS-PHIEP, Box 17A, Folder: "Abram L. Sachar." This three-page, single-spaced memo is the first draft of the "Sachar Plan."
33. Minutes of the Grand Council Meeting, December 30, 1934, AJHS-PHIEP, Box 7, Folder: "1934."
34. Jean Wertheimer to Grand Superior Louis M. Fushan, March 28, 1936, AJHS-PHIEP, Box 13, Folder: "Judaica Programming."
35. Maurice Jacobs to Louis M. Fushan, April 7, 1936, AJHS-PHIEP, Box 13, Folder: "Judaica Programming." Phi Epsilon Pi's chapter at the University of Cincinnati, established in 1920, closed down in 1935.
36. Theodore Shafton, President of the Chicago Alumni Association, to Dr. A. L. Sachar, December 1, 1936, AJHS-PHIEP, Box 17A, Folder: "Abram L. Sachar." In his letter Shafton attempts to convince Sachar to back down from his position.
37. Abram Sachar to Theodore Shafton, December 4, 1936, in reply to Shafton's letter of December 1, AJHS-PHIEP, Box 17A, Folder: "Abram L. Sachar."
38. See Wice-Jacobs correspondence, August 16, 1933 to February 2, 1937, AJHS-PHIEP, Box 17A, Folder: "David H. Wice." The folder includes handwritten notes and diagrams of the proposed new ritual.
39. Maurice Jacobs to Rabbi David H. Wice, January 21, 1937, AJHS-PHIEP, Box 17A, Folder: "David H. Wice."
40. Wice's reply to Jacobs, February 2, 1937, AJHS-PHIEP, Box 17A, Folder: "David H. Wice."
41. Minutes of the December 1936 convention, AJHS-PHIEP, and "Proposed Revised Initiation Ritual," 1939, AJHS-PHIEP, Box 46, Folder: "Ritual Manual." The typescript ritual is 22 pages long.
42. Samuel J. Sherman to Maurice Jacobs, November 20, 1936, reporting on the revolt against the Sachar Plan at the recent Chicago alumni meeting, AJHS-PHIEP, Box 13, Folder: "Judaica Programming."

43. Maurice Jacobs to Samuel J. Sherman, November 21, 1936, 2, AJHS-PHIEP, Box 13, Folder: "Judaica Programming."
44. A. D. Schwarz, review of *The Jews of Germany*, by Marvin Lowenthal, ZBTQ 18, 3 (December 1936): 17.
45. L. Elliot Grafman, *Pledge Manual of Phi Epsilon Pi* (1937), AJHS-PHIEP, Box 46A, Folder: "Publications." The folder contains several editions of Grafman's ten pledge lessons, accompanied by comments from the fraternity's executive secretary, which date from 1937 to the entrance of the U.S. into World War II in 1941.
46. Grafman, 15.
47. Grafman, 17.
48. Grafman, 18.
49. Grafman, 22, 26.
50. The historian Jenna Weissman Joselit has written on this theme in an article entitled "The Importance of Being Nice," presented at the annual conference of the Association for Jewish Studies, December 12, 1993, in Boston, MA.
51. "Zeta Beta Tau Manual for Chapter Administration," 1st ed. (1937; revised December 1, 1941), 13, Fane Papers, Box 33 Folder: "Miscellaneous ZBT 1941–1945."
52. Harold Riegelman, excerpt of remarks to the Fortieth Convention, ZBTQ 20, 4 (March 1939): 12.
53. Riegelman, remarks to Fortieth Convention, 12.
54. Executive Secretary James C. Hammerstein, visitation report on Chi [McGill] Chapter, March 17, 1935, Supreme Council Minutes, 171, SAM.
55. Supreme Council Minutes, December 8, 1936, SAM.
56. Executive Board Minutes, April 21–27, 1941, New York City, 39, AEPhi, Box 6, Notebook 1: "Council Minutes 1934–1941."
57. For discussion of the American Student Union (ASU) and its possible connection with the Communist party, see letter to all chapters from Gertrude Montel, Chairman of the Social Relations Committee, September 18, 1939, AEPhi, Box 6, Notebook 2: "Council Minutes and Correspondence August 1937–September 1939," Subject: "American Student Union." Also see Box 6, Notebook 1: "Executive Board Minutes December 11–15, 1939," 7, in which Gertrude Montel quotes California's *Oakland Tribune*, (November 29, 1939, that of 28 students on the National Executive Board of the ASU, 14 were members of the Young Communist League. AEPhi's fears concerning the ASU are supported by descriptions of the organization published annually in the NYU yearbook, the *Washington Square College Album*, from 1938 to 1940 (for the 1939 album, see 68–69; for 1940, see 73). While the 1938 feature describes the organization and its goals in admiring tones, by 1940 it had apparently been completely discredited as a Young Communist League organization whose policy was "directed by Josef Stalin," and the majority of students who had been members resigned. For photocopies of these yearbook articles and other information on radical student politics at NYU in the late 1930s, I am indebted to Susan Aprill of the New York University Archives.
58. For the sorority's descriptions and discussion concerning the Naomi Bloom affair at NYU, see Mickey Greenberg, First Province Director, to Reba B.

Cohen, March 21, 1941, subject: "Naomi Bloom"; Florence S. Orringer,Field
Secretary, to Reba B. Cohen, March 26, 1941, subject: "Naomi Bloom, Zeta";
and Mickey Brown Greenberg to Reba B. Cohen, March 30, 1941, which
memo contains the text of a statement in the NYU student newspaper that
was authored by the Chairman of the Discipline Committee, AEPhi, Box
6, Notebook 1: "Council Minutes 1934–1941." Extensive coverage and editorials concerning the incident appear in NYU's *Washington Square College
Bulletin* newspaper beginning on Monday, March 10, 1941 (volume 9, number 30) through Eleanor Roosevelt's visit reported in the issue of April 9,
1941. Documents in the NYU Archives relating to the incident include a
letter to Dean Alexander Baltzly from Robert B. Dow, a faculty member of
the Discipline Committee, dated March 5, 1941 and describing fully what
had happened in the NYU cafeteria (see RG 12,0, Series 2, Box 2, Folder 3,
Student Affairs Office WSC, Dow, Robert, 1938–43); an open letter to the
administration by the New York College Teachers Union Local 537 (American Federation of Teachers) dated March 8, 1941, and signed by professor of
education Robert K. Speer, president of the union; correspondence between
NYU Chancellor Harry Woodburn Chase and Robert K. Speer ("I await an
explanation") dated March 11, 13, and 20, 1941 (see RG. 3.0.5, Box 59,
Folder 2, Harry W. Chase Papers, Speer, Prof. Robert M., School of Education 1933–1944). A copy of a flyer calling for a student strike and noon
demonstration at the Garibaldi statue, headed "Defend Academic Freedom—
Reinstate the 7 Students!" appears in RG 3.0.5, Box 59, Folder 4, Harry
W. Chase Papers, Student Organizations and Publications, 1933–1944. For
copies of all these documents, I am grateful to Susan Aprill of the New York
University Archives.
59. One of the buttons is preserved in the records of the NYU Student Affairs
    Office (RG. 12,0, Series 2, Box 2 Folder 3, Student Affairs Office WSC,
    Dow, Robert 1938–43).
60. "Mrs. Roosevelt Addresses Council for Student Equality on U.S. Race Prob-
    lem: Advocates Same Policy as Bulletin on NYU Negro Sports Problem,"
    Washington Square College Bulletin, Wednesday, April 9, 1941, 1 (with pho-
    tograph).
61. Mickey Brown Greenberg to Reba B. Cohen, March 30, 1941, AEPhi, Box
    6, Notebook 1: "Council Minutes 1934–1941," in which she reports on her
    visit with the Dean of Women and pleads leniency for Naomi Bloom.
62. Florence S. Orringer to Reba B. Cohen, March 26, 1941, subject: "Naomi
    Bloom," AEPhi, Box 6, Notebook 1: "Council Minutes 1934–1941."
63. Irma Loeb Cohen (Mrs. Adolph Loeb, Zanesville, OH) to Louise Wolf,
    April 9, 1941, AEPhi, Box 6, Notebook 1: "Council Minutes 1934–1941."
64. Lee Dover, Zeta Beta Tau Manual for Chapter Administration (1937) [here-
    after cited as *ZBT Manual*] 82.
65. *ZBT Manual,* 55.
66. *ZBT Manual,* 73.
67. *ZBT Manual,* 89, s.v. "Important Miscellania."
68. Landon Laird, *Kansas City Star,* August 3, 1936. The item was reprinted,
    obviously with great pride, by Lee Dover in his "C., F., & S," editorial section

(named after his customary closing for letters, an abbreviation standing for "Cordially, fraternally, and sincerely") in ZBTQ 18, 3, December 1936, 5.

69. Joan Loewy Cohn, "Greek P's and Q's," *Columns* 22, 1 (January 1938): 84.
70. See Joan Loewy Cohn, "Greek P's and Q's," *Columns* 23, 1 (January 1939): 50, and 23, 2 (March 1939): 93. "How to Use a Pastry Tube" first appeared in a column "RSVP," in *Columns* 17, 3 (May 1933): 43.
71. Joan Loewy Cohn, "Greek P's and Q's," in *Columns* 23, 2 (March 1939): 93.
72. Joan Loewy Cohn, "Greek P's and Q's," March 1939.
73. *ZBT Manual*, 31, s.v. "Unfair Standards."
74. The details of the procedure are given in an article by Leon Gross, "Janus and the Beauty Surgeon," ZBTQ 14, 4 (May 1930): 15–16.
75. Lee Dover to Irwin Tober, President of Omega (University of Missouri) Chapter, October 9, 1941, Fane Papers, Box 33, Folder: "ZBT General Correspondence 1941."
76. For a discussion of this and other specific manifestations of anti-Jewish discrimination in American social institutions, see Belth, ed., *Barriers: Patterns of Discrimination Against Jews.*
77. Lee Dover to Irvin Fane and Morris Ginsberg, Directors of Omega (University of Missouri) Chapter, October 9, 1941, Fane Papers.
78. Irwin Tober to Lee Dover, October 16, 1941, Fane Papers.
79. Lee Dover to Rabbi David Jacobson of Temple Beth-El, San Antonio, Texas, October 21, 1941, Irvin Fane Papers.
80. Lee Dover to Irwin Tober, October 21, 1941, Fane Papers.
81. Lee Dover to Irwin Tober, October 21, 1941.
82. See clipping, "Iowa U. Is Given Until May 6 to 'Clean Up All Vice Charges,'" *Des Moines Register and Tribune*, April 9, 1935, 1, AJHS-PHIEP, Box 16, Folder: "Anti-Defamation League."
83. Richard E. Gutstadt to Maurice Jacobs, form letter, April 10, 1935, AJHS-PHIEP, Box 16, Folder: "Anti-Defamation League."
84. Gutstadt to Jacobs, April 10, 1935.
85. Richard E. Gutstadt to Maurice Jacobs, June 26, 1935, AJHS-PHIEP, Box 16, Folder: "Anti-Defamation League."
86. Maurice Jacobs to Richard E. Gutstadt, July 3, 1935, AJHS-PHIEP, Box 16, Folder: "Anti-Defamation League."
87. Supreme Council Minutes, February 20, 1934, 52, s.v. "Anti-Semitism," SAM. "A letter was received from Mr. Ullman, President of Beta Sigma Rho [another Jewish fraternity]. Mr. Ullman stated that he had spoken to the American Ambassador to Austria who remarked that the Nazi ascendancy in Austria would be followed by Nazi ascendancy in other parts of the world. Mr. Ullman felt that the Jewish students should have some central body 'to aid them in keeping their own house in order and in minimizing Jewish student opinion in matters of general import.' The executives of Jewish Fraternities recently appointed a committee to consider this entire question. Meetings have been held by the Committee and a plan of action has been prepared which will be submitted to the various Jewish Fraternities for further consideration. Pending receipt of the plan, it was decided not to discuss the matter as it has already been considered at all of our meetings this year."

88. Minutes of Roundtable Discussion on Fraternity Finances, Grand Convention, Cleveland, December 30, 1937, AJHS-PHIEP, Box 7, Folder: "1937."
89. Reba B. Cohen to National Council, January 4, 1939, subject: "Report of Eastern and Western Trips, Recommendations," 3, AEPhi, Box 3, Notebook 12: "Votes and Decisions of National Council 1938–1940."

EPILOGUE

1. Louise W. Wolf to Executive Board, March 8, 1943, AEPhi, Box 4, Notebook 2: "Votes and Decisions of National Council and Executive Board 1942–43." She wrote: "Boys do not always have such lovely manners when alone at home, and they may not change them just because the girls come over. It must be approved by the Dean of Women and chaperoned well with the understanding that the girls are not to linger after meals more than a few minutes and leave the house for the boys—not a dormitory for all." See also "ZBT's on the Menu at Alpha Lambda," *Columns* 27, 3 (May 1943): 57.
2. For one example, see Norman Hanover, comp., " Chi [Syracuse University] in Service Unofficial Message Center," July 1944, AJHS-PHIEP, Box 15, Folder: "World War II Correspondence 1944." Letters from soldiers and wartime chapter newsletters are also evident in the available archives of Sigma Alpha Mu, Phi Sigma Delta, and ZBT, which on the national level published names and addresses of soldiers in a section entitled the "Get Acquainted Bulletin" in its wartime publication, *ZBT Duration News.*
3. ZBTQ 24, 3 (October 1942): 8.
4. ZBTQ 24, 3 (October 1942): 9.
5. "Service-Men's Mail Bag," ZBTQ 24, 3 (October 1942): 8.
6. For one example, see S. A. Weisman, from somewhere in North Africa to the Grand Council, May 13, 1943, Phi Epsilon Pi Collection, Box 15, Folder: "World War II Correspondence 1943."
7. Colonel Harmond D. Spanner, Western Reserve '36, from somewhere in England, September 24, 1942, "Service-Men's Mail Bag," ZBTQ 24, 3 (October 1942): 9.
8. "The Victory Convention," *Zeta Beta Tau Duration News,* 24, 4 (January–February 1943): 1.
9. Jewish men and women served in all branches of the U.S. armed forces. Of the approximately 550,000 who served, 10,500 died, 24,000 were wounded, and 36,000 decorated for gallantry. They were served by 310 Jewish chaplains holding military rank (The *Encyclopedia Judaica,* s.v. "United States of America").
10. Discussion of the "veteran problem" and attempts to ease it appear in virtually all men's fraternity records from 1945 to 1949 as well as in the general fraternity periodicals *Fraternity Month* and *Banta's Greek Exchange.* For one example of such a discussion and reports of how various campuses were dealing with it, see Roundtable Minutes, April 18, 1947, regional convention, Phi Epsilon Pi Collection, Box 18, Folder: "Regional Groups: Mid-Western." The anomalies of attending college immediately after World War II along

with some fear, awe, and admiration of battle-scarred older veterans also figure prominently in informant interviews.

11. Interview with William Schwartz, Executive Director, Sigma Alpha Mu,
University of Oklahoma '50, describing his undergraduate experiences at the
SAM house at Norman, Oklahoma.

12. Jewish fraternity discussion and documentation of the "S" question is voluminous, and the following attitudinal descriptions are based on a full perusal of
these sources, as well as interviews with alumni and alumnae who participated
in the process. A most valuable source is a folder in the ZBT National Office
labeled simply "the 'S' Question," containing the complete transcript (three
hours, 177 pages) of the 1954 debate in which the fraternity, after repeatedly voting the measure down, finally voted to remove the sectarian clause
from its charter. The transcript is entitled "Zeta Beta Tau Fraternity, 56th
Anniversary National Convention, Monte Carlo Hotel, Miami Beach, FL,
August 26–29, 1954." A similar debate and vote took place at the 1953 Sigma
Alpha Mu convention; see SAM Convention and Supreme Council Minutes,
Miami Beach, FL, August 30, 1953. In SAM records, extensive discussion of
the sectarian issue can be found in the following Supreme Council and Convention minutes: November 13, 1945; December 15–16, 1945; December 31,
1946; December 28, 1947; September 16, 1948 (these minutes also include a
resolution of greetings and good wishes to the new State of Israel); December 30, 1949; January 20, February 28, March 28, April 30, and August 30,
all in 1950; September 5, 1951; August 29, 1952; January 20, 1953; March
15, 1953; and, for the last time before the final vote, April 9, 1953. The debate was less complex and less legally charged for all the other Jewish groups,
none of whom actually had sectarian clauses in their constitutions, although
they had always been known as Jewish. For examples of Phi Epsilon Pi's adjustment to losing potential Jewish members to Gentile fraternities and the
ostracism they faced as a "sectarian" fraternity, see Correspondence, 1947–
1950, AJHS-PHIEP, Box 12, Folder: "Extension Committee". For Sigma
Delta Tau, see the minutes of the 19th Biennial Convention (June 23–27,
1958), the 20th Biennial Convention (June 23–27, 1960) and the 22nd Biennial Convention (June 22–26, 1964). For Alpha Epsilon Phi reactions,
see AEPhi, Box 4, Notebook 5: "Council Votes July 1948–December 1949,"
where the first impact of the anti-discrimination movement is felt; National
Dean to National Council, October 16, 1953, subject: "Eta chapter," AEPhi,
Box 4, Notebook 12: "Council Votes 1953"; Elizabeth Eldridge to Joan Cohn,
February 25, 1957, subject: "Elliott Bill No. 758," AEPhi, Box 5, Notebook
1: "National Council Votes 1956–1957" [on a bill before the California leg-
islature sponsored by Burton Elliott requiring all sororities, fraternities, and
private organizations on all the fifty state-supported California campuses to
reveal their constitutions and prove that there were no discriminatory clauses
in them]. On the same subject see memoranda on the Elliot Bill dated March
8, 1957; April 4, 1957; April 12, 1957 (this memo includes the full text of the
proposed bill); and April 14, 1957. Among all the Jewish fraternity leaders,
the most passionate and outspoken opponent of changing his group's Jewish identity was executive secretary George S. Toll of Alpha Epsilon Pi, a

folder of whose personal correspondence can be found at the AEPi national
office.

13. Leonard Dinnerstein, in his essay "Antisemitism Exposed and Attacked,
1945–1950," in *Uneasy at Home: Antisemitism and the American Jewish Experience* (New York: Columbia University Press, 1987), describes in detail the
post-war gearing up of Jewish communal and defense agencies to collectively
battle antisemitisn in the courts and legislative bodies of the nation (pp. 178–
196). Contrary to some assertions, American antisemitism did not simply
evaporate in the wake of World War II. Returning veterans at first faced as
much discrimination in housing, employment, and higher education as they
ever had. However, post-war conditions of relative tolerance and economic
prosperity, as well as the belief that bigotry did not serve the national interests of the United States, created a window of opportunity and an impetus for
American Jews to unify, rally around a common cause, and for the first time
gain widespread support from sympathetic Gentile allies.

14. See George S. Toll, memorandum to all chapters, March 22, 1952; "Special
Report to the Supreme Board of Governors," December 30, 1952; "Report of
the Executive Secretary," 1954; "Remarks at the 1955 Convention," August
25, 1955; "1954–55 Executive Office Report," August 25, 1955 (esp. 5–7);
"1955–1956 Executive Office Report," August 22, 1956, 5–8; and "Special
Report to the Supreme Board of Governors," January 28, 1958, AEPi.

15. Johnson, 230–235.

16. On the New York State ban, see "Eta Chapter," [Albany] October 18, 1953,
AEPhi, Box 4, Notebook 12: "Council Votes 1953." A campus-by-campus
review of changing fraternity legislation appears in Krapin, 78–88.

17. Joan L. Cohn to National Council and National Honorary Advisors, subject: "Report on NADWC Meeting," April 14, 1957, AEPhi, Box 1, Folder:
"Miscellaneous."

18. AJHS-PHIEP, Box 13, Folder: "Negro-Jewish Relations."

19. This observation was made by George S. Toll, the executive secretary of Alpha Epsilon Pi and most vociferous opponent of dropping the Jewish sectarian clauses. See George S. Toll, memo, "Fraternities' Secretaries and Editors
Association meeting, July 13–16, Absecon, New Jersey," AEPI.

20. Seth Cagin and Philip Dray, *We are Not Afraid: The Story of Goodman, Schwerner, and Chaney and the Civil Rights Campaign for Mississippi* (New York:
Macmillan, 1988), 257.

21. Eric Pooley, "Doctor J: The Rise of Afrocentric Conspiracy Theorist Leonard
Jeffries and his Odd Ideas about Blacks and Whites," *New York Magazine*,
September 2, 1991, 35. In interviews Jeffries seemed to remember his term
as "Rex" or president of the Pi Lambda Phi chapter fondly and referred to it
as a time when he was "King of the Jews."

22. The writer, who was himself Catholic, wrote that the Columbia chapter's
straying from its Jewish roots was a constant source of tension with the national office; in 1960, the Phi Sigma Delta chapter house at Missouri still
kept kosher.

23. In addition to the Alfred Rogers incident at the University of Connecticut,
in 1949 the Phi Epsilon Pi chapter at Rutgers University summarily declared

406 NOTES TO EPILOGUE

itself truly nonsectarian and made a deliberate attempt to pledge non-Jews and eliminate any of its Jewish identity, against the wishes of the national (AJHS-PHIEP, Box 28, Folder: "Lambda," May 3, 1949). In 1952 an Alpha Epsilon Pi member at the University of Manitoba resigned from the fraternity in protest over its membership policies and reported his feelings to the local Anglo-Jewish Press (memorandum, December 16, 1952, George S. Toll Correspondence, AEPi.)

24. A typical example occurred at Washington and Lee University in the fall of 1950. Dr. A. M. Ginsberg of Kansas City, a ZBT alumnus, and his family "had their hearts set" on their son Robert becoming a ZBT there. However, Robert had recently received letters from two non-Jewish fraternities asking him for rushing dates. "His father, naturally concerned about the future welfare of his son, is disturbed by this development," wrote ZBT's executive secretary to the head of the W&L chapter, on the chance that the boy had been overlooked by them. "Of course I have not overlooked the possibility that some of the non-Jewish fraternities on your campus have changed their policy and are now interested in pledging some of the top Jewish boys. If this is true, it will present a serious problem," Lee Dover to Richard Marcus, President of the Alpha Epsilon Chapter of ZBT, September 6, 1950, Fane Papers, Box 34, Folder: "ZBT 1950."

25. Maurice Jacobs, "The Case for Jewish Fraternities," in *The National Jewish Monthly*, November 1961, 40.

26. Millie Wolff in "Which Way Fraternities—What's the Answer?" *Jewish Digest*, 5, no. 12 (September 1960): 1–7.

27. Johnson, *Fraternities in Our Colleges* (1972), 213.

28. The debate took place Saturday morning, August 28, 1954, at ZBT's convention in Miami Beach. For a description and analysis of the proceedings along with excerpts from the verbatim transcript of the debate (it ultimately covered 221 typed pages) see Sanua, *Here's to Our Fraternity*, 196–207.

29. Horowitz, 220–221 and 289: "No one surveying the campus scene in 1959 could have predicted the 1960s."

30. S. Norman Feingold, Iris Sexter, Karen Rose, and Ronald S. Kaiser, *An Analysis of Major Trends in Jewish College Enrollment: A Resource for Educational and Vocational Guidance Counselors* (Washington, DC: B'nai B'rith Vocational Service, 1968) 2, 10.

31. For examples of the unsuccessful attempt of a Jewish sorority to stem the tide of members leaving the house and going to live in independent apartments, along with discussion of their disaffiliation, see AEPhi, Box 5 Notebook 9: "Vote Sheets 1959–60 Beta-Omega" and Box 5, Notebook 10: "Vote Sheets September 1960–June 1961 Beta-Omega."

32. See Mary Margaret Garrard, "What's New on Campus—III," *Columns* 56, 4 (Summer 1972): 1. After this issue, the magazine ceased publication until 1977.

33. Anonymous interview. The group of women were gathered at a synagogue to celebrate the Bar Mitzvah of one of their sons.

34. Blanche Greenberger to Mrs. Isadore J. Kahn (president El Paso Alumnae Association), July 13, 1965, AEPhi, Box 1, "Miscellaneous."

35. Benjamin M. Kahn, "The World in which we Live: Reality and Challenge," in *New Frontiers for Jewish Life on the Campus* (Washington, DC: B'nai B'rith Hillel Foundations, 1968), 9. For interesting comparative data on the political attitudes of Jewish and non-Jewish students and faculty, see Steinberg, 153–166.
36. Nathan Glazer, "The Jewish Role in Student Activism," *Fortune* (January 1969): 112–129. In this same period Yale psychologist Kenneth Kenniston, in his study of student radicals, was popularizing the so-called "red diaper baby" hypothesis to explain that prominence, i.e. that radical Jewish students were products of nonauthoritarian homes and parents who had themselves been social activists in the 1930s.
37. Glazer, "The Jewish Role in Student Activism," 112.
38. Mitchell Gerber (Phi Epsilon Pi, Columbia '70), interview by author via telephone, June 17, 1991
39. William Schwartz of Sigma Alpha Mu, interview. For insights on the student rebellions of the 1960s, see also Horowitz, 220–244.
40. Historically Jewish sororities still in existence are Alpha Epsilon Phi, Phi Sigma Sigma, Sigma Delta Tau, and Delta Phi Epsilon. None ever merged. Of the fraternities, Phi Epsilon Pi, Phi Sigma Delta, Phi Alpha, and Kappa Nu were all incorporated into Zeta Beta Tau; Beta Sigma Rho and Phi Beta Delta merged with Pi Lambda Phi; Sigma Omega Psi and Sigma Tau Phi merged with Alpha Epsilon Pi; and Omicron Alpha Tau, Alpha Mu Sigma, and Tau Delta Phi all ceased to function, although there are reports that loyal followers of the last are attempting a comeback. Of the remaining Jewish Greek-letter groups, Alpha Epsilon Pi by far places the most stress on its historic Jewish identity.
41. See Marianne R. Sanua, "Stages in the Development of Jewish Life at Princeton University," *American Jewish History* 76, 4 (June 1987): 391–415.

Bibliography

PRIMARY SOURCES

AEPi	Alpha Epsilon Pi Fraternity archives, Indianapolis, IN
AEPhi	Alpha Epsilon Phi Sorority archives, Stamford, CT
AJC	American Jewish Committee Archives, Jacob Blaustein Library, New York City
AJHS-PHIEP	Phi Epsilon Pi Collection, American Jewish Historical Society, Center for Jewish History, New York City
HUC-AJA	Hebrew Union College/American Jewish Archives, Cincinnati, OH
SAM	Sigma Alpha Mu Fraternity archives, Carmel, IN
SDT	Sigma Delta Tau Sorority archives, Indianapolis, IN
ZBT	Zeta Beta Tau Fraternity archives, New York City

PERIODICALS CONSULTED

The American Jewish Year Book
The American Hebrew
The Hillel Digest
Banta's Greek Exchange
Fraternity Monthly
The Scroll of Alpha Epsilon Pi
The Columns of Alpha Epsilon Phi
The Phi Epsilon Pi Quarterly
The Octagonian of Sigma Alpha Mu
The Zeta Beta Tau Quarterly
The Menorah Journal

SECONDARY LITERATURE

Anson, Jack L., Jr., and Robert F. Marchesani, Jr., eds. *Baird's Manual of American College Fraternities*. 20th ed. Indianapolis: Baird's Manual Foundation, 1991. (Also, earlier editions from 1915, 1920, 1923, 1927, 1930, 1935, 1940, and 1963.)

Baruch, Bernard. *My Own Story*. New York: Henry Holt, 1957.

Belth, Nathan C. *A Promise to Keep: A Narrative of the American Encounter with Anti-Semitism*. New York: Times, 1979

Belth, Nathan C., ed. *Barriers: Patterns of Discrimination Against Jews*. Washington, D.C.: Anti-Defamation League of B'nai B'rith, 1958.

Borowitz, Eugene B. *The Masks Jews Wear: The Self-Deceptions of American Jewry*. New York: Simon and Schuster, 1973.

Broun, Heywood, and George Britt. *Christians Only: A Study in Prejudice*. New York: Vanguard Press, 1931.

Canby, Henry Seidel. *Alma Mater: The Gothic Age of the American College*. New York: Farrar and Rinehart, 1936.

Carnes, Mark C. *Secret Ritual and Manhood in Victorian America*. New Haven: Yale University Press, 1989.

Center for the Study of the College Fraternity. *Annotated Bibliography: Research Studies and Articles, 1950–1970*. Bloomington: University of Indiana, 1970.

Clark, Thomas Arkle. *The Fraternity and the College*. Menasha, WI: George Banta Publishing Co., 1931.

Cohen, Naomi W. *Encounter With Emancipation: The German Jews in the U.S., 1830–1914*. Philadelphia: Jewish Publication Society, 1984.

Cuddihy, John Murray. *The Ordeal of Civility: Freud, Marx, Levi-Strauss, and the Jewish Struggle with Modernity*. 2nd. ed. Boston: Beacon Press, 1987.

Current, Richard Nelson. *Phi Beta Kappa in American Life: The First Two Hundred Years*. New York: Oxford University Press, 1990.

Diner, Hasia. *A Time for Gathering: The Second Migration, 1820–1880*. Baltimore: Johns Hopkins University Press, 1992.

Dinnerstein, Leonard. *Antisemitism in America*. New York: Oxford University Press, 1994.

———"Education and the Advancement of American Jews." *American Education and the European Immigrant, 1840–1940*, ed. Bernard J. Weiss. Urbana: University of Illinois Press, 1982.

———*Uneasy at Home: Anti-Semitism and the American Jewish Experience*. New York: Columbia University Press, 1987.

Dobkowski, Michael N. *The Tarnished Dream: The Basis of American Anti-Semitism*. Westport, CT: Greenwood Press, 1979.

Edman, Irwin. "Reuben Cohen Goes to College." *The Menorah Journal* 12 (April–May 1926): 127–37.

Epstein, Joseph. "Memoirs of a Fraternity Man." *Commentary* 52, no. 1 (July 1971):59–64.

Fass, Paula S. *The Damned and the Beautiful: American Youth in the 1920s*. New York: Oxford University Press, 1977.

Feingold, Henry L. "Investing in Themselves: The Harvard Case and the Origins of the Third American-Jewish Commercial Elite." *American Jewish History* 77, no. 4 (June 1988): 530–553.

——. *A Time for Searching: Entering the Mainstream, 1920–1945.* Baltimore: Johns Hopkins University Press, 1992.

Friesel, Evyatar. "The Age of Optimism in American Judaism, 1900–1920." *A Bicentennial Festschrift for Jacob Rader Marcus,* ed. Bertram Wallace Korn. New York: Ktav, 1976.

Gerber, David A., ed. *Anti-Semitism in American History.* Urbana: University of Illinois Press, 1986.

Gilman, Sander L. *Jewish Self-Hatred: Anti-Semitism and the Hidden Language of the Jews.* Baltimore: Johns Hopkins University Press, 1986.

Glazer, Nathan. *American Judaism.* 2nd. ed., revised. Chicago: University of Chicago Press, 1972.

——. "The Jewish Role in Student Activism." *Fortune,* January 1969, 112–129.

Glazer, Nathan, and Daniel Patrick Moynihan. *Beyond the Melting Pot: The Negroes, Puerto Ricans, Jews, Italians, and Irish of New York City.* Cambridge: MIT Press, 1970.

Gordon, Lynn D. "The Gibson Girl Goes to College: Popular Culture and Women's Higher Education in the Progressive Era, 1890–1920." *American Quarterly* 39, no. 2 (summer 1987).

Gorelick, Sherry. *City College and the Jewish Poor: Education in New York, 1880–1924.* New Brunswick: Rutgers University Press, 1981.

Goren, Arthur A. *The American Jews: Dimensions of Ethnicity.* Cambridge: Harvard University Press, 1982.

——. *New York Jews and the Quest for Community: The Kehillah Experiment, 1908–1922.* New York: Columbia University Press, 1970.

Gottheil, Richard J. H. *The Life of Gustav Gottheil: Memoir of a Priest in Israel.* Philadelphia: Jewish Publication Society, 1914.

Haskins, Charles Homer. *The Rise of the Universities.* Ithaca: Cornell University Press, 1957.

Higham, John. *Send These to Me: Jews and Other Immigrants in Urban America.* New York: Atheneum, 1975.

——. *Strangers in the Land: Patterns of American Nativism, 1860–1925.* 2nd. ed. New Brunswick: Rutgers University Press, 1988.

Horowitz, Lefkowitz Helen. *Campus Life: Undergraduate Cultures from the End of the 18th Century to the Present.* New York: Knopf, 1987.

Horvitz, Eleanor F., and Benton H. Rosen. "The Jewish Fraternity and Brown University." *Rhode Island Jewish Historical Notes,* 8, no. 3 (November 1981): 299–344.

Hyman, Joseph. "After Twenty-Five Years." *The Frater* (Pi Lambda Phi Fraternity) vol. 16 (August 1933).

Intercollegiate Menorah Association. *The Menorah Movement.* Ann Arbor, Michigan, 1914.

Iota Alpha Pi Sorority. "The First Sixty Years." *The Heights,* New York, 1964.

Jacobs, Maurice. "Fraternities, Jewish." *Universal Jewish Encyclopedia*, vol. 4. New York: 1941.

Johnson, Clyde Sanfred. *Fraternities in Our Colleges*. New York: National Interfraternity Foundation, 1972.

Joselit, Jenna Weissman. "Without Ghettoism: A History of the Intercollegiate Menorah Association, 1906–1930." *American Jewish Archives* 30, no. 2 (Nov. 1978): 133–154.

Jospe, Raphael, and Samuel Fishman, eds. *Go and Study: Essays and Studies in Honor of Alfred Jospe*. Washington, DC: B'nai B'rith Hillel, 1980.

Kessner, Thomas. *The Golden Door: Italian and Jewish Immigrant Mobility in New York City, 1880–1915*. New York: Oxford University Press, 1977.

Klingenstein, Susanne. *Jews in the American Academy 1900–1940: The Dynamics of Intellectual Assimilation*. New Haven: Yale University Press, 1991.

Lee, Alfred McClung. *Fraternities Without Brotherhood: A Study of Prejudice on the American Campus*. Boston: The Beacon Press, 1955.

Leemon, Thomas A. *The Rites of Passage in a Student Culture: A Study of the Dynamics of Transition*. New York: Teachers College Press, 1972.

Levine, David O. *The American College and the Culture of Aspiration, 1915–1940*. Ithaca: Cornell University Press, 1988.

Levinger, Lee J. *The Jewish Student in America: A Study Made by the Research Bureau of the B'nai B'rith Hillel Foundations*. Cincinnati, Ohio: B'nai B'rith, 1937.

Liebman, Charles. *The Ambivalent American Jew: Politics, Religion, and Family in American Jewish Life*. Philadelphia: Jewish Publication Society, 1973.

Linfield, H. S. "The Communal Organization of the Jews of the United States, 1927." *American Jewish Yearbook* v. 31 (1929–1930).

Martin, Ida Shaw. *The Sorority Handbook*. Third Edition. Roxburgh Press: Boston, 1909.

McWilliams, Carey. *A Mask for a Privilege: Anti-Semitism in America*. Boston: Little, Brown and Company, 1948.

Moore, Deborah Dash. *At Home in America: Second-Generation New York Jews*. New York: Columbia University Press, 1981.

———*To the Golden Cities: Pursuing the American Jewish Dream in Miami and L.A.* New York: Free Press, 1994.

Nathan, Marvin. *The Attitude of the Jewish Student in the Colleges and Universities Toward His Religion*. New York: Block Publishing Co., 1932.

Nelson, Thomas W., Jr. *The Undergraduate Experiences of Alumni Who Support Their Alma Mater*. Bloomington: Center for the Study of the College Fraternity, 1988.

Oren, Dan A. *Joining the Club: A History of Jews and Yale*. New Haven: Yale University Press, 1985.

Pelcovits, N. A. "What about Jewish Anti-Semitism? A Prescription to Cure Self-Hatred." In *Commentary* 3, no. 2 (February 1947): 118–125.

Rischin, Moses. *The Promised City: New York's Jews, 1870–1914*. Cambridge: Harvard University Press, 1977.

Ritterband, Paul, and Harold S. Wechsler. *Jewish Learning in American Universities: The First Century*. Bloomington: Indiana University Press, 1994.

Rosovsky, Nitza. *The Jewish Experience at Harvard and Radcliffe.* Cambridge: Harvard University Press, 1986.

Rozenblit, Marsha L. *The Jews of Vienna 1867–1914: Assimilation and Identity.* Albany: State University of New York Press, 1983.

Rudolph, Frederick. *The American College and University: A History.* New York: Knopf, 1962.

Rudy, Willis. *The College of the City of New York: A History.* New York: The City College Press, 1949.

Samuel, Maurice. *The Gentleman and the Jew: Twenty-Five Centuries of Conflict in Manners and Morals.* New York: Behrman House, Inc., 1977.

Sanua, Marianne R. "Non-Recognition of Jewish Fraternities: The Cases of Columbia and Brown Universities." *American Jewish Archives,* 45, no. 2, (fall/winter 1993): 125–145.

——. "Stages in the Development of Jewish Life at Princeton University." *American Jewish History* v. 76, n. 4, June 1987.

——. " 'We Hate New York': Negative Images of the Promised City as a Source for Jewish Fraternity and Sorority Members, 1920–1940." *An Inventory of Promises: a Festschrift for Moses Rischin,* Jeffrey S. Gurock, ed. Brooklyn, NY: Carlson Publishing, 1995.

——. *Here's to Our Fraternity: One Hundred Years of Zeta Beta Tau, 1898–1998.* Hanover: University Press of New England and the ZBT Foundation, 1998.

——"Jewish College Fraternities in the U.S., 1895–1945: An Overview." *Journal of American Ethnic History* 19, no. 2 (winter 2000): 1–42.

Sarna, Jonathan D., ed. *The American Jewish Experience.* New York: Holmes and Meier, 1986.

Shapiro, Edward S. "The Friendly University: Jews in Academia Since World War II." *Judaism* (summer 1997): 365–374.

——. *A Time for Healing: American Jewry Since World War II.* Baltimore: Johns Hopkins University Press, 1992.

Sheldon, Henry D. *Student Life and Customs.* New York: Appleton and Co., 1901.

Shubow, Joseph Shalom, ed. *The Brandeis Avukah Volume of 1936: A Collection on Contemporary Zionist Thought Dedicated to Justice Louis D. Brandeis.* New York: Avukah, the American Student Zionist Federation and Stratford Publishers, 1936.

Solberg, Winton U. "The Early Years of the Jewish Presence at the University of Illinois." *Religion and American Culture* 2, no. 2 (Summer 1992): 215–45.

Sorin, Gerald. *A Time for Building: The Third Migration 1880–1920.* Baltimore: Johns Hopkins University Press, 1992.

Steinberg, Stephen. "How Jewish Quotas Began." *Commentary* 52, no. 3 (Sept. 1971): 67–76.

Steinberg, Stephen. *The Academic Melting Pot: Catholics and Jews in American Higher Education.* New York: McGraw Hill, 1974.

Suntag, Sidney S. *The History of Tau Epsilon Phi: 75 Years of Friendship, 1910–1985.* Atlanta: The TEP Foundation, Inc., 1986.

Svonkin, Stuart. *Jews Against Prejudice: American Jews and the Fight for Civil Liberties.* New York: Columbia University Press, 1997.

Synnott, Marcia Graham. "Anti-Semitism and American Universities: Did Quotas Follow the Jews?" *Anti-Semitism in American History*, ed. David A. Gerber. Urbana and Chicago: University of Illinois Press, 1986.

———. *The Half-Opened Door: Discrimination and Admissions at Harvard, Yale, and Princeton, 1900–1970.* Westport, CT: Greenwood Press, 1979.

Toll, George S. *Alpha Epsilon Pi: The First Sixty-Five Years, 1913–1978.* The Alpha Epsilon Pi Foundation, Inc., 1980.

———. "Colleges, Fraternities, and Assimilation." *Journal of Reform Judaism* 32, no. 4 (summer 1985): 93–103.

Veysey, Laurence R. *The Emergence of the American University.* Chicago: University of Chicago Press, 1970.

Wechsler, Harold S. *The Qualified Student: A History of Selective College Admissions in America.* New York: John Wiley & Sons, 1977.

———. "Rabbi Bernard C. Ehrenreich: A Northern Progressive Goes South." *Jews of the South: Selected Essays from the Southern Jewish Historical Society*, ed. Samuel Proctor and Louis Schmier. Macon, GA: Mercer University Press, 1984.

———. "The Rationale for Restriction: Ethnicity and College Admission in America, 1910–1980." *American Quarterly* 36 (winter 1984): 643–667.

Weil, Clarence. *Zeta Beta Tau: The First Twenty-Five Years.* New York: Zeta Beta Tau, 1923.

UNPUBLISHED THESES AND PAPERS

Greenebaum, Gary T. "The Jewish Experience in the American College and University: The Factors Making for Acceptability of Jews in American Colleges and Universities from the Close of the Civil War to the End of World War II." Rabbinic thesis, Hebrew Union College, Cincinnati, OH, 1978, 131 pp., AJA.

Mason, Steven J. "The Jewish Fraternity as a Jewish Socializing Agency." Rabbinic thesis, Hebrew Union College, Cincinnati, OH, 1976 109 pp., AJA.

Ruder, Jay Stanley. "Greeks, Barbarians, and Jews: The Early Years of American Jewish College Fraternities." BA Honors Thesis, Harvard College, Cambridge, 1976.

Slade, Irving Leonard. "An Introductory Survey of Jewish Student Organizations in American Higher Education." Ed.D. dissertation, Columbia Teachers College, New York, 1966.

Index of Names

Abrahams, Harris S., *P2–14*
Abrahamson, Emmanuel, 152
Abramowitz, Herman, 52, 286, *P1–3*
Abramson, Lorraine, *P2–8*
Acker, Jesse, 63, 64, 73, 130
Adler, Marilyn, *P2–8*
Adler, Milton, 147, *P1–16*
Adler, Walter, 130
Adler, William F., *P1–11*
Album, Margie, *P2–16*
Alhadeff, Charles, 382n. 29
Alhadeff, Jack, 382n. 29
Alhadeff, Jerry, 382n. 29
Alperin, Alberta, 215
Alpern, Lillian Gordon, 312
Alpert, Bernice, *P2–10*
Amster, Bertram W., *P1–14*
Annenberg, Walter, 198
April, Israel, *P1–11*
Arbuse, David I., 151–52
Arden, Abraham (A. A. Brill), 53
Arnstine, James M., *P1–13*
Asimov, Isaac, 118
Aurbach, Arthur B., *P2–1*

Baird, William Raimond, 360n. 12
Baloff, Edward, *P2–14*
Bamberger, Eddie, 107
Bamberger family, 375n. 34
Baron, Salo, 25
Barron, Moses Dr., 165

Barsha, John S., *P1–12*
Baruch, Bernard, 41
Beck, Ida, 310, *P1–7*
Belzer, Doris, *P2–8*
Bergman, Bernard A., 144, 169–70
Berk, William L., 294
Berman, Betty, *P2–10*
Berman, Esther, *P2–16*
Bernard, Boris, 114
Bernard, Jack A., *P2–14*
Bernhardt, Joshua, 300
Bernstein, Irwin L., *P1–11*
Bernstein, Jean, *P2–8*
Bernstein, Rose Posner, 309
Bernstein, Sarah, *P2–8*
Bickart, Morton Francis, 220
Bitker, Henry P., *P1–10*
Bloch, Alvin P., 289
Bloch, Bernhard (Bernard Block), 55, 286
Bloom, Howard A., *P1–14*
Bloom, Naomi, 252, 253
Bloom, Stella Caplan, 160
Bloomfield, Simon R., *P1–11*
Blumberg, Abraham, *P1–2*
Blume, Robert L., 296
Bow, Clara, 96
Braekman, Jenny, 252
Brandeis, Louis D., 59, 121
Brandt, Jacob Julian, *P1–2*
Brav, Ernie, 108

Index of Colleges and Universities

Index of Subjects

Accents, Jewish, 44, 169, 170–71, 214
Activists, Jewish student, 277–78, 407n. 36
Adelphean Society, 35
Admissions restrictions. *See* Selective admissions
"Adonis," 111
African American students, 39, 115, 190, 192–93, 253; alternative fraternity system, 46; membership in Jewish fraternities in 1950s, 270–71
Alcohol consumption; 18, 97, 104, 166, 254, 276; during Prohibition, 98–100
Aleph Zaddik Aleph (AZA), 18
Alpha Delta Gamma, 46
Alpha Delta Phi, 35, 182, 186, 271
Alpha Delta Pi, 35
Alpha Epsilon Phi (AEPhi), 19, 20; African-American membership, 271; application forms for, 156; attempts to establish chapter at William and Mary, 184–85; avoiding "Depression-product" schools, 210; career information, 239; chapter rolls, 310–12; exaggerated emphasis on etiquette, 255–56; fear of antisemitism on eve of World War II, 262; first national

convention, *P1–20*; founders, Barnard College, 1909, *P1–7*; founding, 81; general scholarships to help combat antisemitism, 251; Jewish observances, 272; Miami University chapter, 209; national convention of 1934, *P2–4*; and National Panhellenic Congress, 192–95; 1930 through 1934, 199; non-acceptance in local councils, 189–91; "Petitioning Groups Not Accepted," 158, 212–18; question of Gentile membership, 159–61; and residential discrimination against Jewish college women, 226; response to political activism of member, 252–54; rushing, 180–81; songs, 350–52; Sophie Newcomb chapter, 211; Syracuse University, 1920, *P1–20*; at the University of California, Berkeley, 190–91; in World War II, 266; Appendix B, 320–21, 323, 325–42; *P1–12, P2–15*
Alpha Epsilon Pi (AEPi); 13, 19, 20; chapter closings during Depression, 177; chapter closure at Georgia Institute of Technology, 127–28; chapter rolls, 303–7; convention dinner, 1922, *P1–16*; convention locations, 82;

Freemasons, 32, 34
The Freshman, 96

Gambling and card-playing (in chapter
house), 108
Gamma Phi Beta Society, 35
Gentile fraternities: acceptance of
Jewish students after World War
II, 29; antisemitism, 43–44,
83–84; refusal to duel with Jews,
32. *See also* Greek-letter societies
"Gentlemen," 248–49, 262
"Geographical distribution," 126, 127,
146, 202
Georgia Institute of Technology, 63,
73, 113, 127, 145
German American Bund, 230
German Jewish refugee students, 26,
56
German Jewish Student Rescue Fund,
236
German Jews, 31, 40-41, 62, 65, 69,
77, 103, 130, 193, 200, 229, 247;
in ZBT, 53, 69, 78, 100–101,
153–54. *See also* Jews, division
between German and Russian
German university student life, 31, 104
Germany, 103–4, 106, 229, 244,
247–48
"Ghetto Jew," 171, 215
GI Bill of Rights, 26, 29, 268
Grades. *See* Scholarship
Grand Tour of Europe, 103, 199
"Greasy grind," 153, 156, 214
Great Depression, 26, 95, 173–81,
197–206, 220, 227, 239
Greek and Latin (in university
curriculum), 36, 219
Greek-letter societies: anti-Jewish
discrimination, 43–44, 83–84,
181; exclusionism, 39–40;
"Golden Age" of, 95–96;
growing unpopularity of during
Depression, 175–76; history of in
America, 32–37; legitimacy and
guarantees of official support, 37–
39; loss of relevance in 1960s, 276;

national (multi-chapter) college
social fraternities, 18; revival
in the late 1970s and 1980s,
278. *See also* Gentile fraternities;
Jewish Greek fraternities; Jewish
Greek sororities; Jewish Greek
subsystem
"Group B," "Second Division" or
"Associate" membership in local
fraternity councils, 83, 189–91,
192, 232–34

"Harvard Student Opinion on the
Jewish Question," 122–23
Hats and headcovering for men, 88,
280
Hazing, 31, 33, 88, 176, 268, 275
Higher education: antisemitism,
42–44, 83–86; enrollment
expansion in 1920s, 95; Jewish
immigrant influx, 118–19; quotas
for Jews and Roman Catholics,
120
Hillel Foundations, 42, 88, 203, 205,
223–26, 243, 272, 279, 281
"The Home Fraternity," 53, 54
House plans, 176
Humility and patience, as reaction to
antisemitism, 150
Humor, 100–101, 145–46, 166–68

I. C. Sororis, 35
Identity, Jewish. *See* Jewish Identity
Identity crisis, of Jewish fraternities,
47–68, 150–52, 241–48
Immigration quota system, 115, 121,
127
"Imports," 109
Indiana Jewish Chronicle, 153
Indianapolis, 183, 210
Initiation rituals, 93, 246
In loco parentis, 259, 276–77
Intercollegiate Menorah Association,
57, 126, 164, 373n. 6
Interfaith dating, 109, 157
Interfaith marriages, 28, 50, 91, 145,
151–52, 271, 273–74, 280

www.ingramcontent.com/pod-product-compliance
Lightning Source LLC
Chambersburg PA
CBHW050641270326
41927CB00012B/2830